SINS 11

nakaba suzuki presents

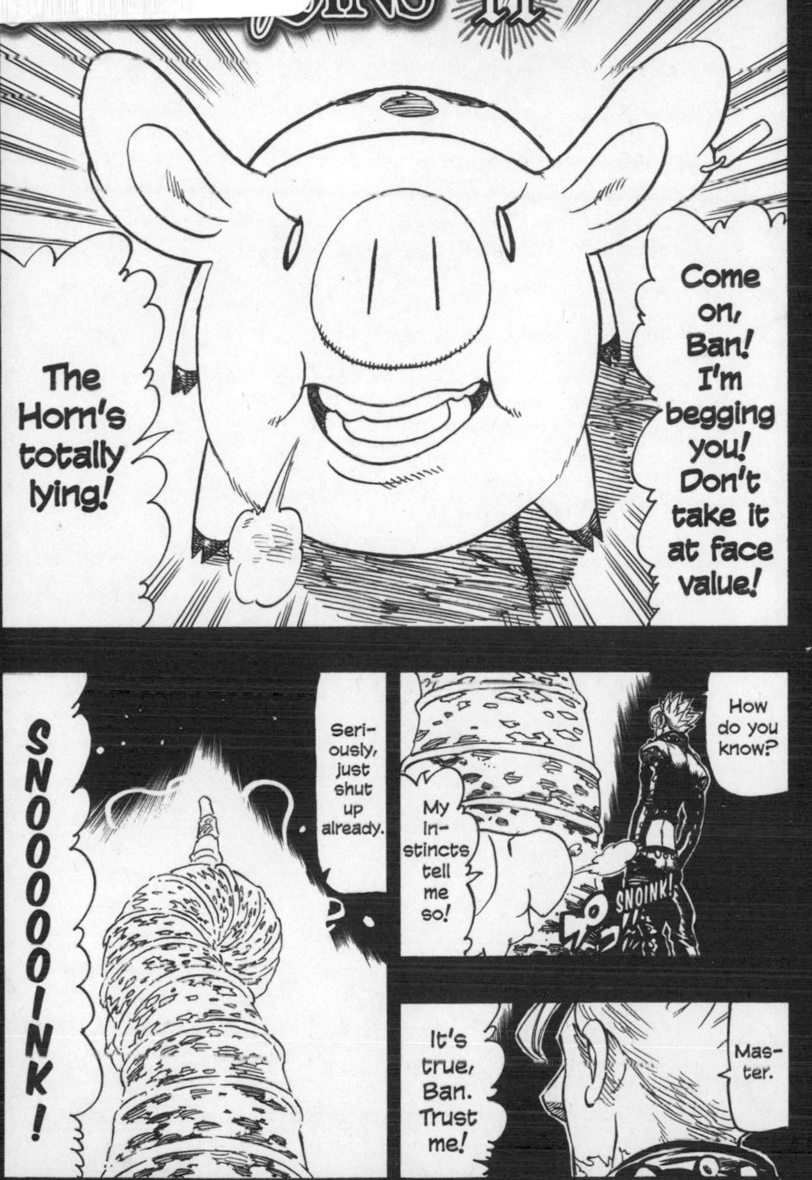
Come on, Ban! I'm begging you! Don't take it at face value!
The Horn's totally lying!
How do you know?
My instincts tell me so!
SNOINK!
Master.
It's true, Ban. Trust me!
Seriously, just shut up already.
SNOOOOOOINK!

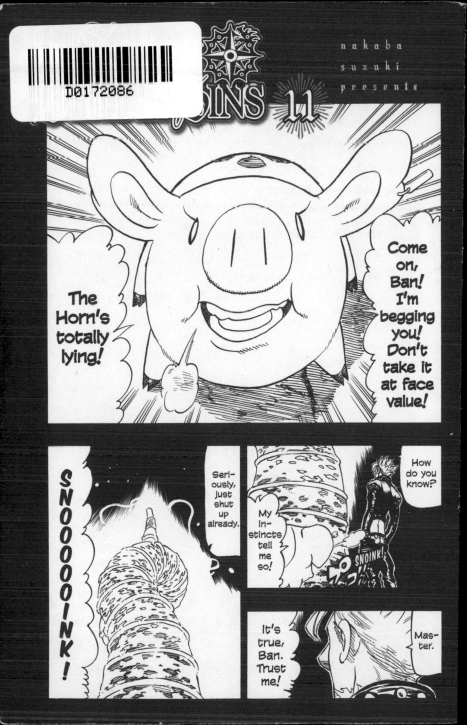

CONTENTS

BOAR HAT

The Seven Deadly Sins

Chapter 79 - Once More

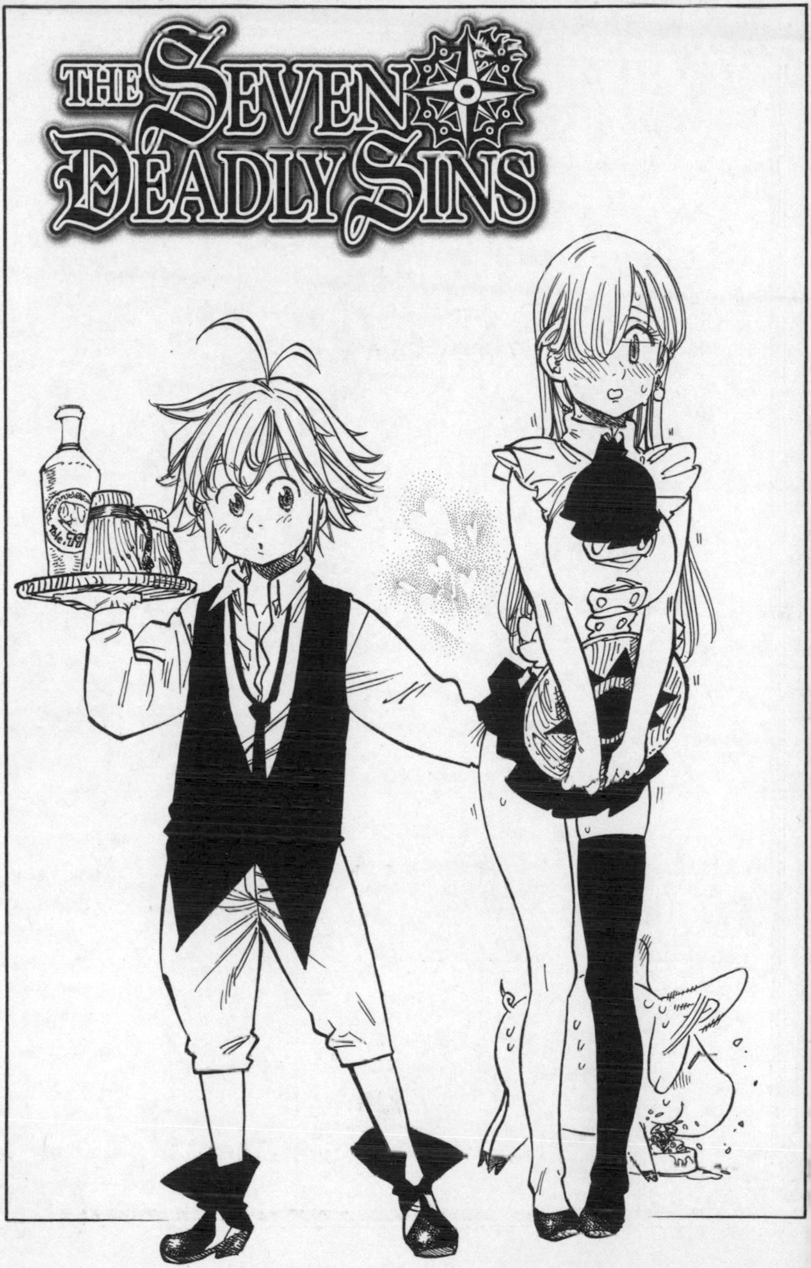
THE SEVEN DEADLY SINS

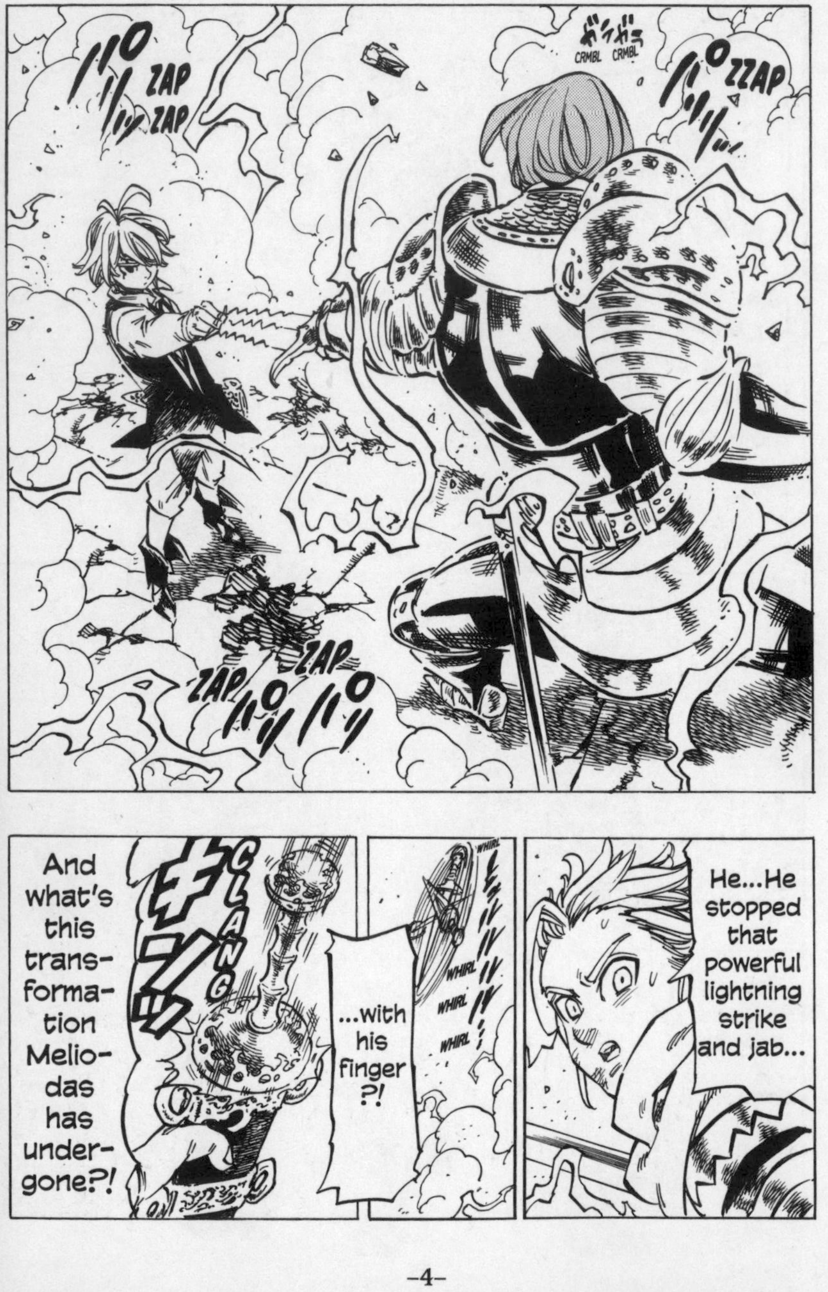
CRMBL CRMBL
ZZAP
ZAP ZAP
ZAP ZAP
He...He stopped that powerful lightning strike and jab...
...with his finger?!
WHIRL WHIRL WHIRL WHIRL
CLANG
And what's this transformation Meliodas has undergone?!

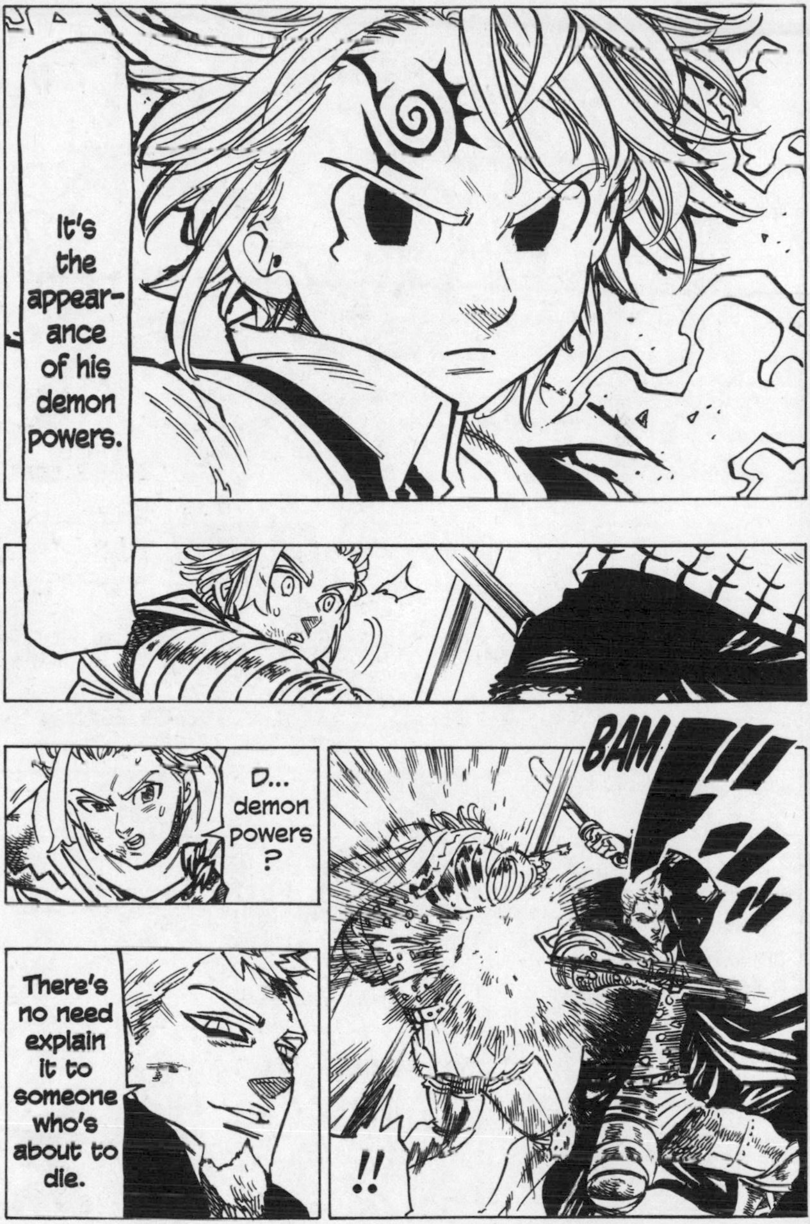
It's the appearance of his demon powers.
BAM
!!
D... demon powers ?
There's no need explain it to someone who's about to die.

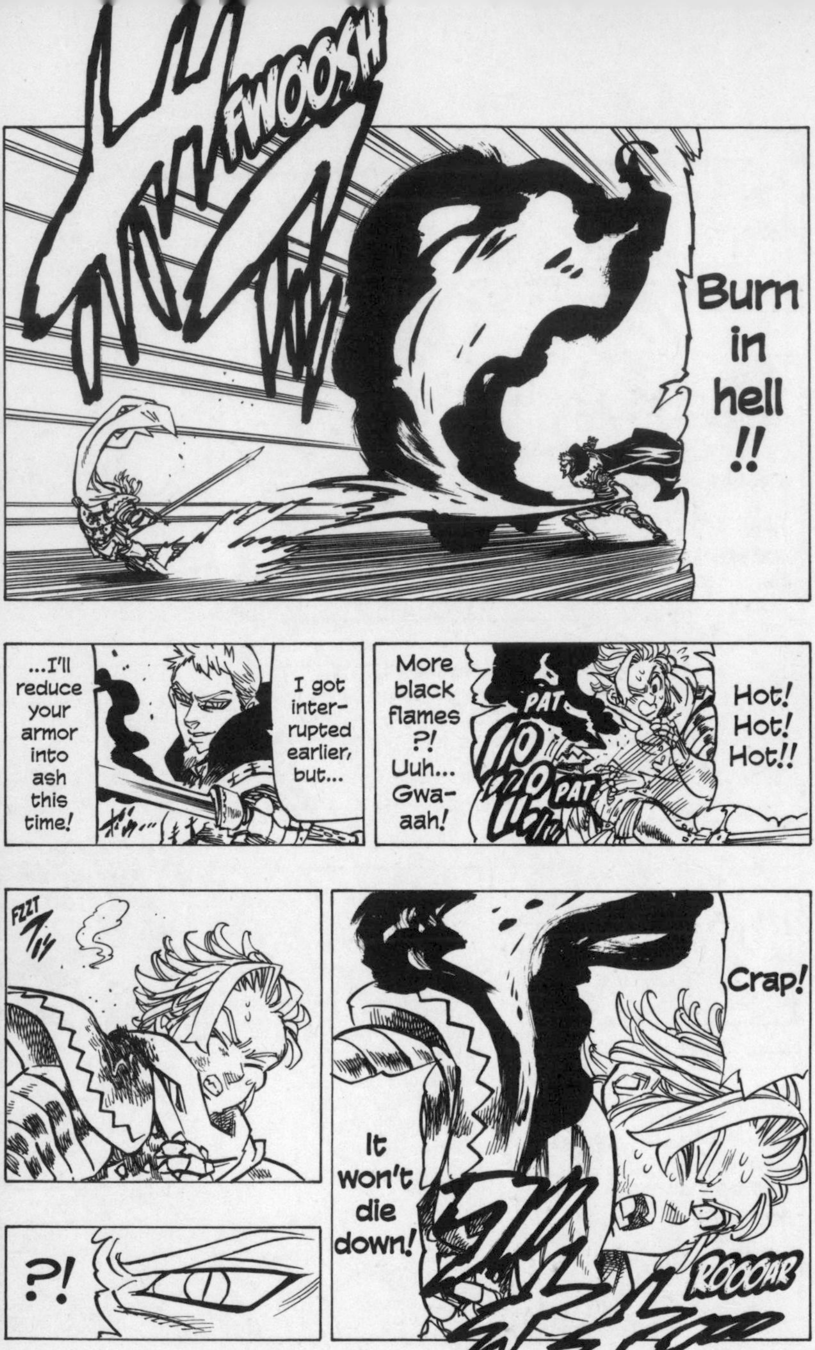
FWOOSH
Burn in hell!!
Hot! Hot! Hot!!
PAT
PAT
More black flames?! Uuh... Gwa-aah!
I got inter-rupted earlier, but...
...I'll reduce your armor into ash this time!
Crap!
It won't die down!
ROOOAR
FZZT
?!

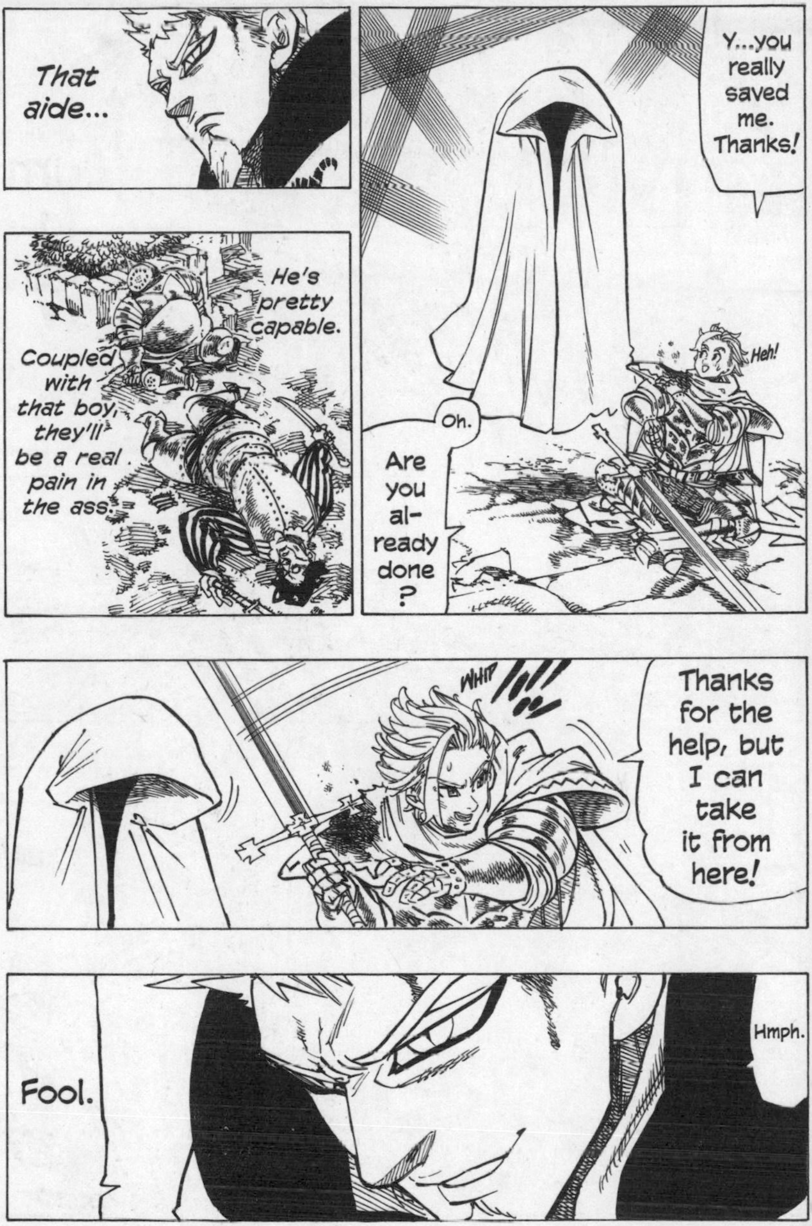
Y...you really saved me. Thanks!
Heh!
Oh.
Are you al-ready done?
That aide...
He's pretty capable.
Coupled with that boy, they'll be a real pain in the ass.
Thanks for the help, but I can take it from here!
WHIP
Hmph.
Fool.

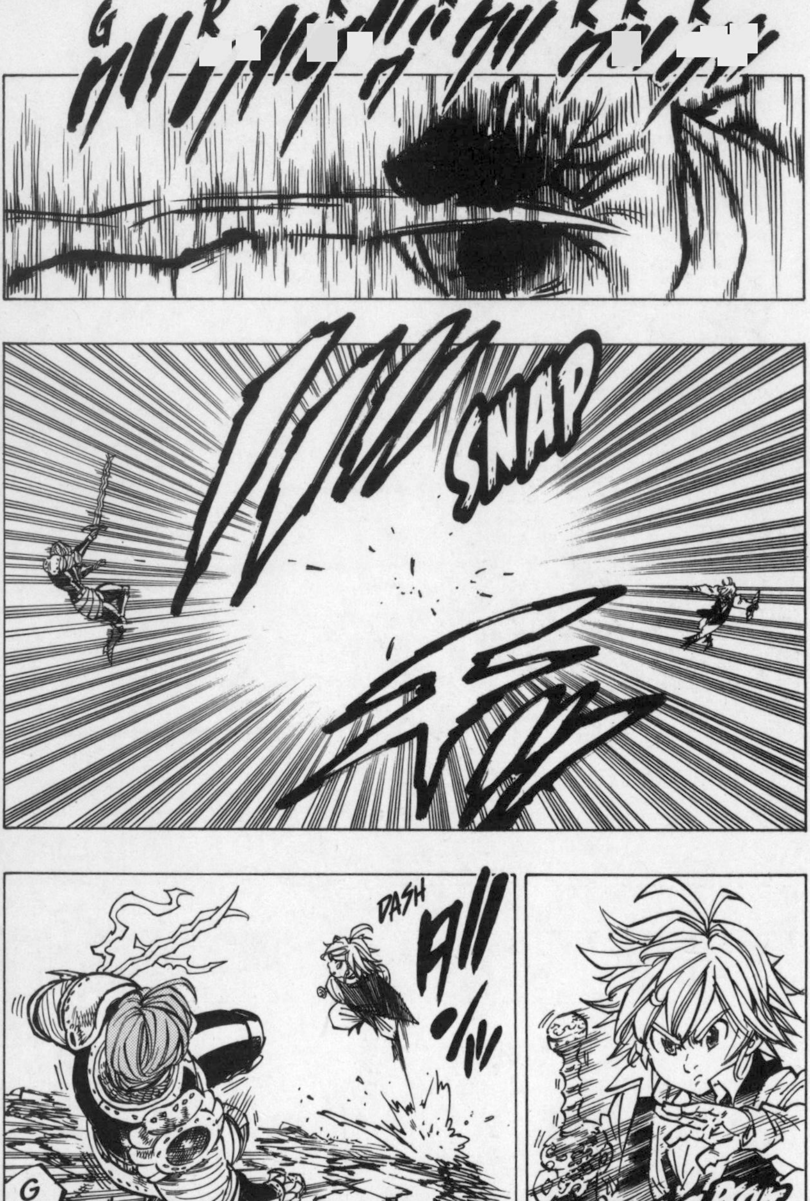
GRRRKKK
SNAP
PSHT
DASH
GSSH

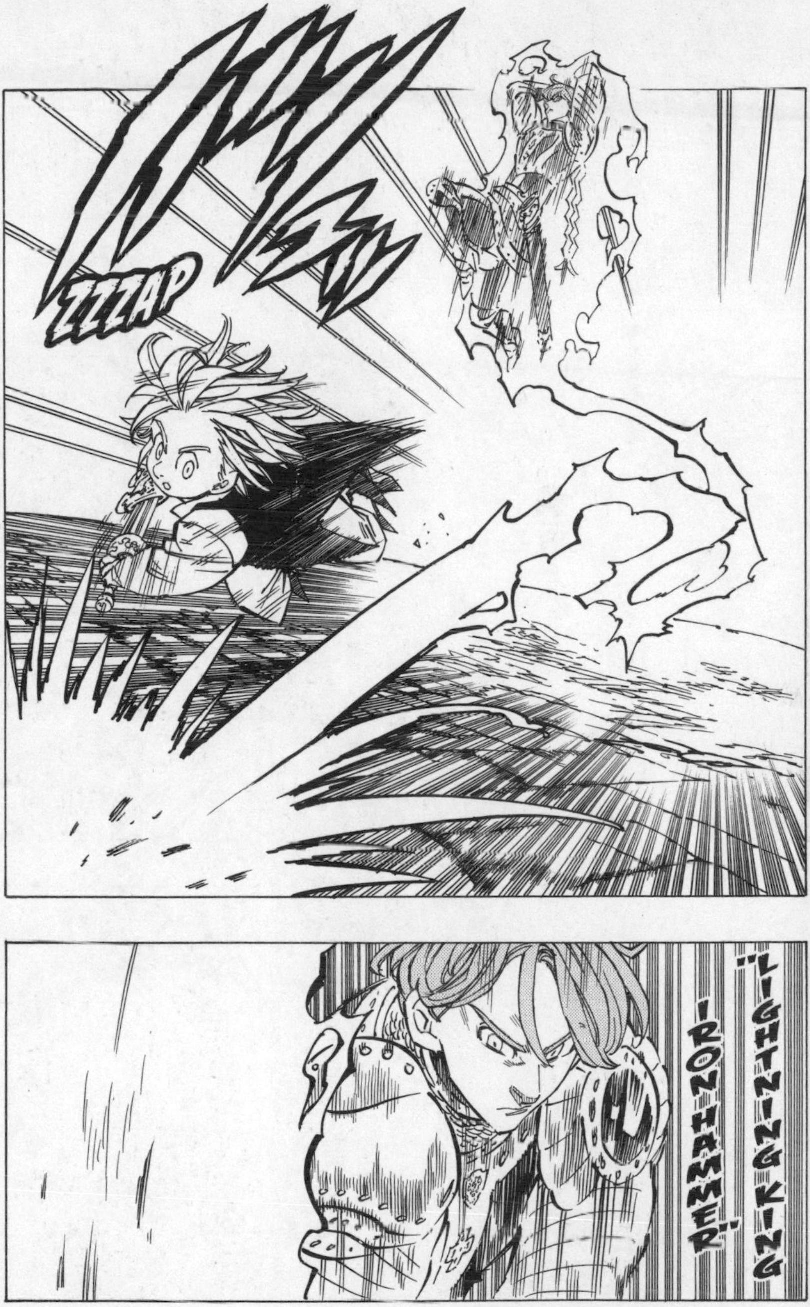
ZZZZAP
...LIGHTNING KING
IRON HAMMER...

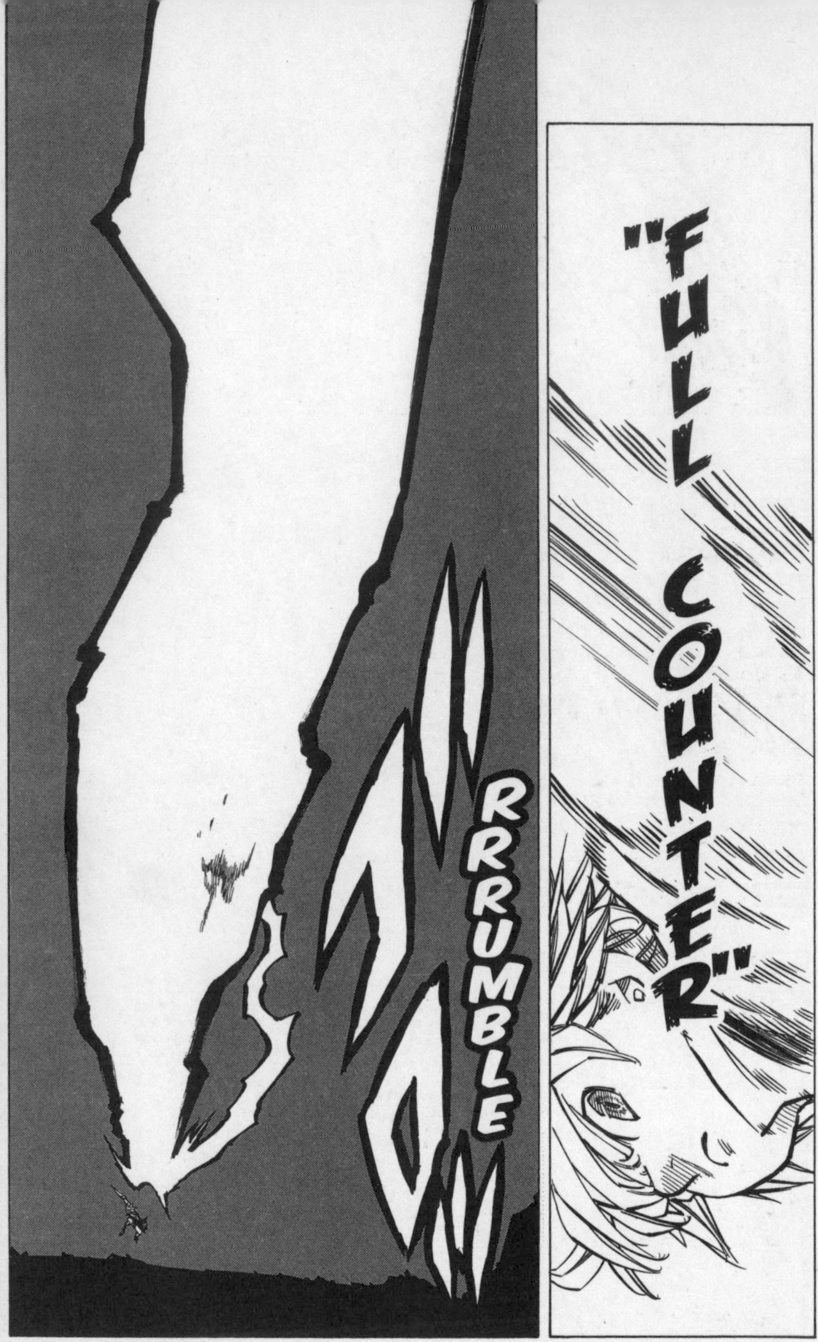
"FULL COUNTER"
RRRUMBLE

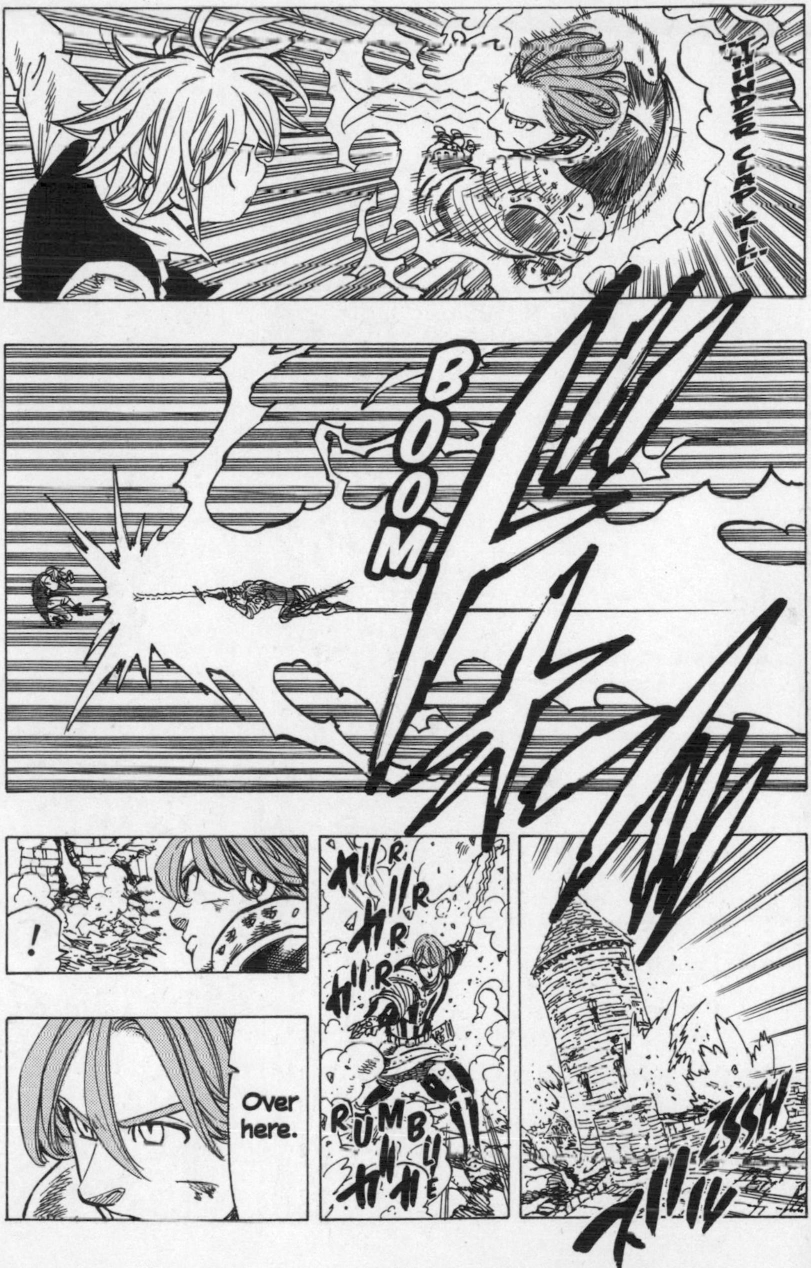
THUNDER CLAP KILL
BOOM
ZSSH
RUMBLE
!
Over here.

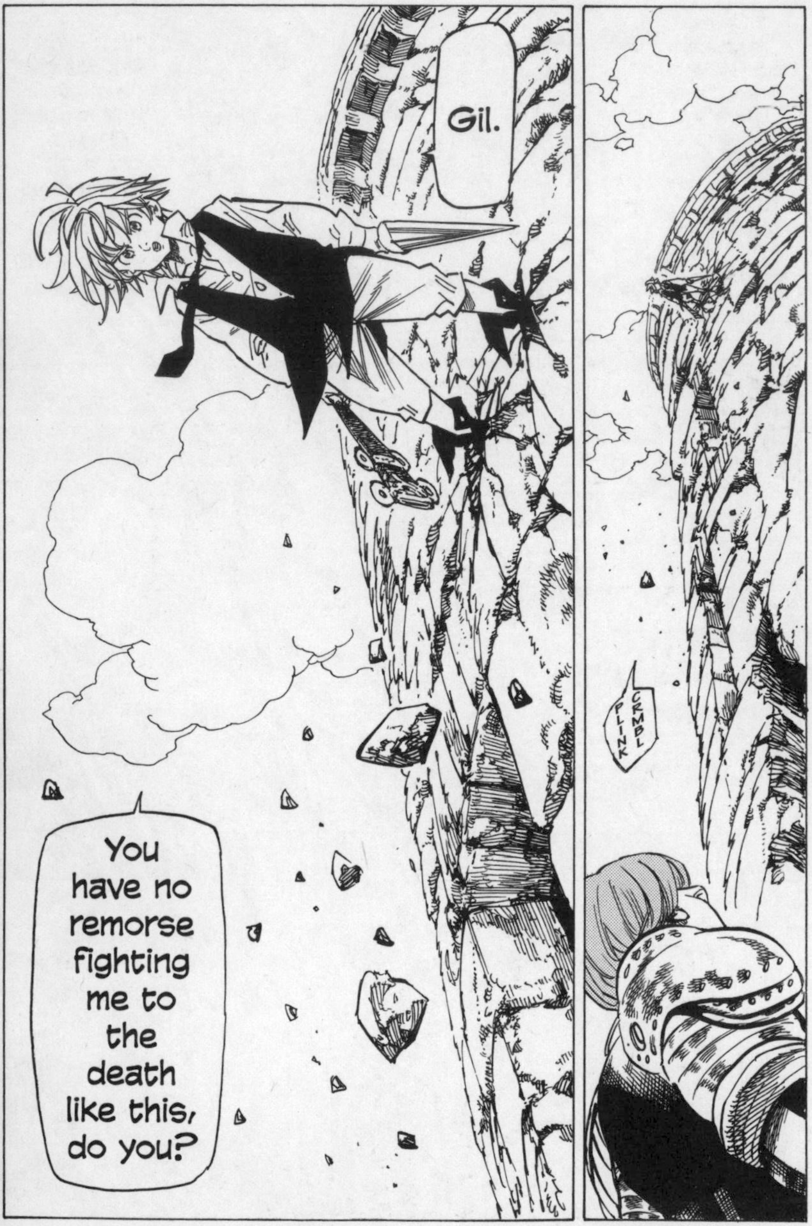
CRMBL
PLINK
Gil.
You have no remorse fighting me to the death like this, do you?

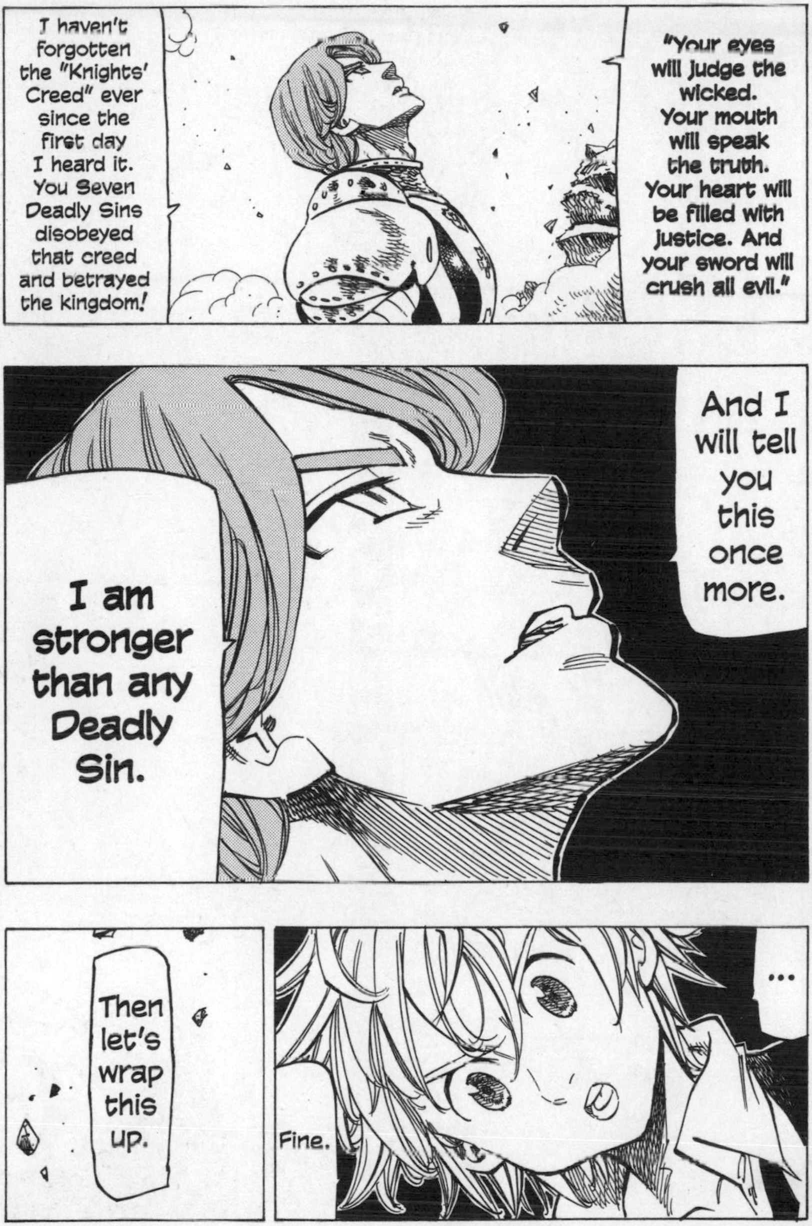
"Your eyes will judge the wicked. Your mouth will speak the truth. Your heart will be filled with justice. And your sword will crush all evil."
I haven't forgotten the "Knights' Creed" ever since the first day I heard it. You Seven Deadly Sins disobeyed that creed and betrayed the kingdom!
And I will tell you this once more.
I am stronger than any Deadly Sin.
...
Fine.
Then let's wrap this up.

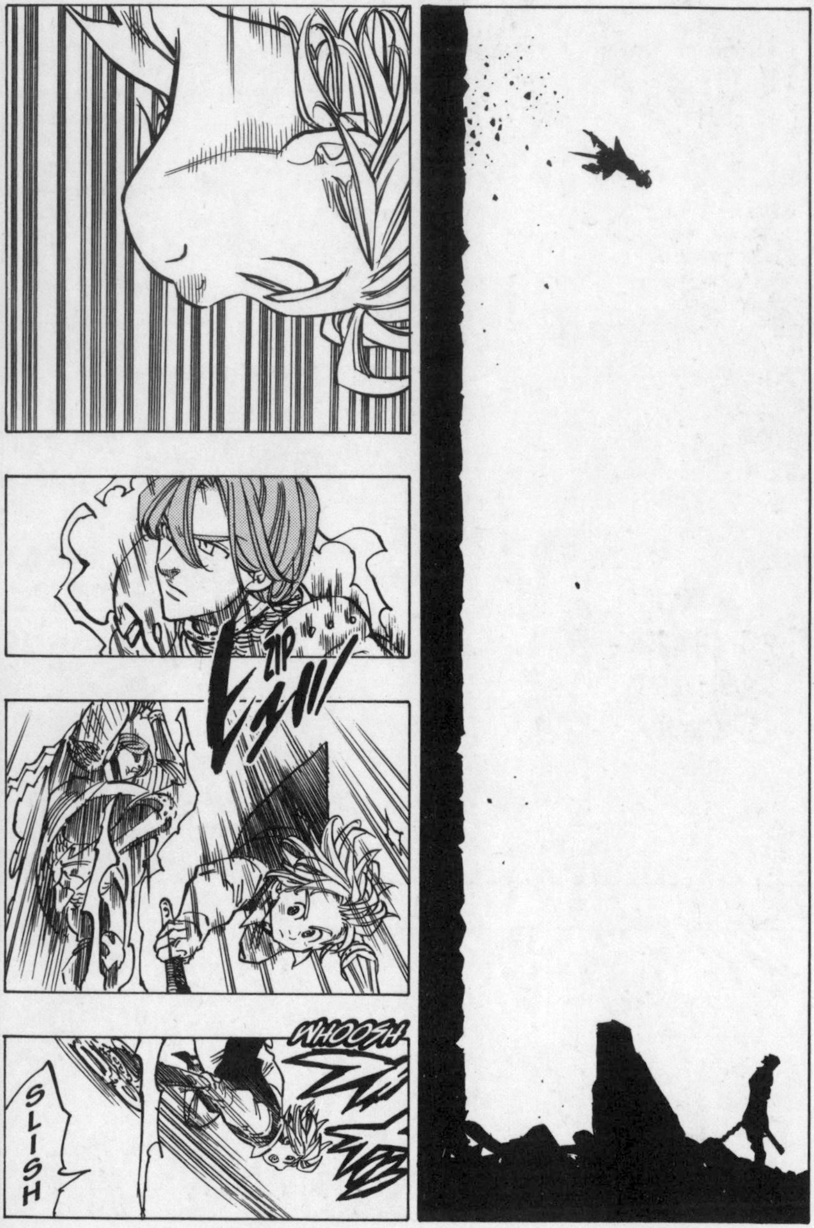
ZIP
WHOOSH
SLISH

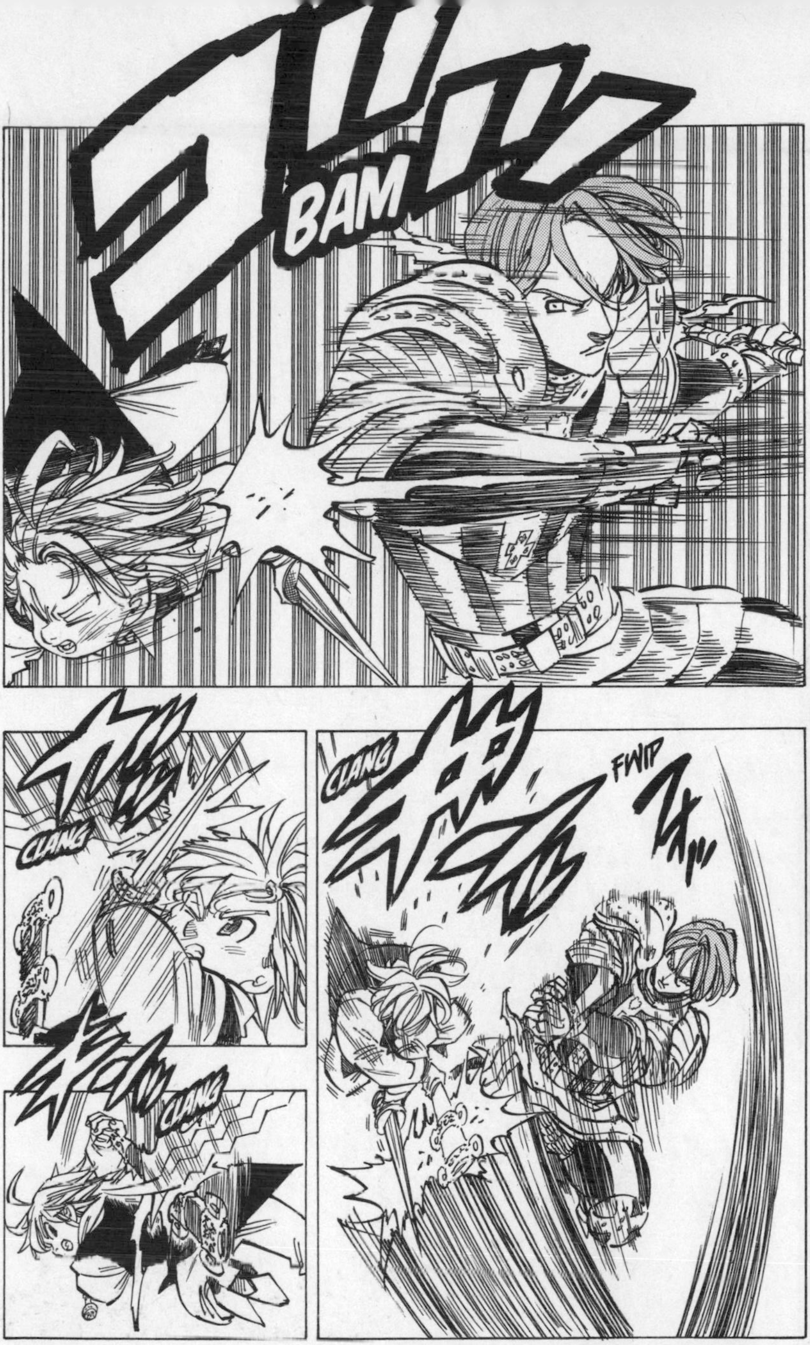
BAM
FWIP
CLANG
CLANG
CLANG

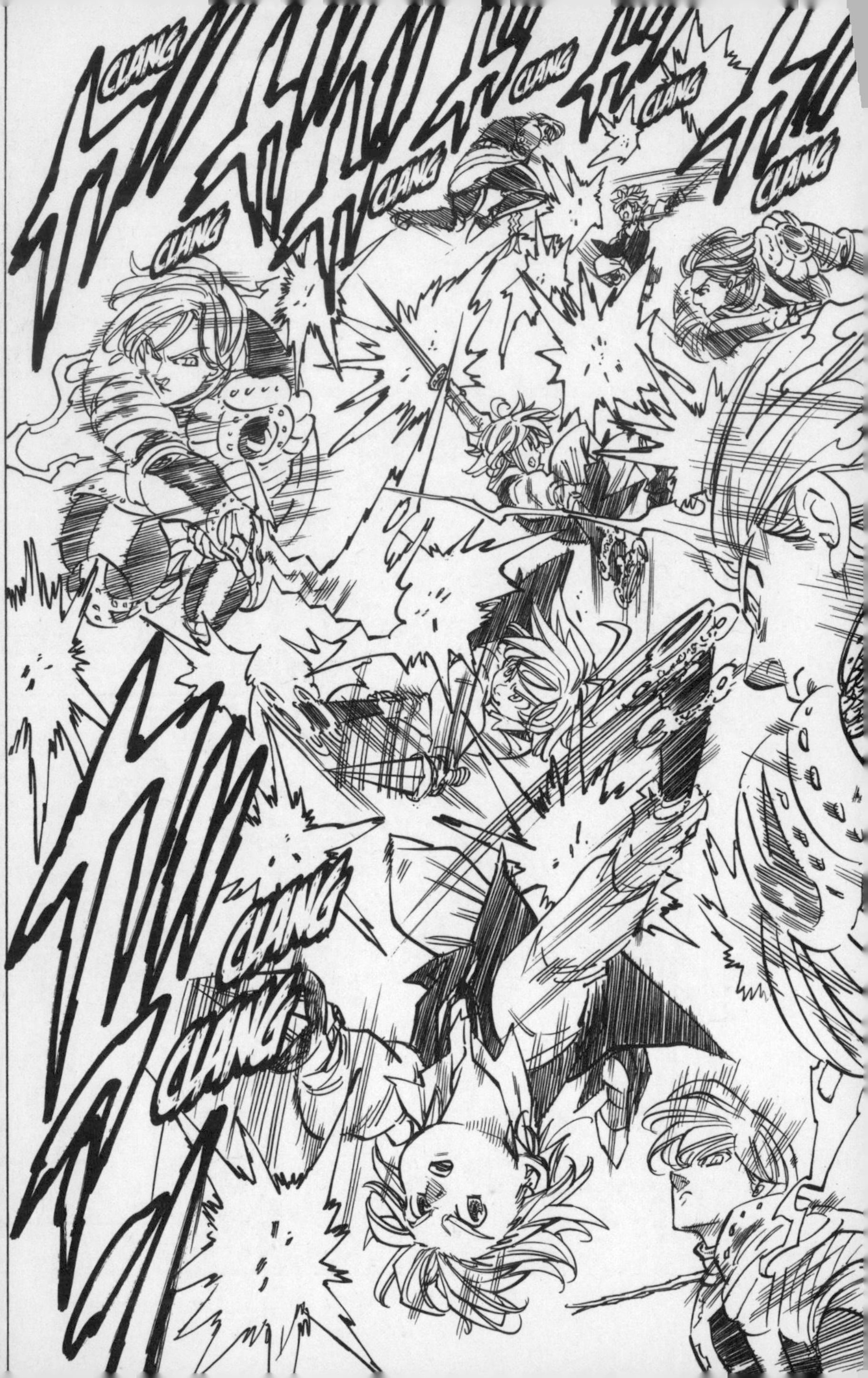
CLANG
CLANG
CLANG
CLANG
CLANG
CLANG
CLANG
CLANG

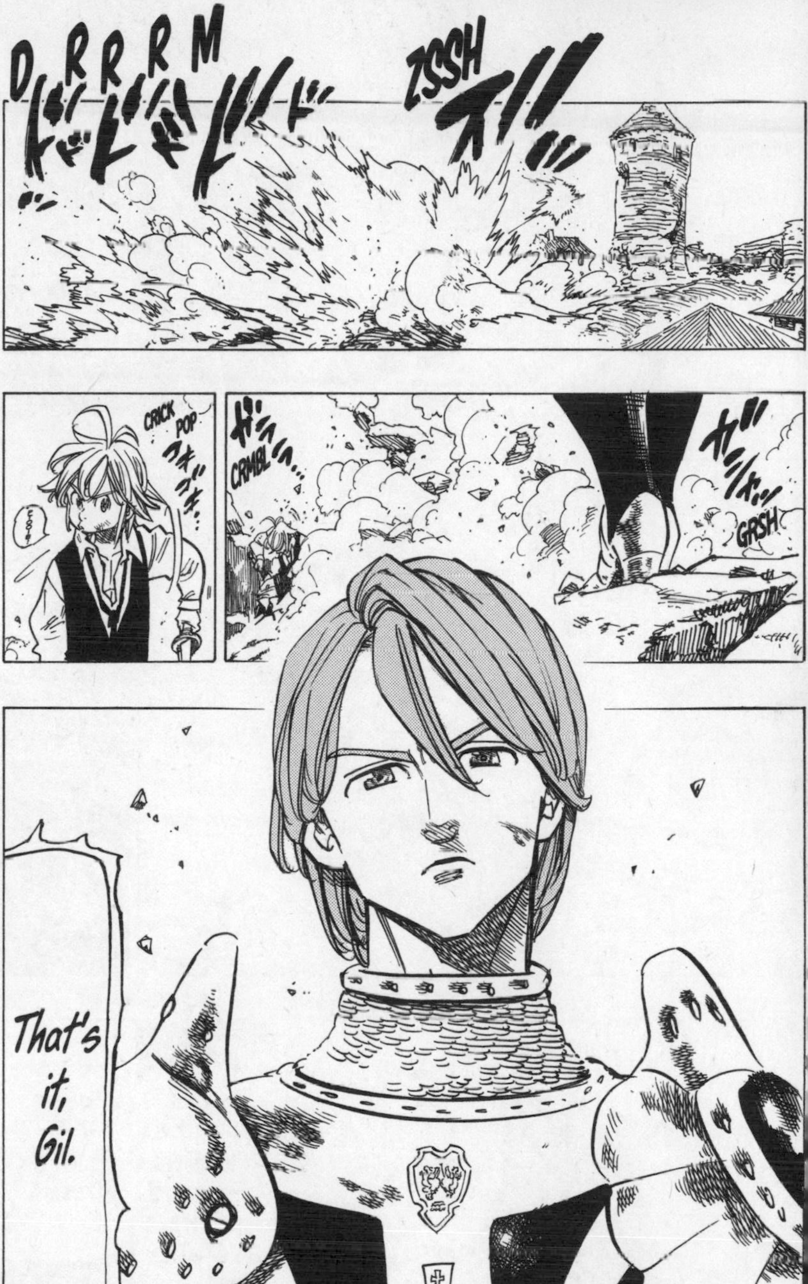
DRRRRM
ZSSH
GRSH
CRMBL
CRICK POP
That's it, Gil.

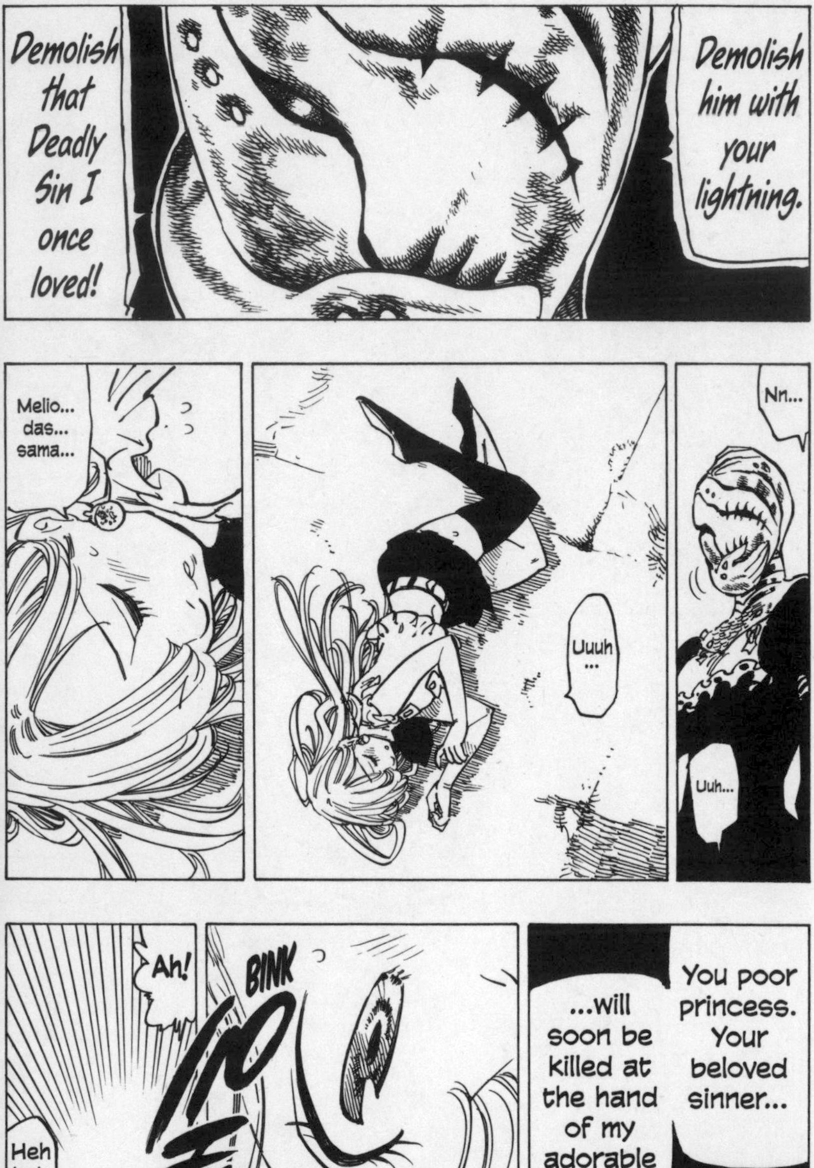
Demolish him with your lightning.
Demolish that Deadly Sin I once loved!
Nn...
Uuh...
Uuuh...
Melio... das... sama...
You poor princess. Your beloved sinner...
...will soon be killed at the hand of my adorable knight.
BINK
Ah!
Heh heh ...

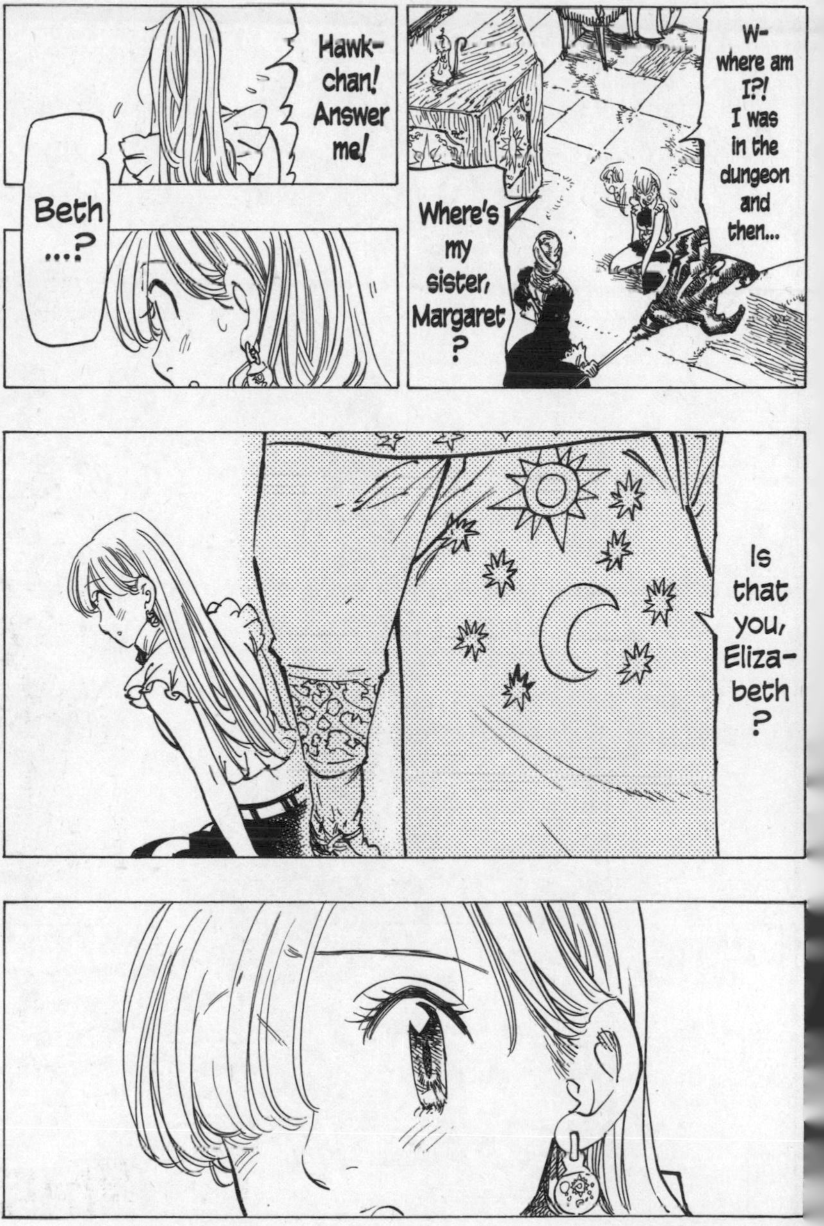
W-where am I?! I was in the dungeon and then...
Where's my sister, Margaret?
Hawk-chan! Answer me!
Beth...?
Is that you, Eliza-beth?

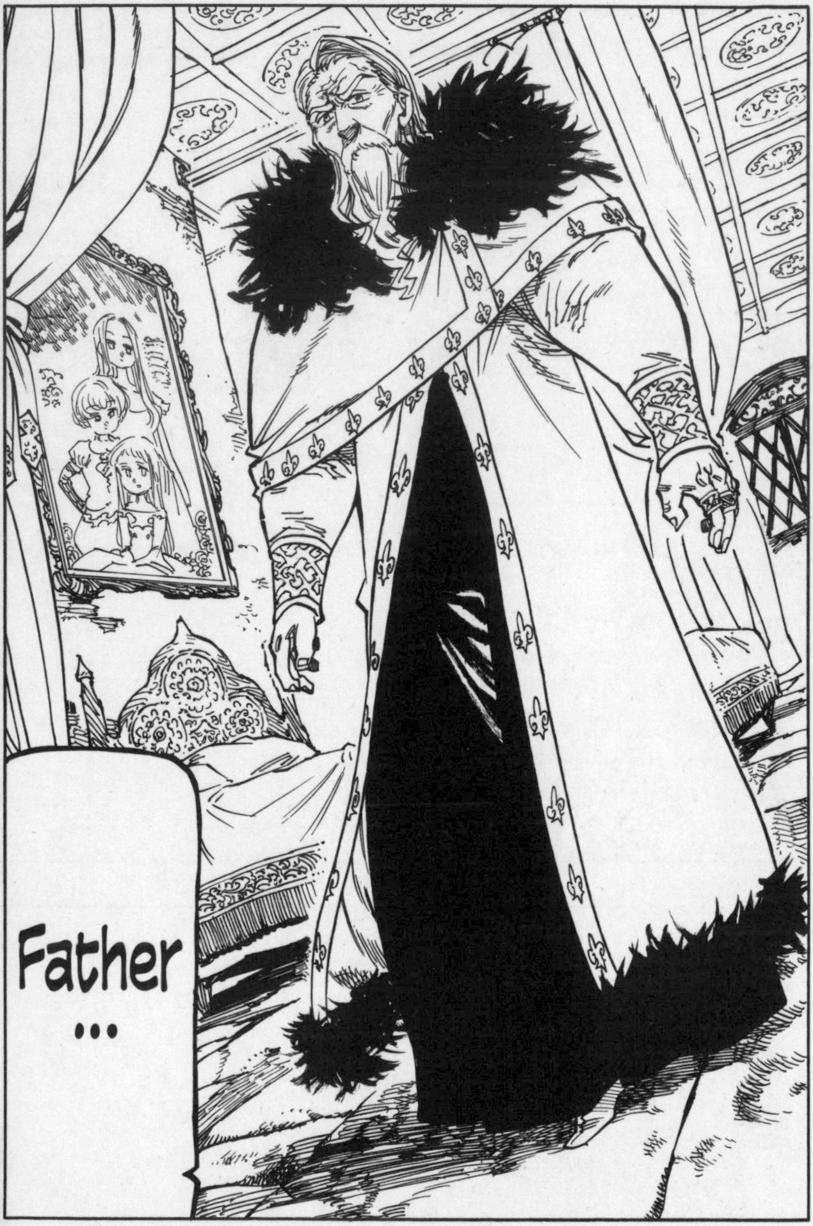
Father
...

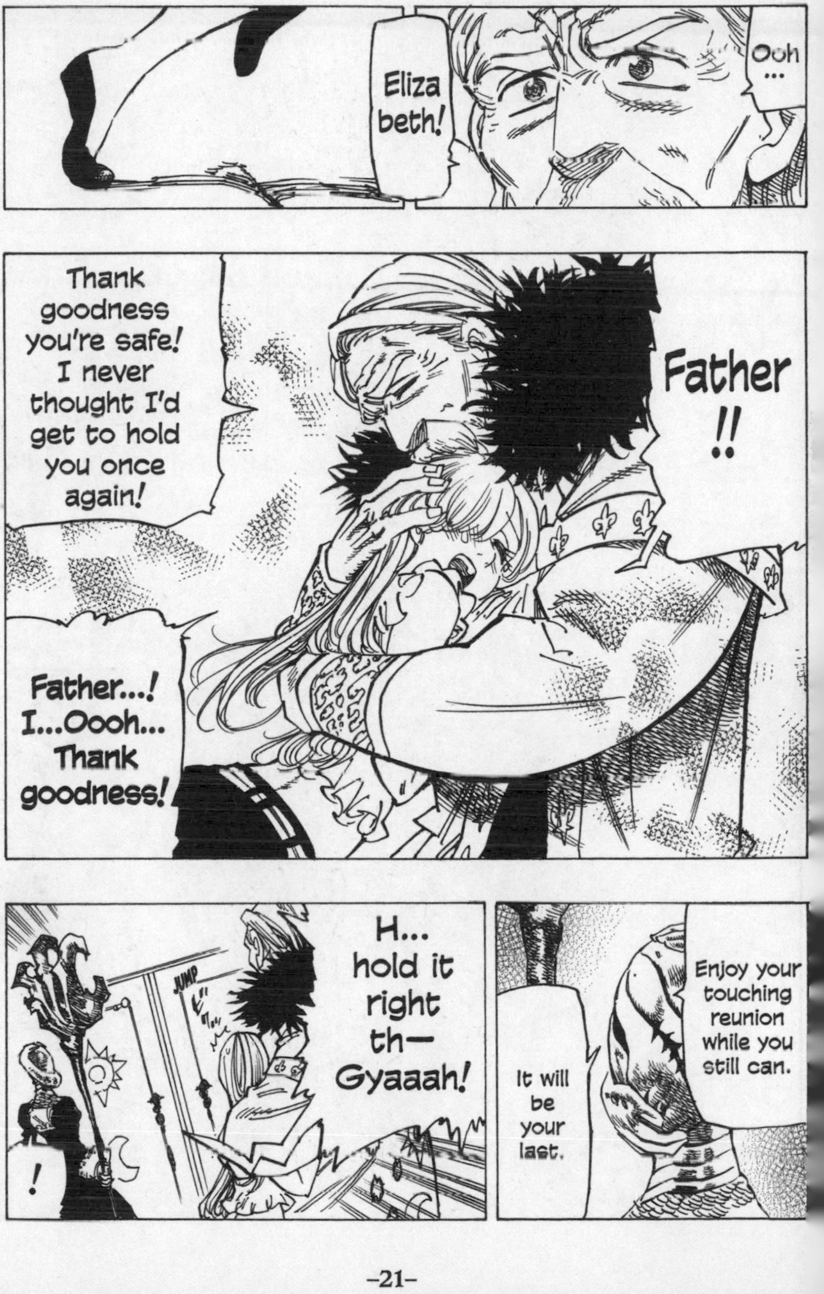
Ooh...
Elizabeth!
Father!!
Thank goodness you're safe! I never thought I'd get to hold you once again!
Father...! I...Oooh... Thank goodness!
Enjoy your touching reunion while you still can.
It will be your last.
H... hold it right th— Gyaaah!
JUMP
!

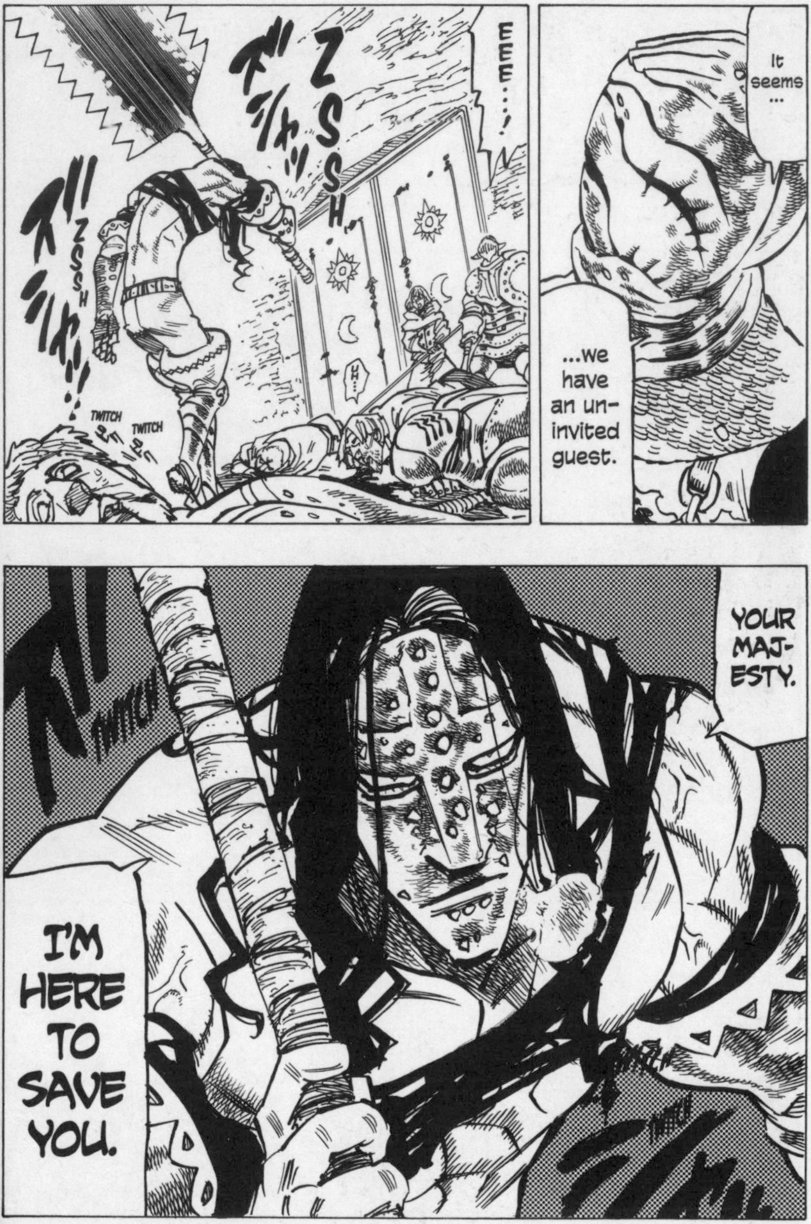
It seems ...
...we have an un-invited guest.
EEE...!
ZSSH.
ZSSH!!
H...
TWITCH
TWITCH
YOUR MAJ-ESTY.
TWITCH
I'M HERE TO SAVE YOU.

Chapter 80 - A Dramatic Surge of Reversal

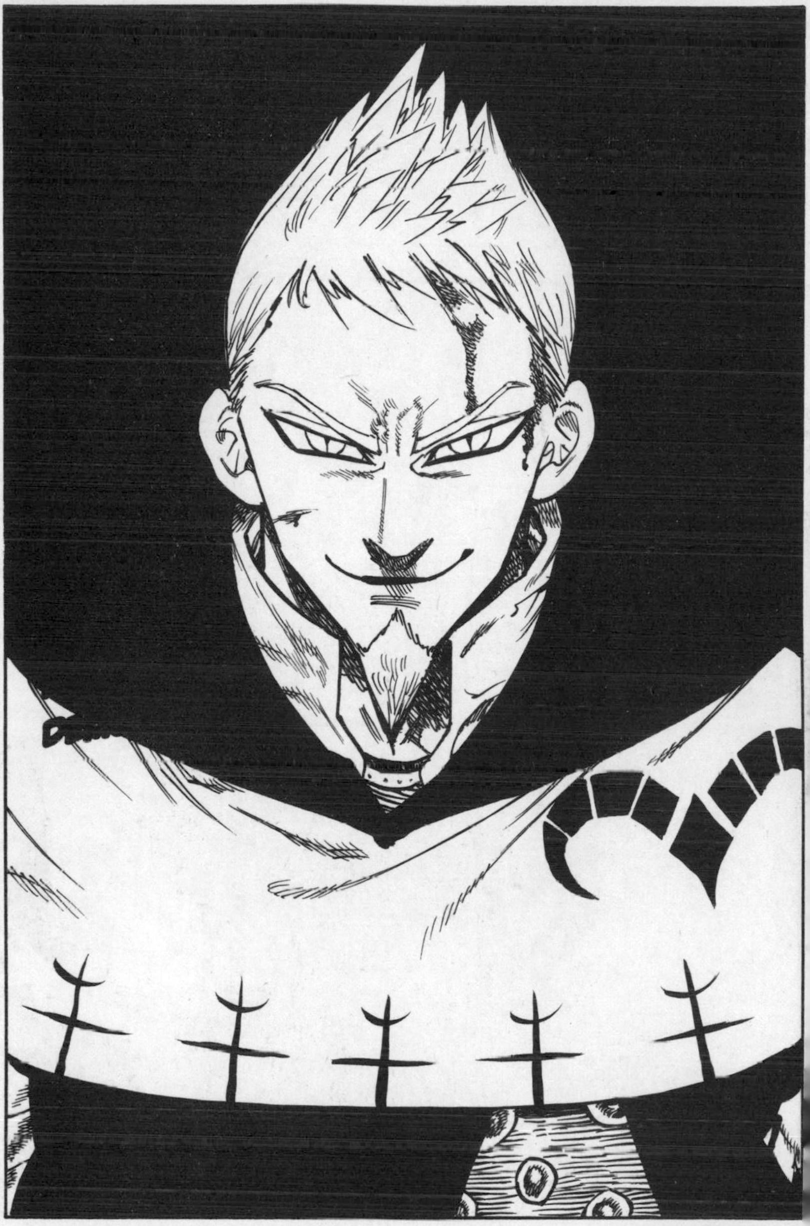

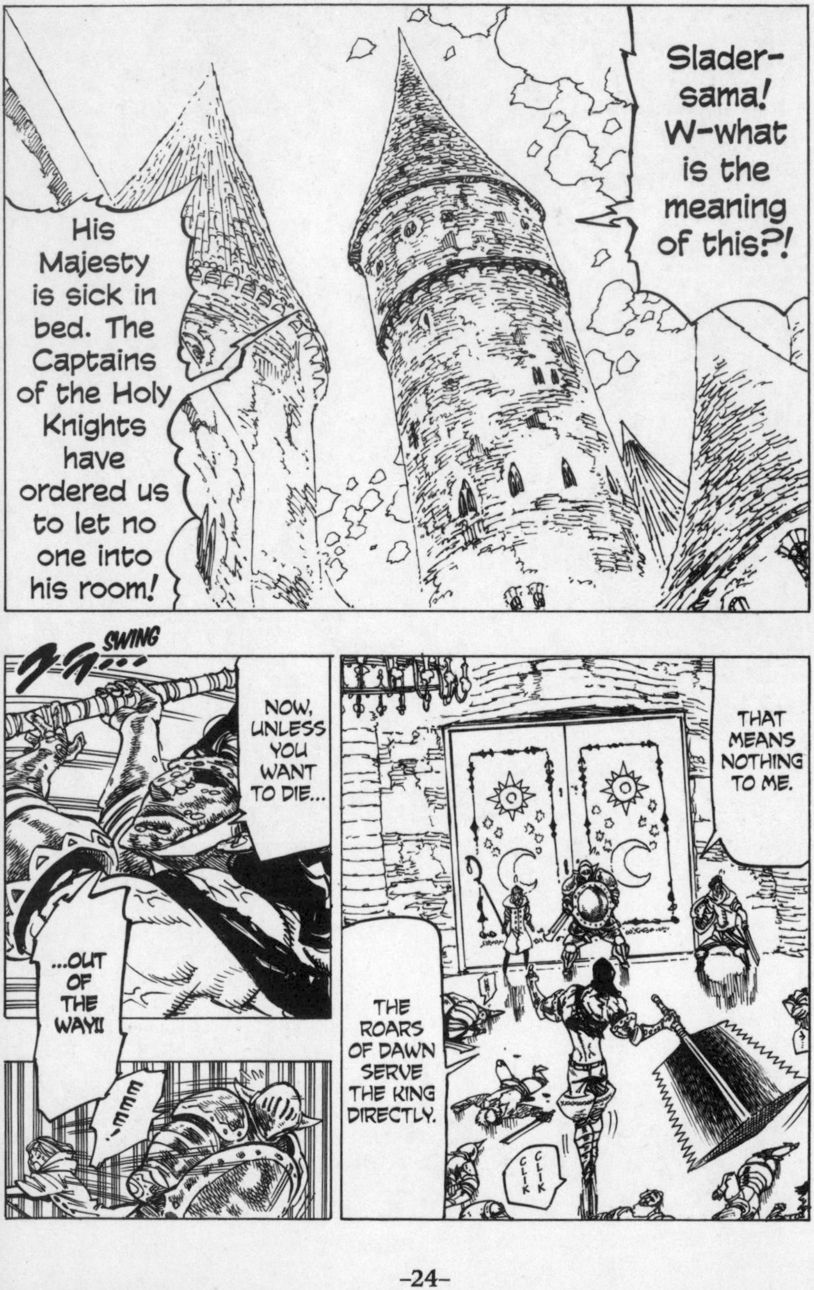
Slader-sama! W-what is the meaning of this?!
His Majesty is sick in bed. The Captains of the Holy Knights have ordered us to let no one into his room!
THAT MEANS NOTHING TO ME.
THE ROARS OF DAWN SERVE THE KING DIRECTLY.
CLIK CLIK
SWING
NOW, UNLESS YOU WANT TO DIE...
...OUT OF THE WAY!!
EEEE

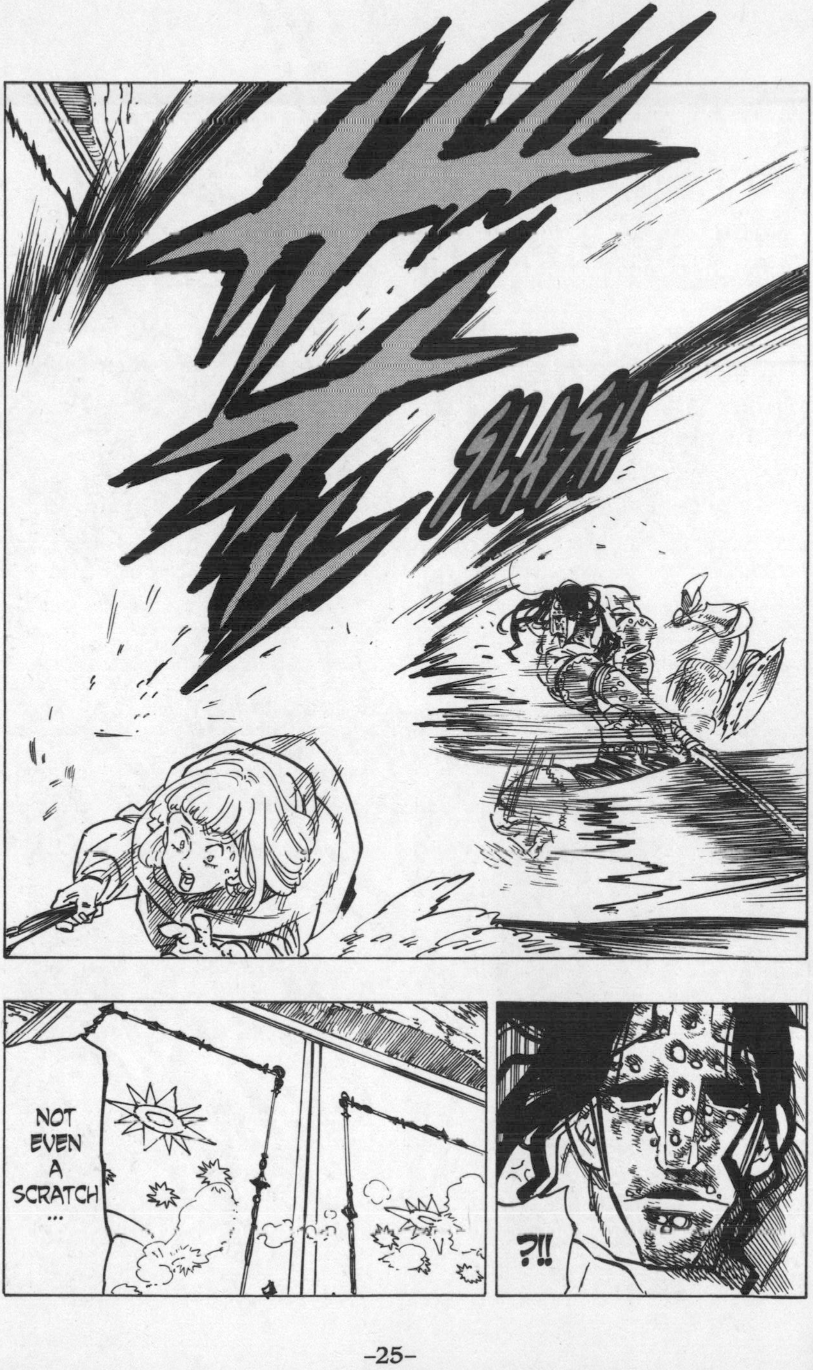
SLASH
?!!
NOT EVEN A SCRATCH ...

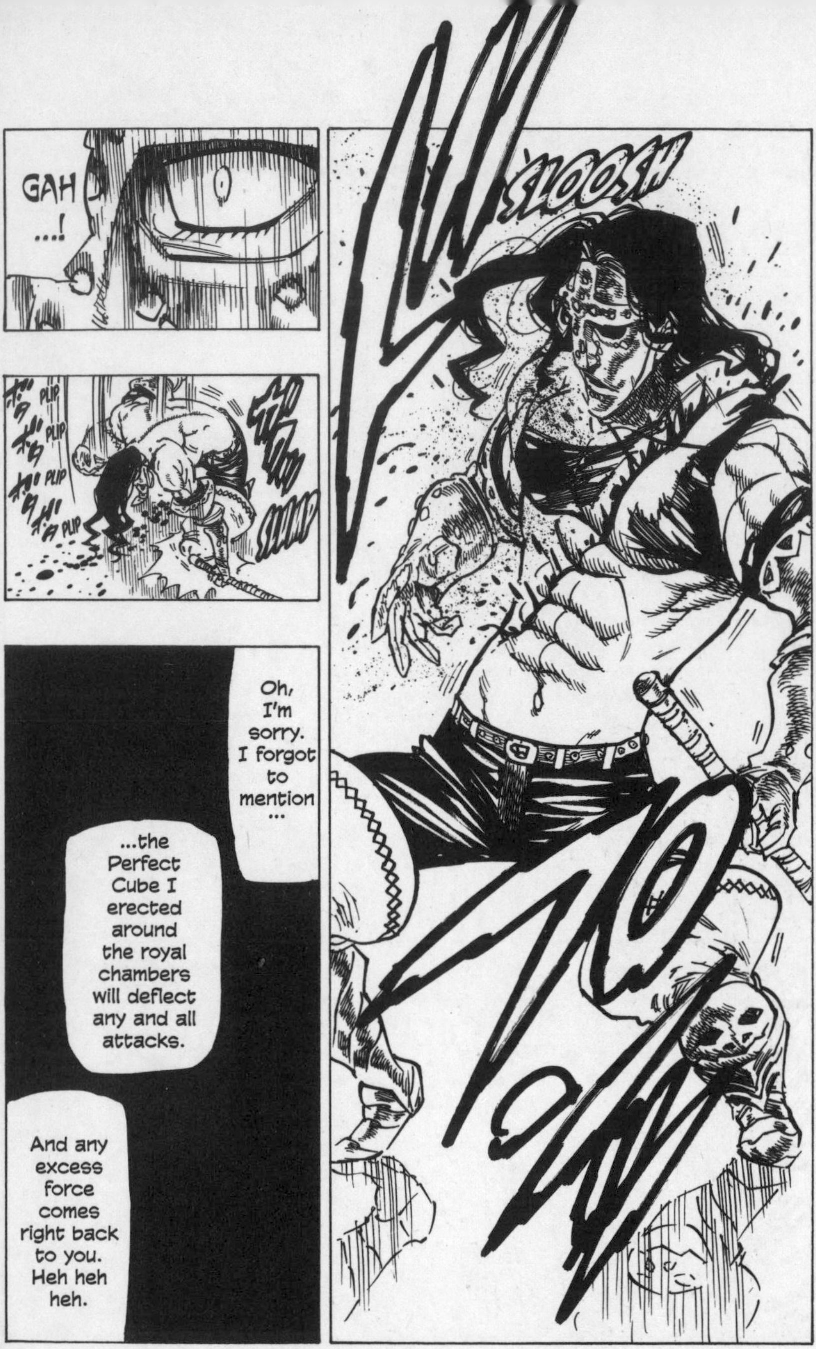
SLOOSH
GAH ...!
PLIP
PLIP
PLIP
PLIP
Oh, I'm sorry. I forgot to mention ...
...the Perfect Cube I erected around the royal chambers will deflect any and all attacks.
And any excess force comes right back to you. Heh heh heh.

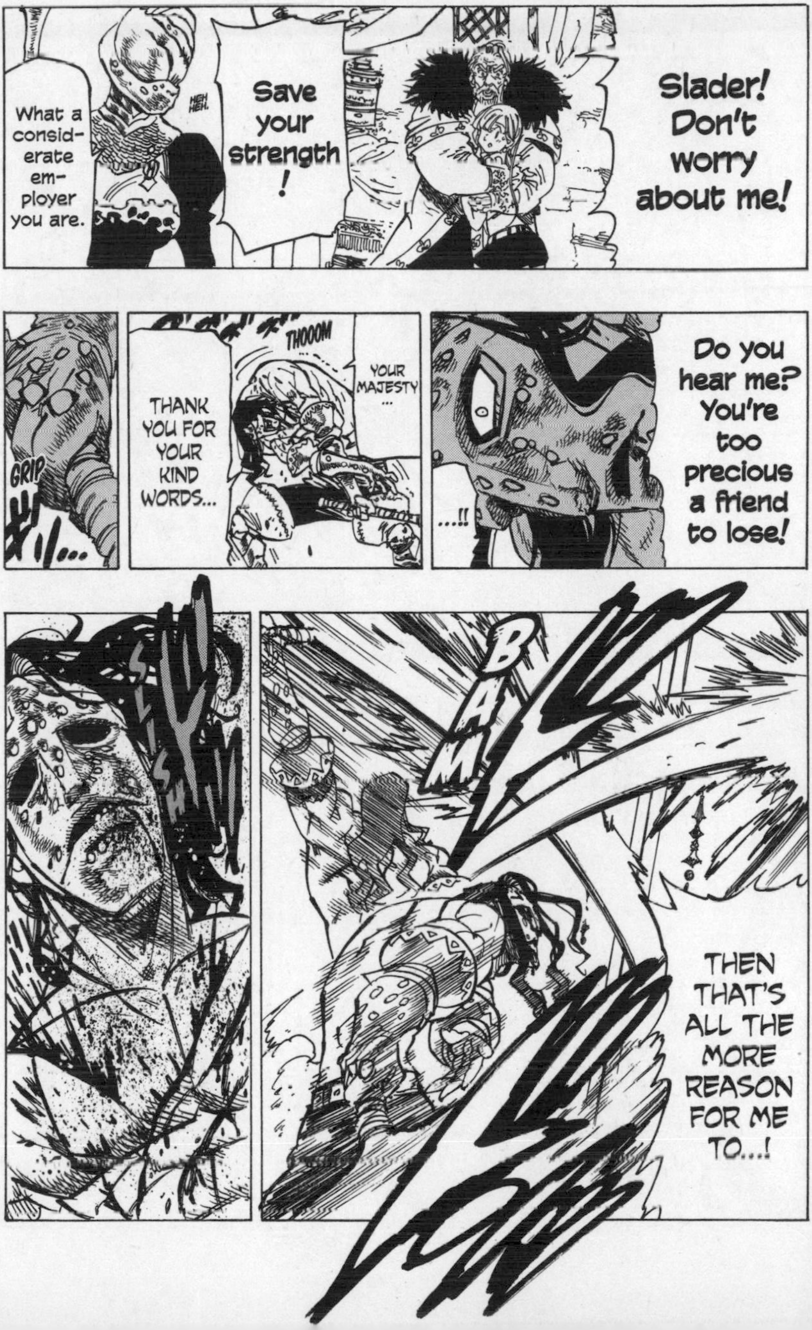
Slader! Don't worry about me!
Save your strength!
HEH HEH.
What a considerate employer you are.
Do you hear me? You're too precious a friend to lose!
...!!
THOOOM
YOUR MAJESTY...
THANK YOU FOR YOUR KIND WORDS...
GRIP
...
BAM
THEN THAT'S ALL THE MORE REASON FOR ME TO...!
SLISH

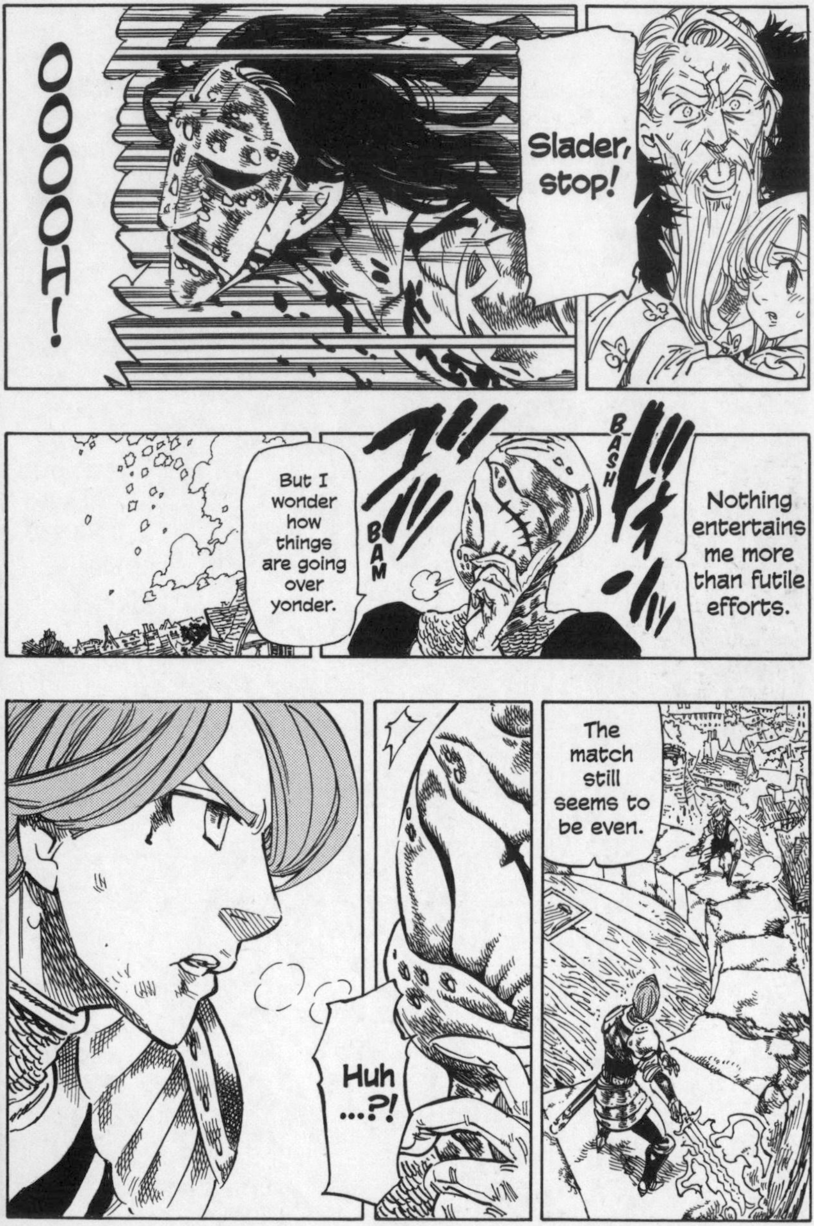
Slader, stop!
OOOOOH!
Nothing entertains me more than futile efforts.
BASH
But I wonder how things are going over yonder.
BAM
The match still seems to be even.
Huh ...?!

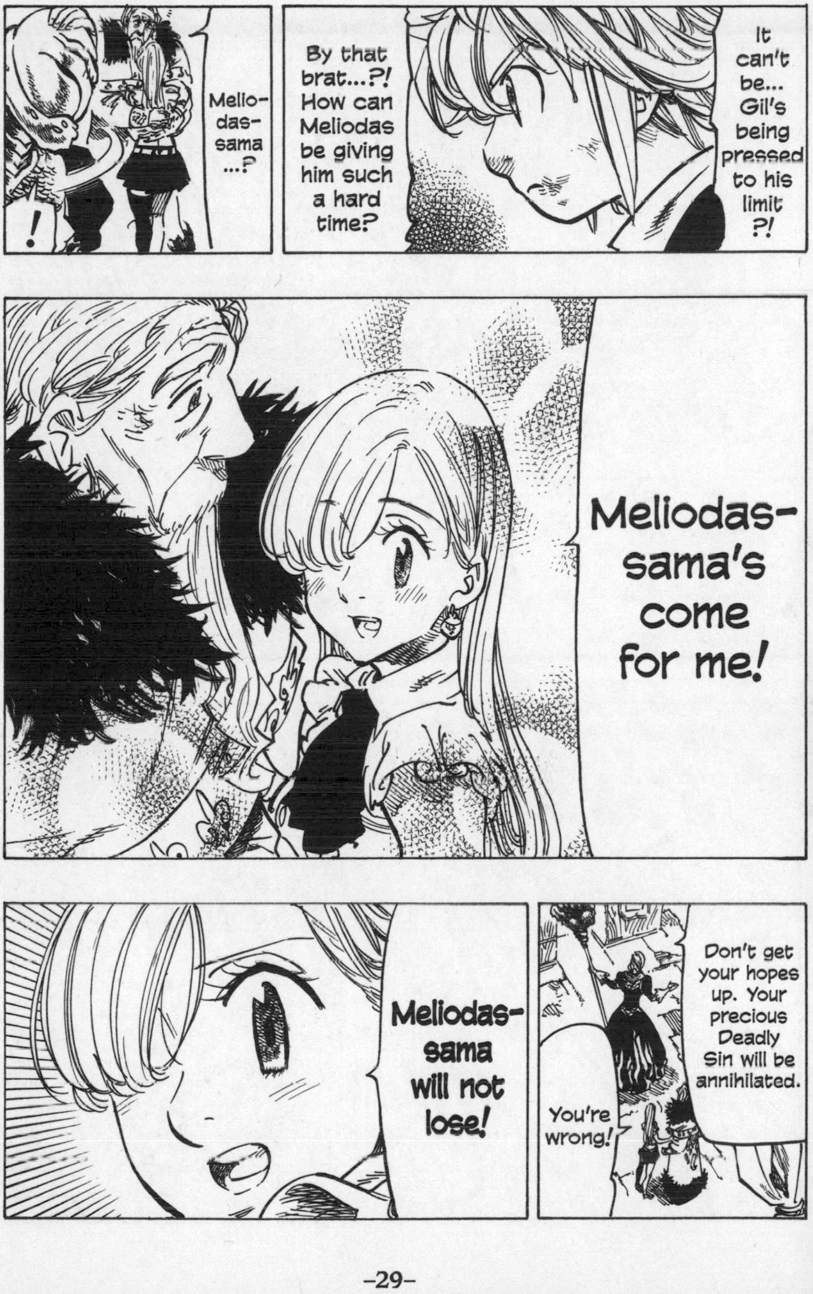
It can't be... Gil's being pressed to his limit?!
By that brat...?! How can Meliodas be giving him such a hard time?
Meliodas-sama ...?
!
Meliodas-sama's come for me!
Don't get your hopes up. Your precious Deadly Sin will be annihilated.
You're wrong!
Meliodas-sama will not lose!

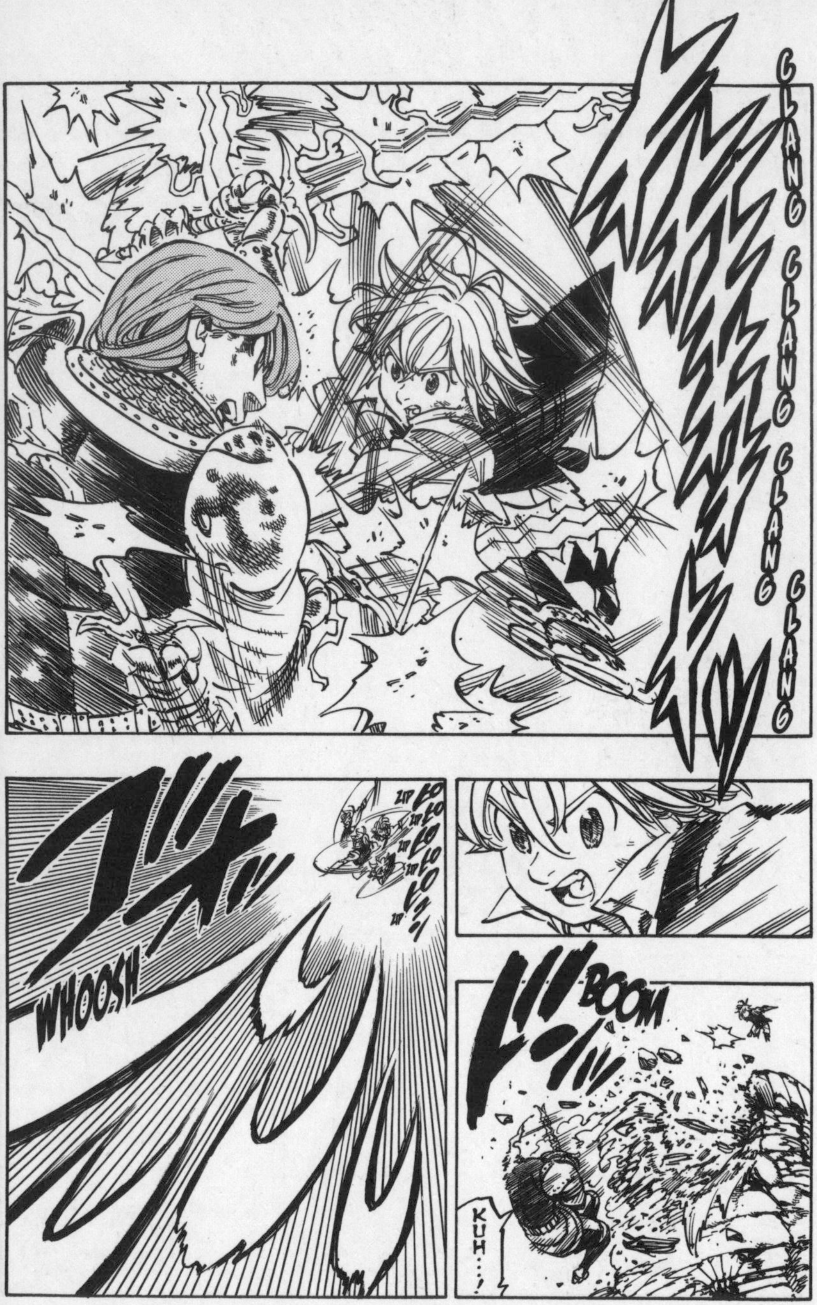
CLANG CLANG CLANG CLANG CLANG
BOOM
KUH...!
ZIP ZIP ZIP ZIP
WHOOSH

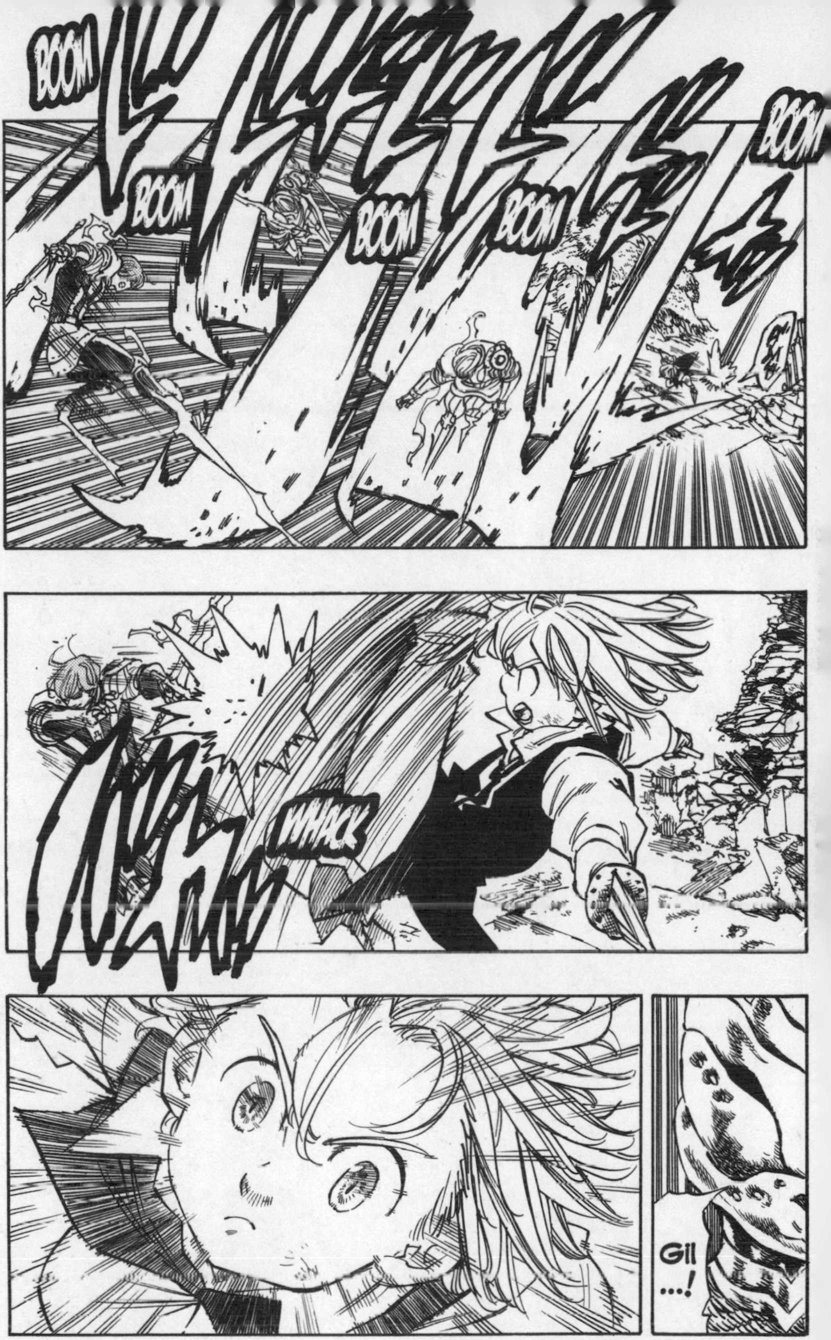
BOOM
BOOM
BOOM
BOOM
BOOM
WHACK
Gi!
...!

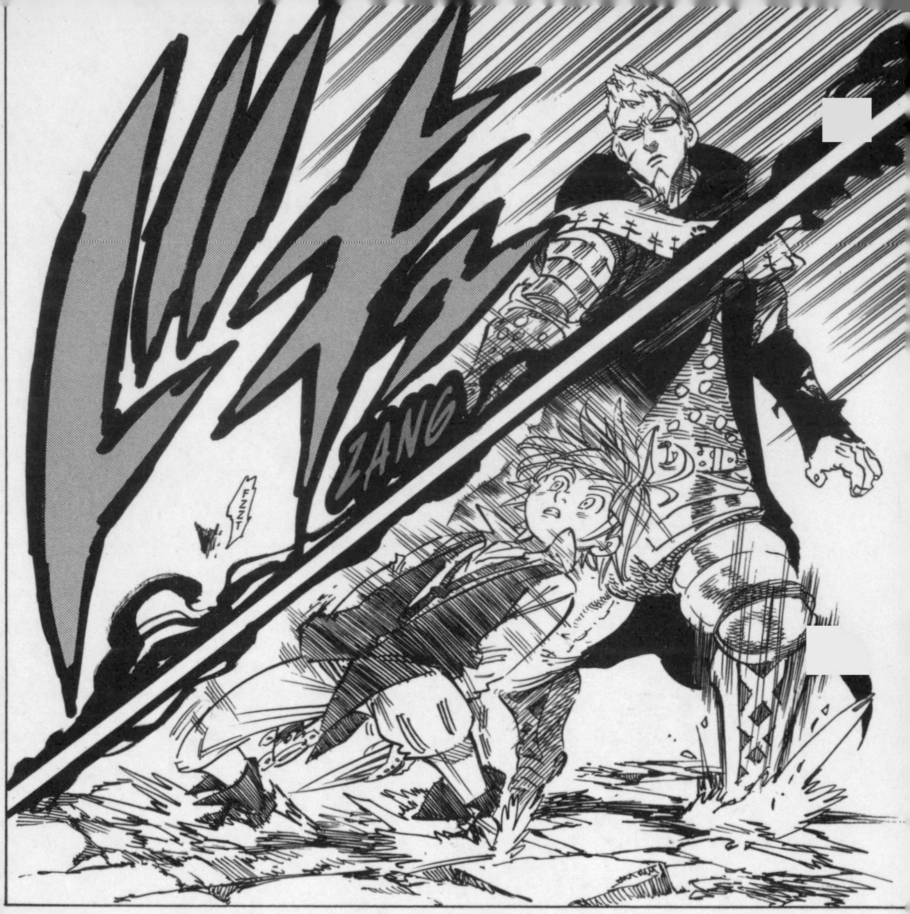
ZANG
FZZT

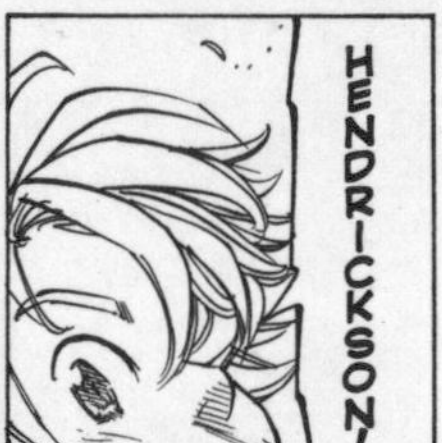
HENDRICKSON!

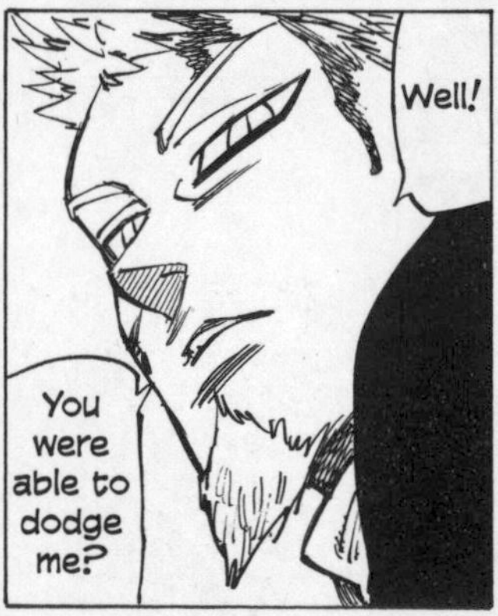
Well!
You were able to dodge me?

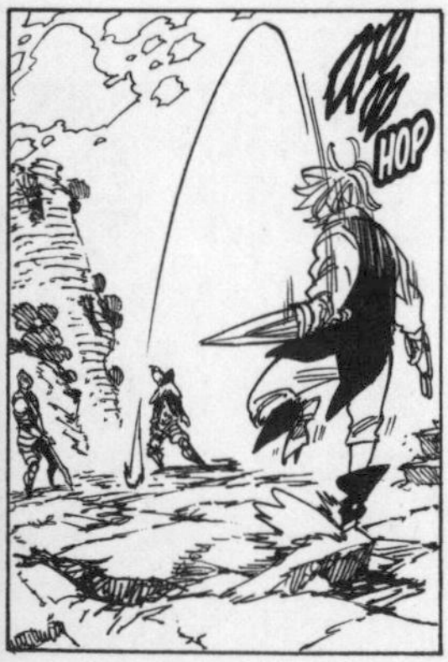
HOP

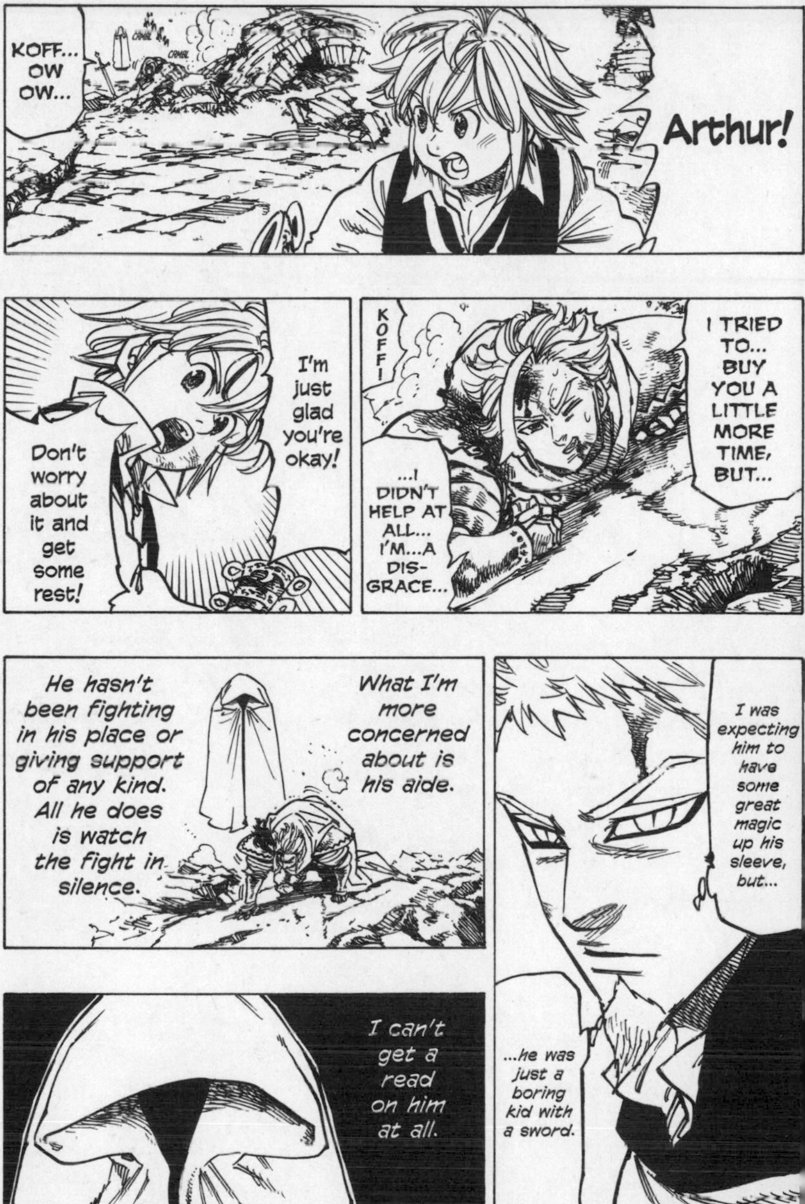
KOFF... OW OW...
CRMBL
CRMBL
Arthur!
KOFF!
I TRIED TO... BUY YOU A LITTLE MORE TIME, BUT...
...I DIDN'T HELP AT ALL... I'M...A DISGRACE...
I'm just glad you're okay!
Don't worry about it and get some rest!
I was expecting him to have some great magic up his sleeve, but...
...he was just a boring kid with a sword.
What I'm more concerned about is his aide.
He hasn't been fighting in his place or giving support of any kind. All he does is watch the fight in silence.
I can't get a read on him at all.

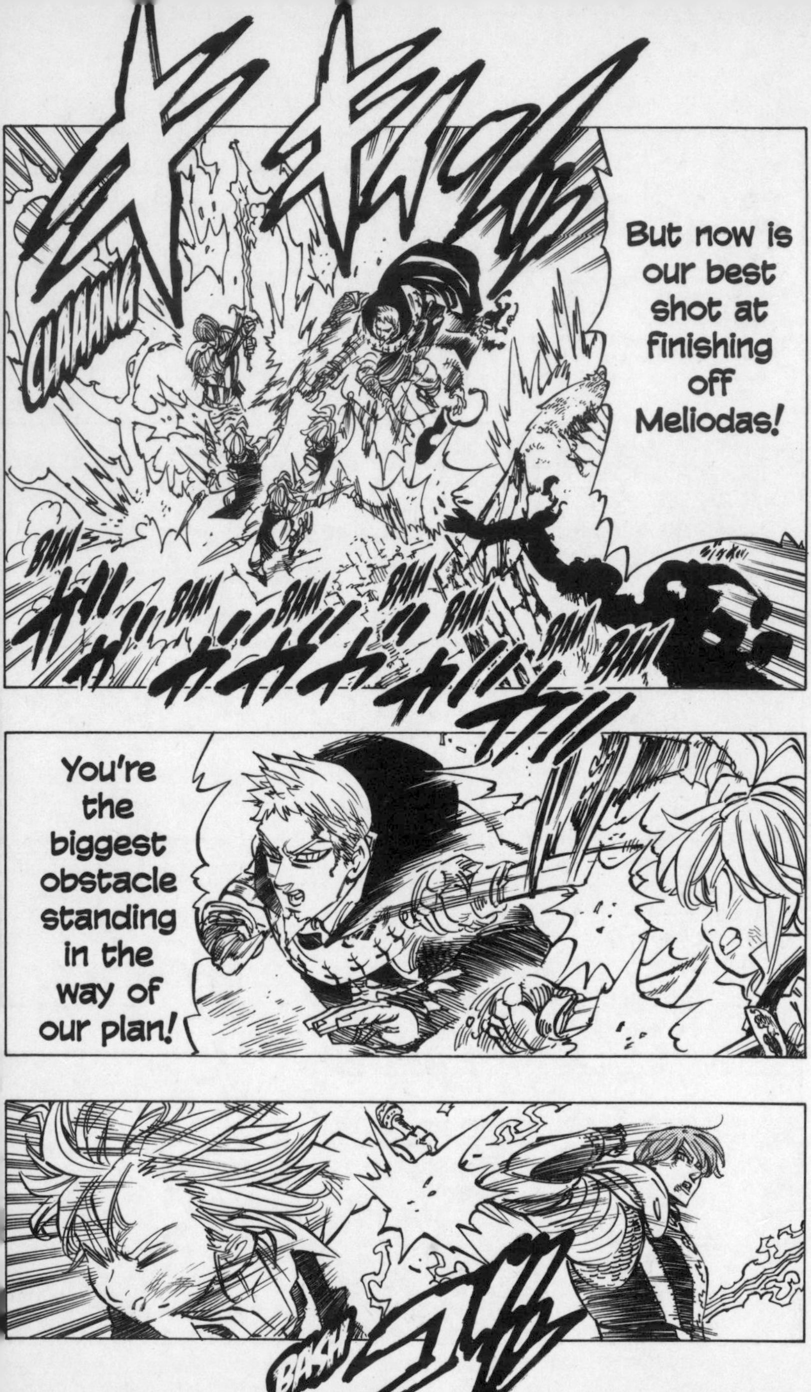
CLAAANG
But now is our best shot at finishing off Meliodas!
BAM BAM BAM BAM BAM BAM BAM
You're the biggest obstacle standing in the way of our plan!
BASH

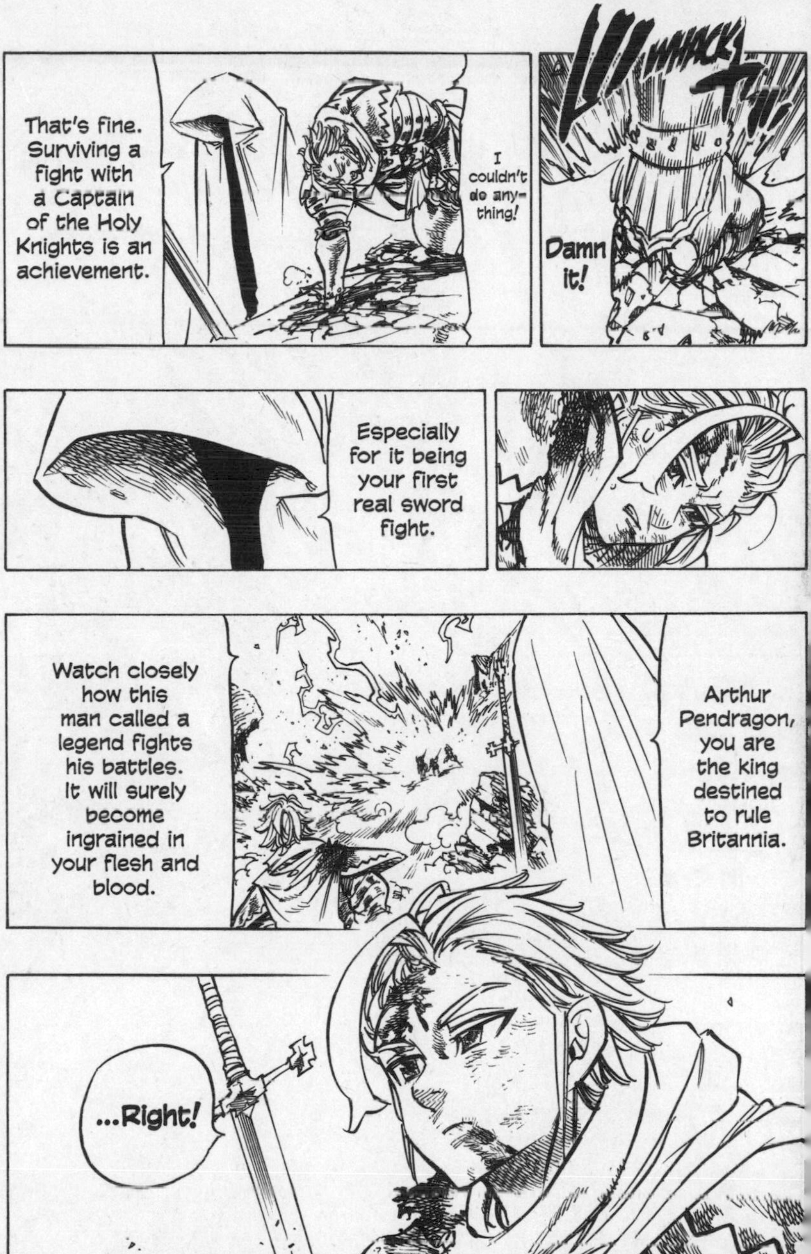
WHACK
Damn it!
I couldn't do anything!
That's fine. Surviving a fight with a Captain of the Holy Knights is an achievement.
Especially for it being your first real sword fight.
Arthur Pendragon, you are the king destined to rule Britannia.
Watch closely how this man called a legend fights his battles. It will surely become ingrained in your flesh and blood.
...Right!

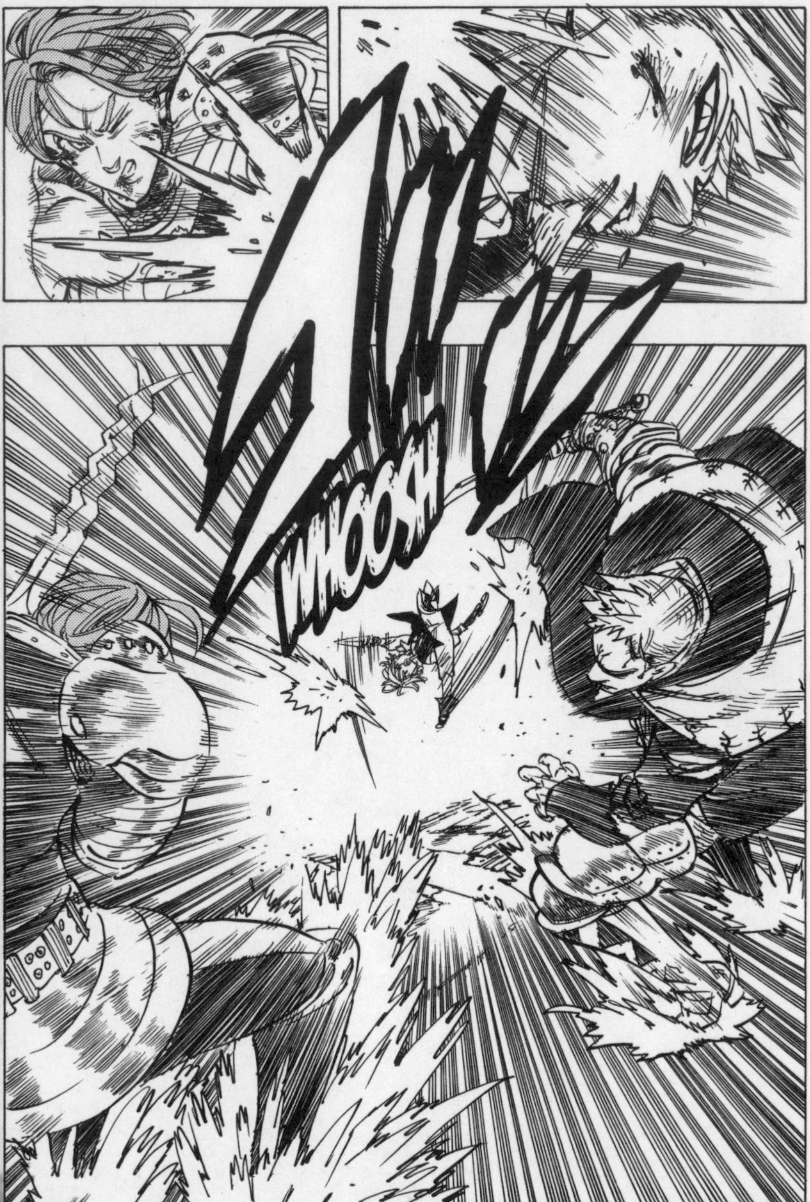
WHOOSH

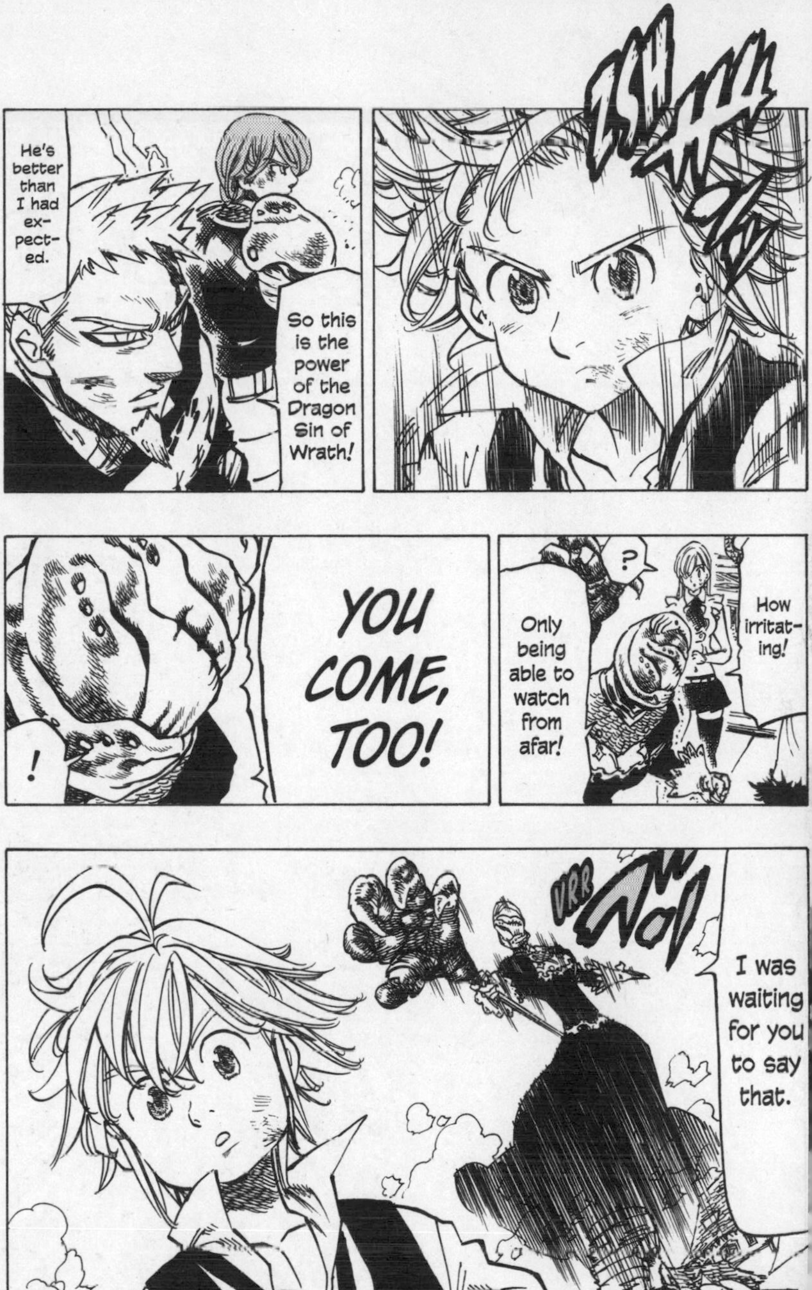
ZSH
So this is the power of the Dragon Sin of Wrath!
He's better than I had expected.
How irritating!
?
Only being able to watch from afar!
YOU COME, TOO!
!
I was waiting for you to say that.
VRR

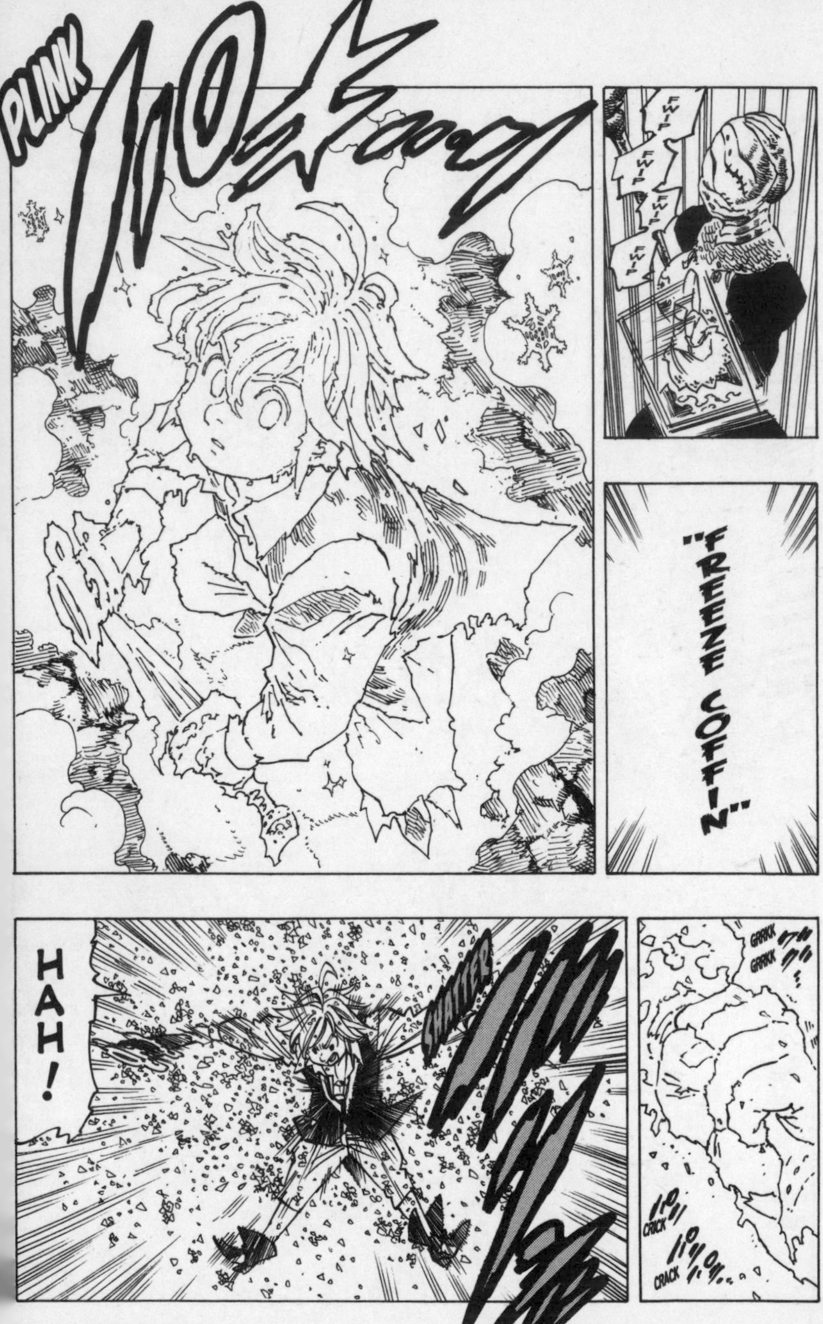
FWIP
FWIP
FWIP
FWIP
"FREEZE COFFIN"
PLINK
GRRKK
GRRKK
CRACK
CRACK
HAH!
SHATTER

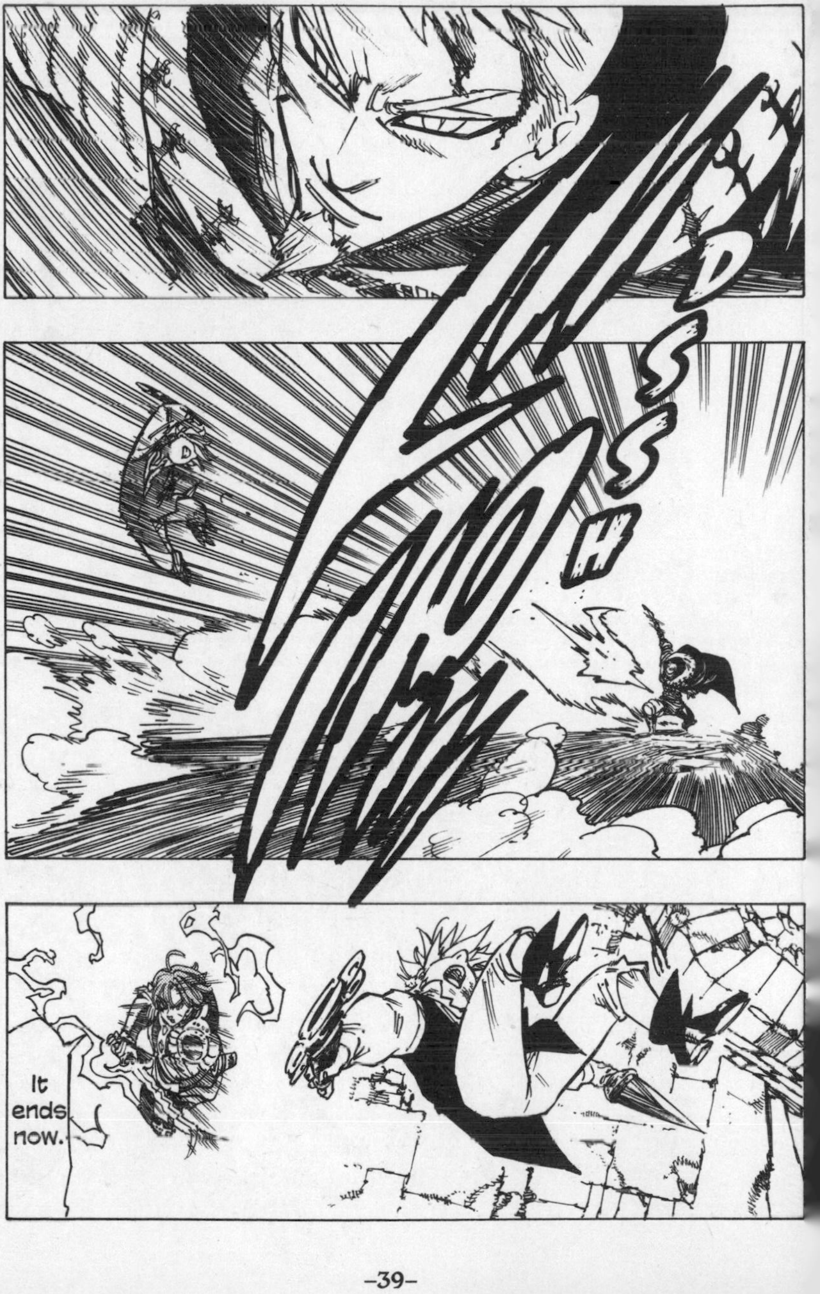
DSSH
It ends now.

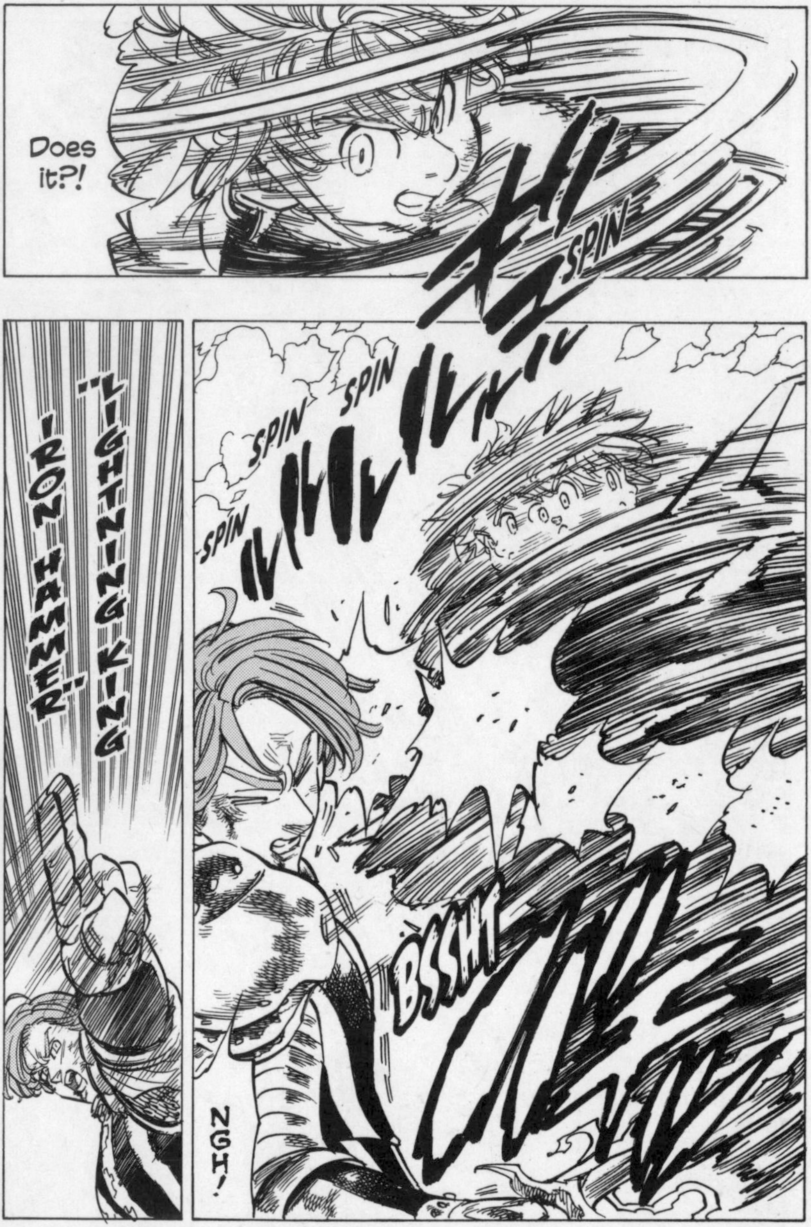
Does it?!
SPIN
SPIN
SPIN
SPIN
SPIN
BSSHT
NGH!
...LIGHTNING KING
IRON HAMMER...

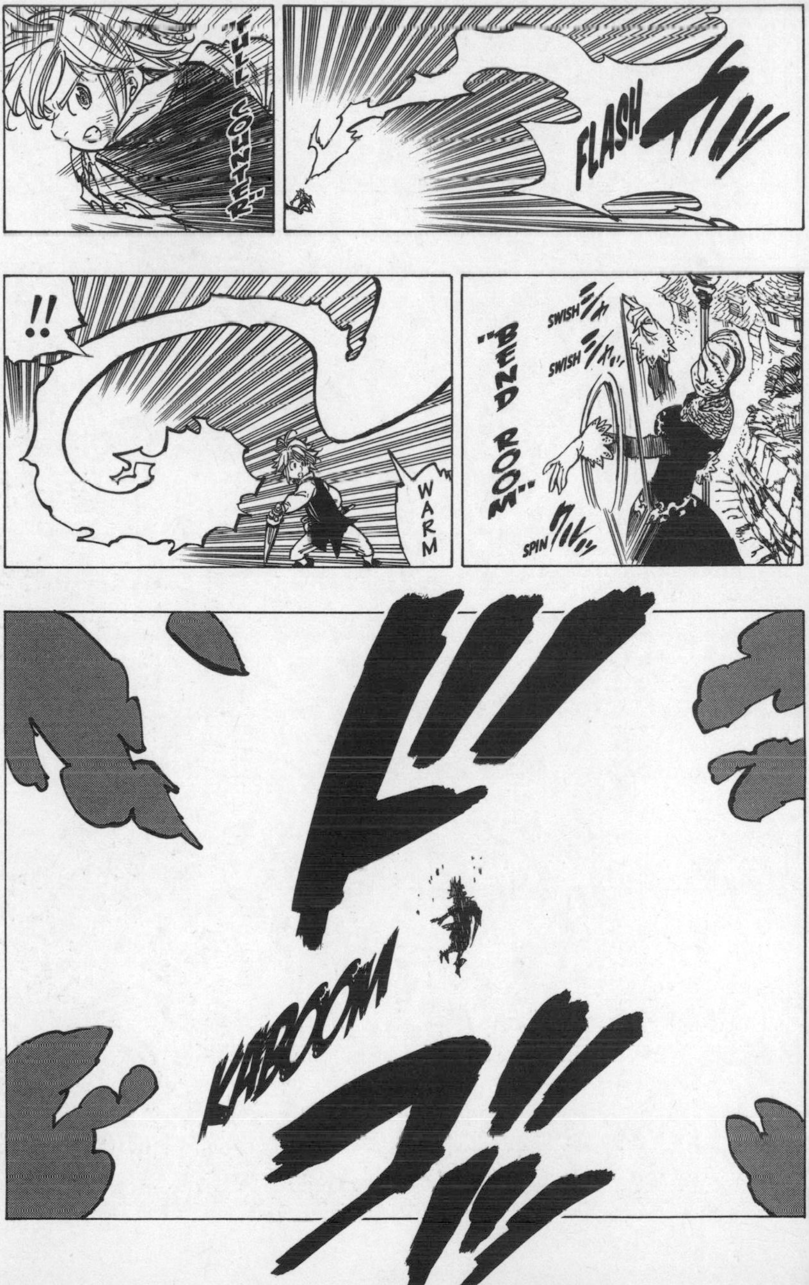
FLASH
...FULL COUNTER...
SWISH
SWISH
...BEND ROOM...
SPIN
!!
WARM
KABOOM

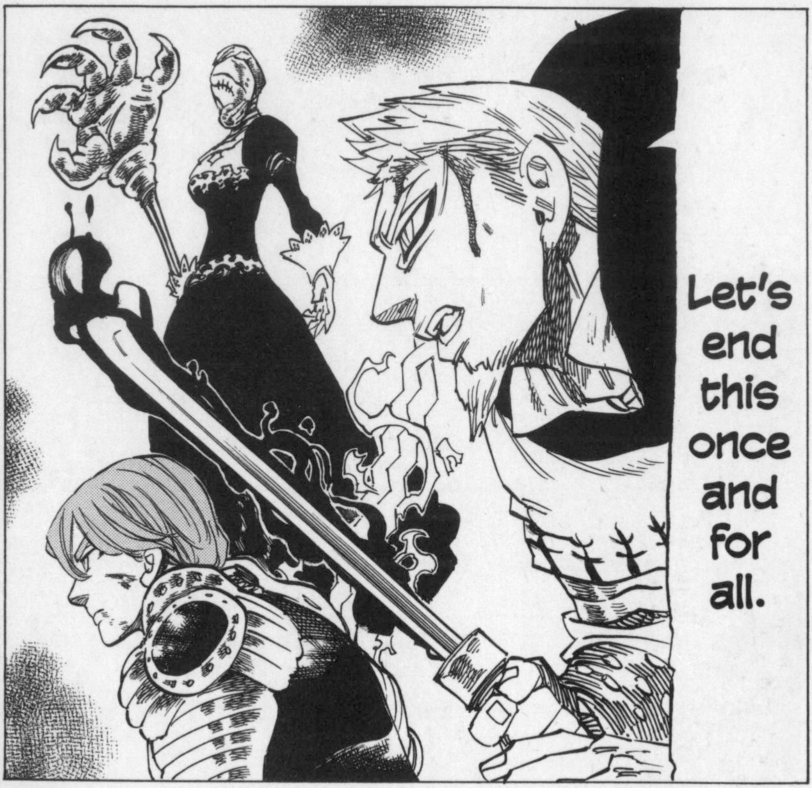
Let's end this once and for all.

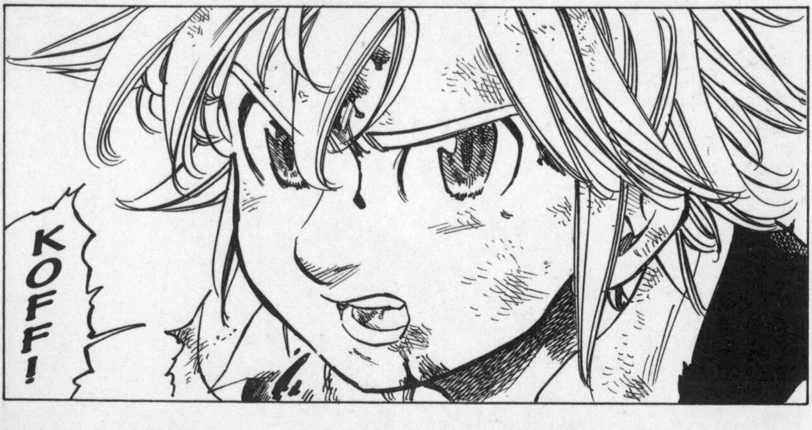
KOFF!

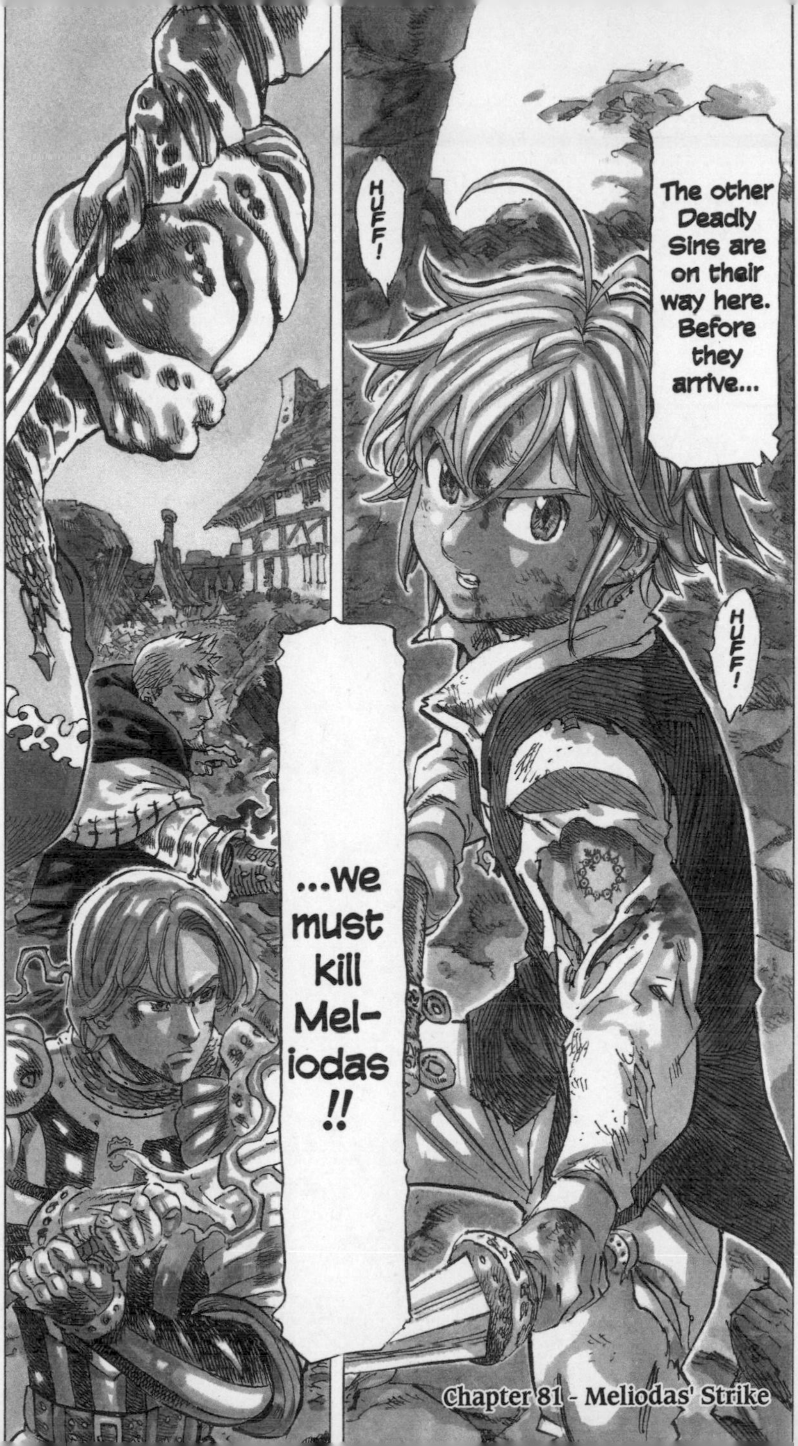
The other Deadly Sins are on their way here. Before they arrive...
HUFF!
HUFF!
...we must kill Meliodas!!

Chapter 81 - Meliodas' Strike

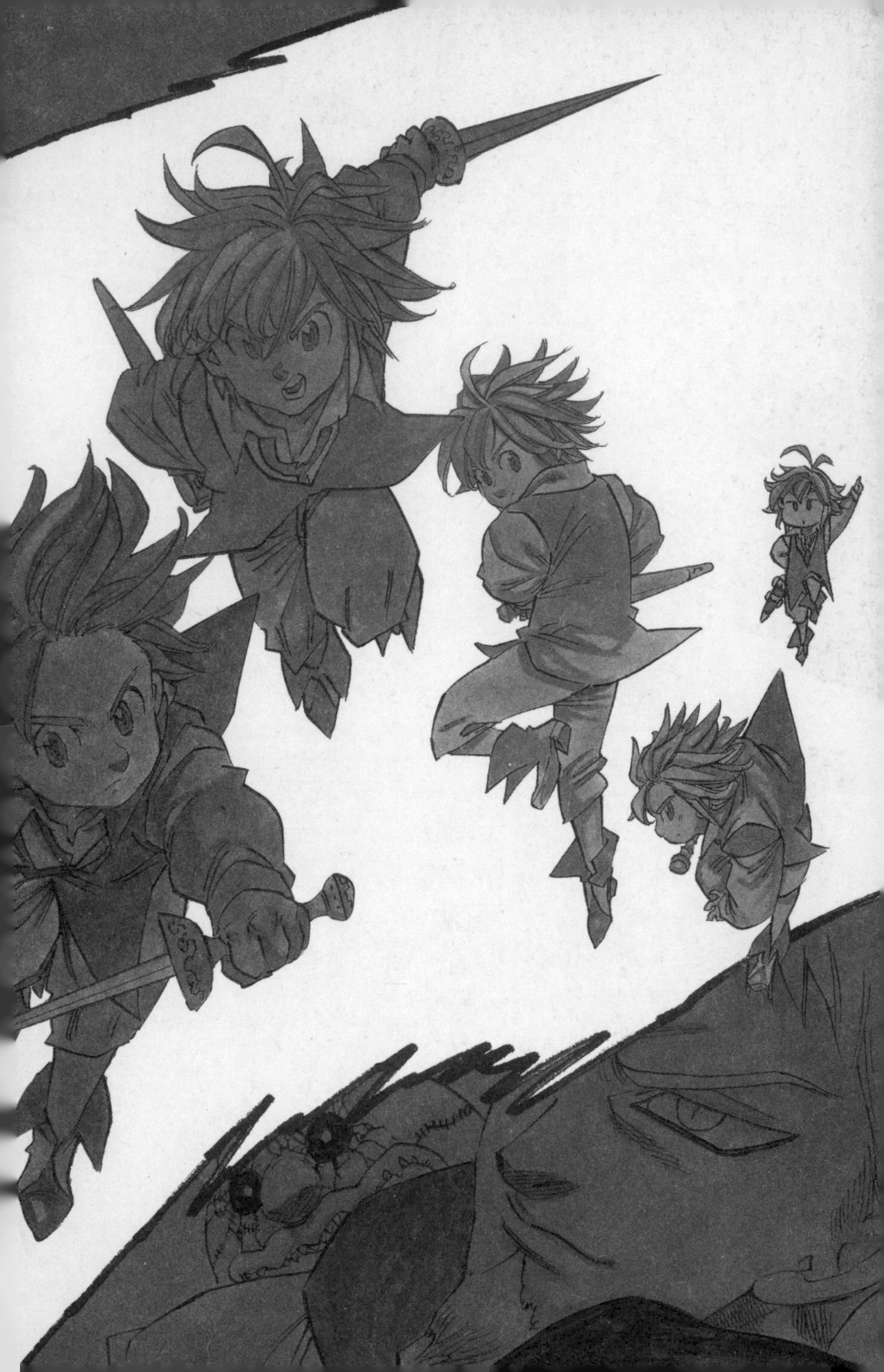

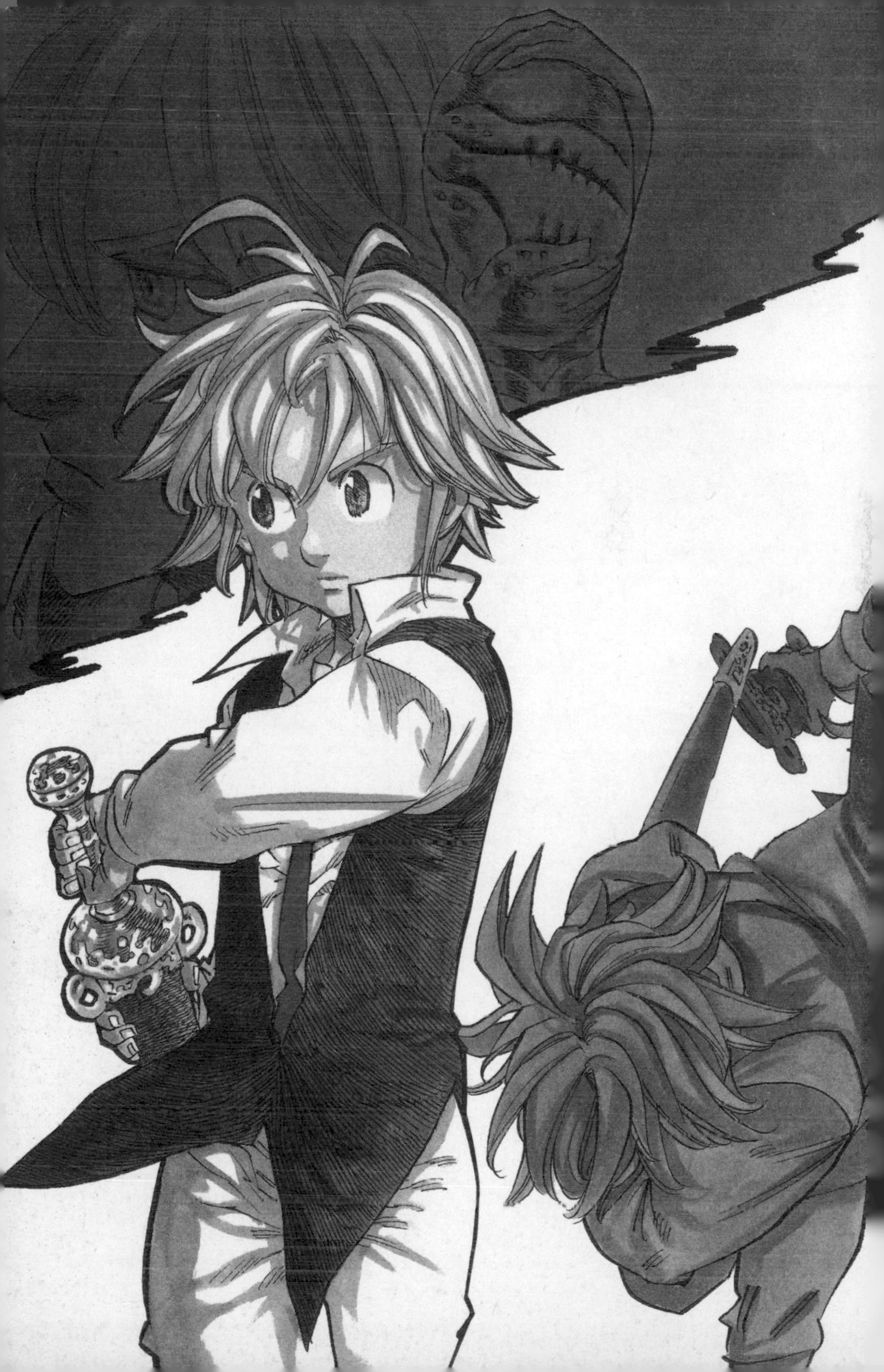

The new king of the Camelot, situated to the south of Britannia. He's still only 16 years old, but his swordsmanship surpasses that of your average Holy Knight. We don't yet know all that his magical powers entail, but though he doesn't carry himself like a dignified king, he's amiable and treats everyone equally.

THE YOUNG KING OF CAMELOT

ARTHUR

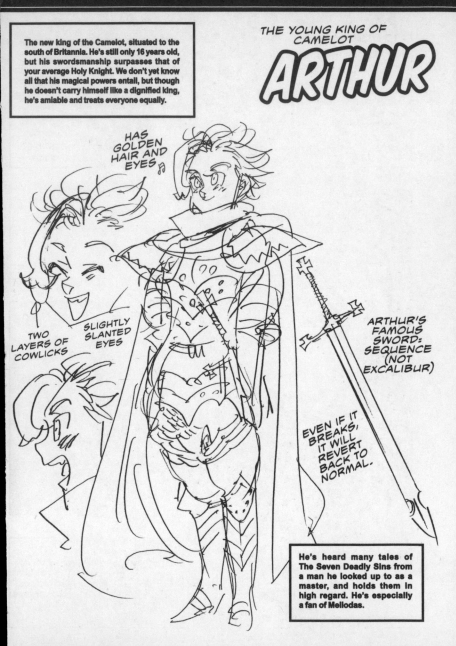

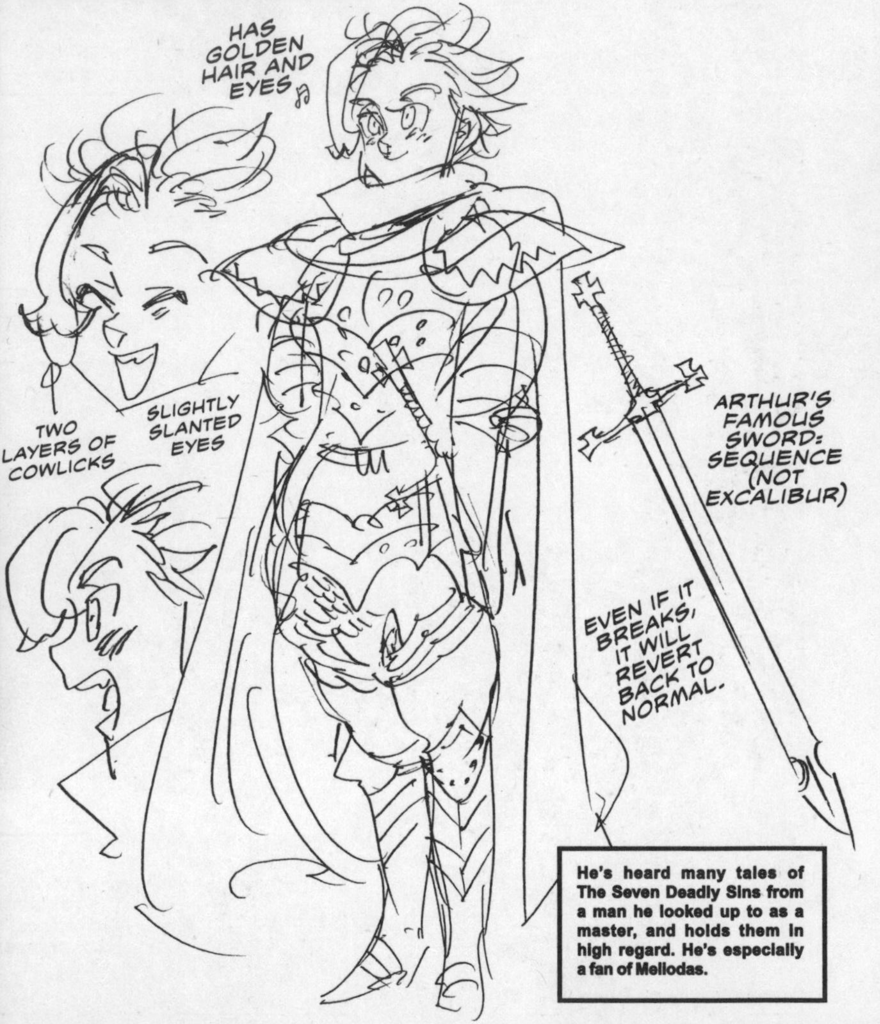
HAS GOLDEN HAIR AND EYES ♪
TWO LAYERS OF COWLICKS
SLIGHTLY SLANTED EYES
ARTHUR'S FAMOUS SWORD: SEQUENCE (NOT EXCALIBUR)
EVEN IF IT BREAKS, IT WILL REVERT BACK TO NORMAL.

He's heard many tales of The Seven Deadly Sins from a man he looked up to as a master, and holds them in high regard. He's especially a fan of Meliodas.

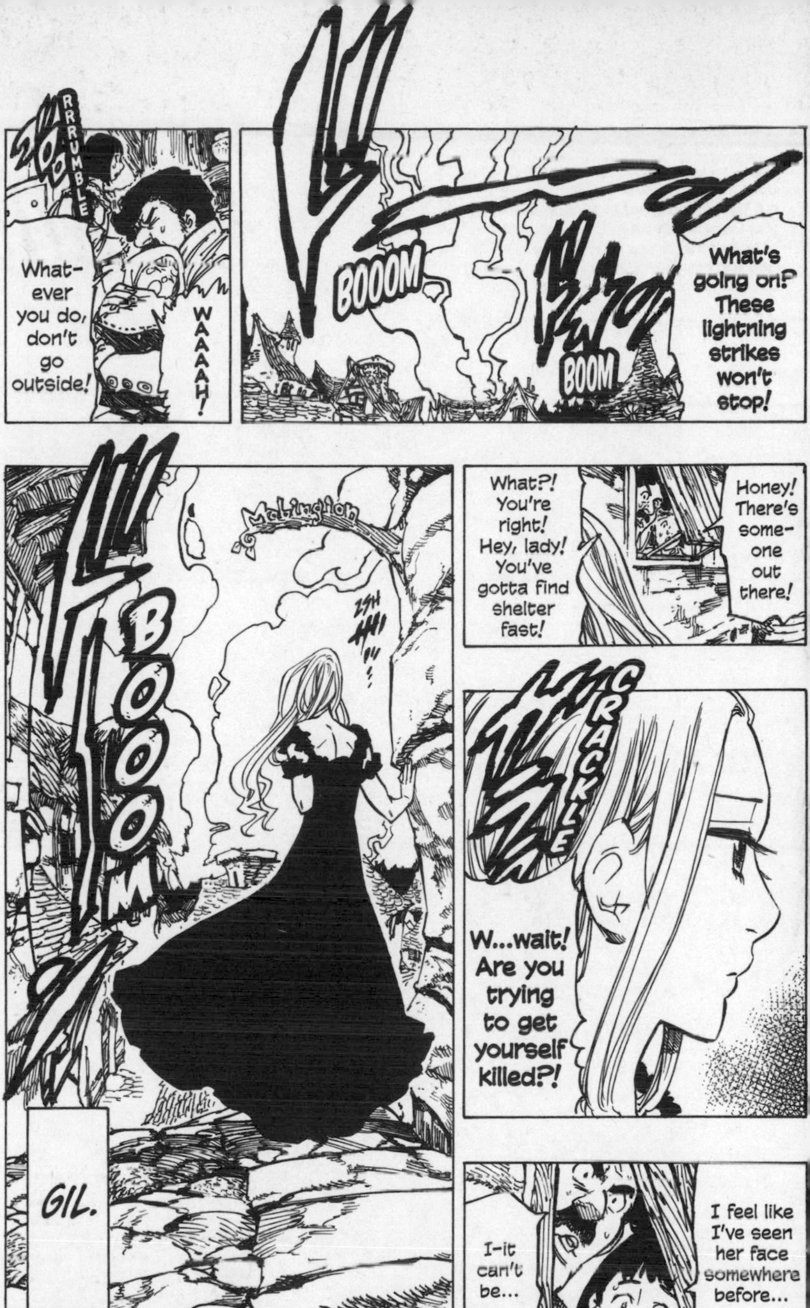
BOOOM
BOOM
What's going on!? These lightning strikes won't stop!
RRRUMBLE
What-ever you do, don't go outside!
WAAAAH!
Honey! There's some-one out there!
What?! You're right! Hey, lady! You've gotta find shelter fast!
CRACKLE
W...wait! Are you trying to get yourself killed?!
I feel like I've seen her face somewhere before...
I-it can't be...
BOOOOM
GIL.

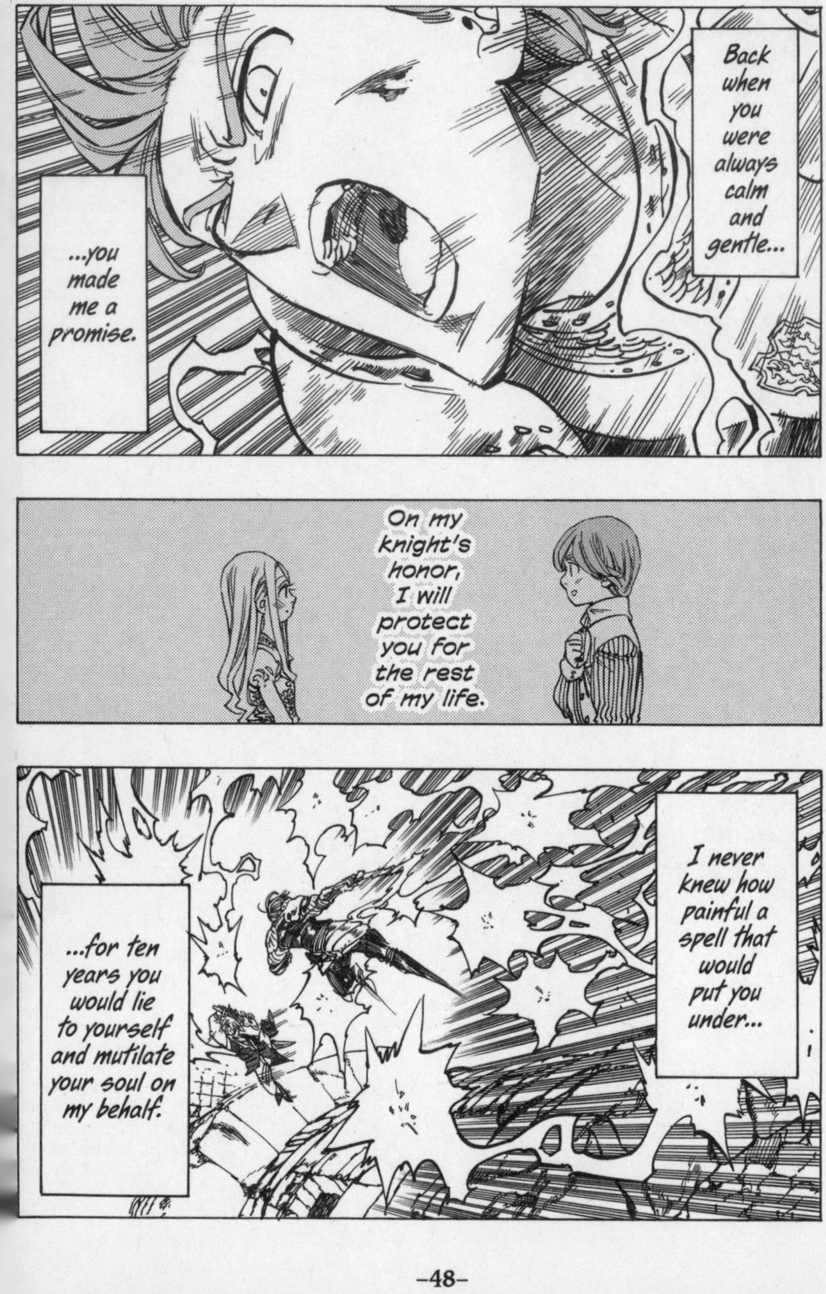
Back when you were always calm and gentle...
...you made me a promise.
On my knight's honor, I will protect you for the rest of my life.
I never knew how painful a spell that would put you under...
...for ten years you would lie to yourself and mutilate your soul on my behalf.

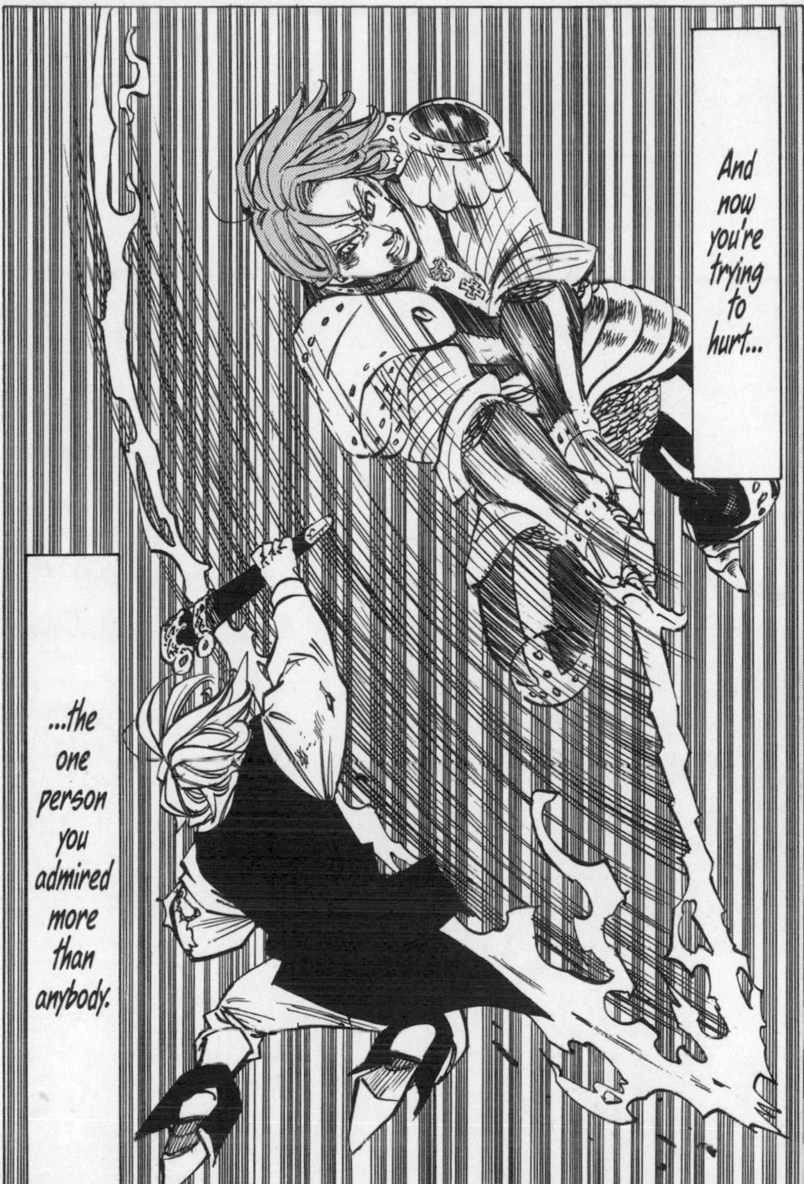
And now you're trying to hurt...
...the one person you admired more than anybody.

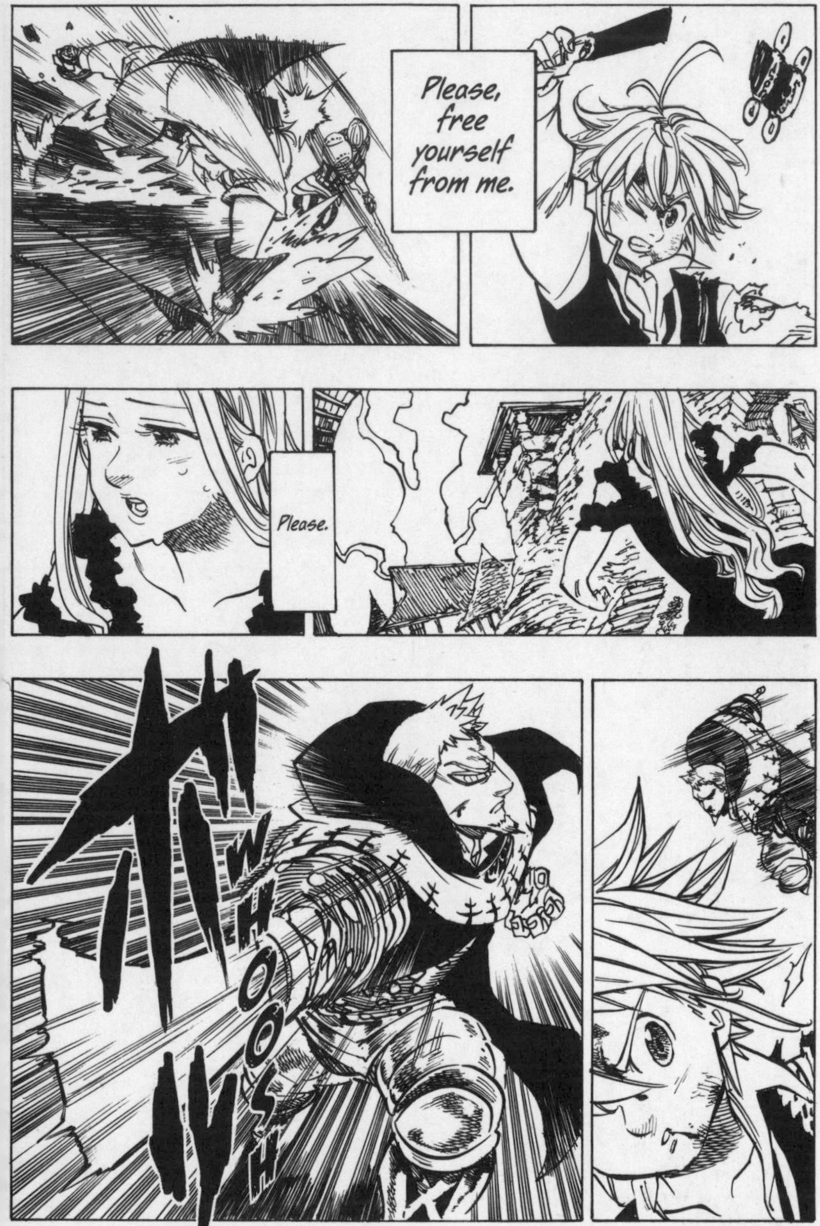
Please, free yourself from me.
Please.
WHOOSH

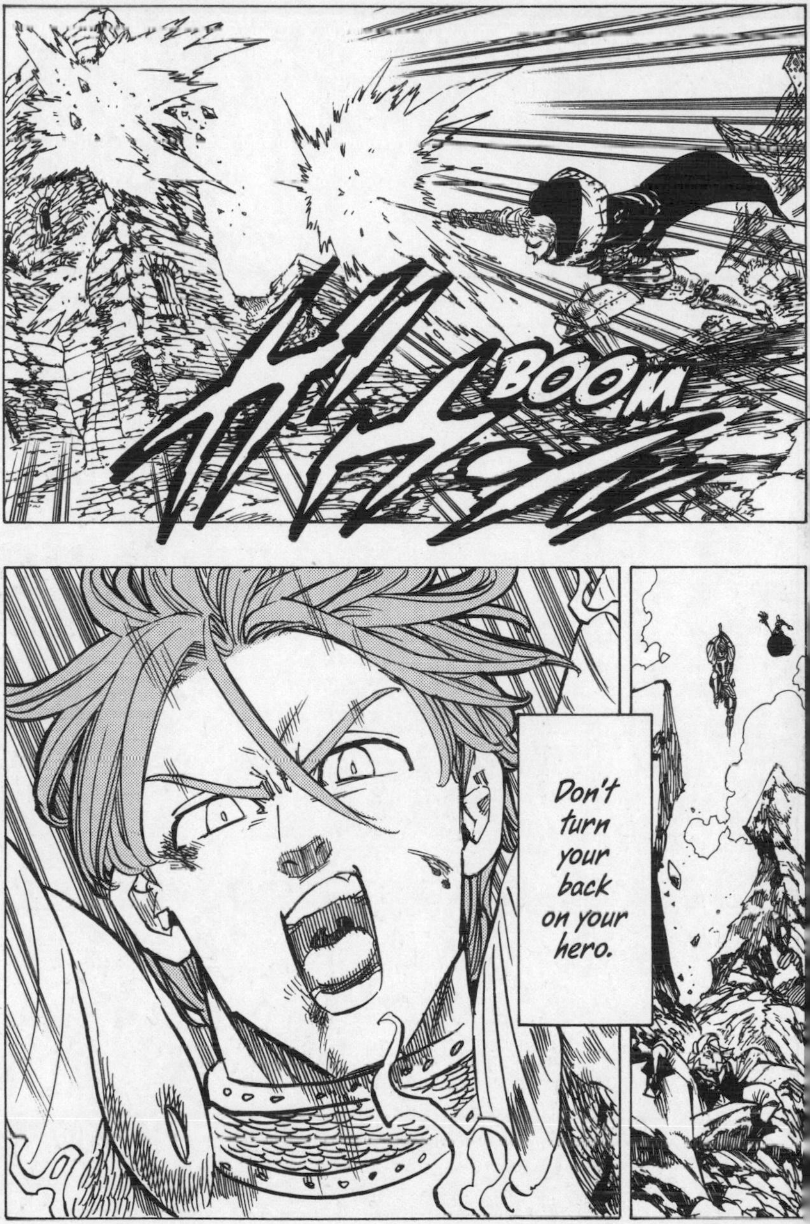
BOOM
Don't turn your back on your hero.

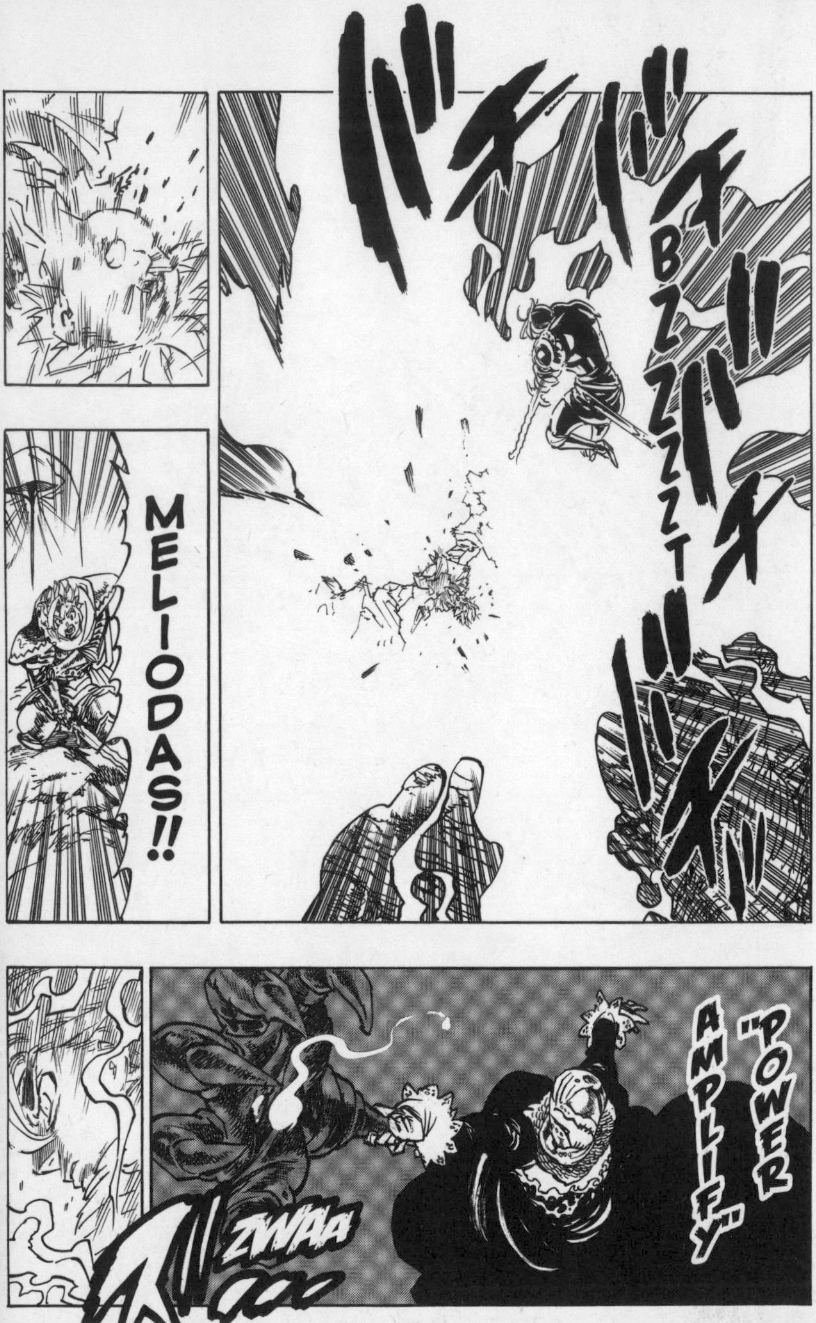
BZZZZZT
MELIODAS!!
"POWER AMPLIFY"
ZWAAAAAA

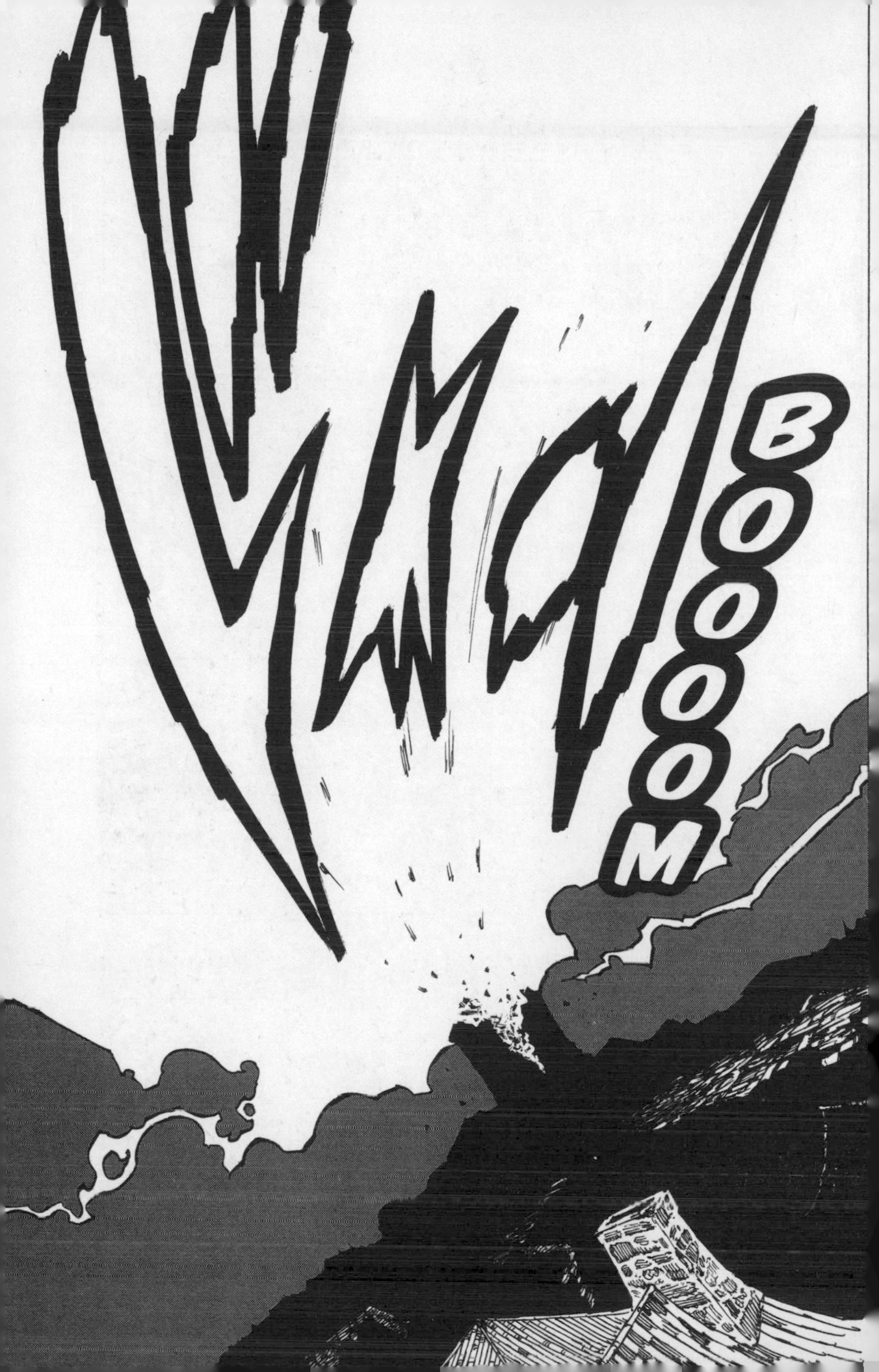
BOOOOOM

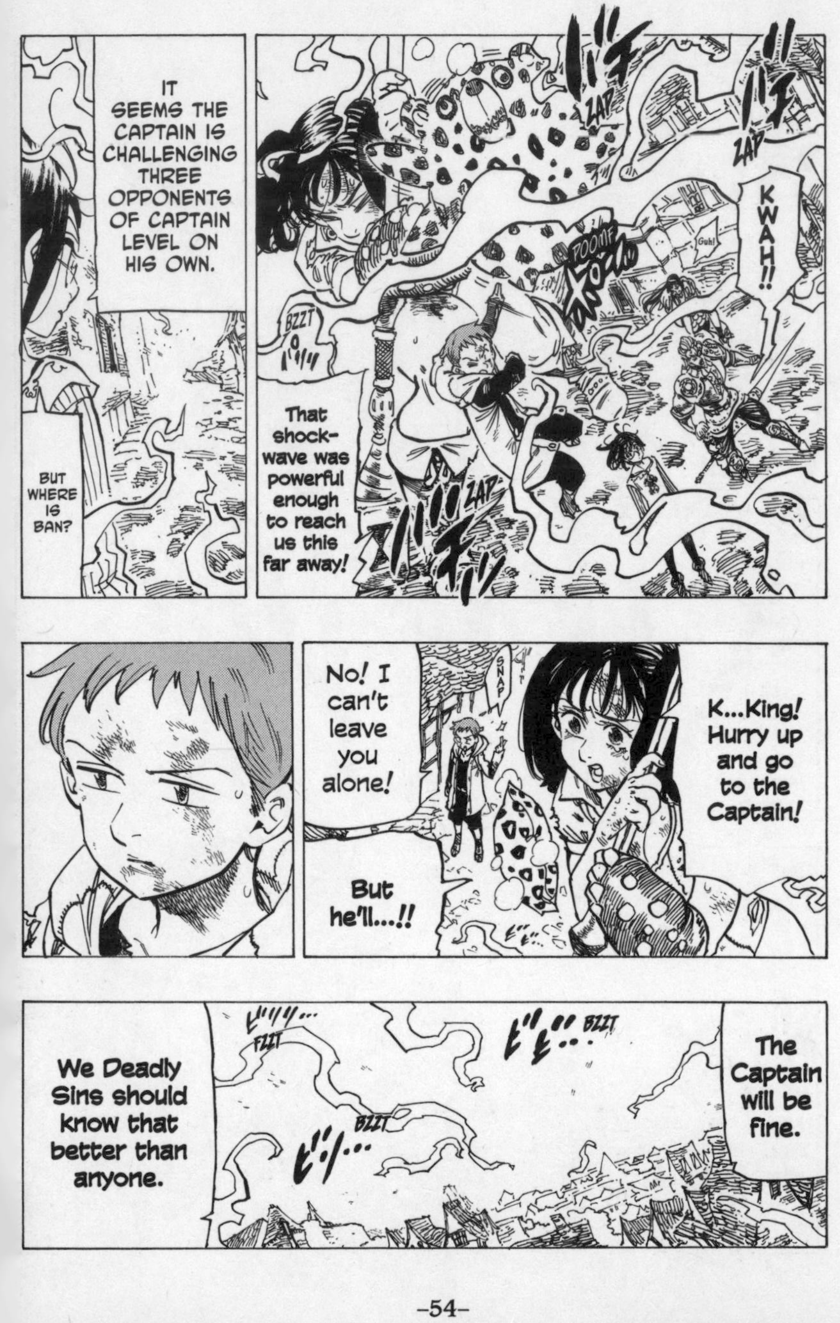
ZAP
ZAP
KWAH!!
Guh!
POOMF
BZZT
That shock-wave was powerful enough to reach us this far away!
ZAP
IT SEEMS THE CAPTAIN IS CHALLENGING THREE OPPONENTS OF CAPTAIN LEVEL ON HIS OWN.
BUT WHERE IS BAN?
K...King! Hurry up and go to the Captain!
SNAP
No! I can't leave you alone!
But he'll...!!
The Captain will be fine.
BZZT
FZZT
BZZT
We Deadly Sins should know that better than anyone.

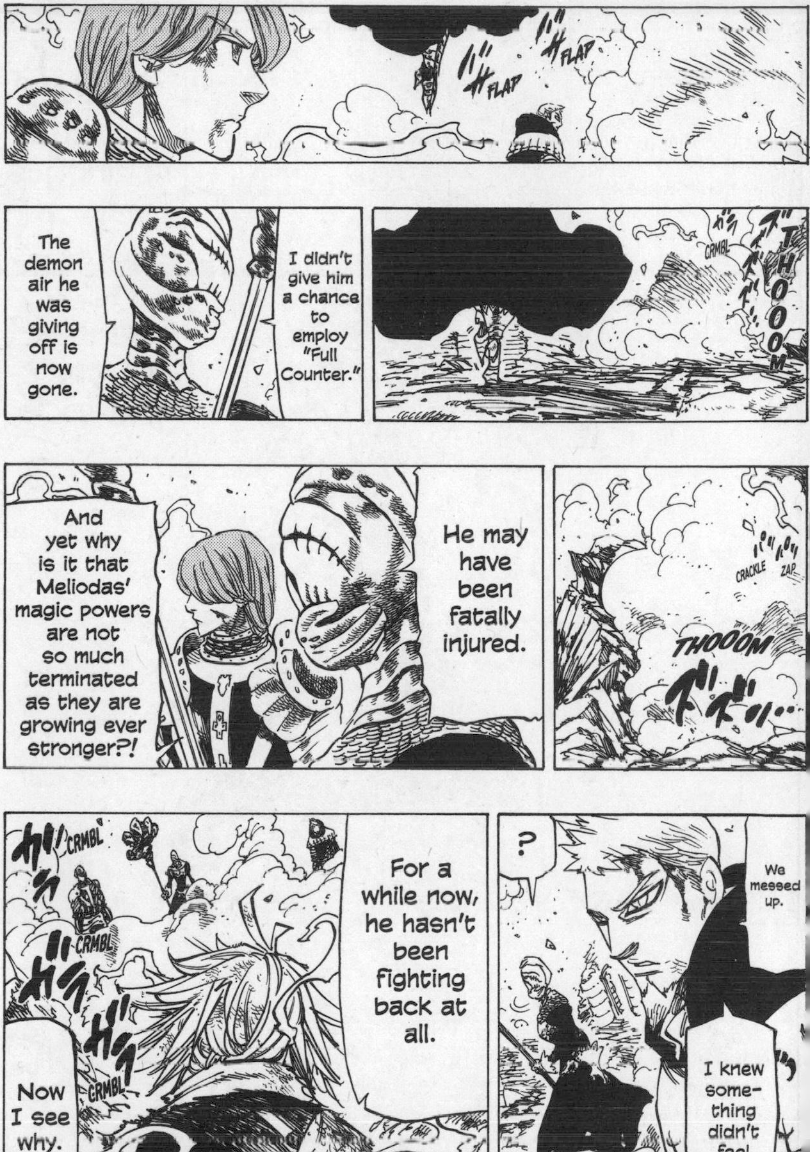
FLAP
FLAP
CRMBL
THOOOOM
I didn't give him a chance to employ "Full Counter."
The demon air he was giving off is now gone.
CRACKLE
ZAP
THOOOM
He may have been fatally injured.
And yet why is it that Meliodas' magic powers are not so much terminated as they are growing ever stronger?!
We messed up.
?
I knew some-thing didn't feel right.
For a while now, he hasn't been fighting back at all.
CRMBL
CRMBL
CRMBL
Now I see why.

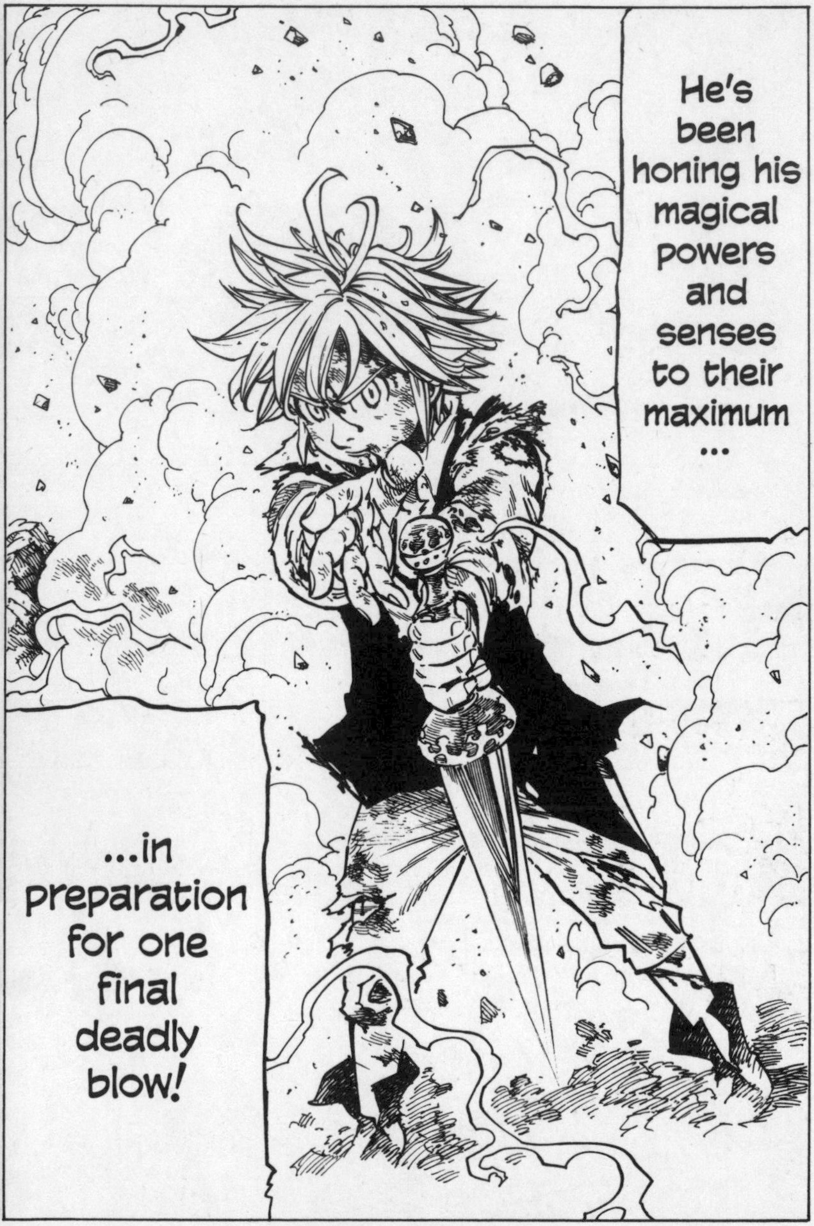
He's been honing his magical powers and senses to their maximum ...
...in preparation for one final deadly blow!

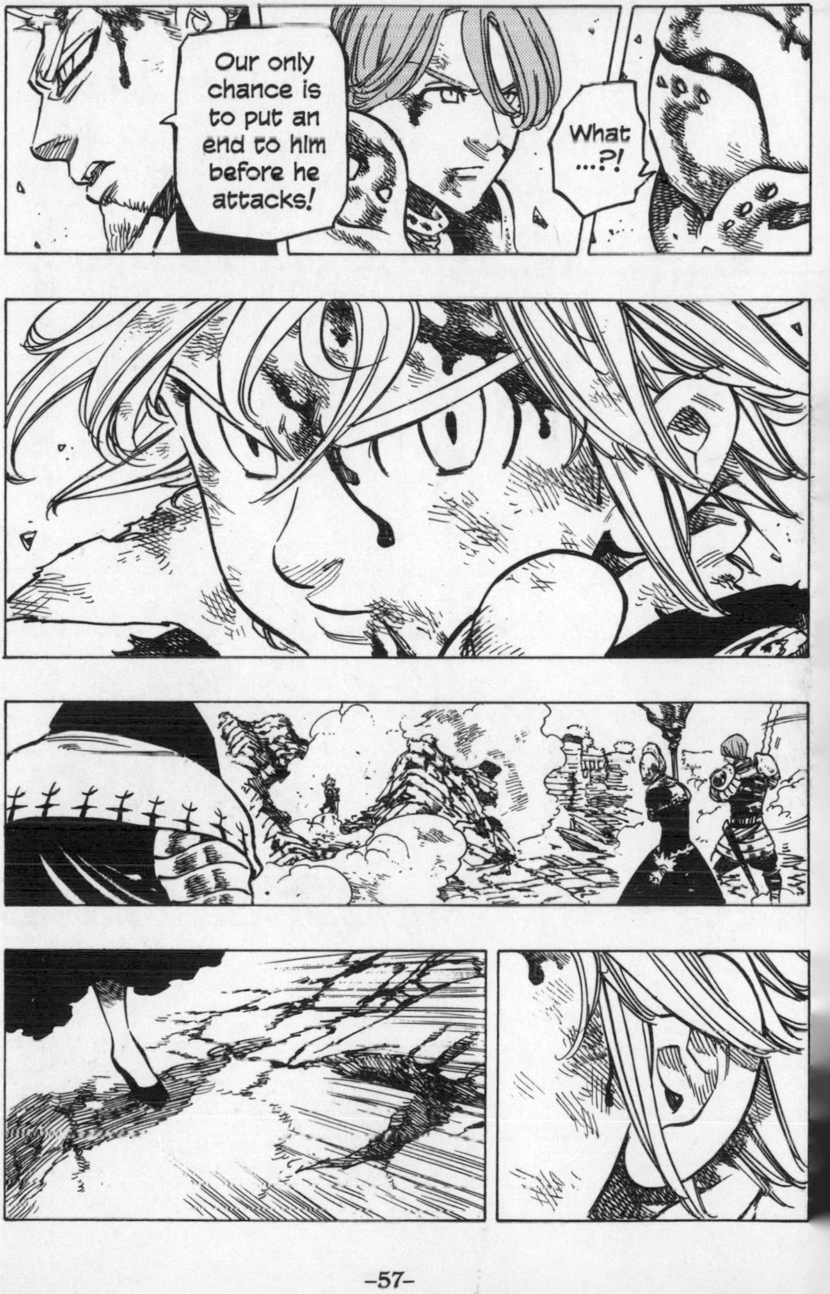
What ...?!
Our only chance is to put an end to him before he attacks!

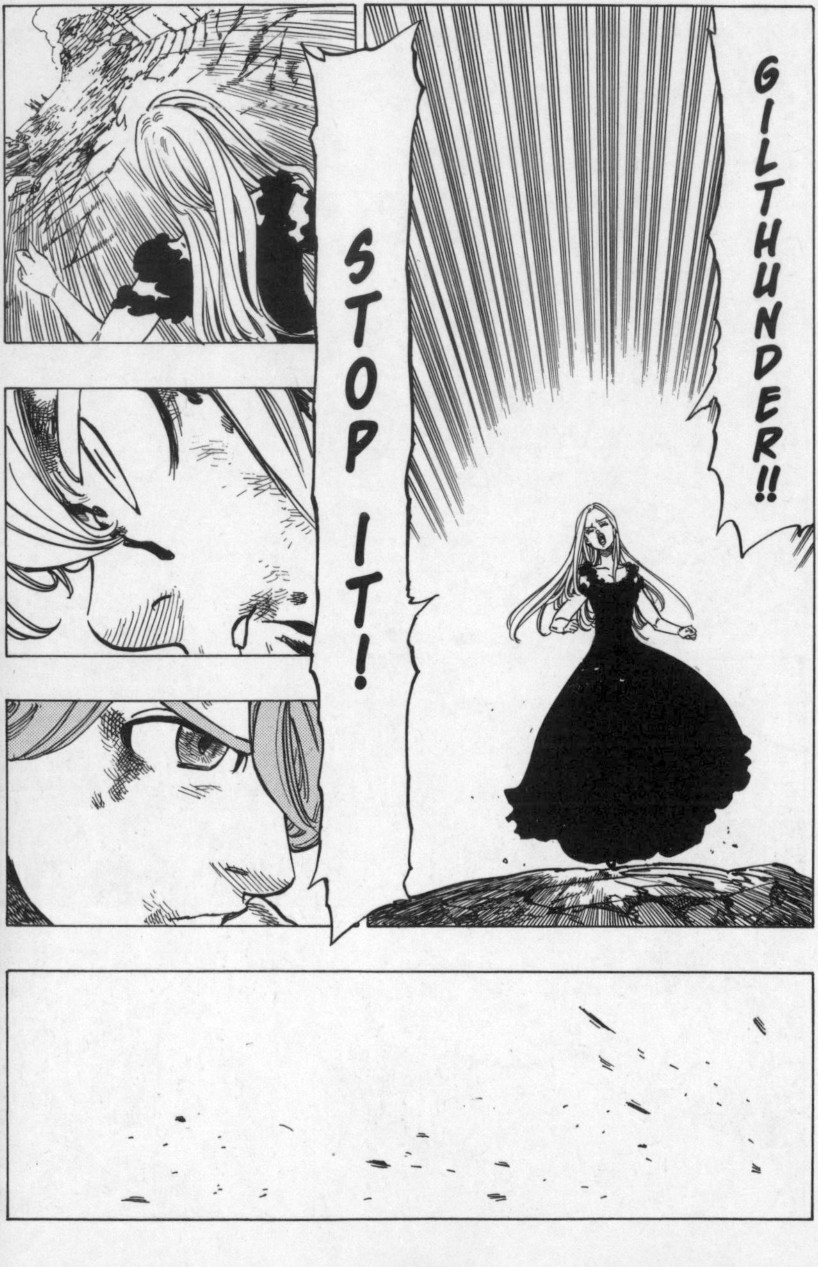
GILTHUNDER!!
STOP IT!

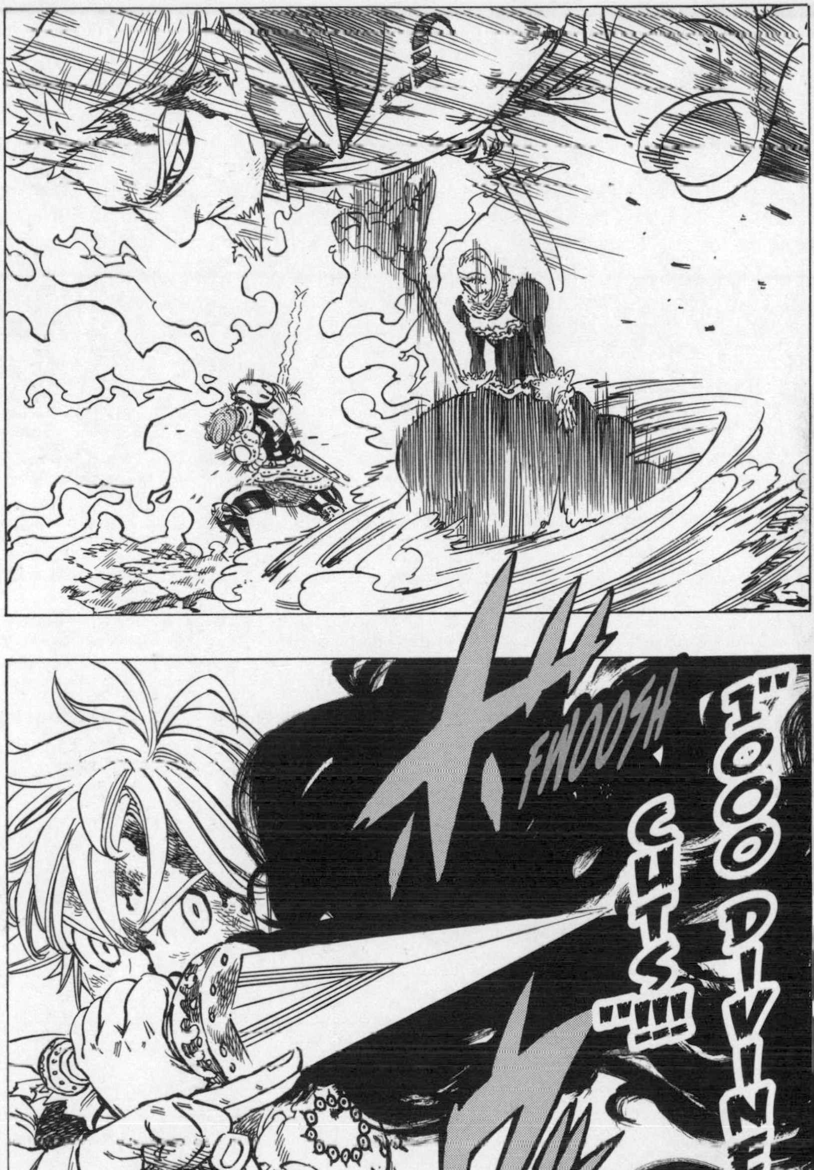
FWOOSH
"1000 DIVINE CUTS"!!!

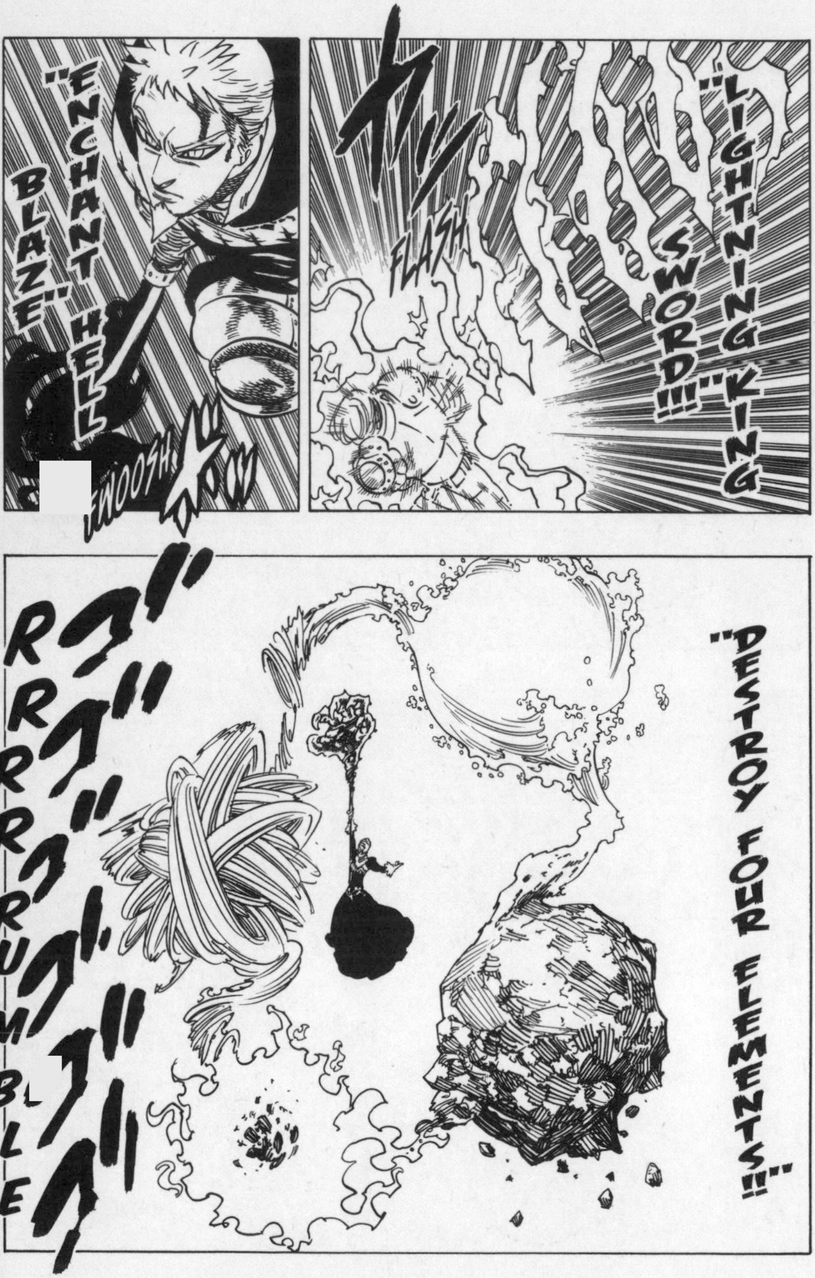
"LIGHTNING KING SWORD!!!"
FLASH
"ENCHANT HELL BLAZE.."
FWOOSH
"DESTROY FOUR ELEMENTS!!!"
RRRRRUMBLE

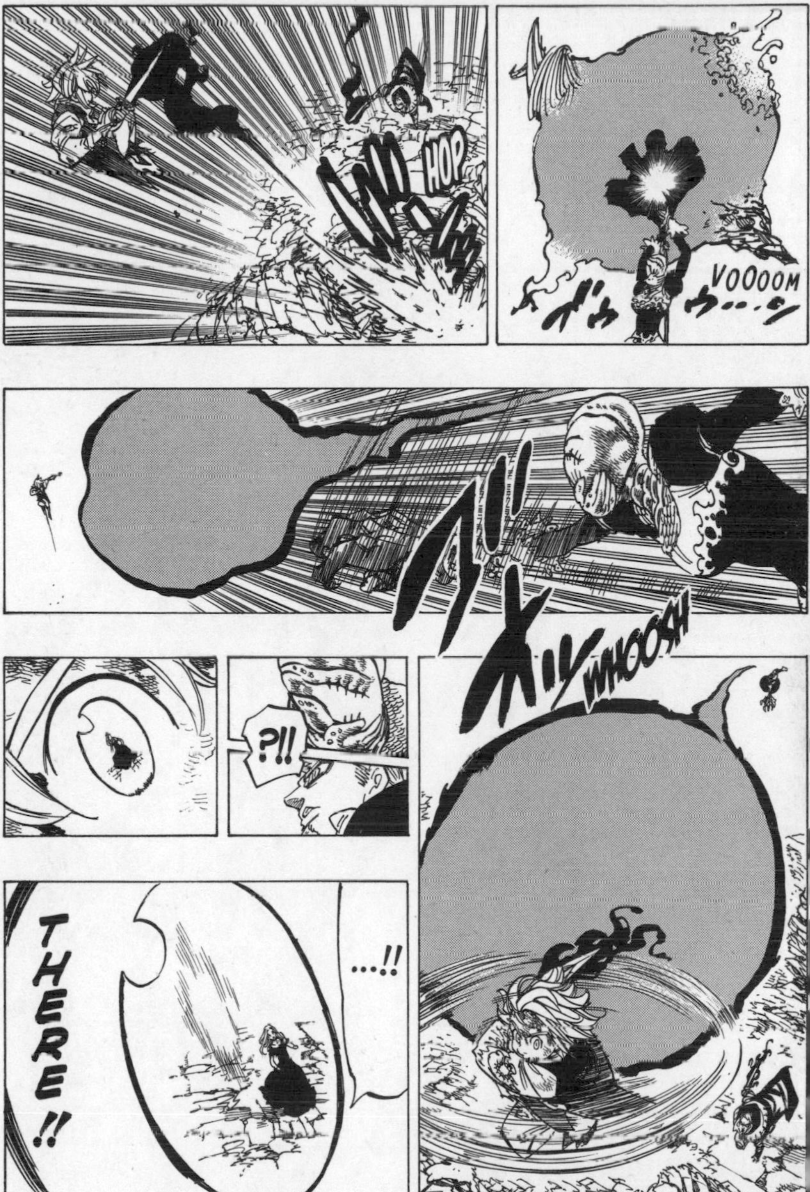
VOOOOM
HOP
WHOOSH
?!!
...!!
THERE!!

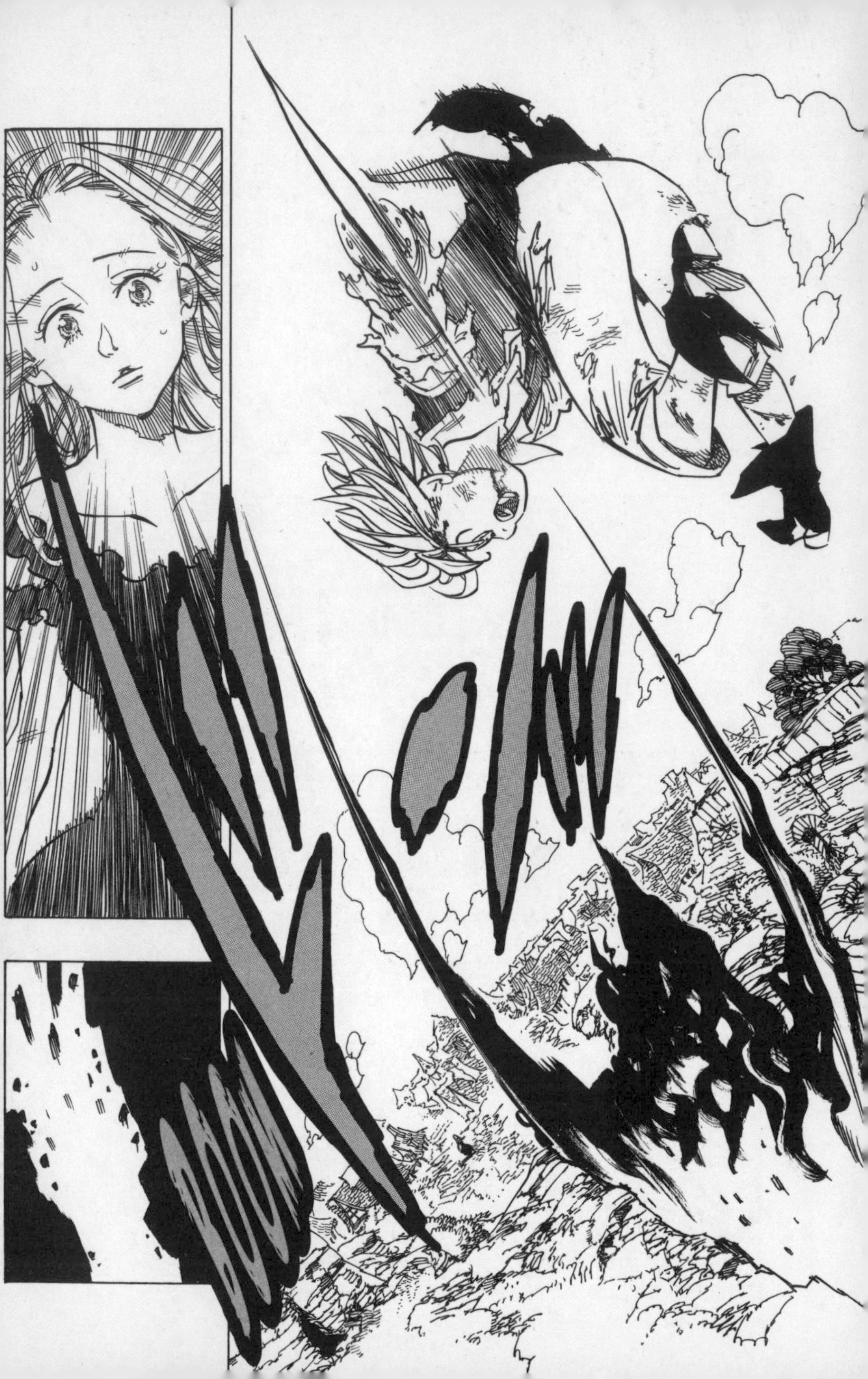

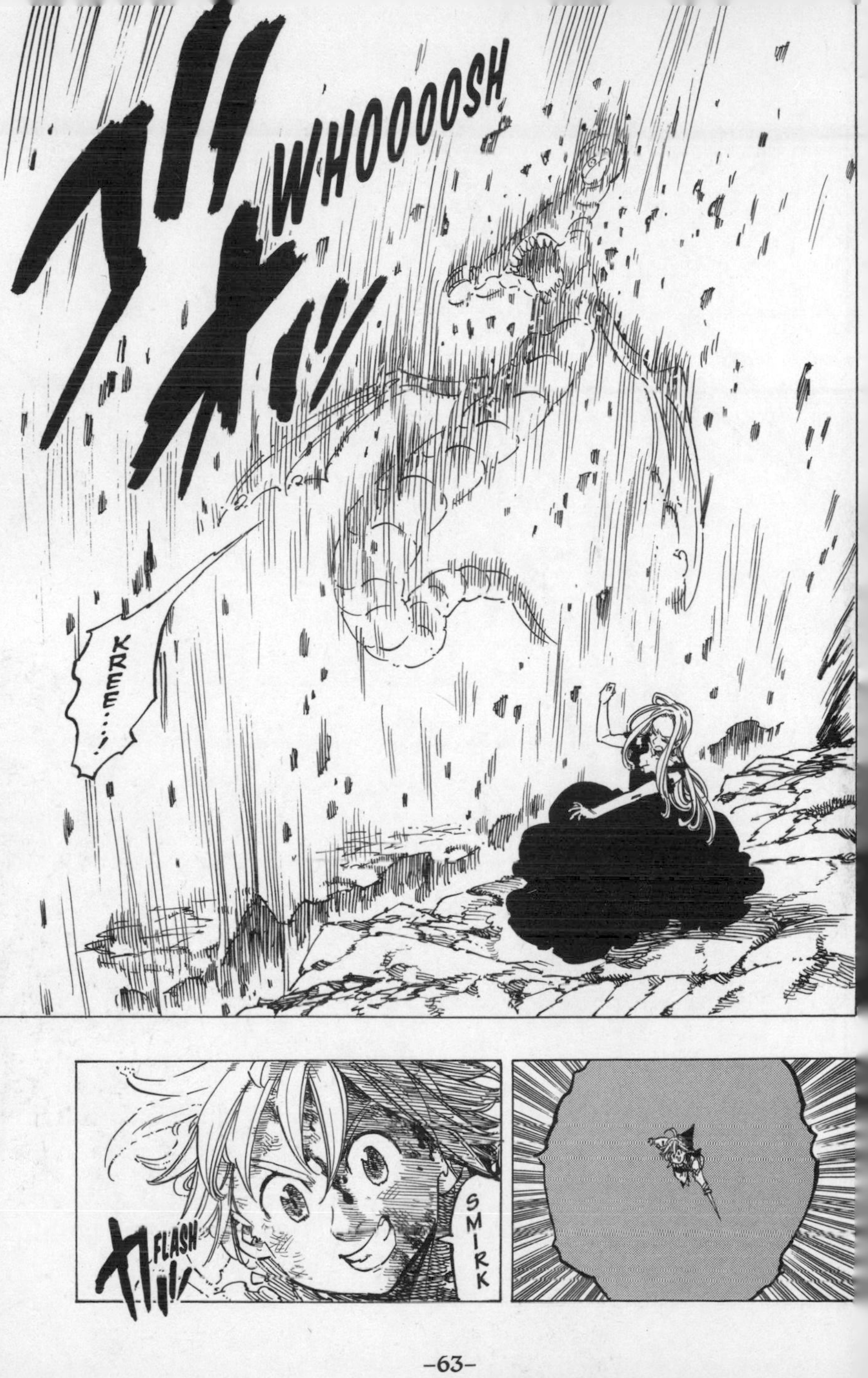
WHOOOOSH
KREE...!
SMIRK
FLASH

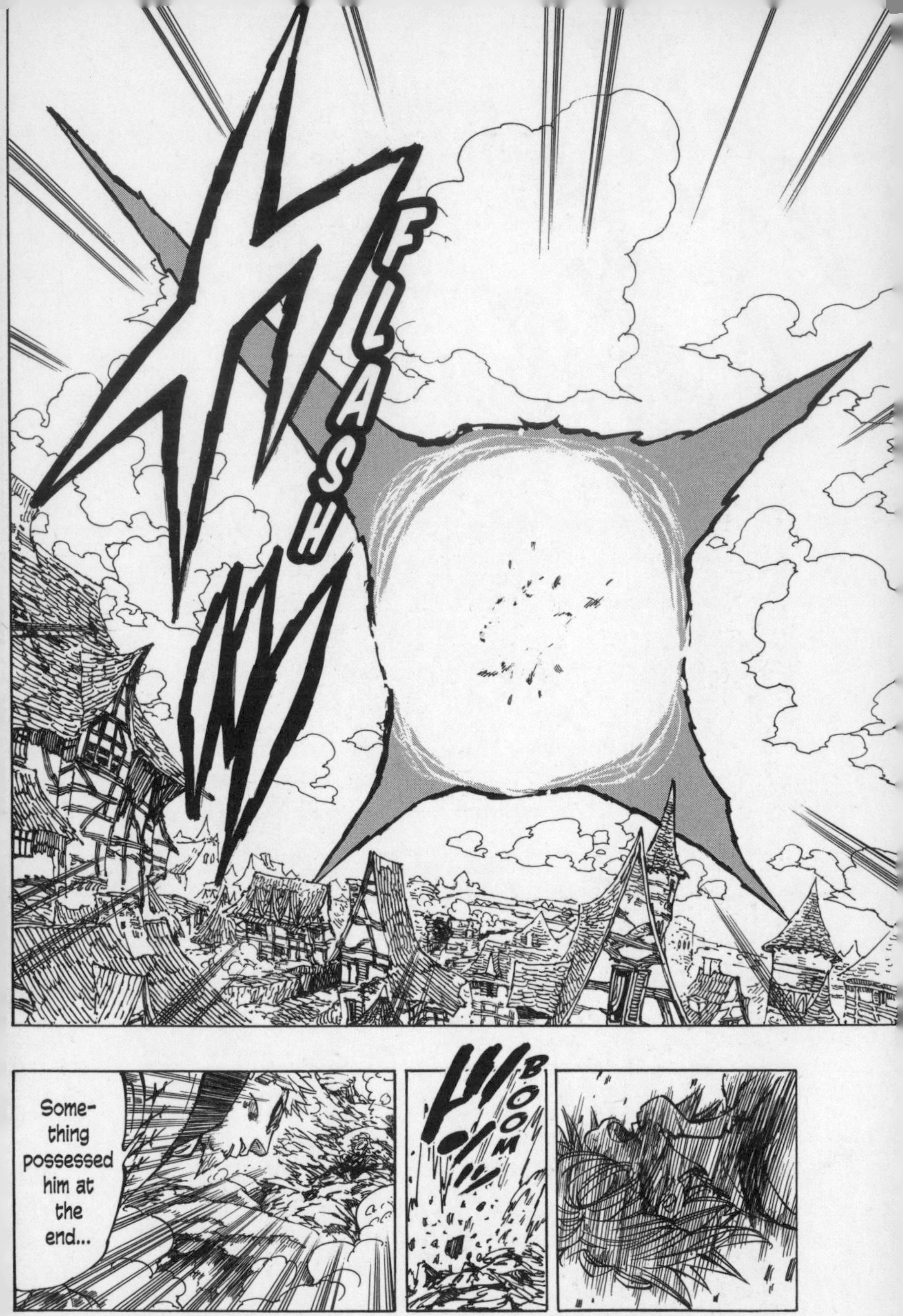
FLASH
BOOM
Something possessed him at the end...

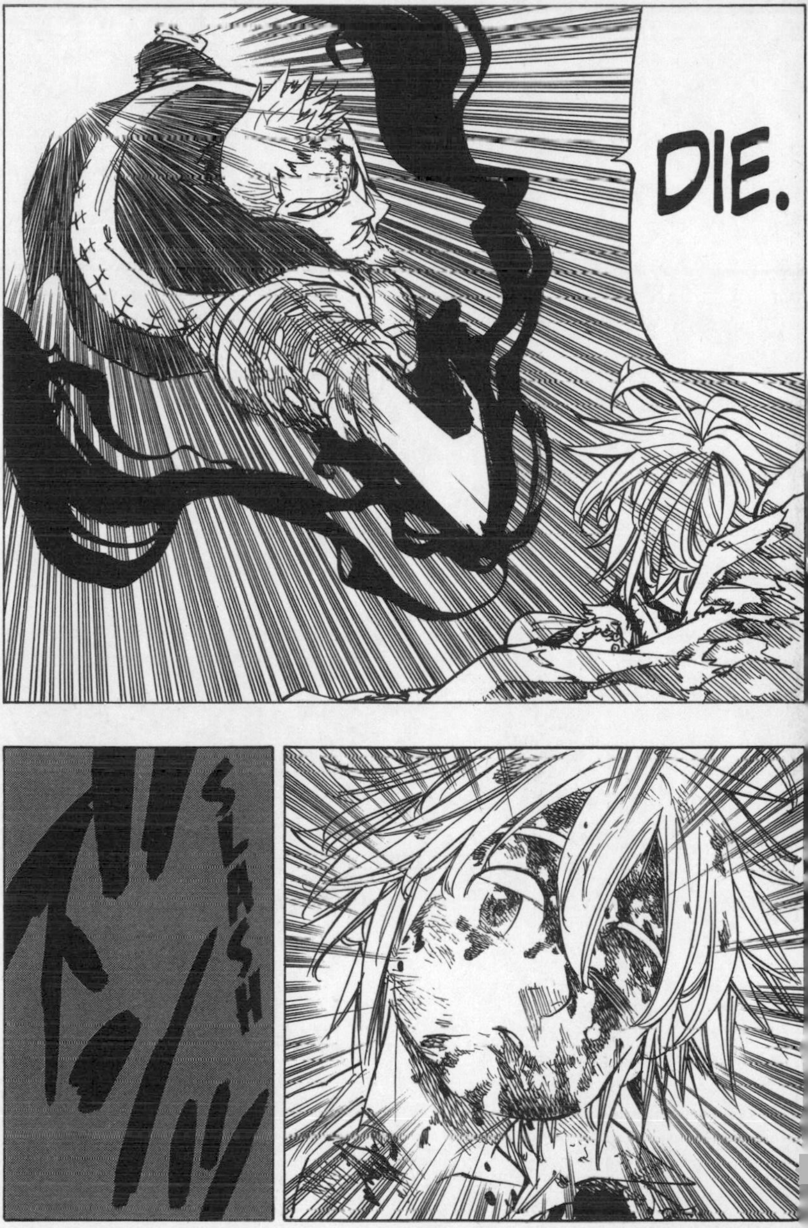
DIE.
SLASH

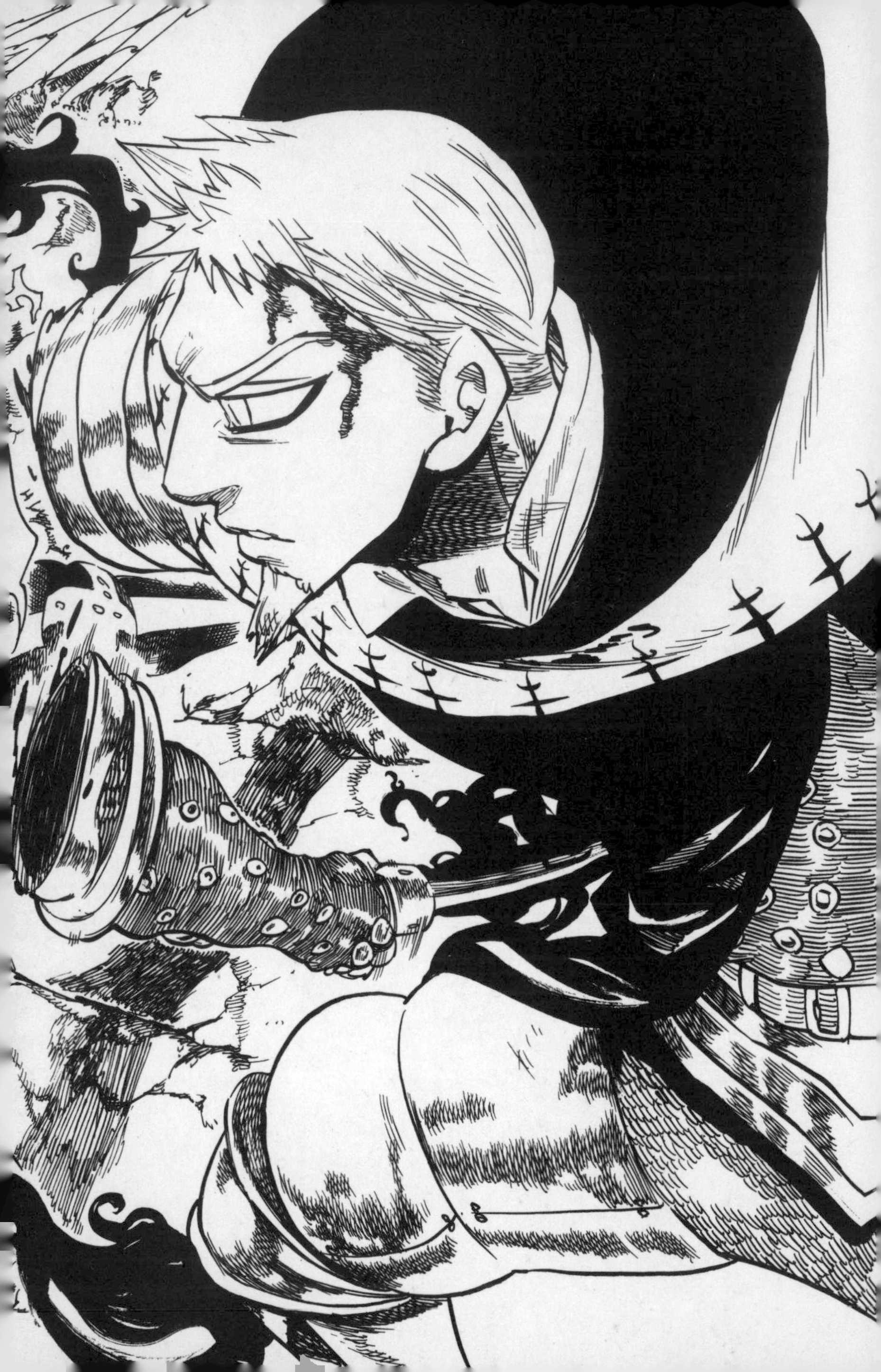

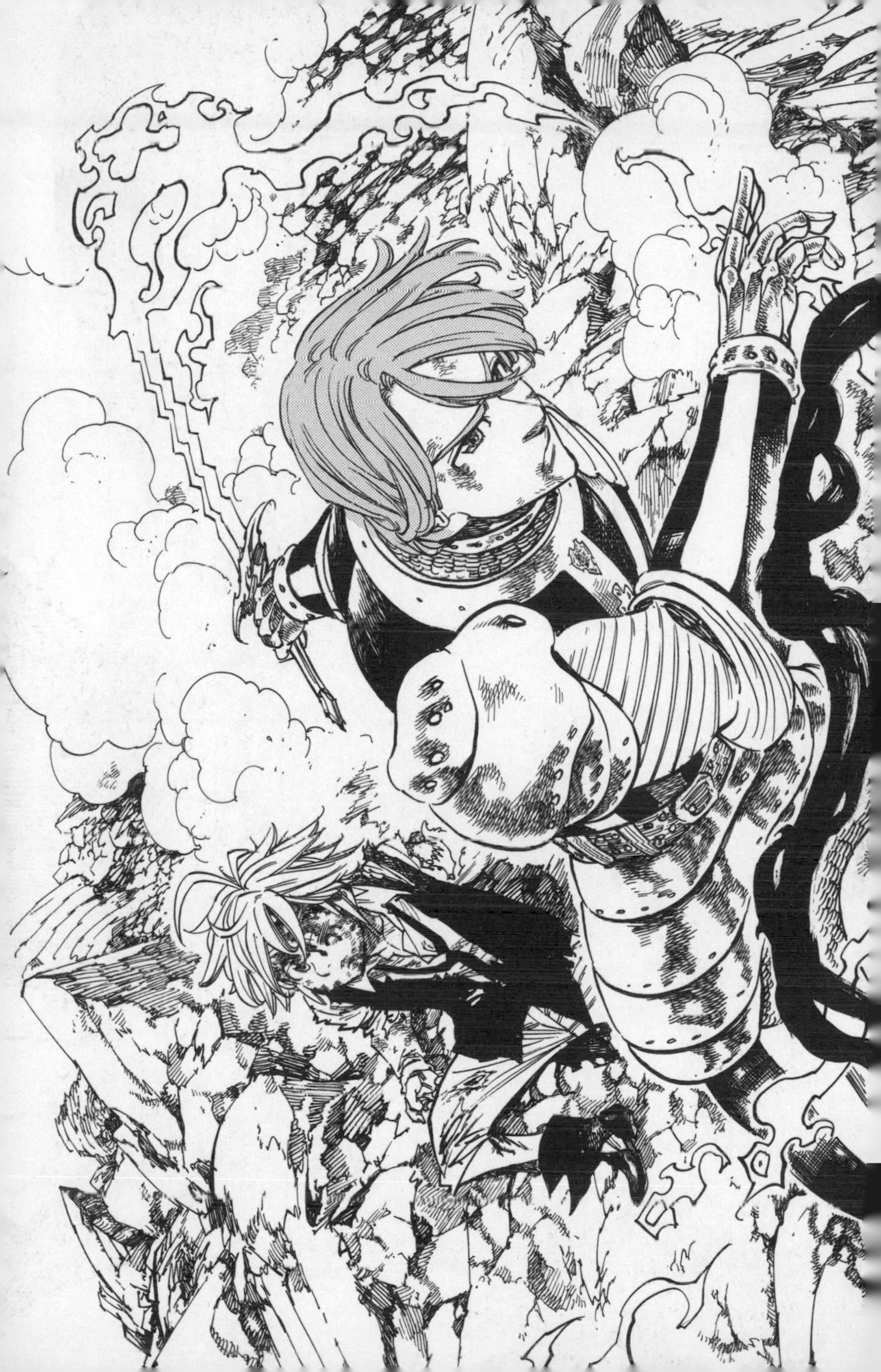

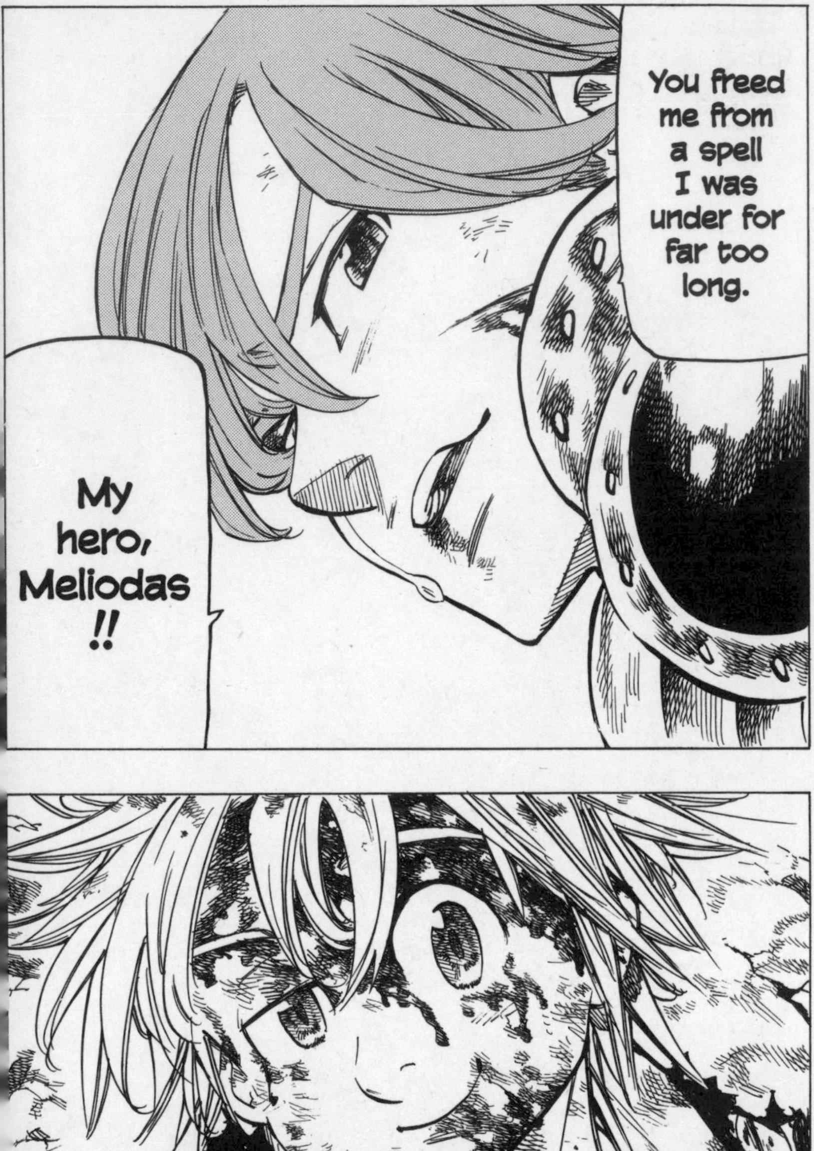
You freed me from a spell I was under for far too long.
My hero, Meliodas!!

THE SEVEN DEADLY SINS

Chapter 82 - The Incantation of Bravery

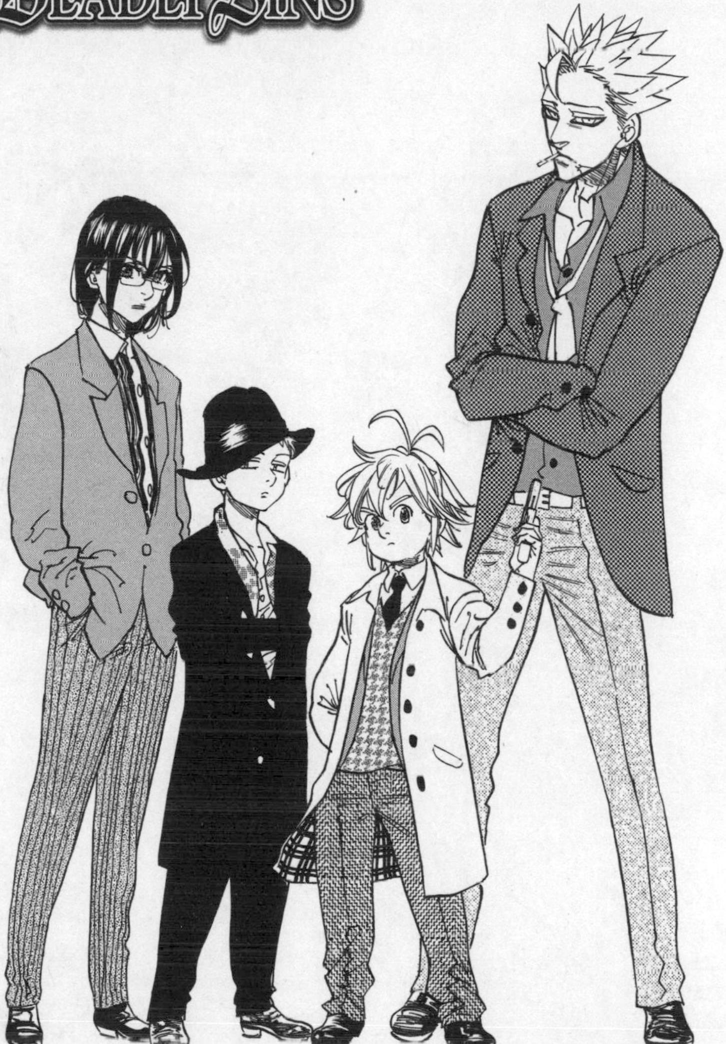

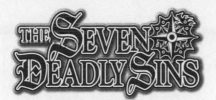

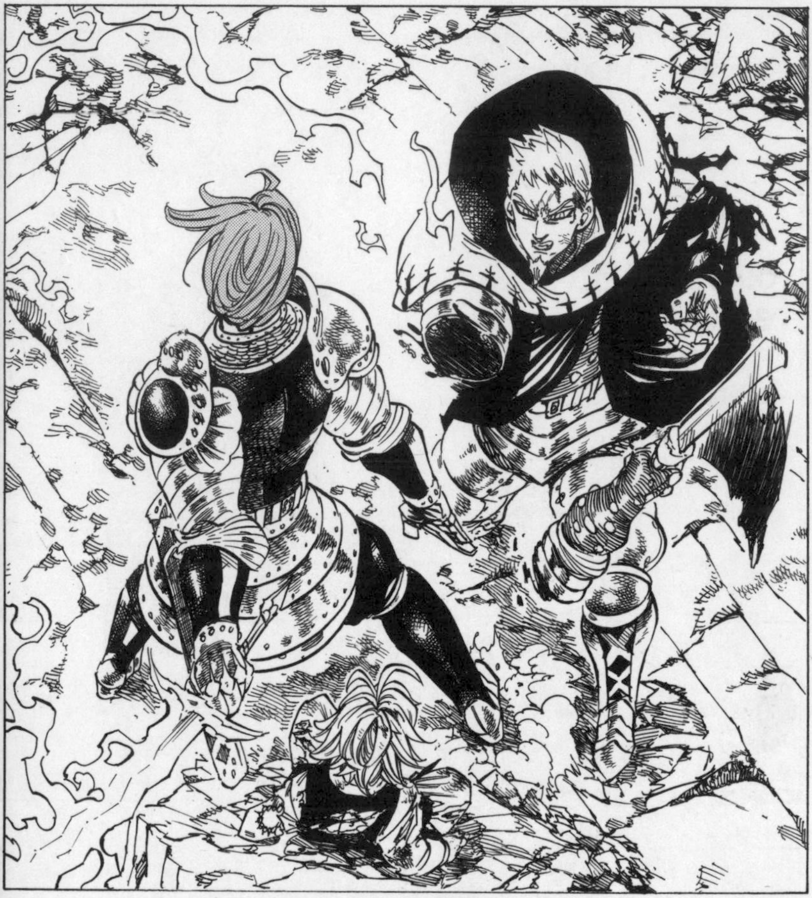

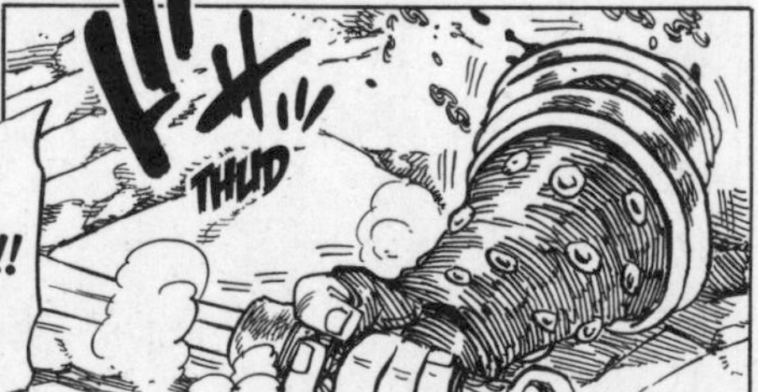
ドサッ
THUD

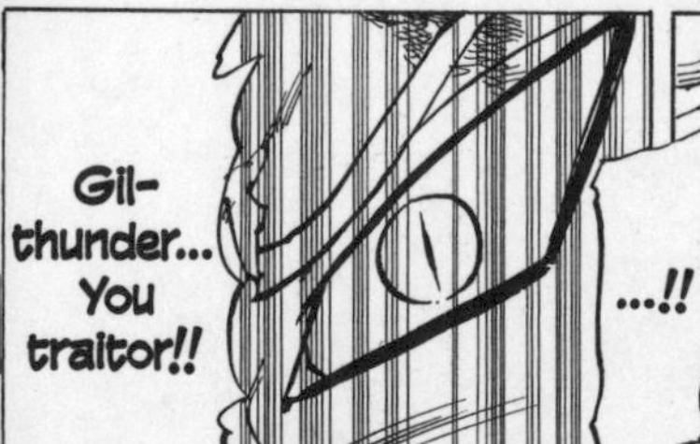
...!!
Gil-thunder... You traitor!!

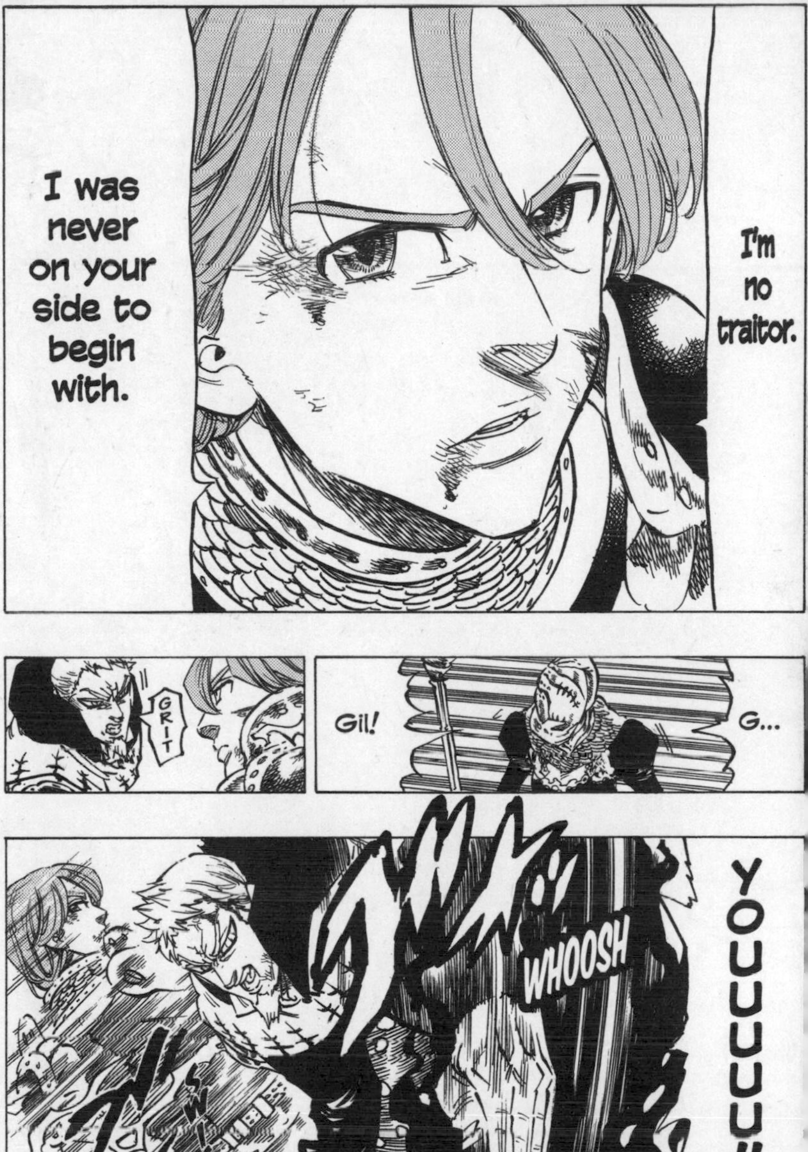
I'm no traitor.
I was never on your side to begin with.
G...
Gil!
GRIT
YOUUUUUU!!
WHOOSH
SWISH

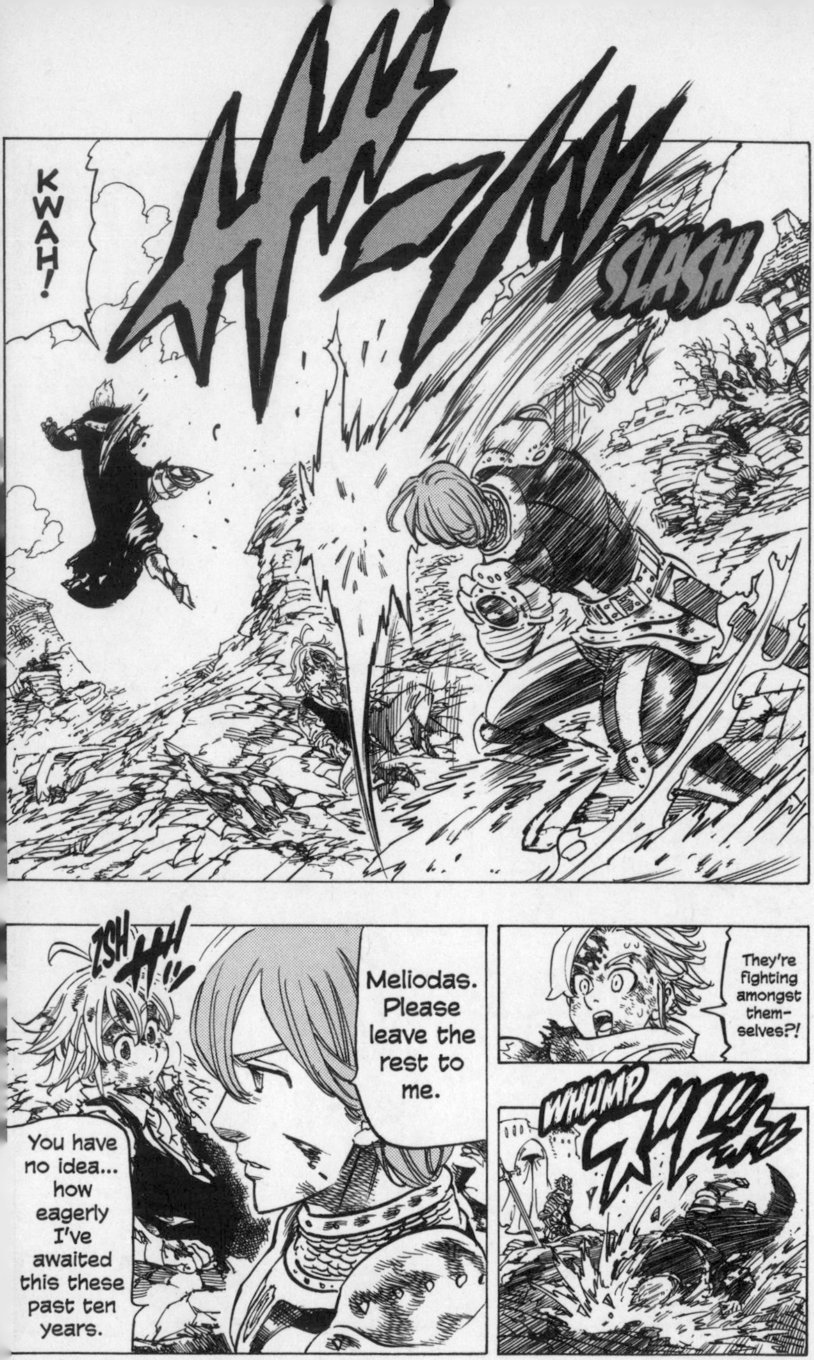
SLASH
KWAH!
They're fighting amongst them-selves?!
WHUMP
Meliodas. Please leave the rest to me.
ZSH
You have no idea... how eagerly I've awaited this these past ten years.

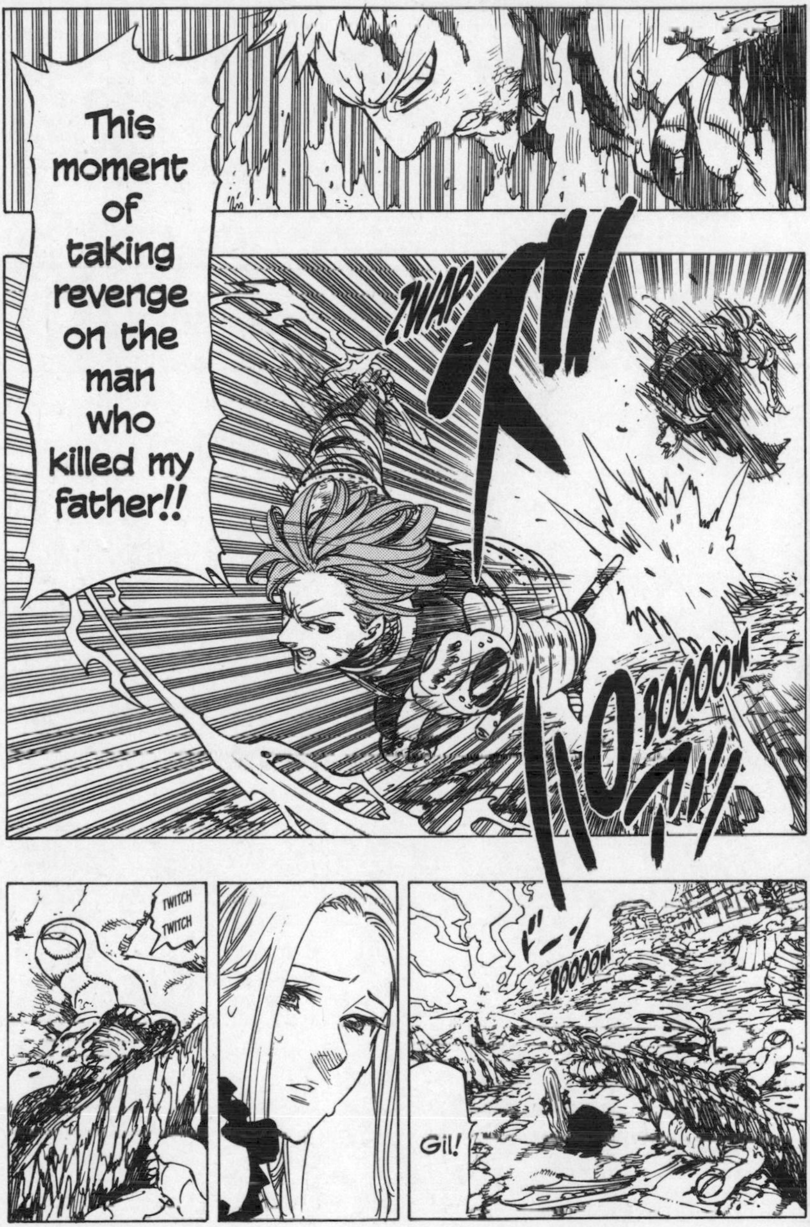
This moment of taking revenge on the man who killed my father!!
ZWAP
BOOOOM
BOOOOM
Gil!
TWITCH
TWITCH

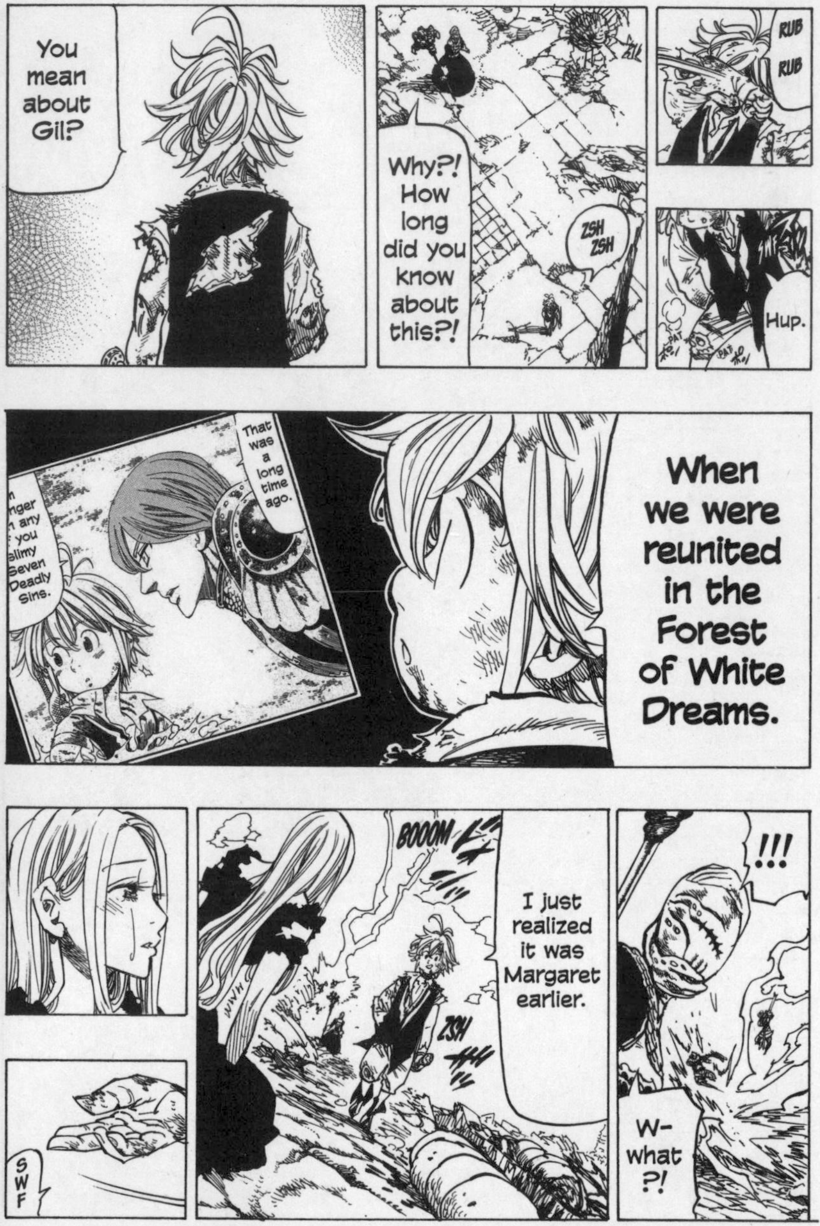
RUB
RUB
Hup.
PAT PAT
Why?! How long did you know about this?!
ZSH ZSH
You mean about Gil?
When we were reunited in the Forest of White Dreams.
That was a long time ago.
slimy Seven Deadly Sins.
!!!
W- what?!
BOOOM
I just realized it was Margaret earlier.
ZSH
SWF

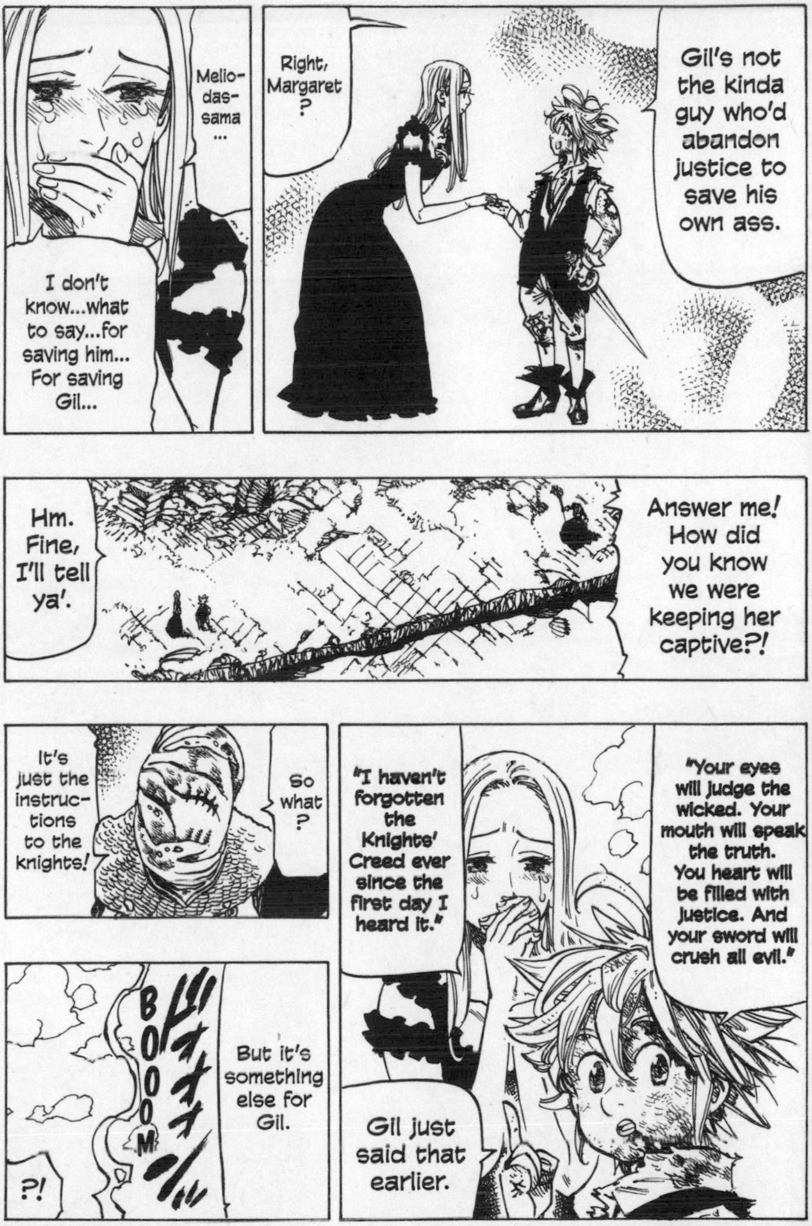
Gil's not the kinda guy who'd abandon justice to save his own ass.
Right, Margaret?
Melio-das-sama...
I don't know...what to say...for saving him... For saving Gil...
Answer me! How did you know we were keeping her captive?!
Hm. Fine, I'll tell ya'.
"Your eyes will judge the wicked. Your mouth will speak the truth. You heart will be filled with justice. And your sword will crush all evil."
"I haven't forgotten the Knights' Creed ever since the first day I heard it."
Gil just said that earlier.
So what?
It's just the instructions to the knights!
But it's something else for Gil.
BOOOOM
?!

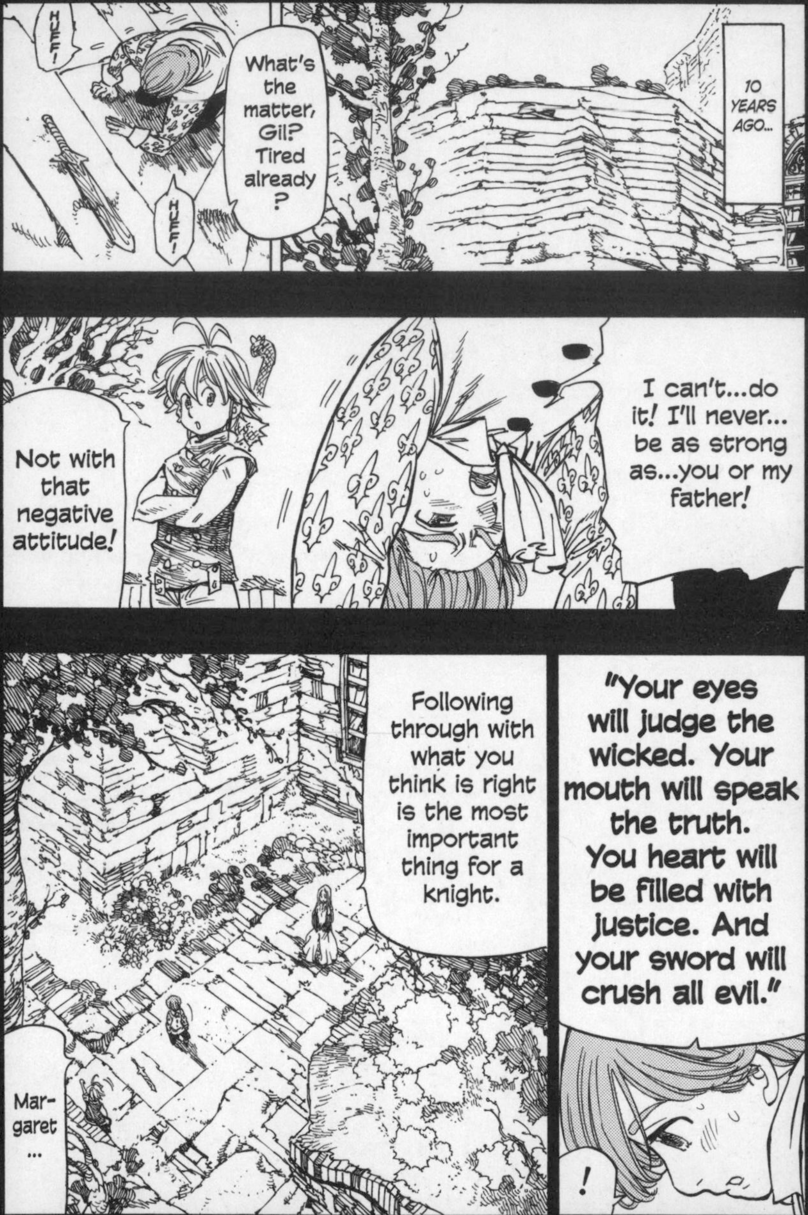
10 YEARS AGO...
What's the matter, Gil? Tired already?
HUFF!
HUFF!
I can't...do it! I'll never... be as strong as...you or my father!
Not with that negative attitude!
"Your eyes will judge the wicked. Your mouth will speak the truth. You heart will be filled with justice. And your sword will crush all evil."
!
Following through with what you think is right is the most important thing for a knight.
Mar-garet ...

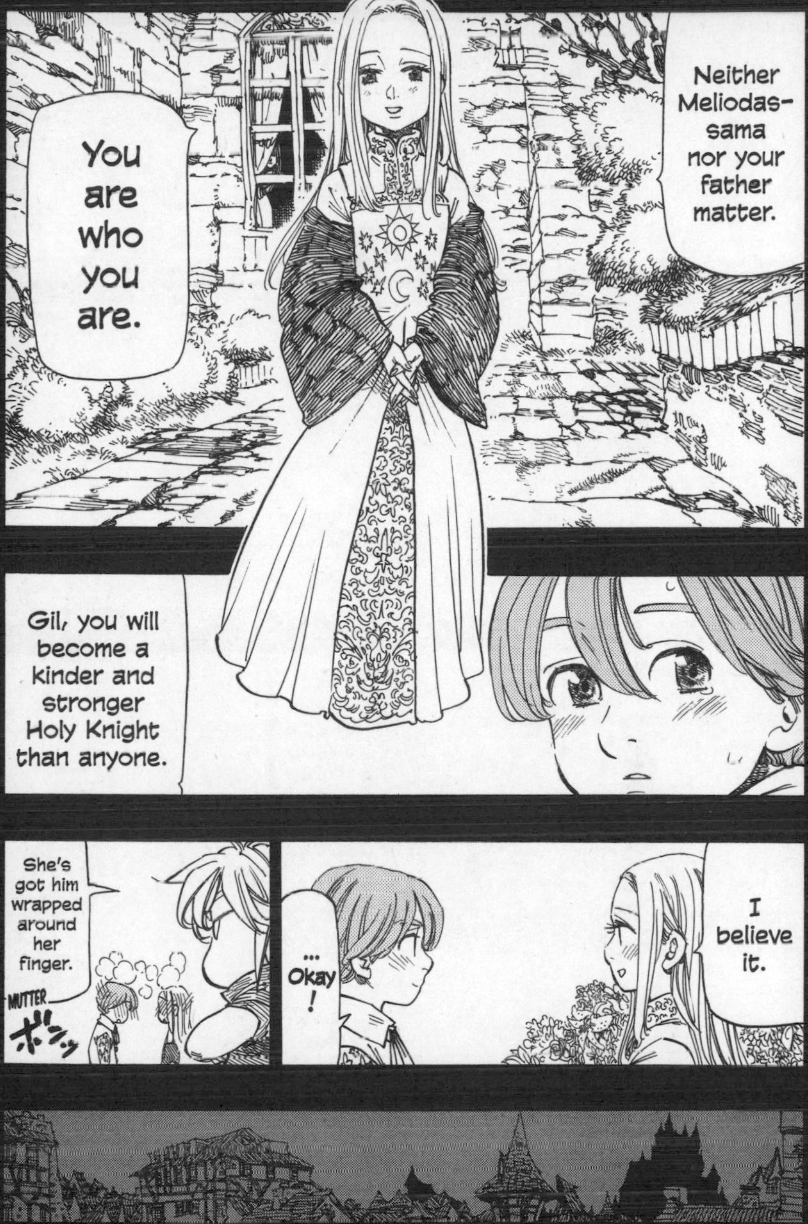
Neither Meliodas-sama nor your father matter.
You are who you are.
Gil, you will become a kinder and stronger Holy Knight than anyone.
I believe it.
... Okay!
She's got him wrapped around her finger.
MUTTER
ボソッ

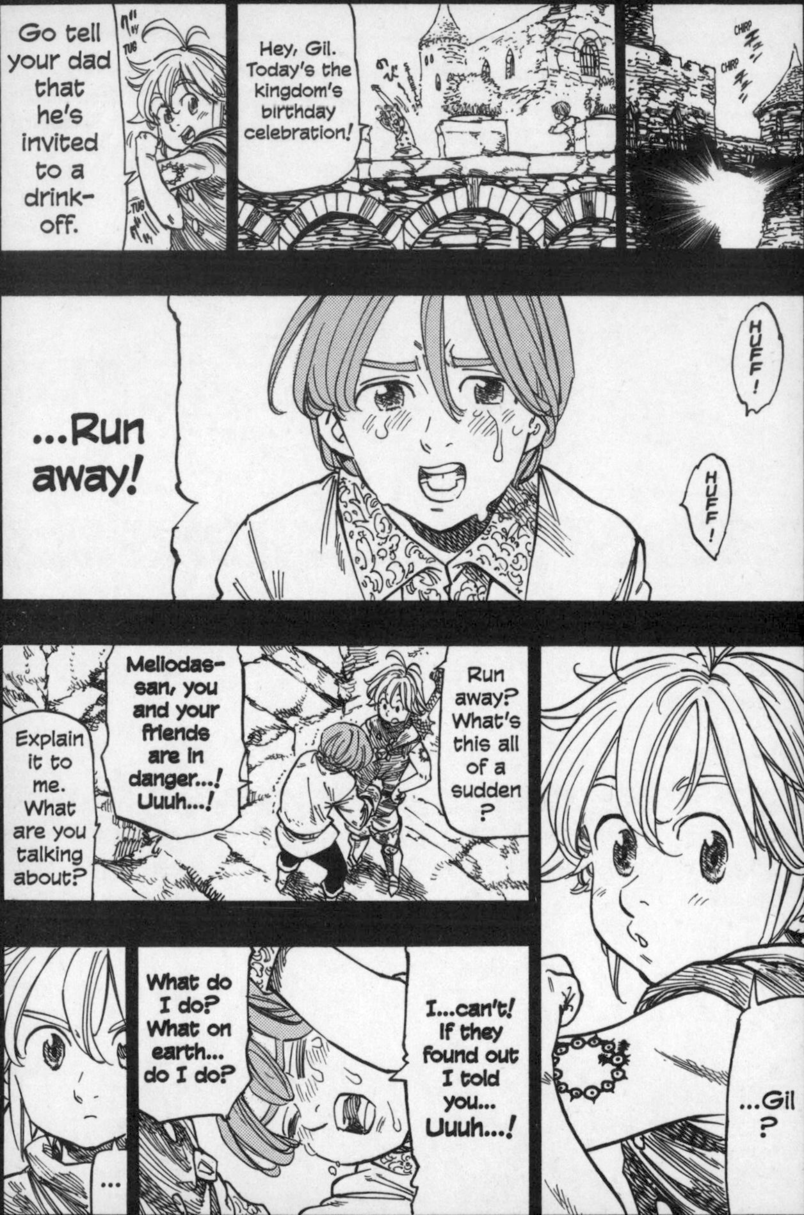
CHIRP
CHIRP
Hey, Gil. Today's the kingdom's birthday celebration!
TUG
Go tell your dad that he's invited to a drink-off.
TUG
HUFF!
HUFF!
...Run away!
...Gil?
Run away? What's this all of a sudden?
Meliodas-san, you and your friends are in danger...! Uuuh...!
Explain it to me. What are you talking about?
I...can't! If they found out I told you... Uuuh...!
What do I do? What on earth... do I do?
...

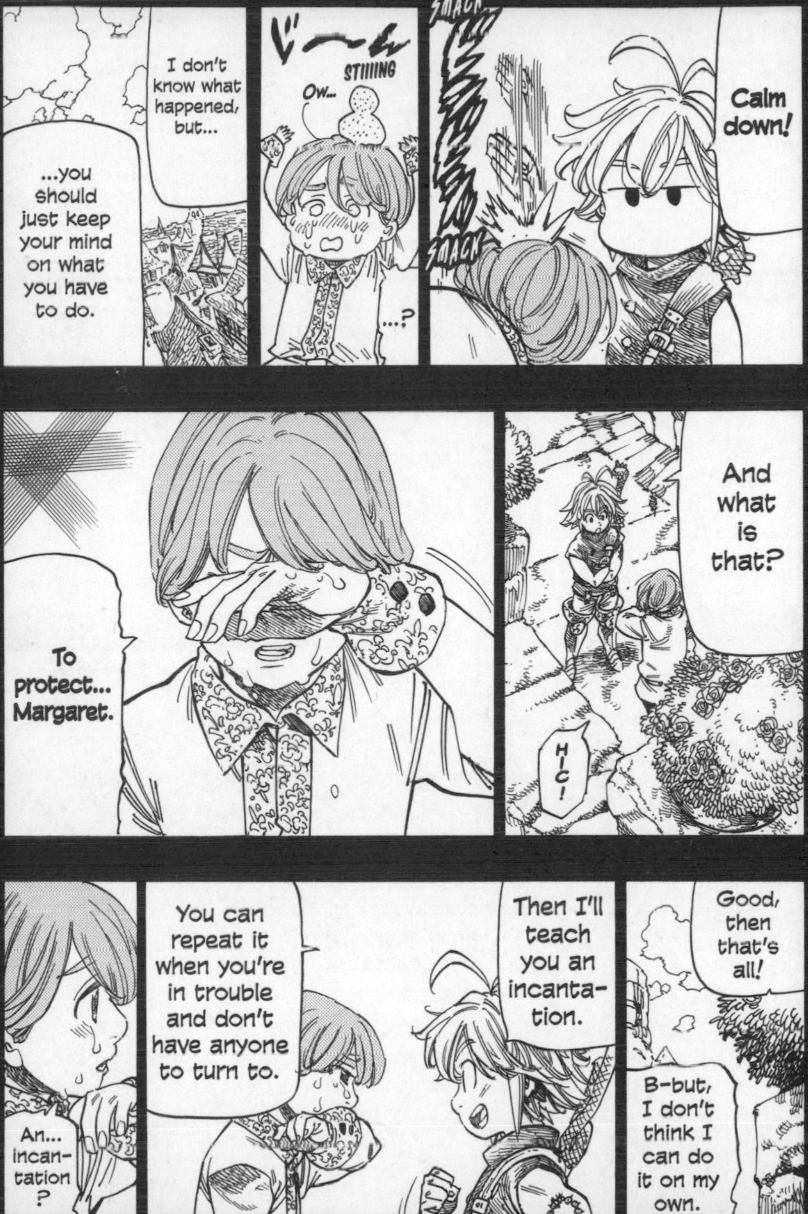
SMACK
SMACK
Calm down!
STIIIING
Ow...
...?
I don't know what happened, but...
...you should just keep your mind on what you have to do.
And what is that?
HIC!
To protect... Margaret.
Good, then that's all!
B-but, I don't think I can do it on my own.
Then I'll teach you an incantation.
You can repeat it when you're in trouble and don't have anyone to turn to.
An... incantation?

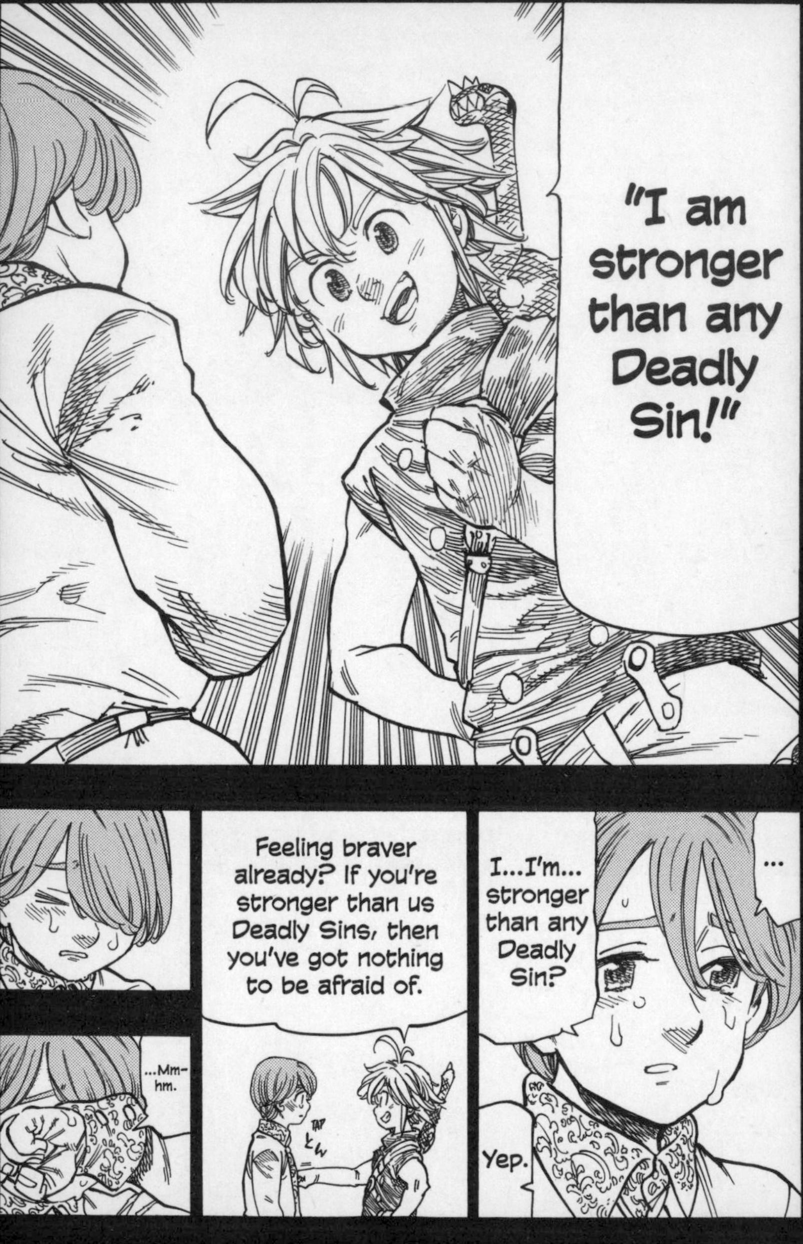
"I am stronger than any Deadly Sin!"
...
I...I'm... stronger than any Deadly Sin?
Yep.
Feeling braver already? If you're stronger than us Deadly Sins, then you've got nothing to be afraid of.
TAP
...Mm-hm.

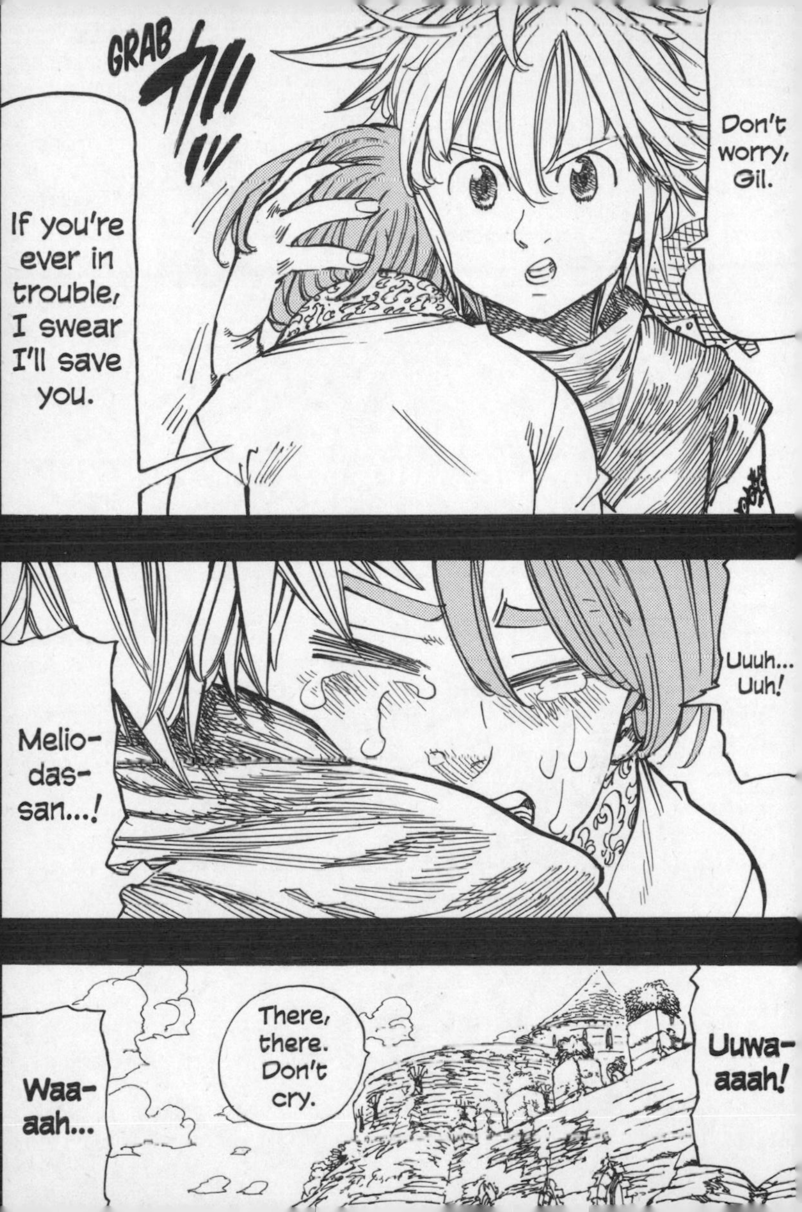
Don't worry, Gil.
GRAB
If you're ever in trouble, I swear I'll save you.
Uuuh... Uuh!
Melio-das-san...!
Uuwa-aaah!
There, there. Don't cry.
Waa-aah...

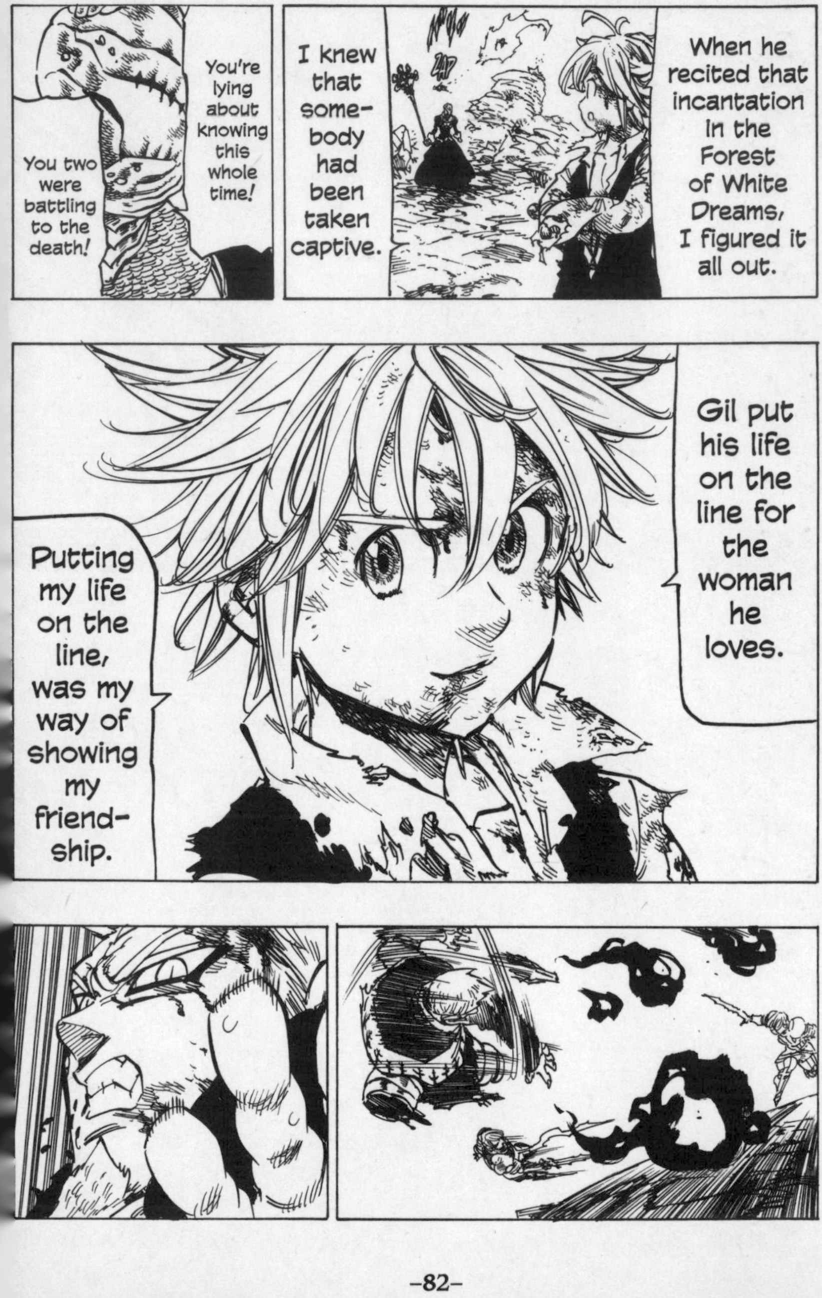
When he recited that incantation in the Forest of White Dreams, I figured it all out.
I knew that somebody had been taken captive.
You're lying about knowing this whole time!
You two were battling to the death!
Gil put his life on the line for the woman he loves.
Putting my life on the line, was my way of showing my friendship.

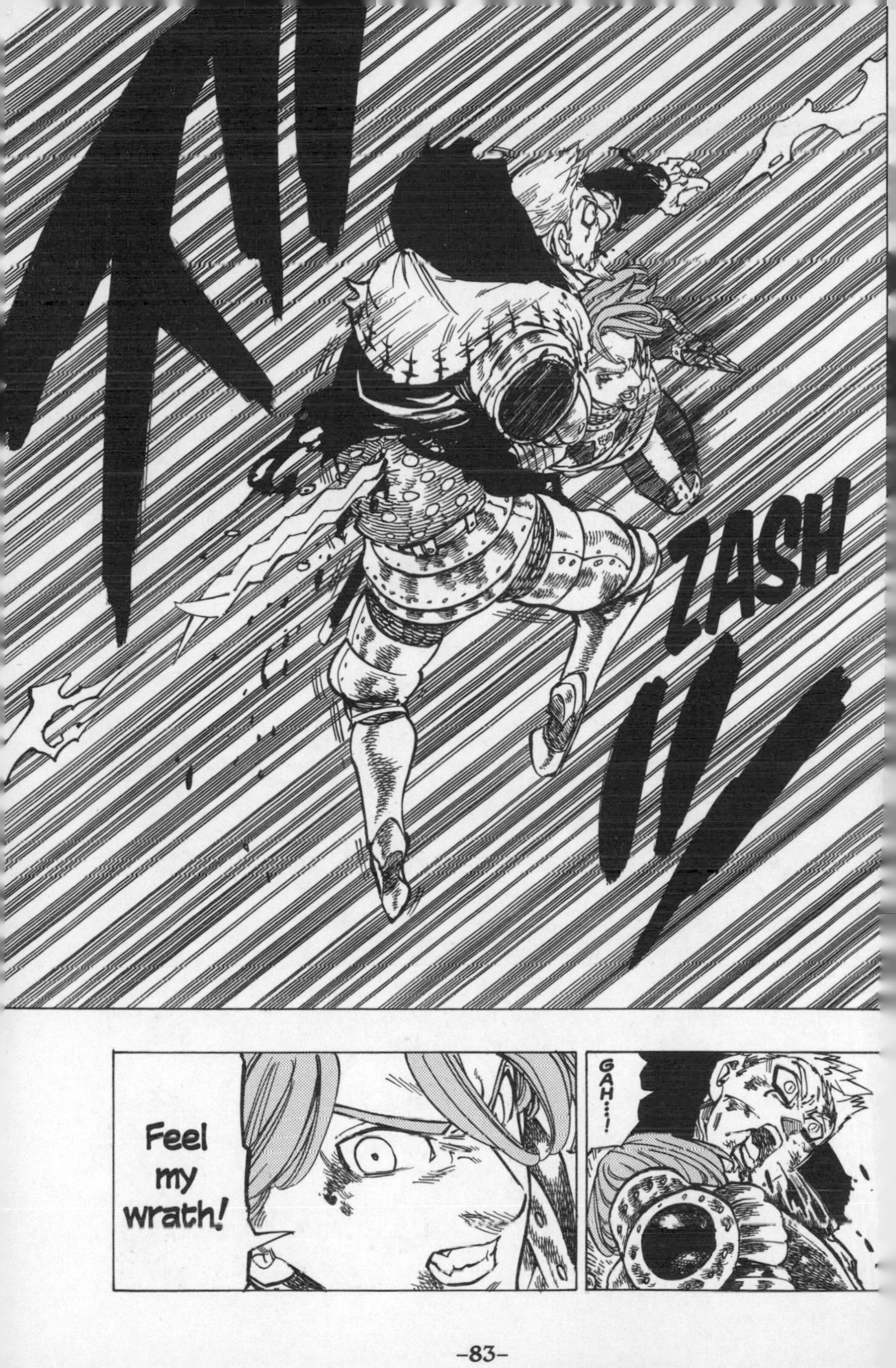
ZASH
GAH...!
Feel my wrath!

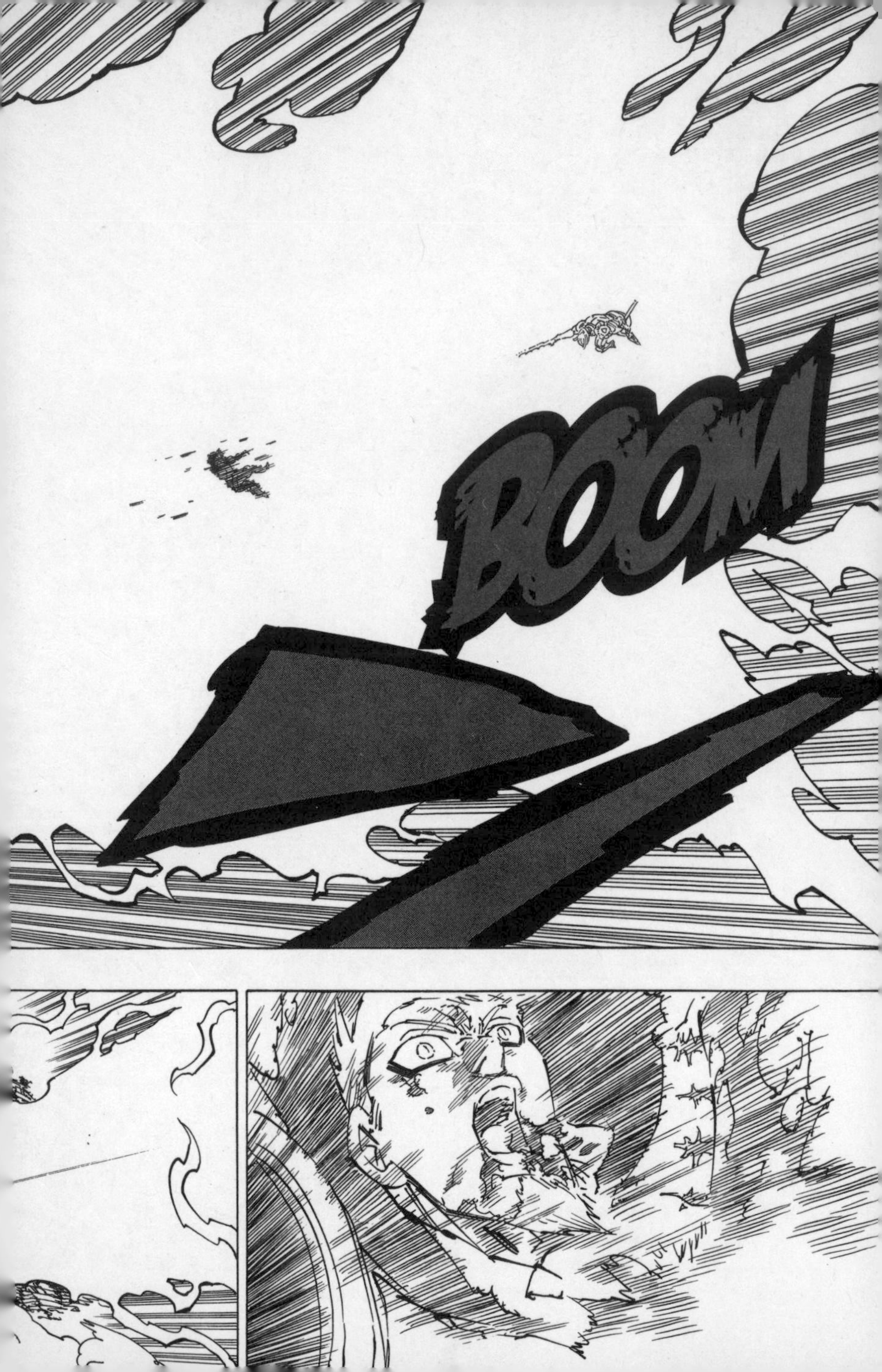
BOOM

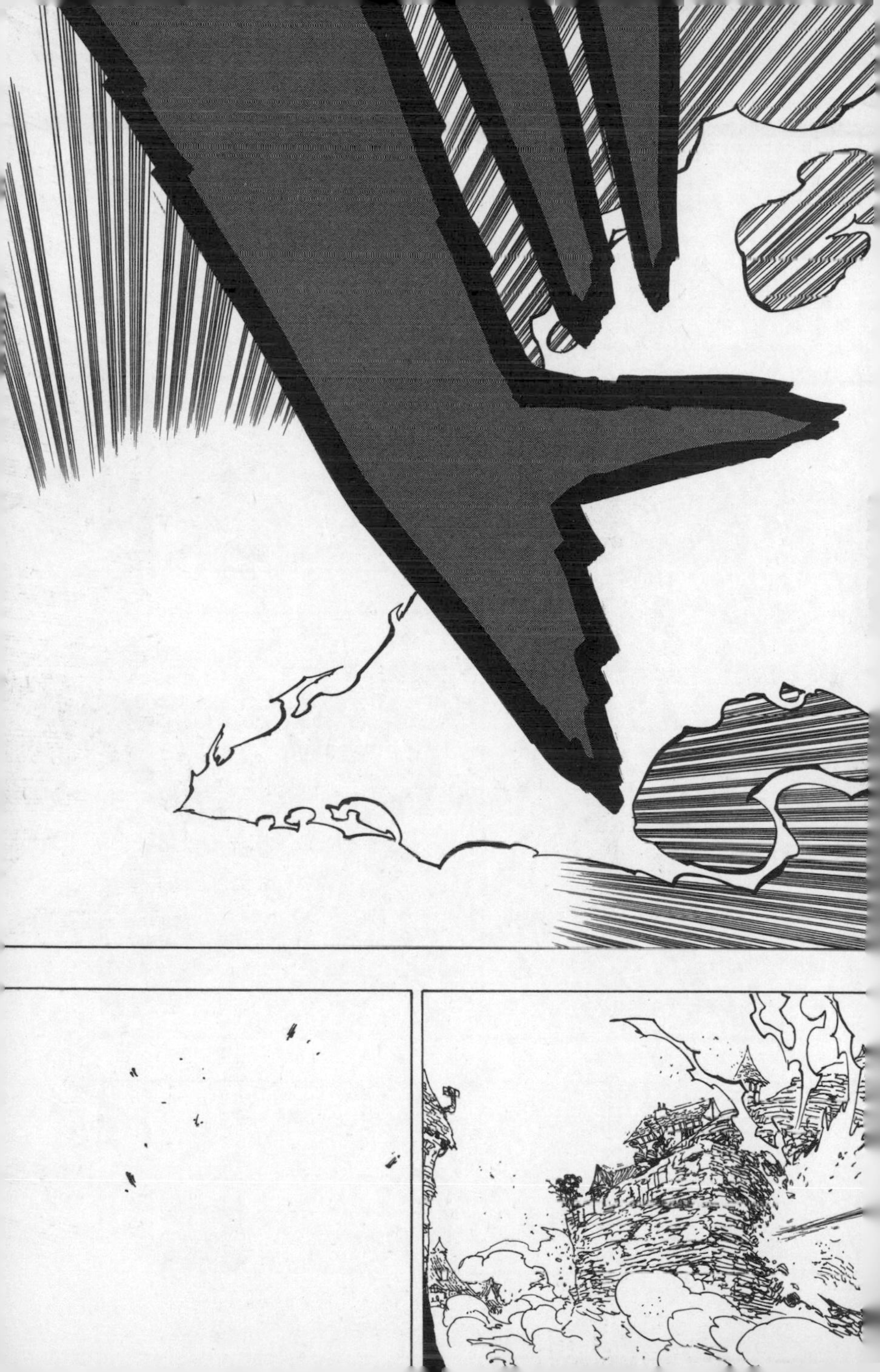

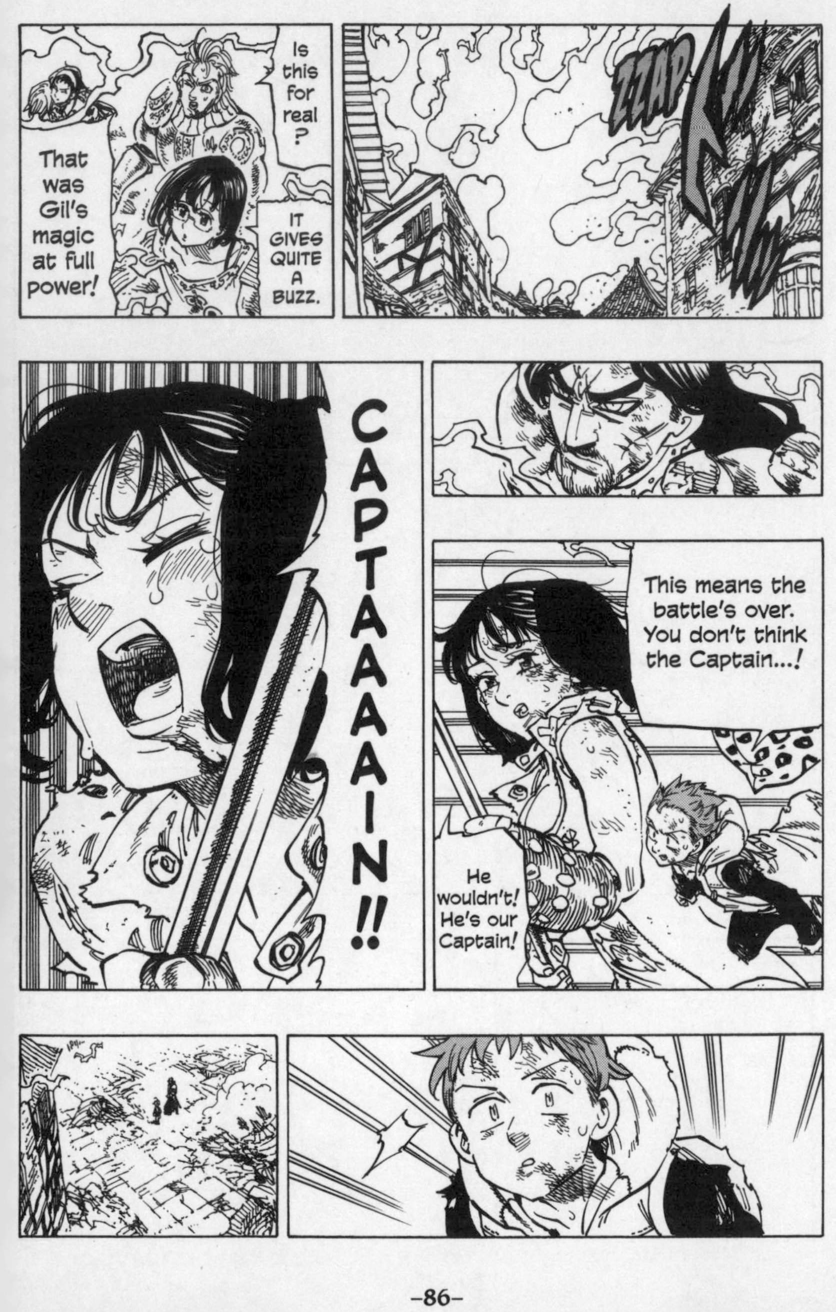
ZZAP
Is this for real?
IT GIVES QUITE A BUZZ.
That was Gil's magic at full power!
This means the battle's over. You don't think the Captain...!
He wouldn't! He's our Captain!
CAPTAAAAAIN!!

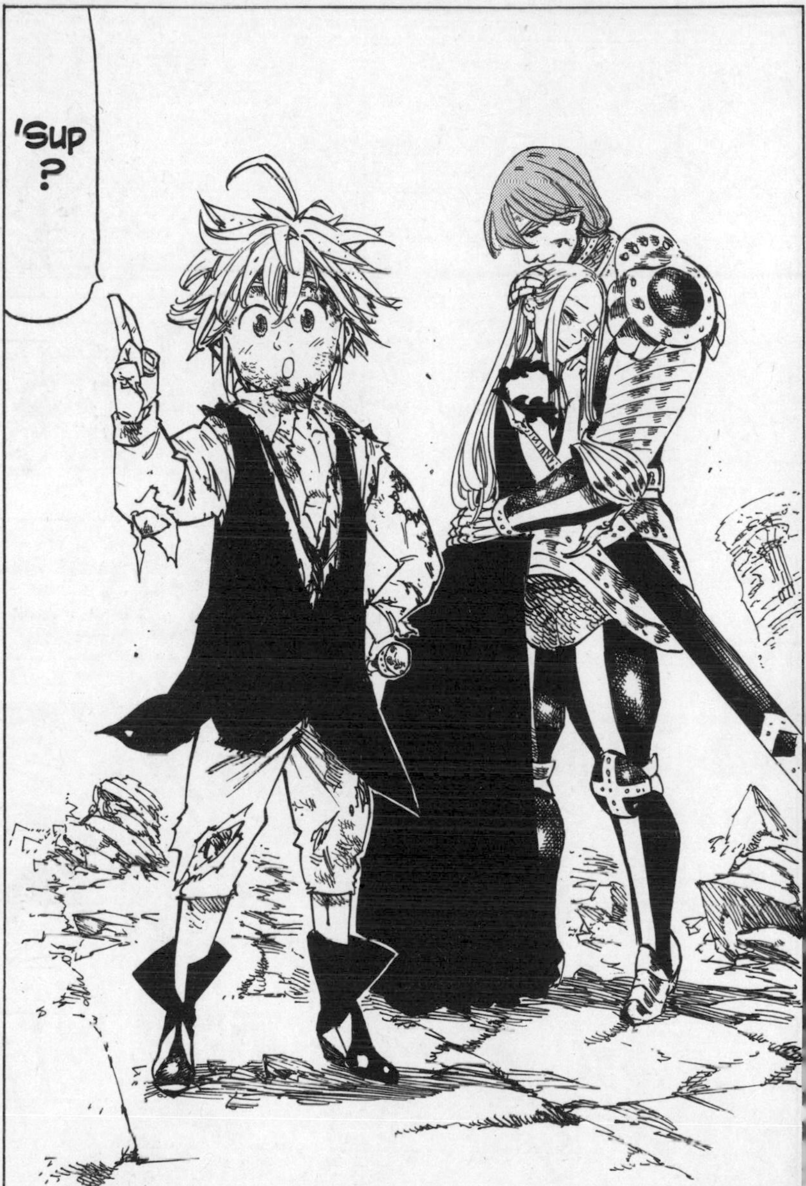
'SUP?

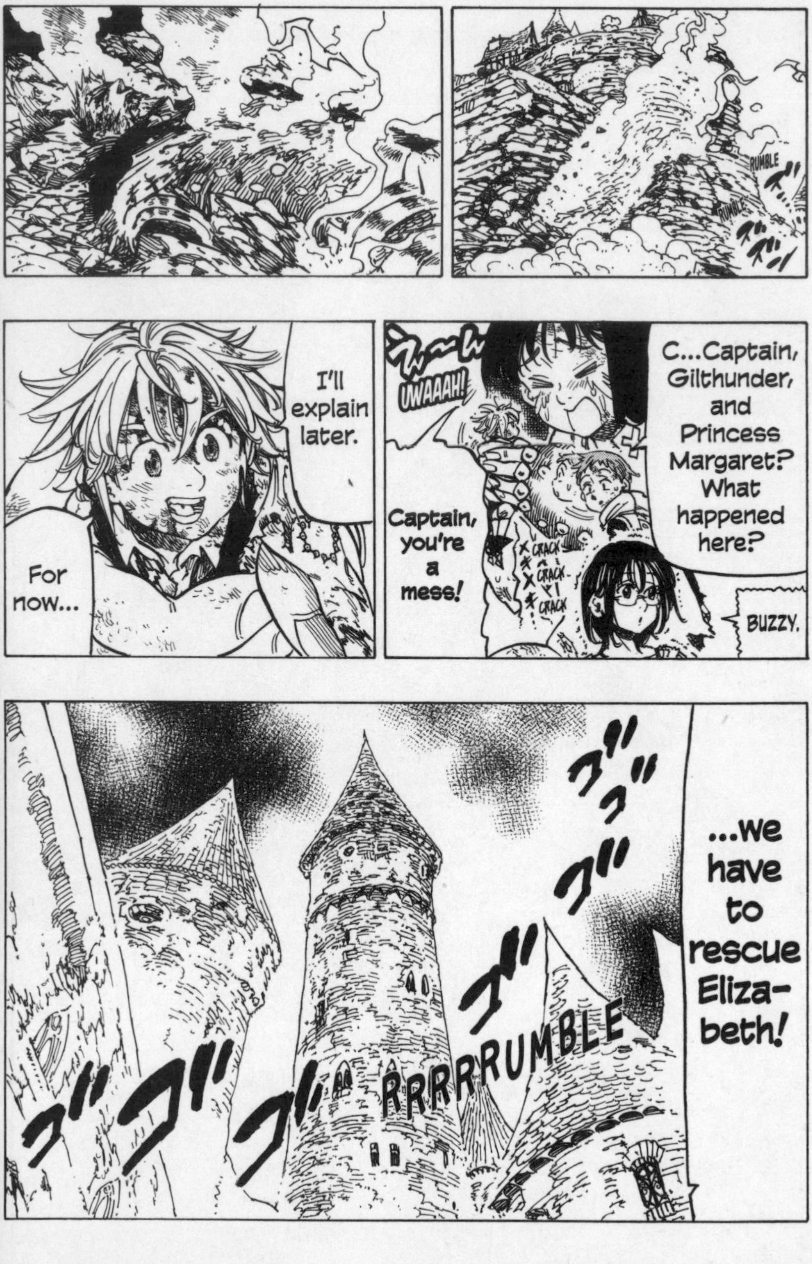
RUMBLE
RUMBLE
C...Captain, Gilthunder, and Princess Margaret? What happened here?
UWAAAH!
Captain, you're a mess!
CRACK
CRACK
CRACK
BUZZY.
I'll explain later.
For now...
...we have to rescue Eliza-beth!
RRRRRUMBLE

Chapter 83 - Blazing Boar

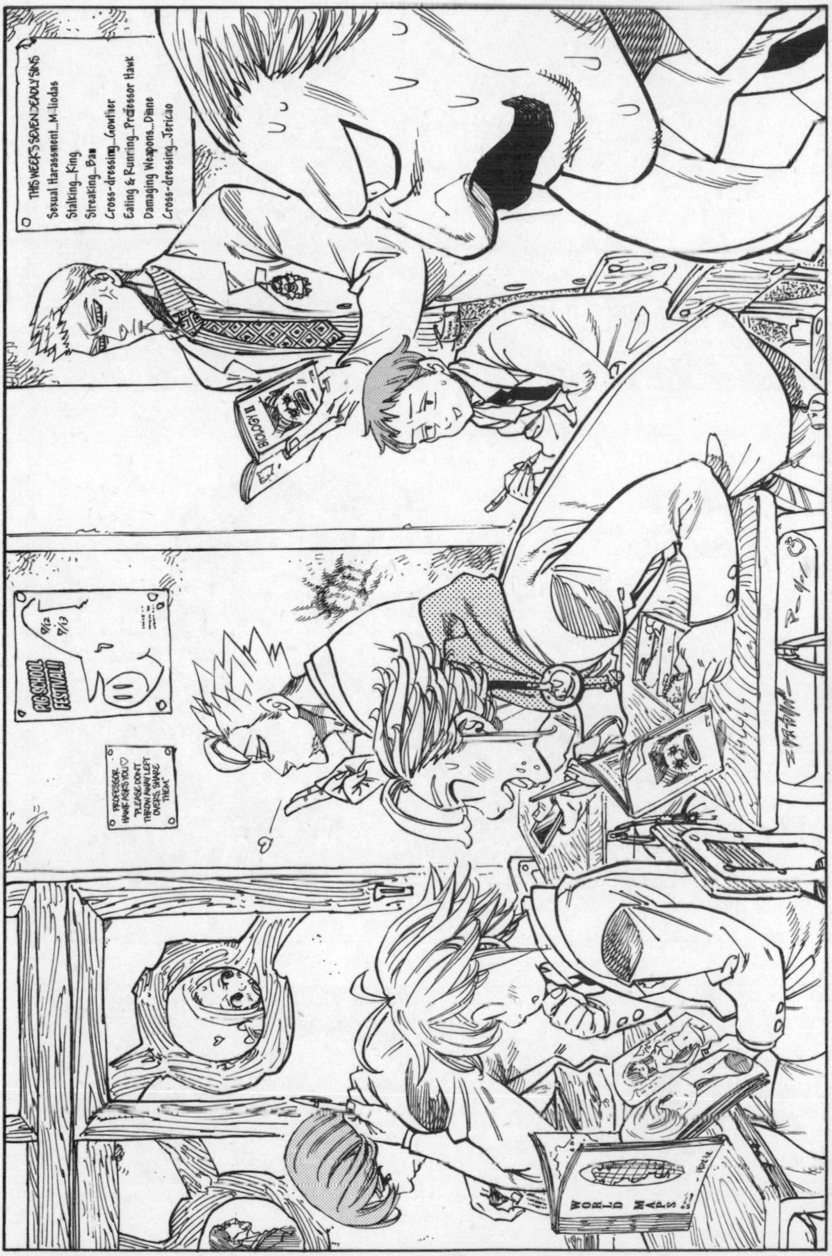
THIS WEEK'S SEVEN DEADLY SINS
Sexual Harassment...Meliodas
Stalking...King
Streaking...Ban
Cross-dressing...Gowther
Eating & Running...Professor Hawk
Damaging Weapons...Diane
Cross-dressing...Jericho
BIOLOGY II
PIG SCHOOL FESTIVAL!!
9/12 9/13
PROFESSOR HAWK ASKS YOU♡ "PLEASE DON'T THROW AWAY LEFT OVERS. SHARE THEM."
WORLD MAPS

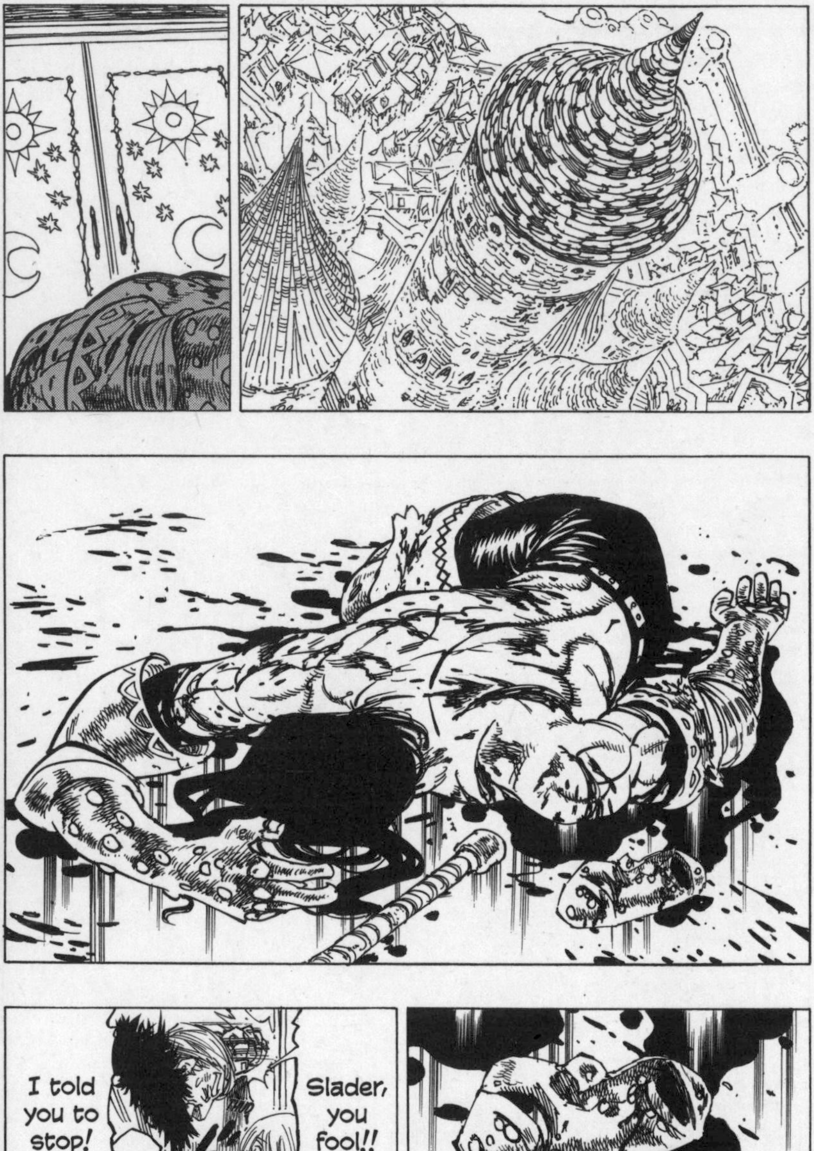
Slader, you fool!!
I told you to stop!
Father!

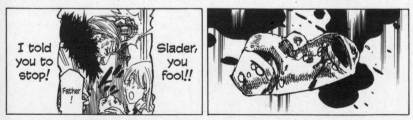

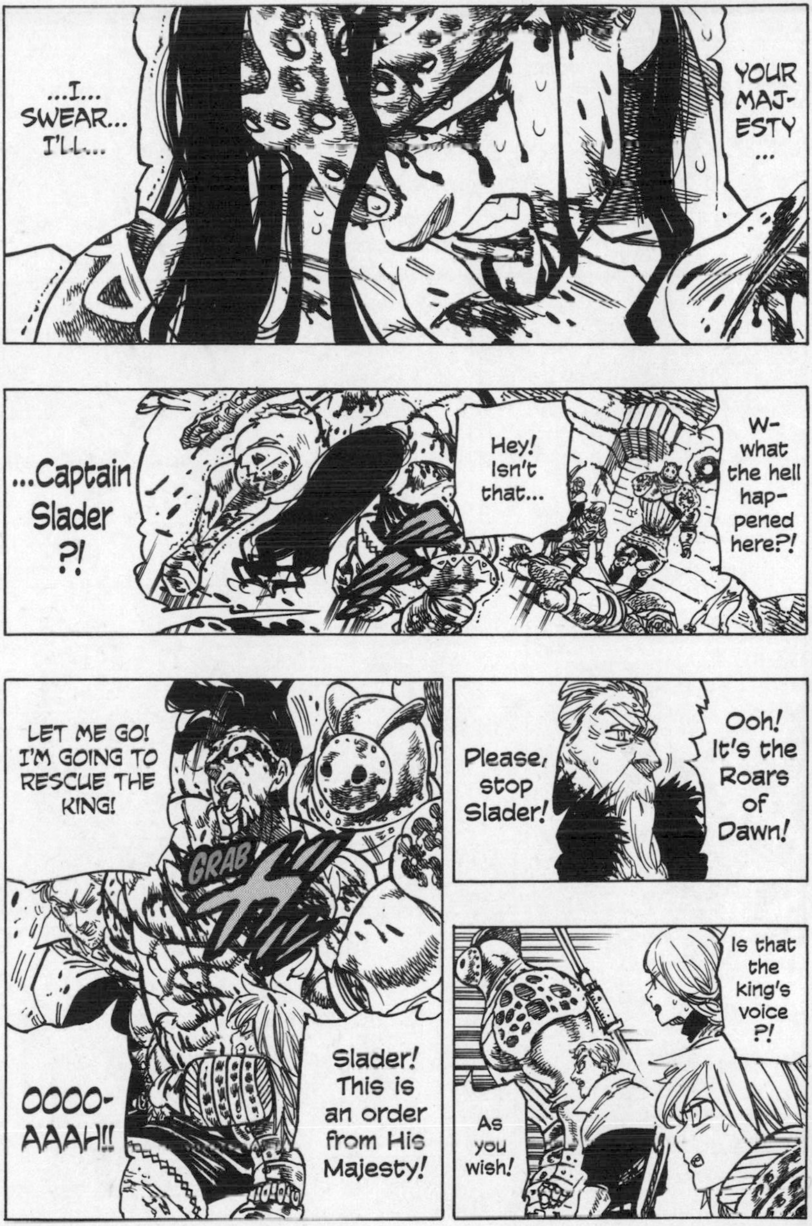
YOUR MAJESTY...
...I... SWEAR... I'LL...
W-what the hell happened here?!
Hey! Isn't that...
...Captain Slader?!
Ooh! It's the Roars of Dawn!
Please, stop Slader!
Is that the king's voice?!
As you wish!
LET ME GO! I'M GOING TO RESCUE THE KING!
GRAB
Slader! This is an order from His Majesty!
OOOO-AAAH!!

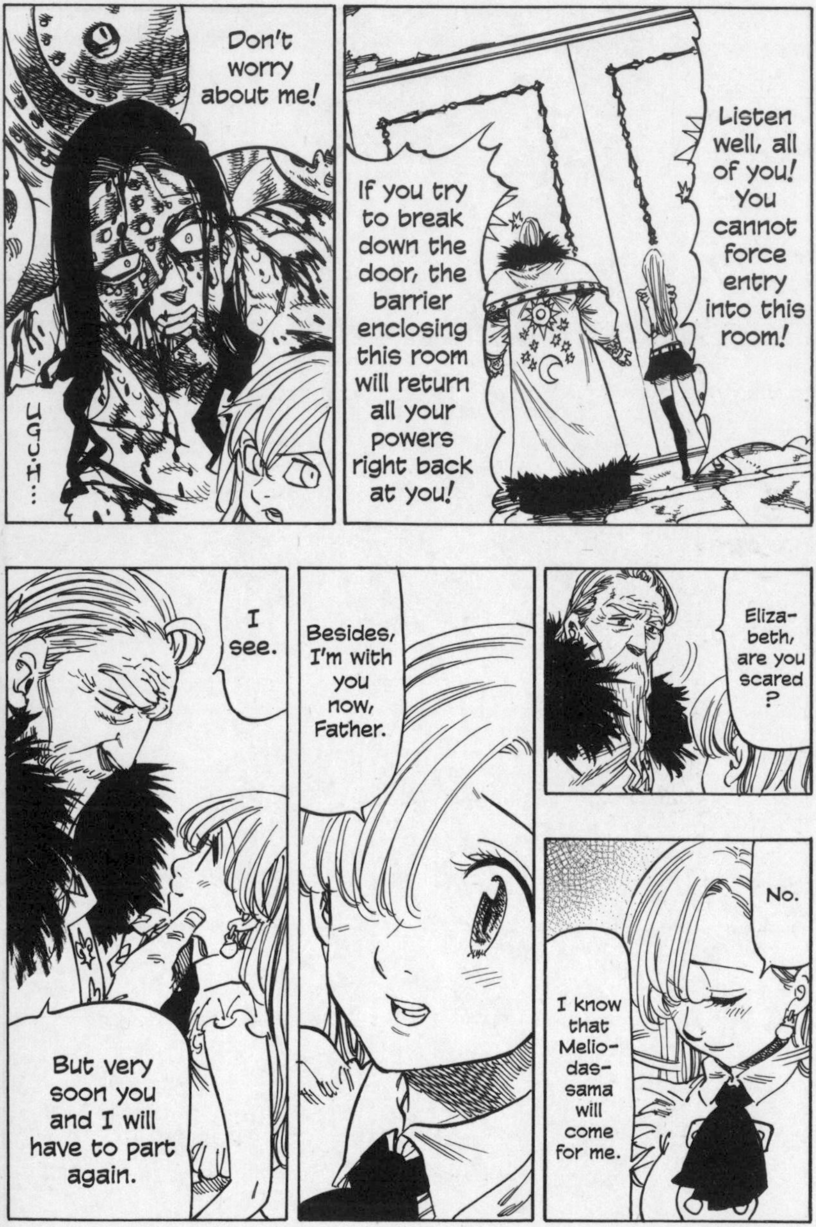
Listen well, all of you! You cannot force entry into this room!
If you try to break down the door, the barrier enclosing this room will return all your powers right back at you!
Don't worry about me!
UGUH...
Eliza-beth, are you scared?
No.
I know that Melio-das-sama will come for me.
Besides, I'm with you now, Father.
I see.
But very soon you and I will have to part again.

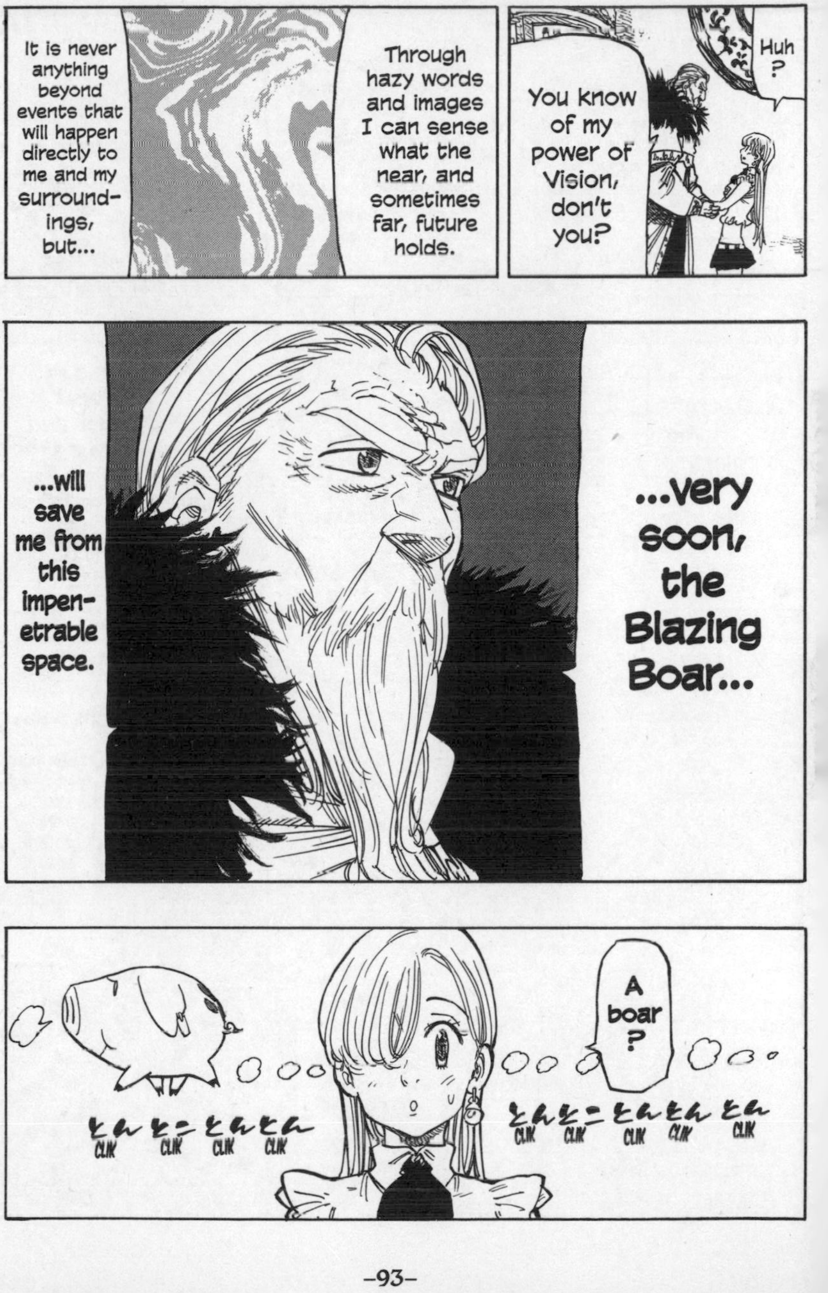
Huh?
You know of my power of Vision, don't you?
Through hazy words and images I can sense what the near, and sometimes far, future holds.
It is never anything beyond events that will happen directly to me and my surroundings, but...
...very soon, the Blazing Boar...
...will save me from this impenetrable space.
A boar?
CLIK CLIK CLIK CLIK CLIK
CLIK CLIK CLIK CLIK

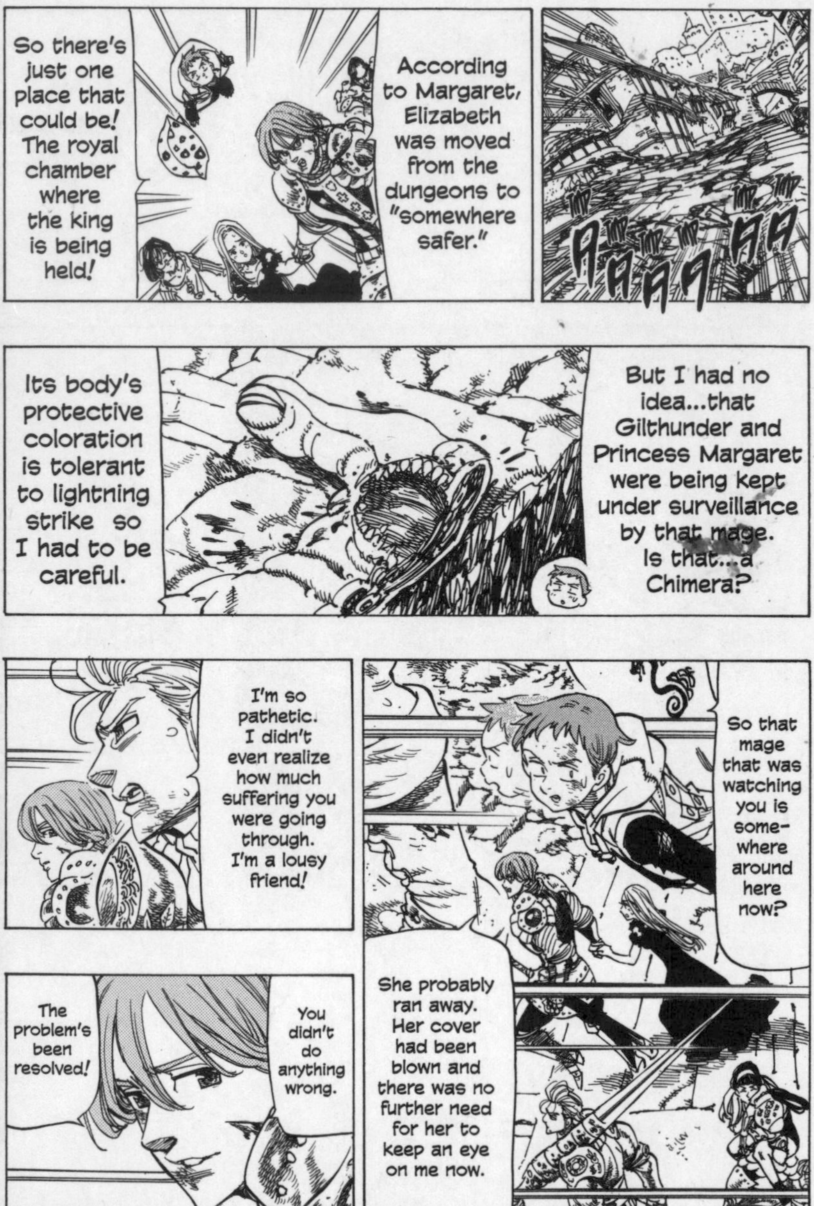
According to Margaret, Elizabeth was moved from the dungeons to "somewhere safer."
So there's just one place that could be! The royal chamber where the king is being held!
But I had no idea...that Gilthunder and Princess Margaret were being kept under surveillance by that mage. Is that...a Chimera?
Its body's protective coloration is tolerant to lightning strike so I had to be careful.
So that mage that was watching you is some-where around here now?
I'm so pathetic. I didn't even realize how much suffering you were going through. I'm a lousy friend!
She probably ran away. Her cover had been blown and there was no further need for her to keep an eye on me now.
You didn't do anything wrong.
The problem's been resolved!

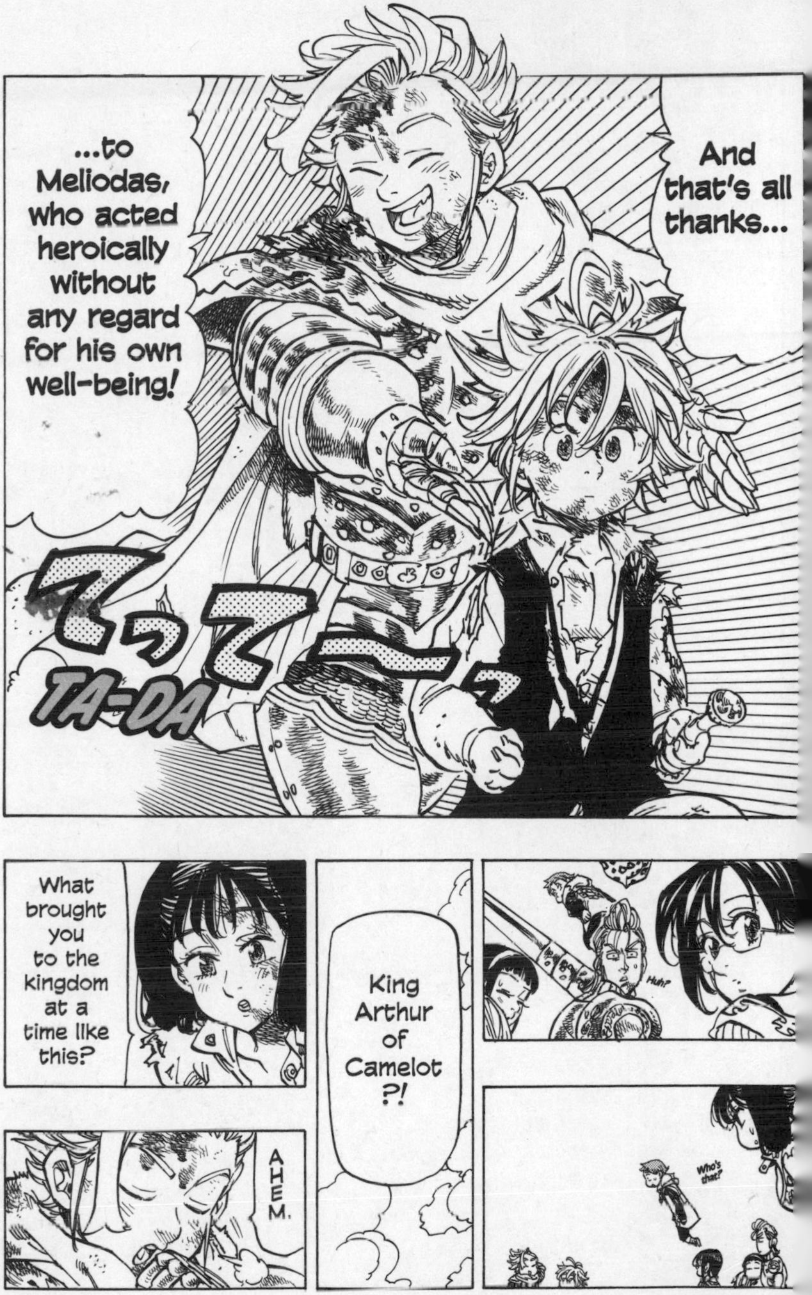
And that's all thanks...
...to Meliodas, who acted heroically without any regard for his own well-being!
TA-DA
Huh?
Who's that?
King Arthur of Camelot ?!
What brought you to the kingdom at a time like this?
AHEM.

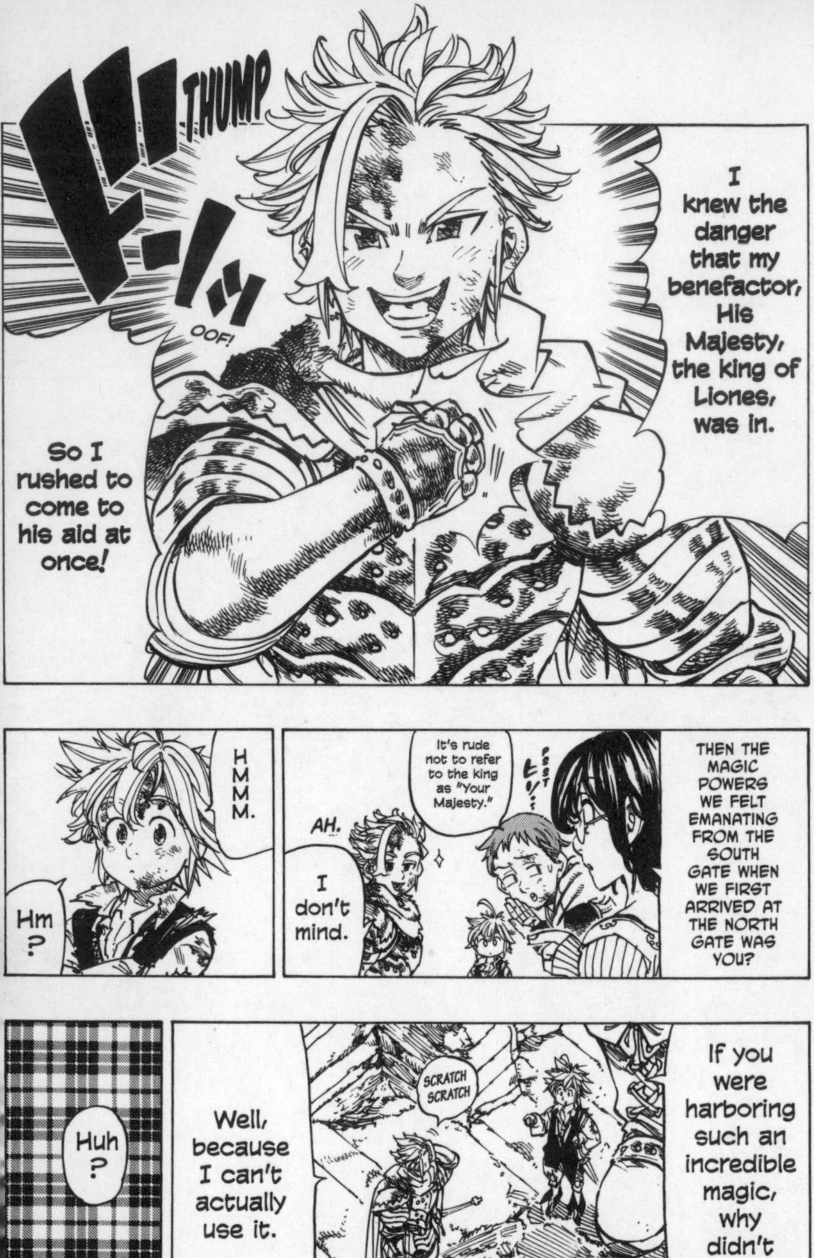
I knew the danger that my benefactor, His Majesty, the king of Liones, was in.
THUMP
OOF!
So I rushed to come to his aid at once!
THEN THE MAGIC POWERS WE FELT EMANATING FROM THE SOUTH GATE WHEN WE FIRST ARRIVED AT THE NORTH GATE WAS YOU?
PSST
It's rude not to refer to the king as "Your Majesty."
AH.
I don't mind.
HMMM.
Hm?
If you were harboring such an incredible magic, why didn't you use it?
SCRATCH SCRATCH
Well, because I can't actually use it.
Huh?

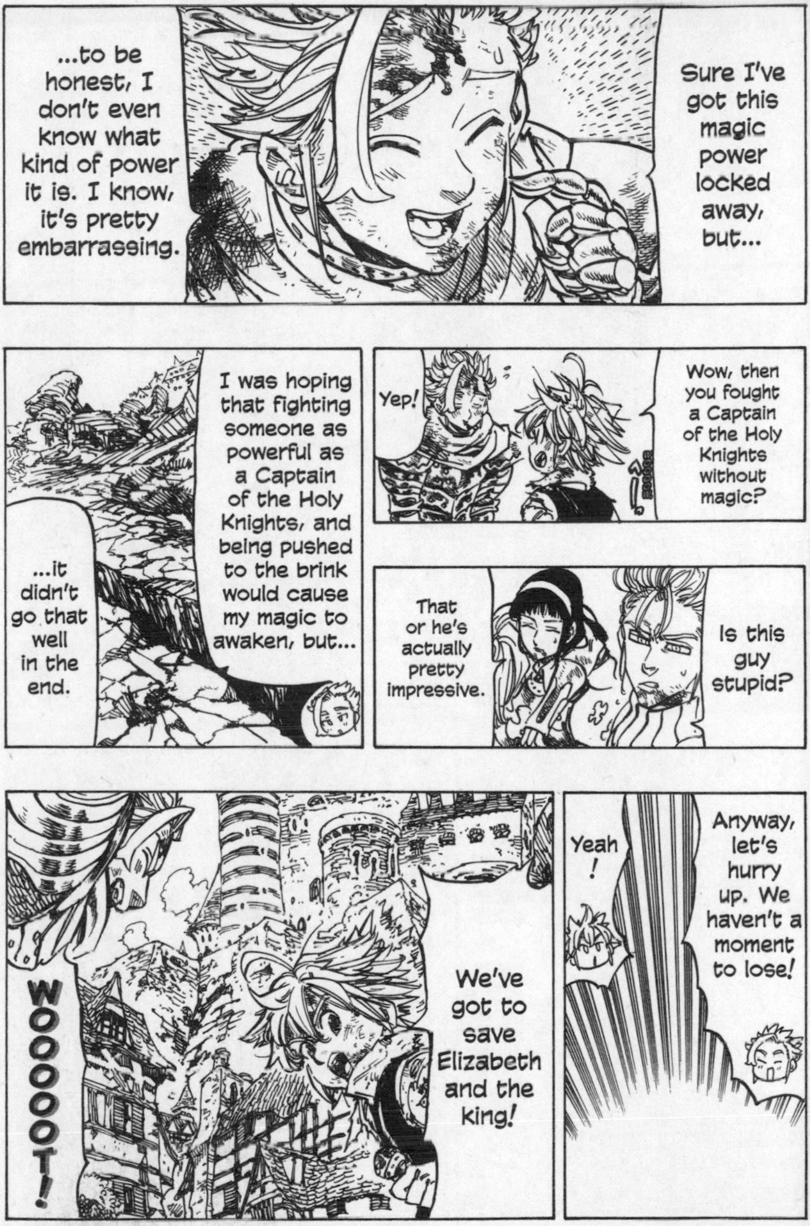
Sure I've got this magic power locked away, but...
...to be honest, I don't even know what kind of power it is. I know, it's pretty embarrassing.
Wow, then you fought a Captain of the Holy Knights without magic?
Yep!
Is this guy stupid?
That or he's actually pretty impressive.
I was hoping that fighting someone as powerful as a Captain of the Holy Knights, and being pushed to the brink would cause my magic to awaken, but...
...it didn't go that well in the end.
Anyway, let's hurry up. We haven't a moment to lose!
Yeah!
We've got to save Elizabeth and the king!
WOOOOOOT!

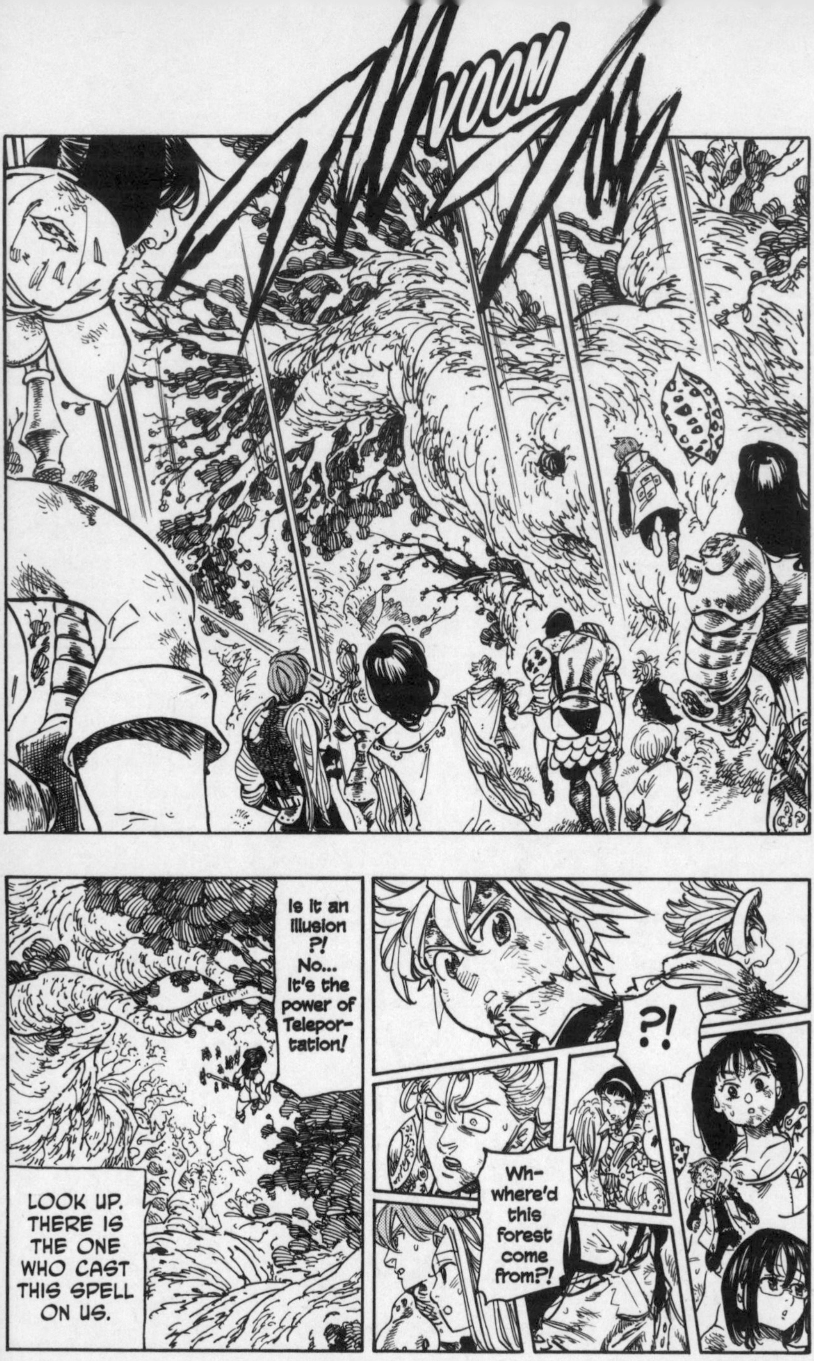
VOOOM
?!
Wh- where'd this forest come from?!
Is it an illusion?! No... It's the power of Teleportation!
LOOK UP. THERE IS THE ONE WHO CAST THIS SPELL ON US.

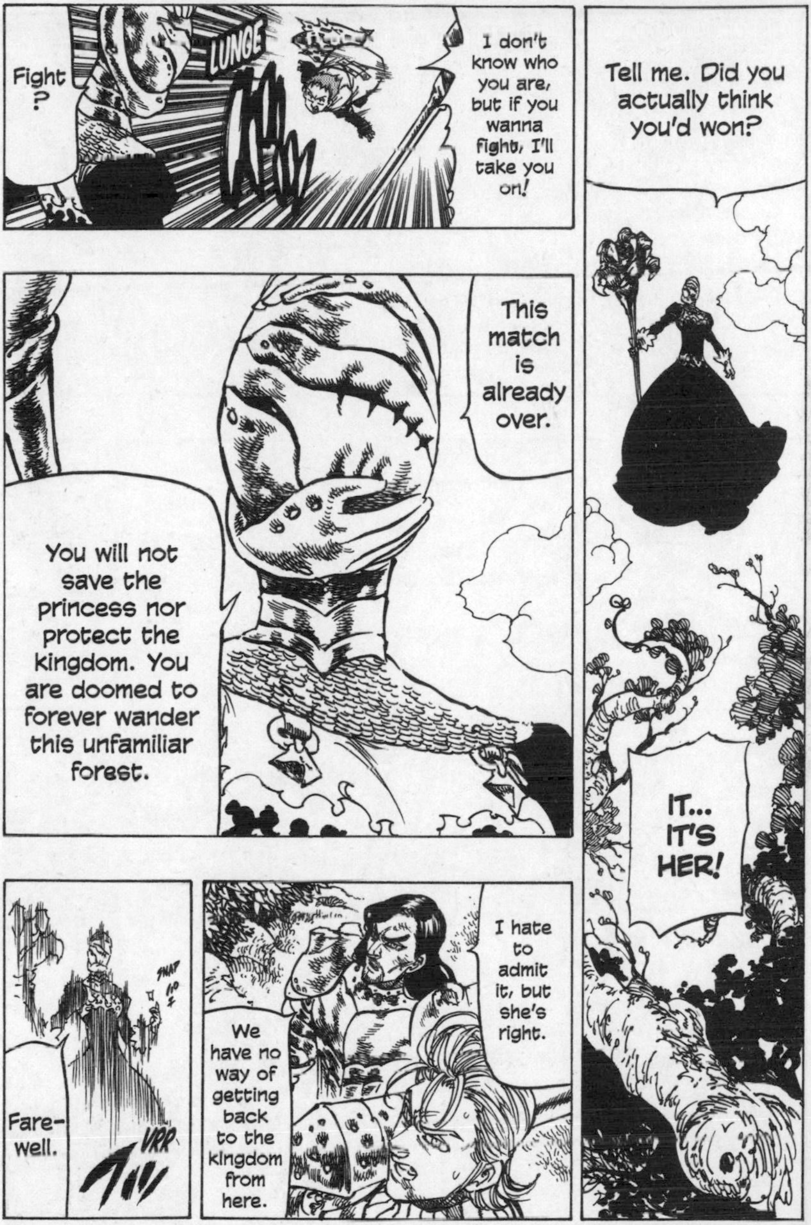
Tell me. Did you actually think you'd won?
IT... IT'S HER!
I don't know who you are, but if you wanna fight, I'll take you on!
LUNGE
Fight ?
This match is already over.
You will not save the princess nor protect the kingdom. You are doomed to forever wander this unfamiliar forest.
I hate to admit it, but she's right.
We have no way of getting back to the kingdom from here.
SNAP
VRR
Fare-well.

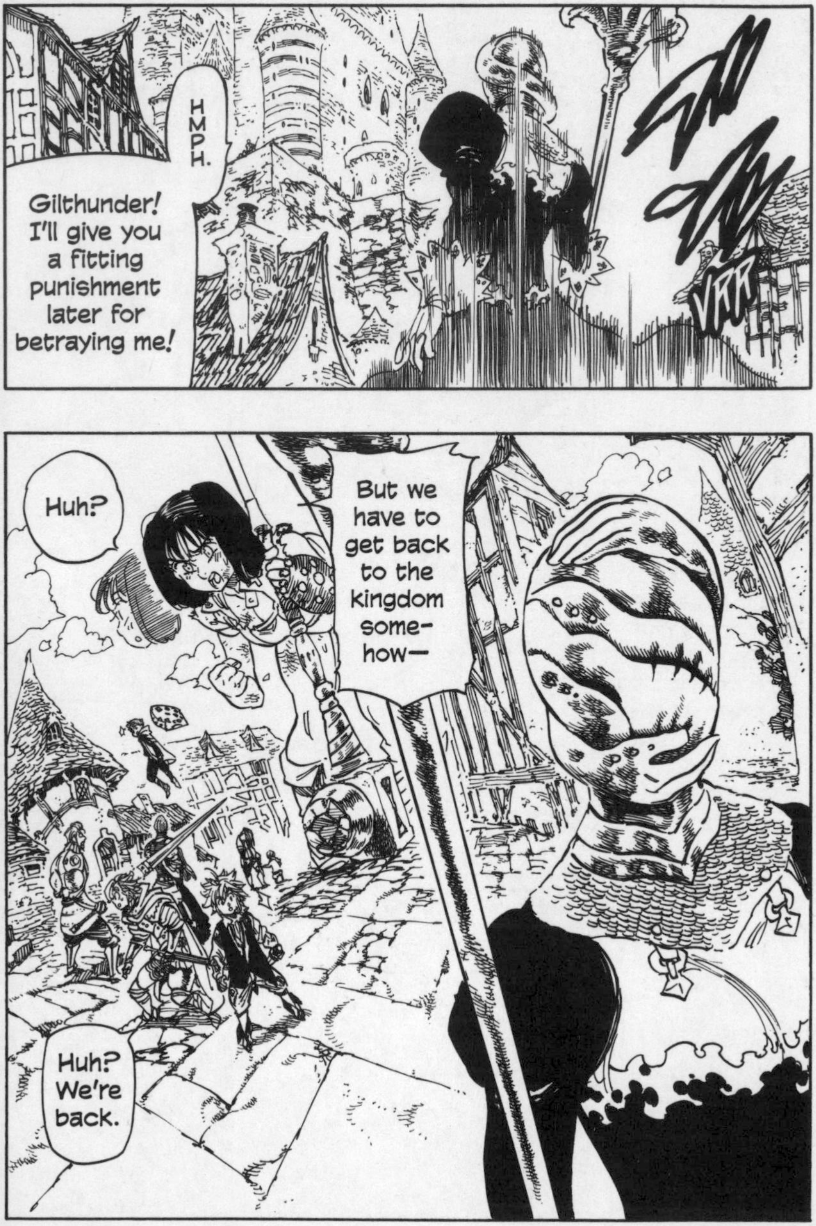
VRR
HMPH.
Gilthunder! I'll give you a fitting punishment later for betraying me!
But we have to get back to the kingdom some-how—
Huh?
Huh? We're back.

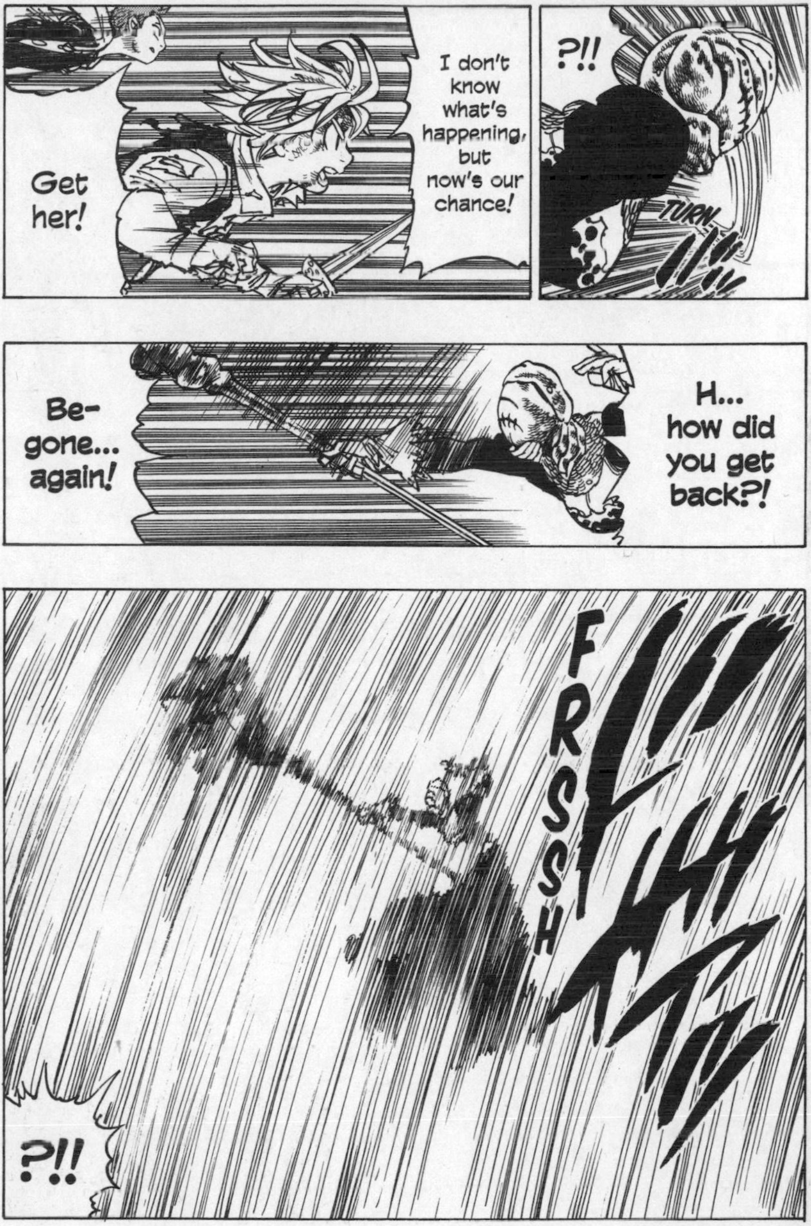
?!!
TURN
I don't know what's happening, but now's our chance!
Get her!
H... how did you get back?!
Be-gone... again!
FRSSH
?!!

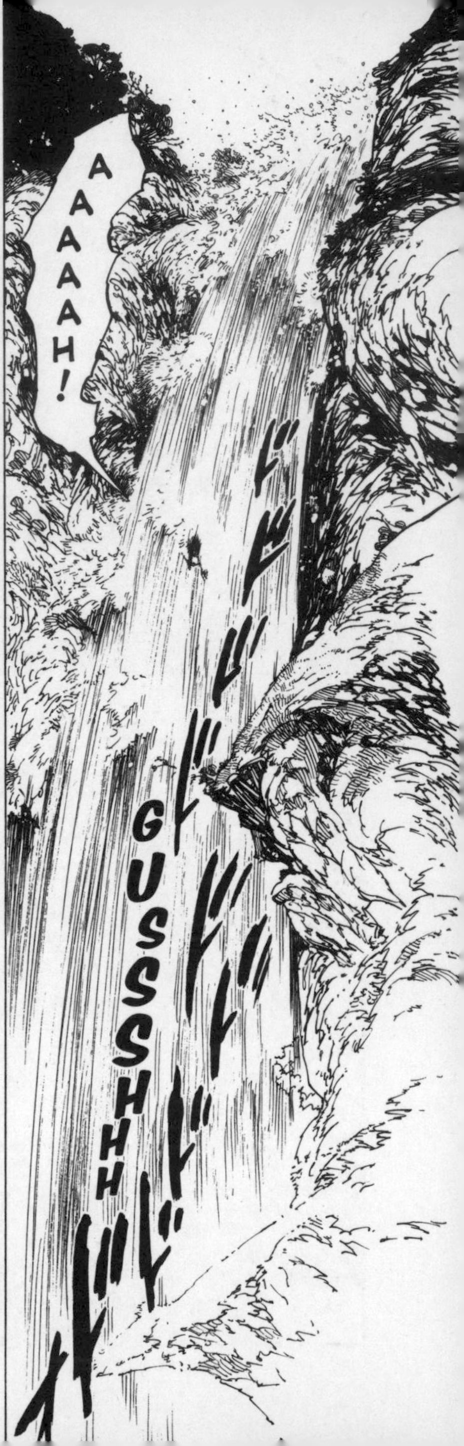
AAAAAH!
GUSSSHHH

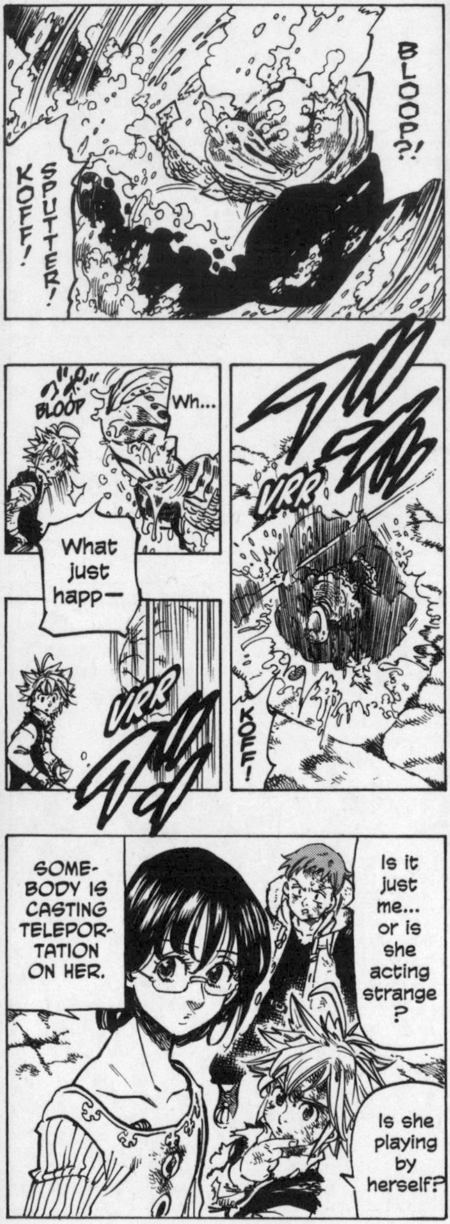
BLOOP?!
SPUTTER!
KOFF!
VRR
KOFF!
Wh...
BLOOP
What just happ—
VRR
Is it just me... or is she acting strange?
Is she playing by herself?
SOME-BODY IS CASTING TELEPOR-TATION ON HER.

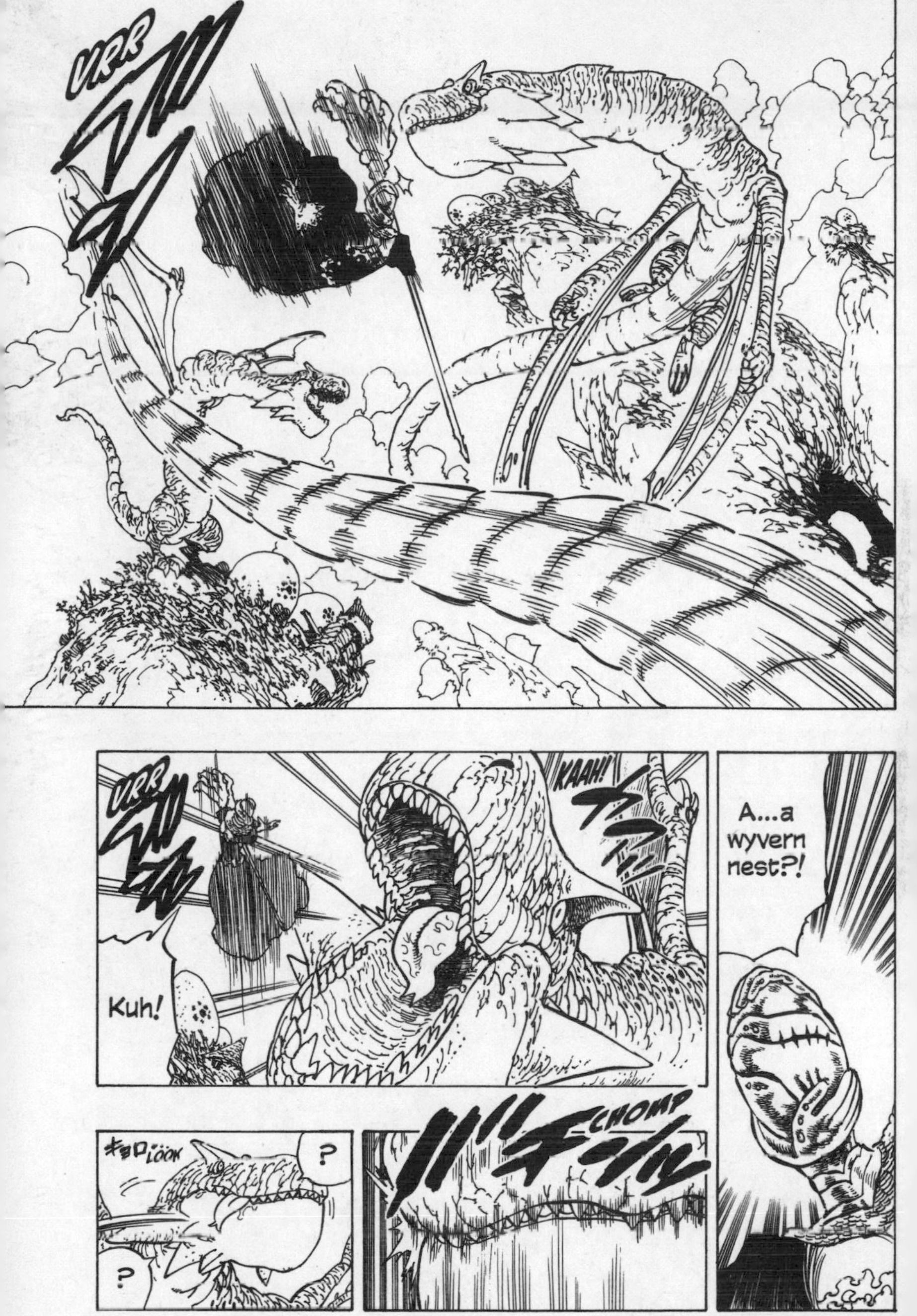
VRR
A...a wyvern nest?!
VRR
KAAH!
Kuh!
CHOMP
キョロ LOOK
?
?

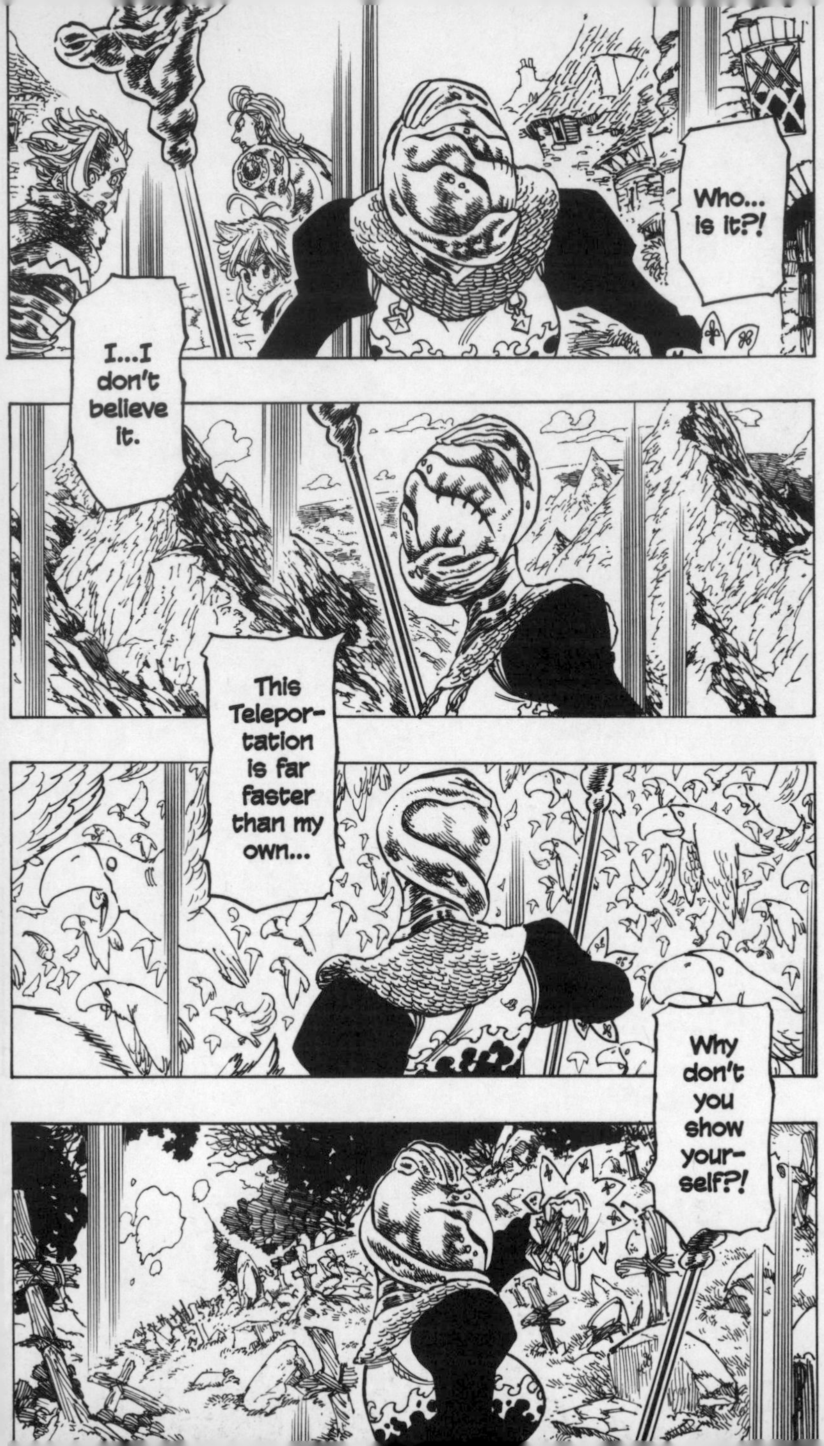
Who... is it?!
I...I don't believe it.
This Teleportation is far faster than my own...
Why don't you show yourself?!

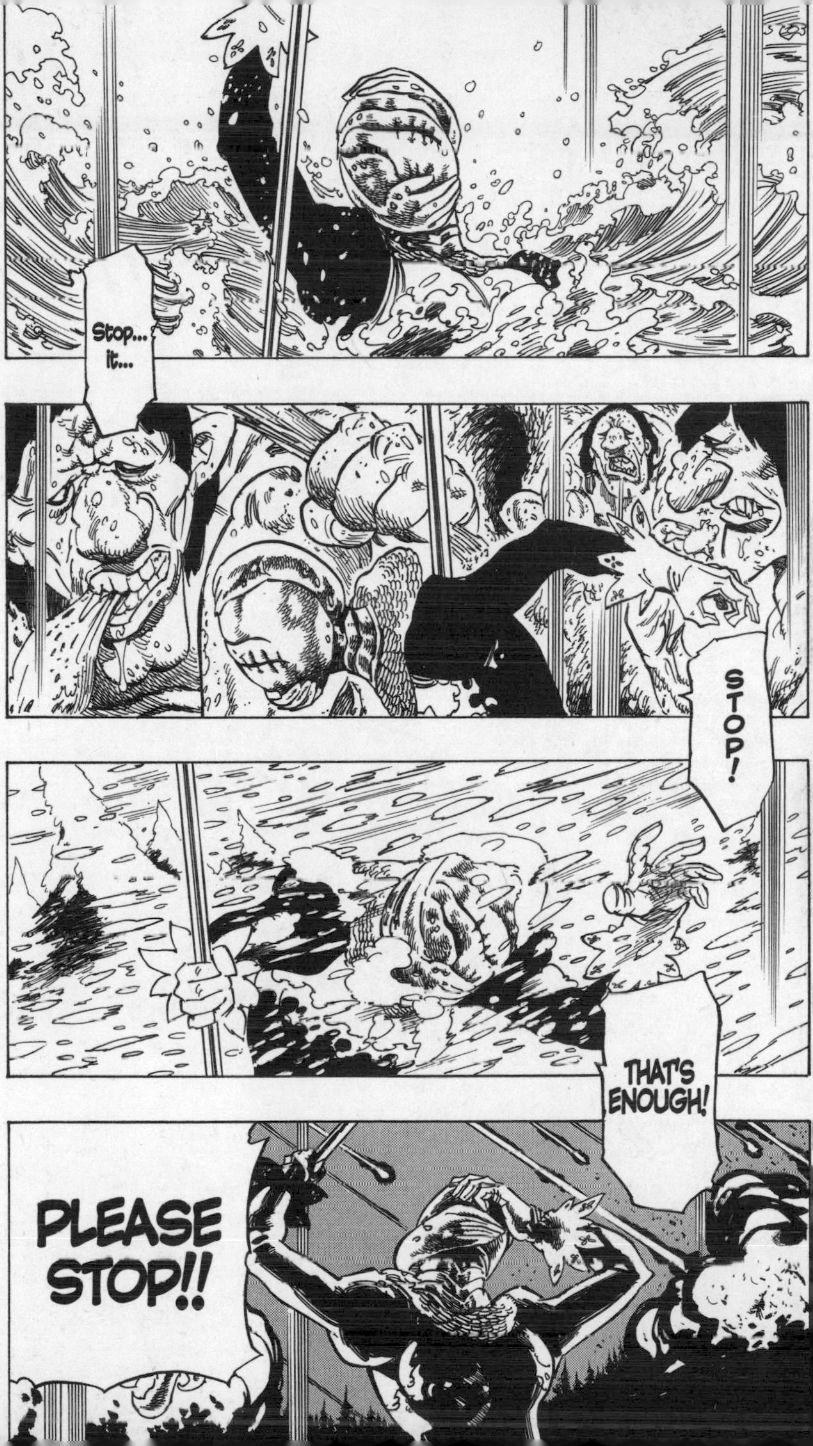
Stop... it...
STOP!
THAT'S ENOUGH!
PLEASE STOP!!

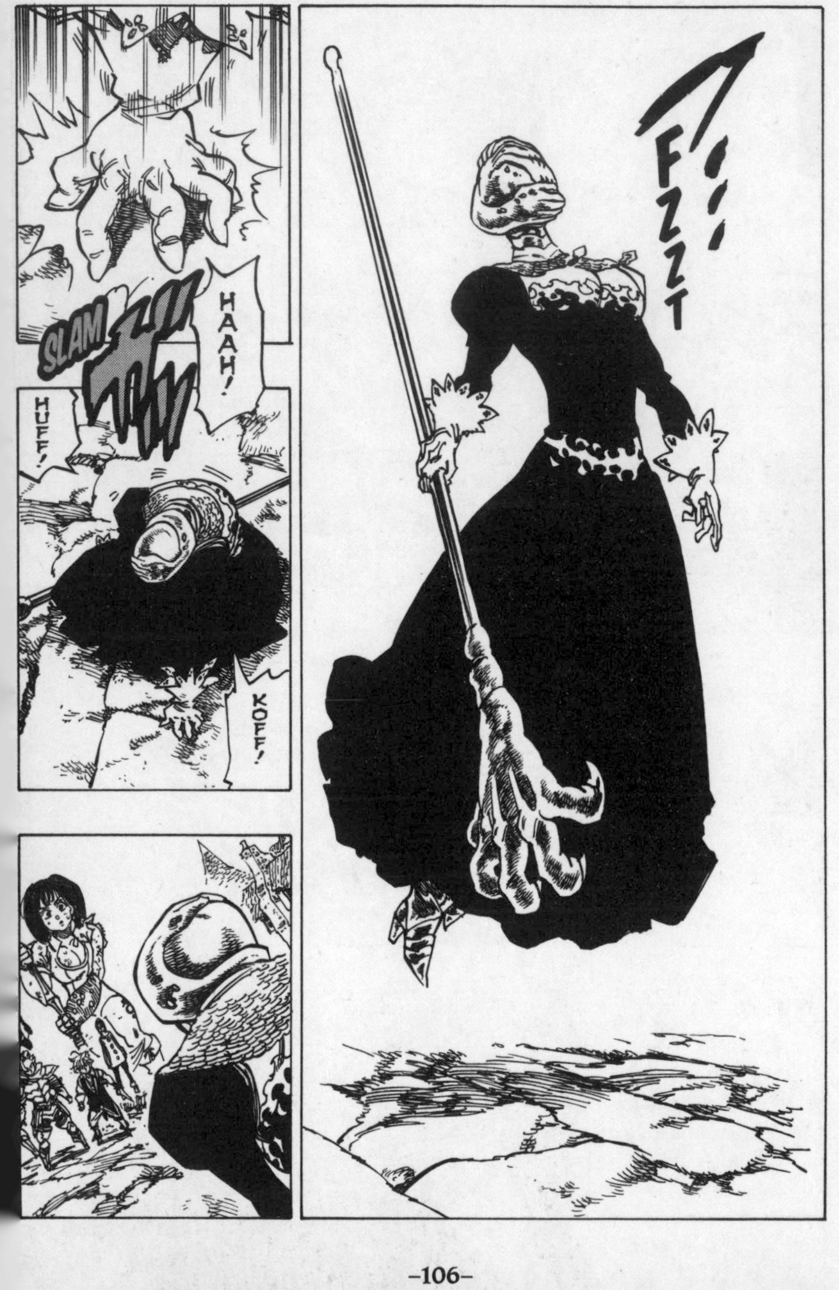
FZZT
SLAM
HAAH!
HUFF!
KOFF!

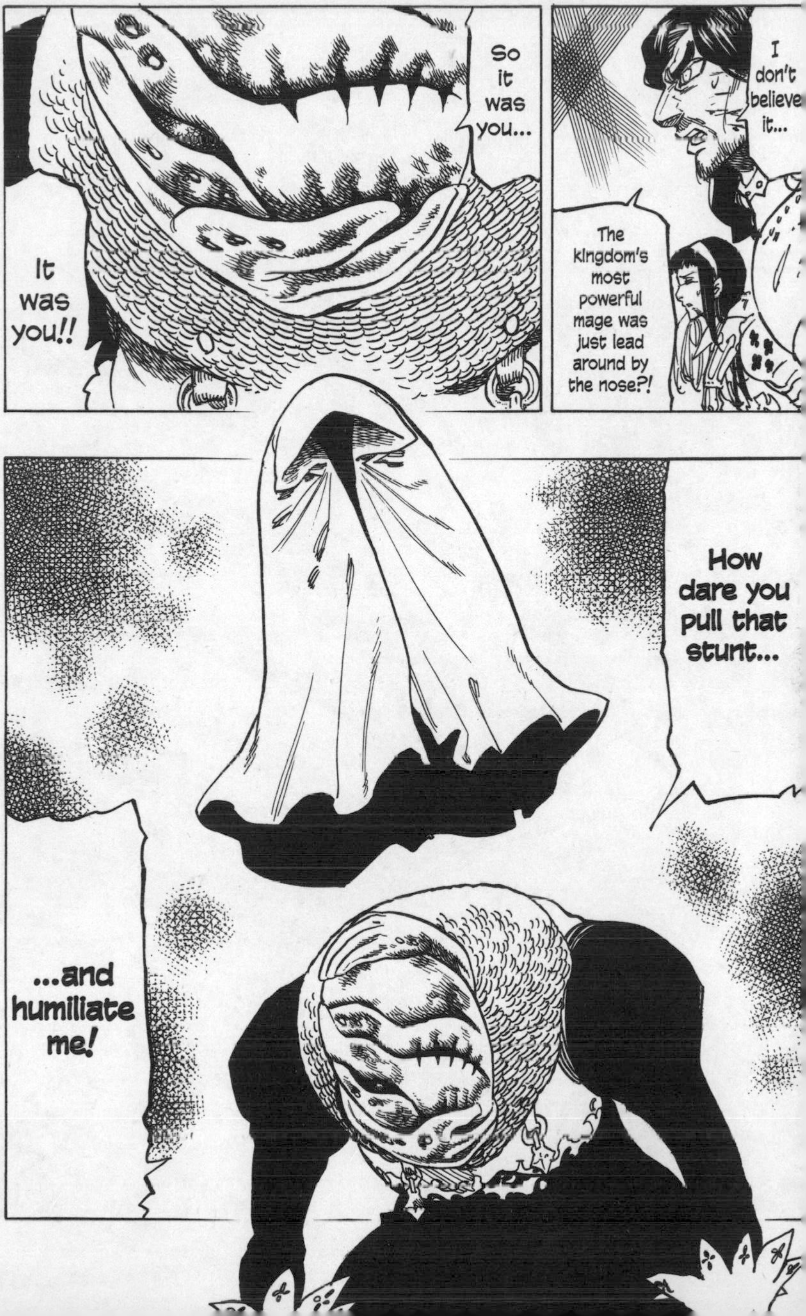
I don't believe it...
The kingdom's most powerful mage was just lead around by the nose?!
So it was you...
It was you!!
How dare you pull that stunt...
...and humiliate me!

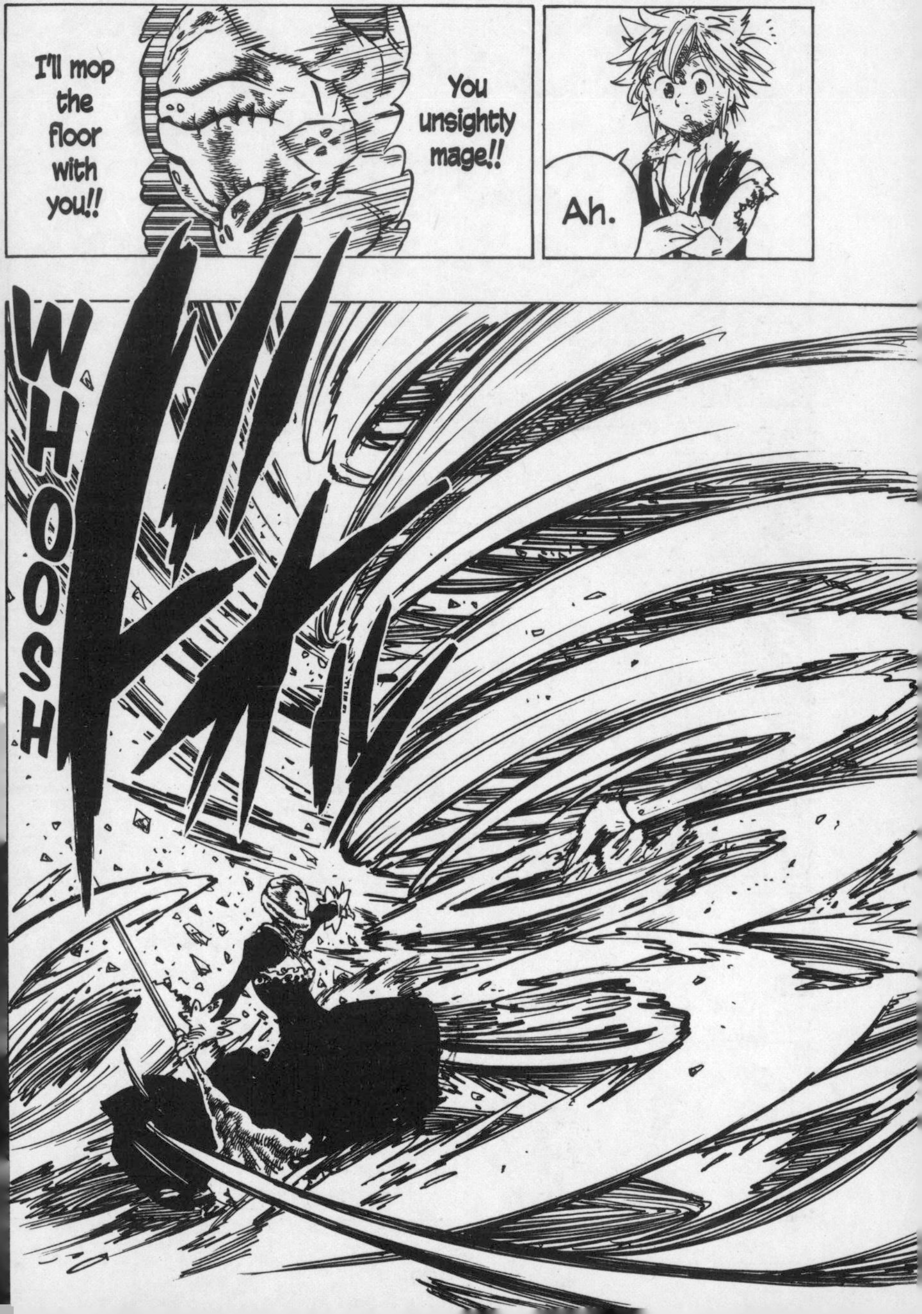
Ah.
You unsightly mage!!
I'll mop the floor with you!!
WHOOSH

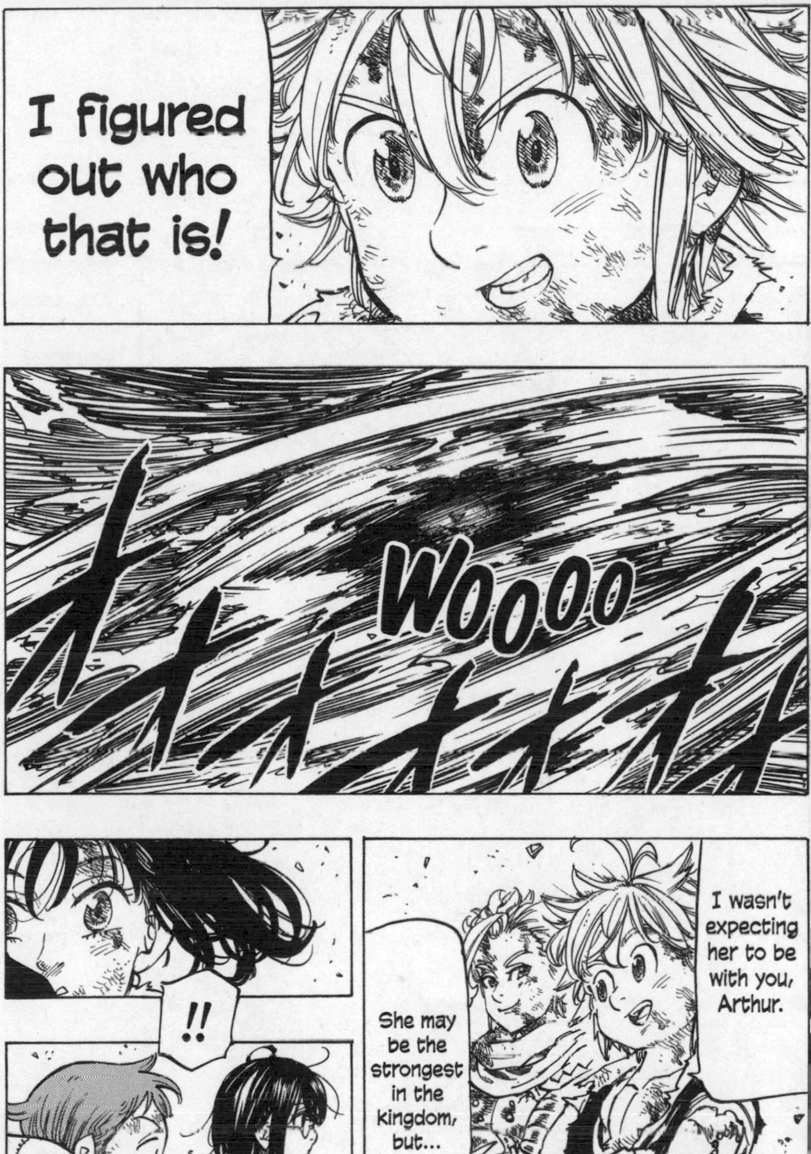
I figured out who that is!
WOOOO
I wasn't expecting her to be with you, Arthur.
She may be the strongest in the kingdom, but...
!!

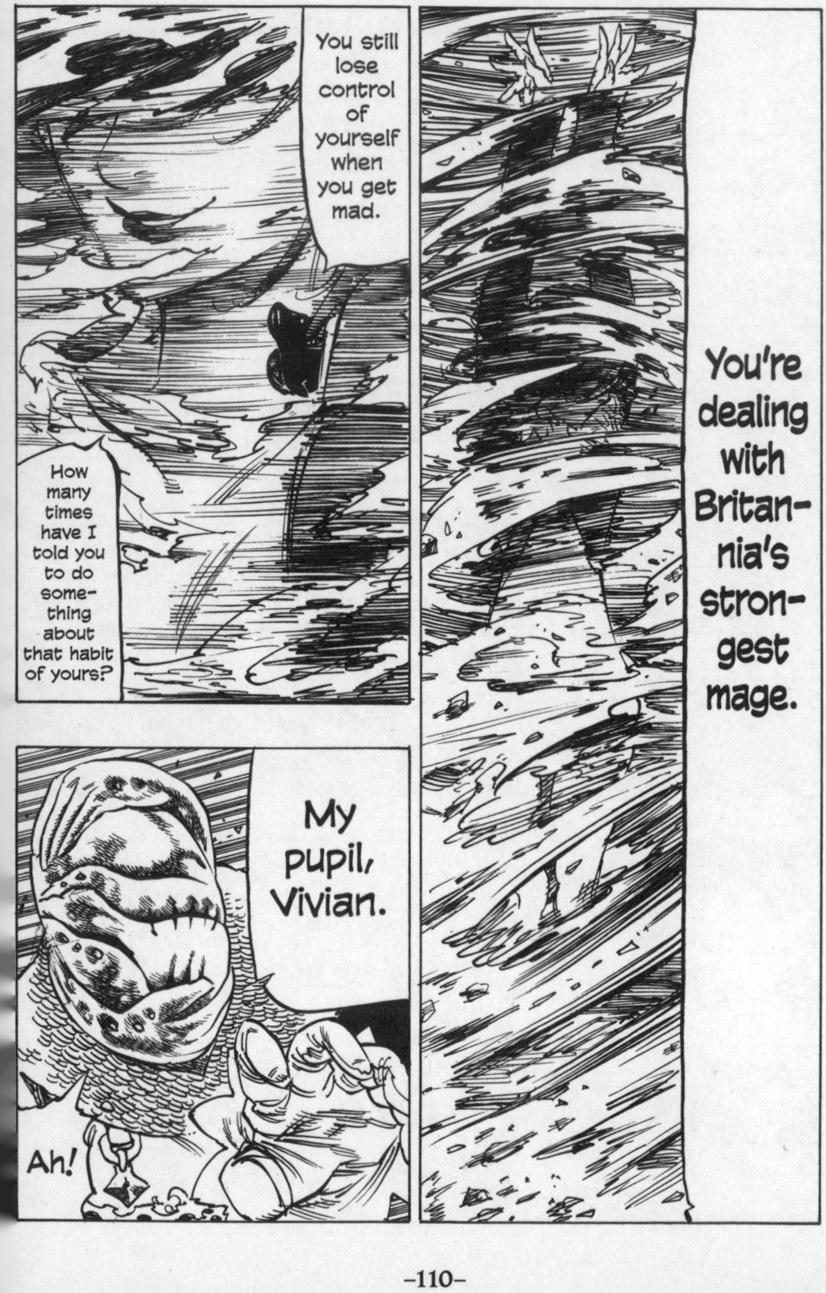
You're dealing with Britan-nia's stron-gest mage.
You still lose control of yourself when you get mad.
How many times have I told you to do some-thing about that habit of yours?
My pupil, Vivian.
Ah!

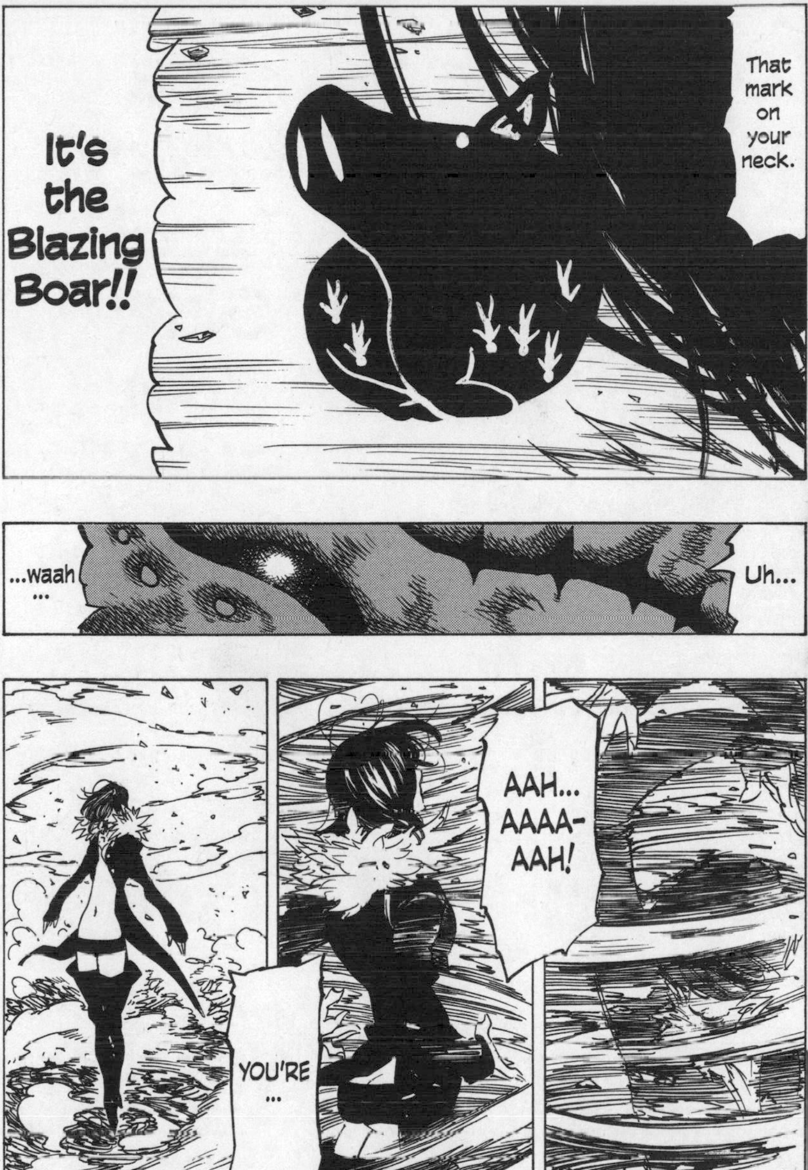
That mark on your neck.
It's the Blazing Boar!!
Uh...
...waah ...
AAH... AAAA-AAH!
YOU'RE ...

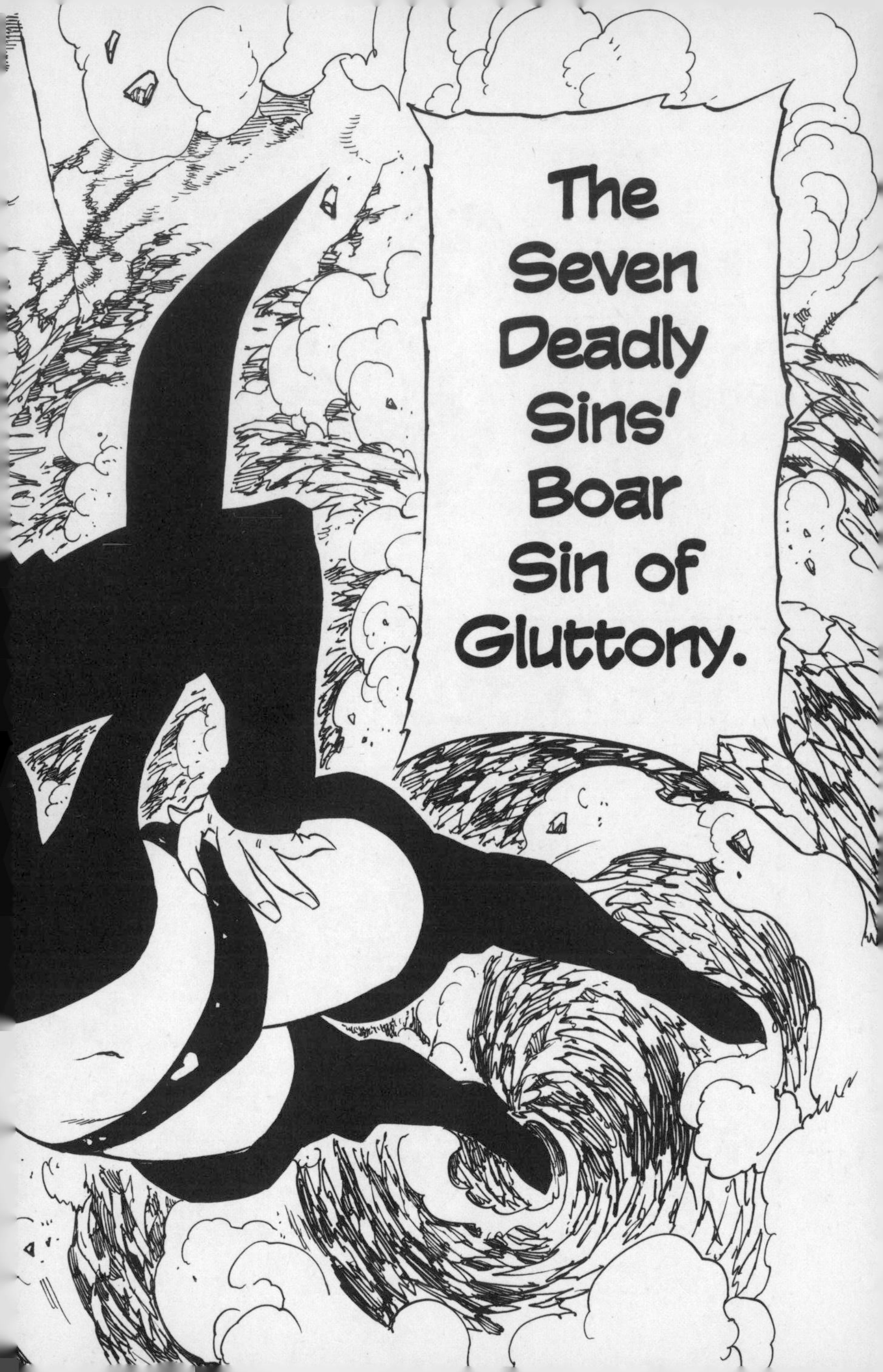
The Seven Deadly Sins' Boar Sin of Gluttony.

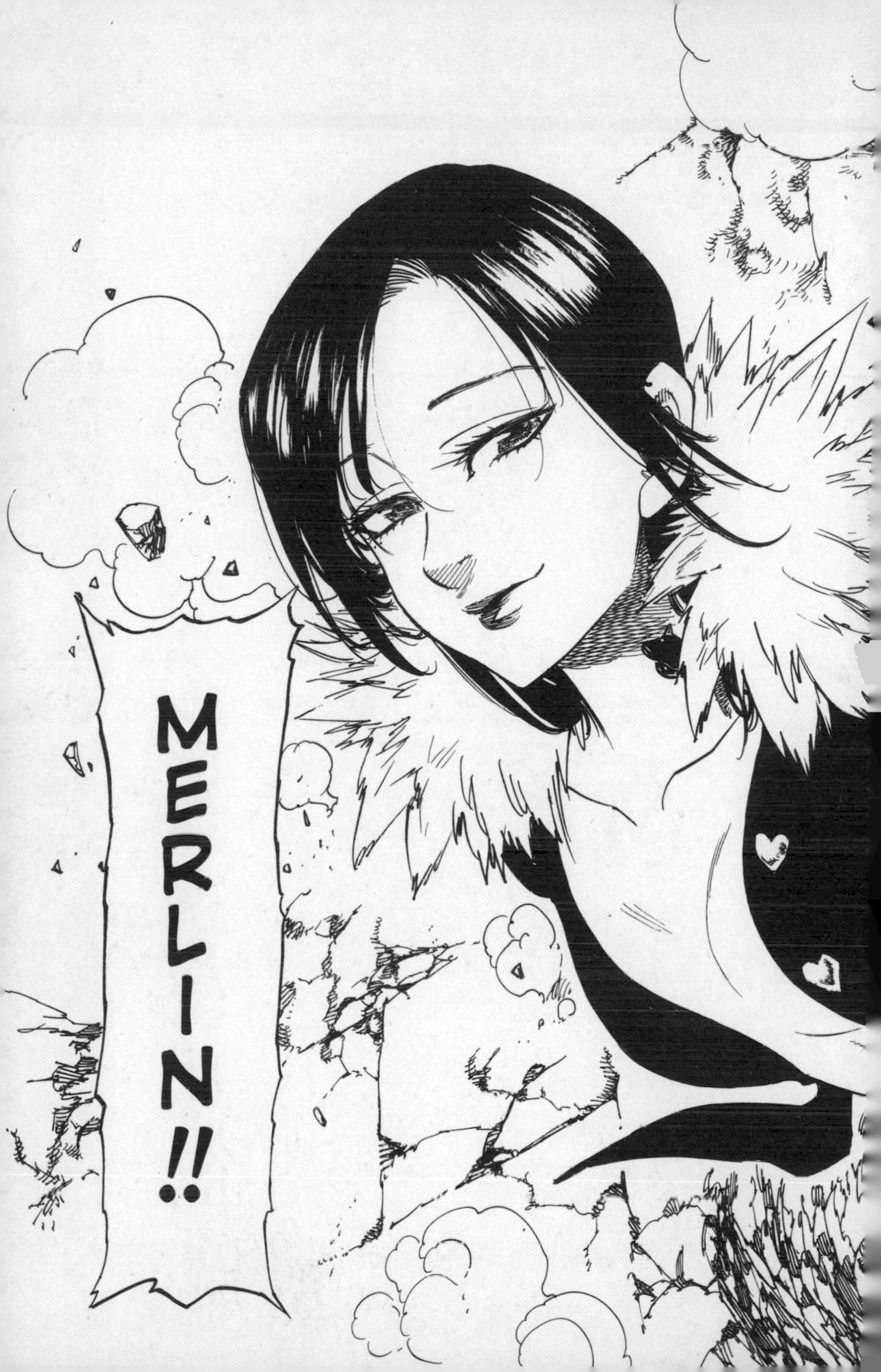
MERLIN!!

Open to the Public for the First Time!! Initial Designs for "The Seven Deadly Sins"

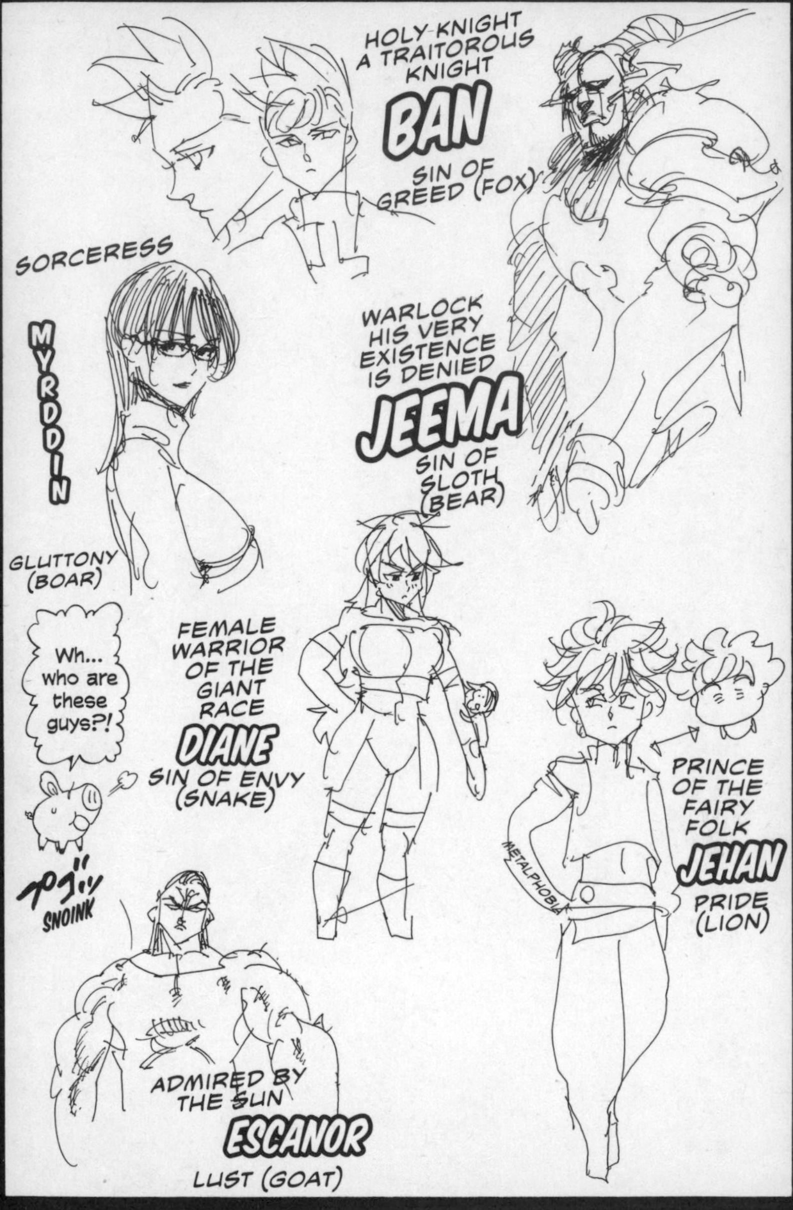
HOLY-KNIGHT
A TRAITOROUS
KNIGHT
BAN
SIN OF
GREED (FOX)
SORCERESS
MYRDDIN
GLUTTONY
(BOAR)
WARLOCK
HIS VERY
EXISTENCE
IS DENIED
JEEMA
SIN OF
SLOTH
(BEAR)
Wh... who are these guys?!
SNOINK
FEMALE
WARRIOR
OF THE
GIANT
RACE
DIANE
SIN OF ENVY
(SNAKE)
PRINCE
OF THE
FAIRY
FOLK
JEHAN
PRIDE
(LION)
METALPHOBIA
ADMIRED BY
THE SUN
ESCANOR
LUST (GOAT)

For more details, go to page 154

Chapter 84 - The Matter Is Settled

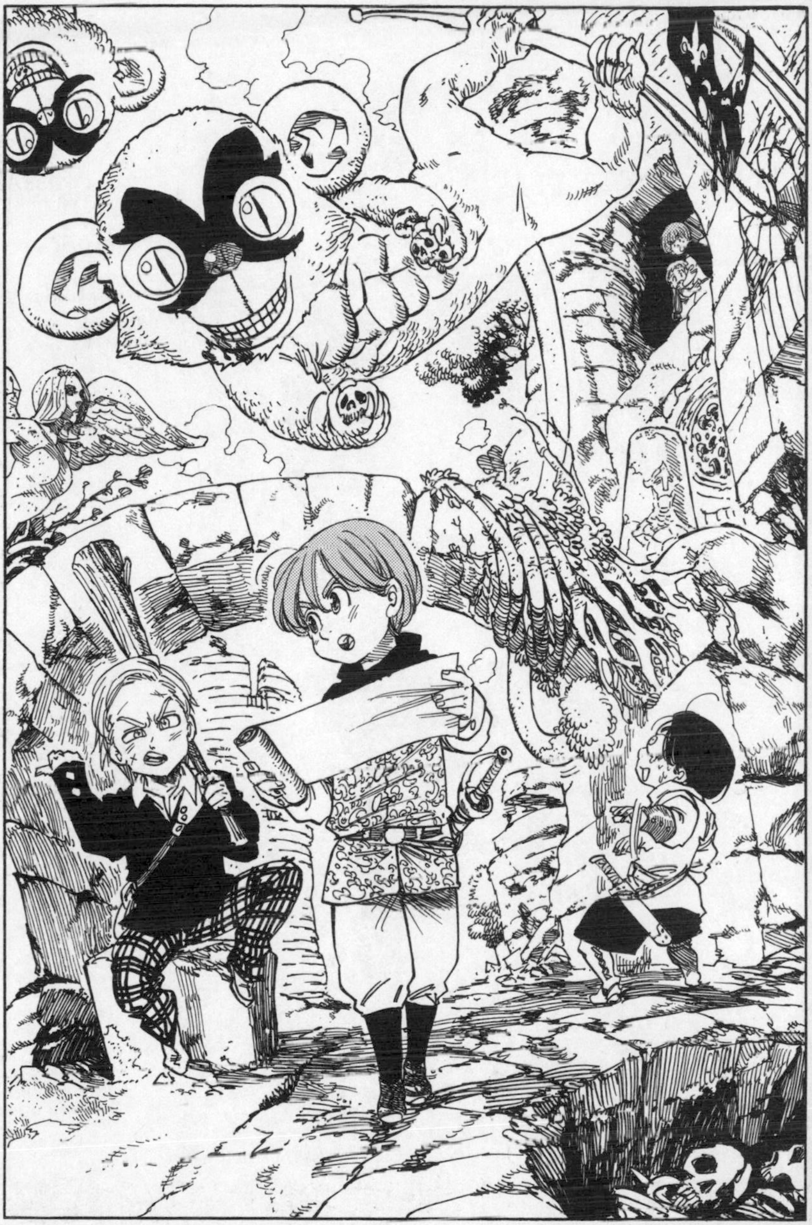

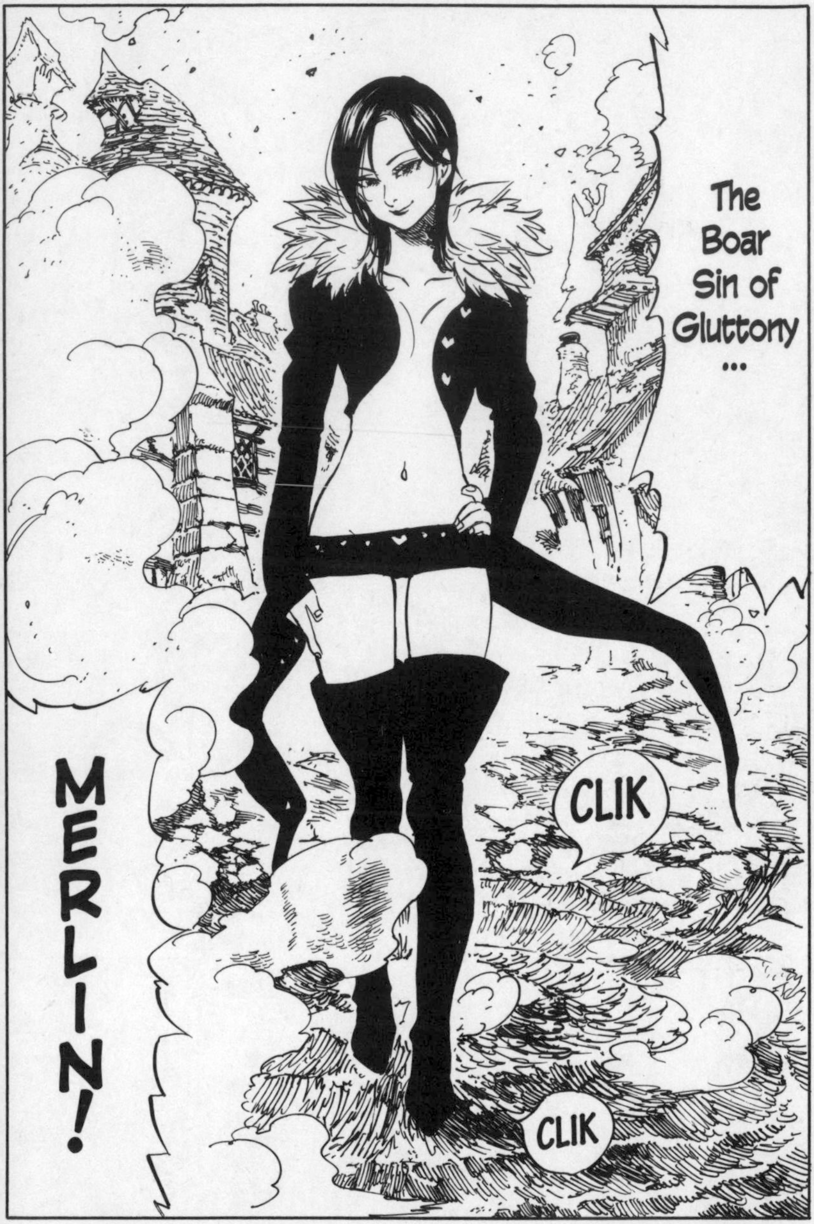
The Boar Sin of Gluttony ...
CLIK
CLIK
MERLIN!

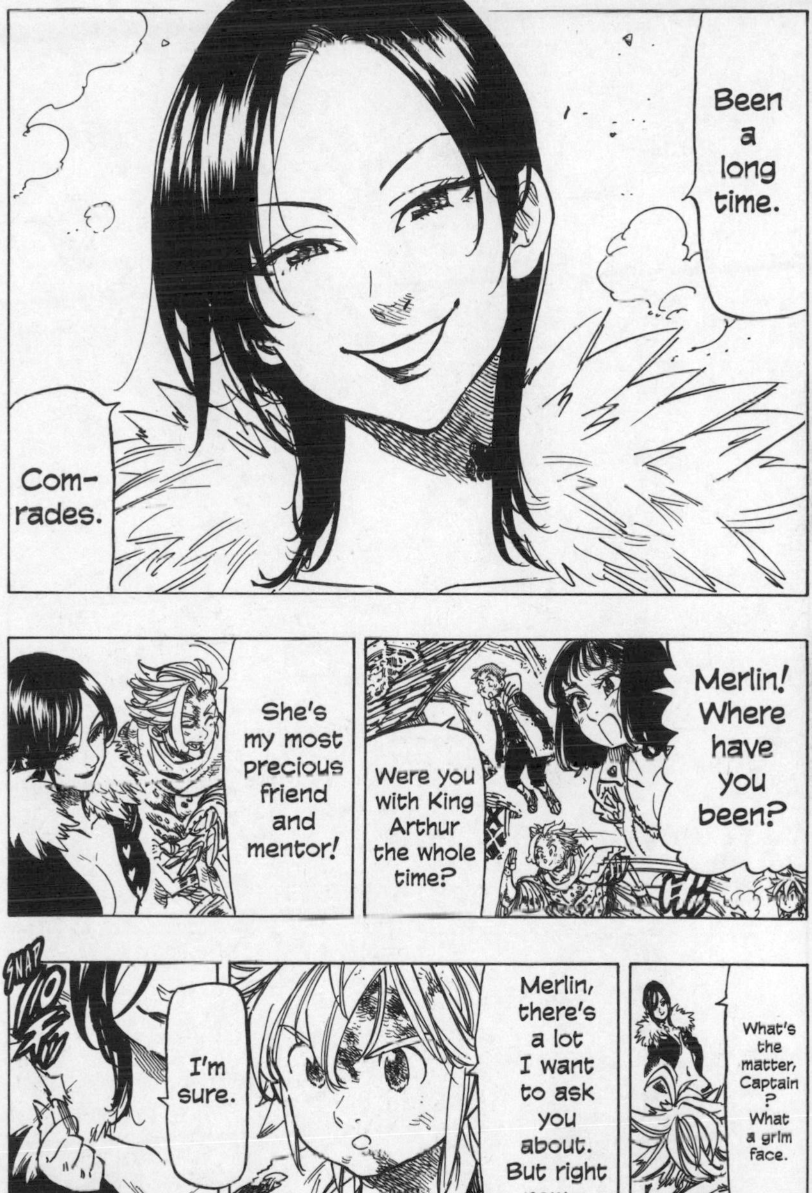
Been a long time.
Comrades.
Merlin! Where have you been?
Were you with King Arthur the whole time?
She's my most precious friend and mentor!
What's the matter, Captain? What a grim face.
Merlin, there's a lot I want to ask you about. But right now—
I'm sure.
SNAP

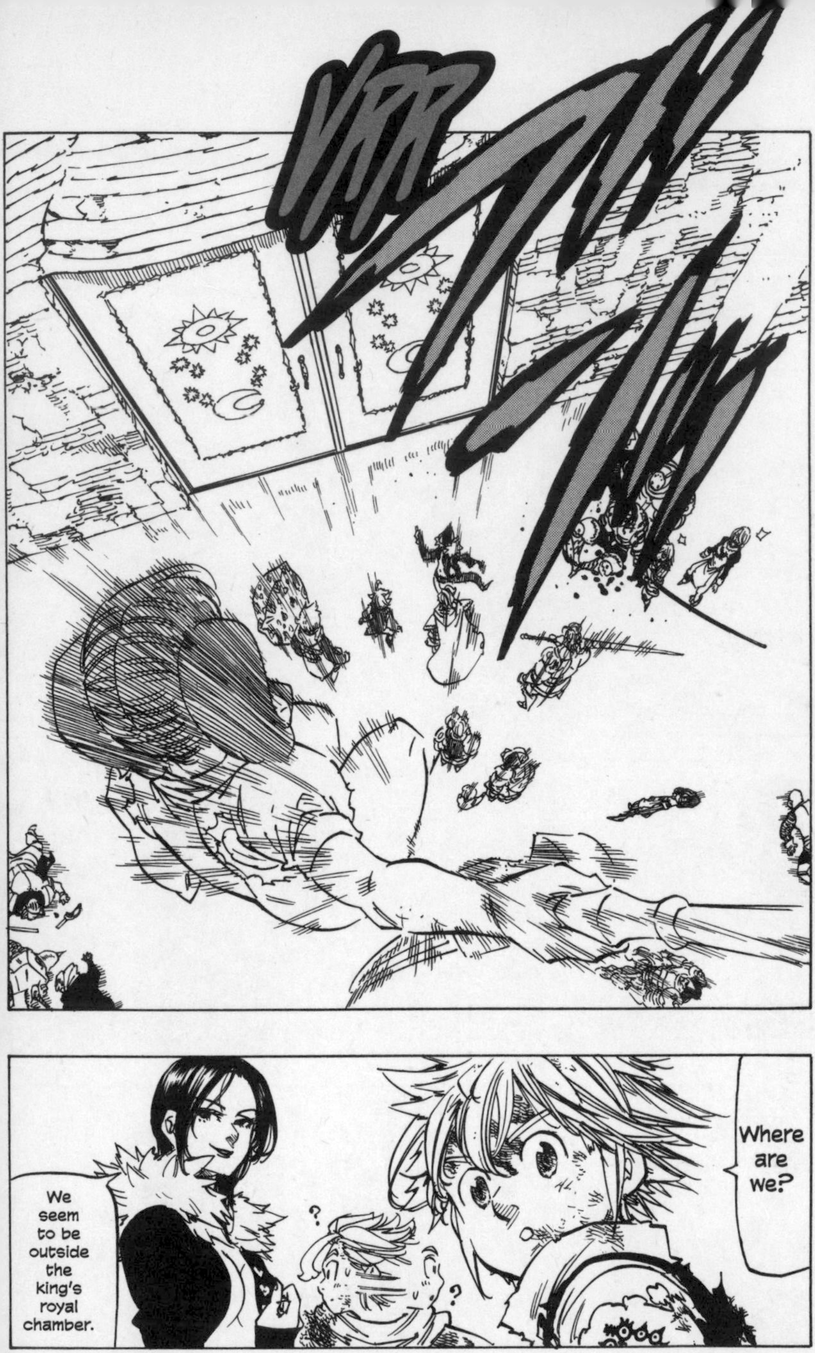
Where are we?
We seem to be outside the king's royal chamber.

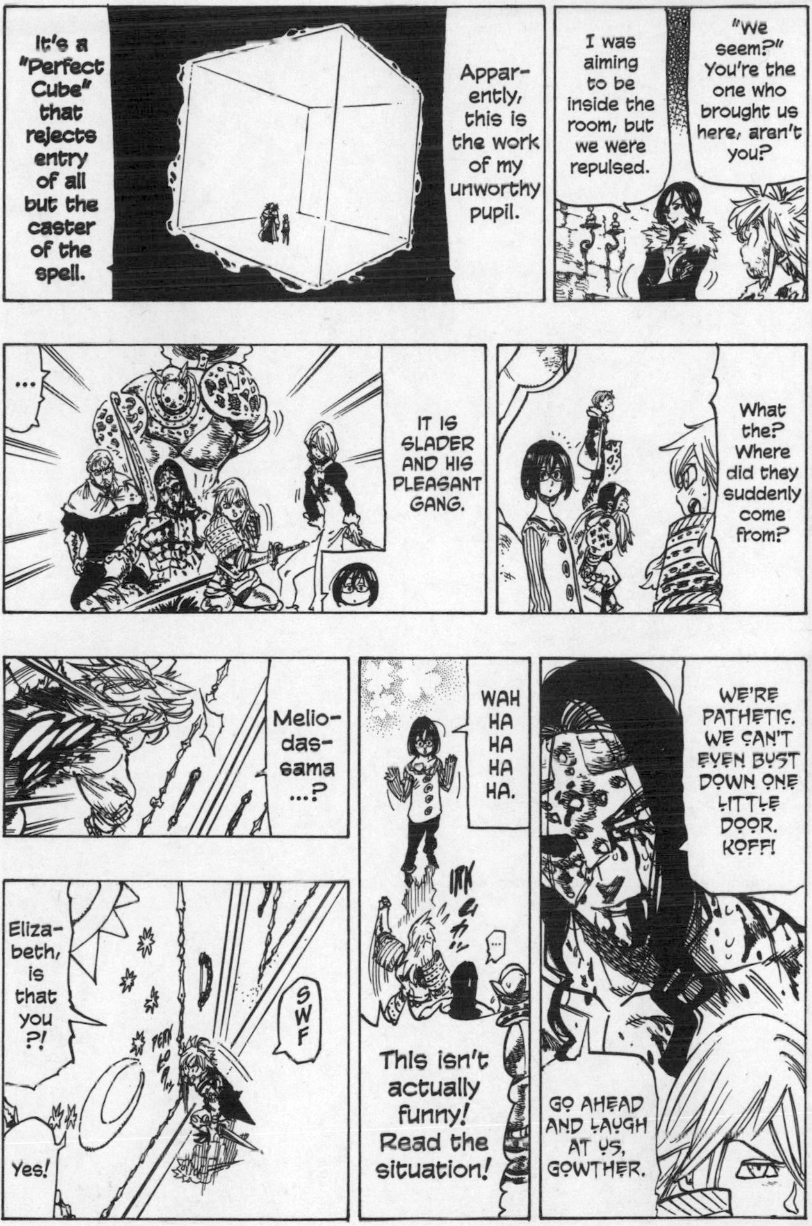

"We seem?" You're the one who brought us here, aren't you?
I was aiming to be inside the room, but we were repulsed.
Apparently, this is the work of my unworthy pupil.
It's a "Perfect Cube" that rejects entry of all but the caster of the spell.
What the? Where did they suddenly come from?
IT IS SLADER AND HIS PLEASANT GANG.
...
WE'RE PATHETIC. WE CAN'T EVEN BUST DOWN ONE LITTLE DOOR. KOFF!
GO AHEAD AND LAUGH AT US, GOWTHER.
WAH HA HA HA HA.
IRK
...
This isn't actually funny! Read the situation!
Melio-das-sama ...?
Elizabeth, is that you?!
SWF
Yes!

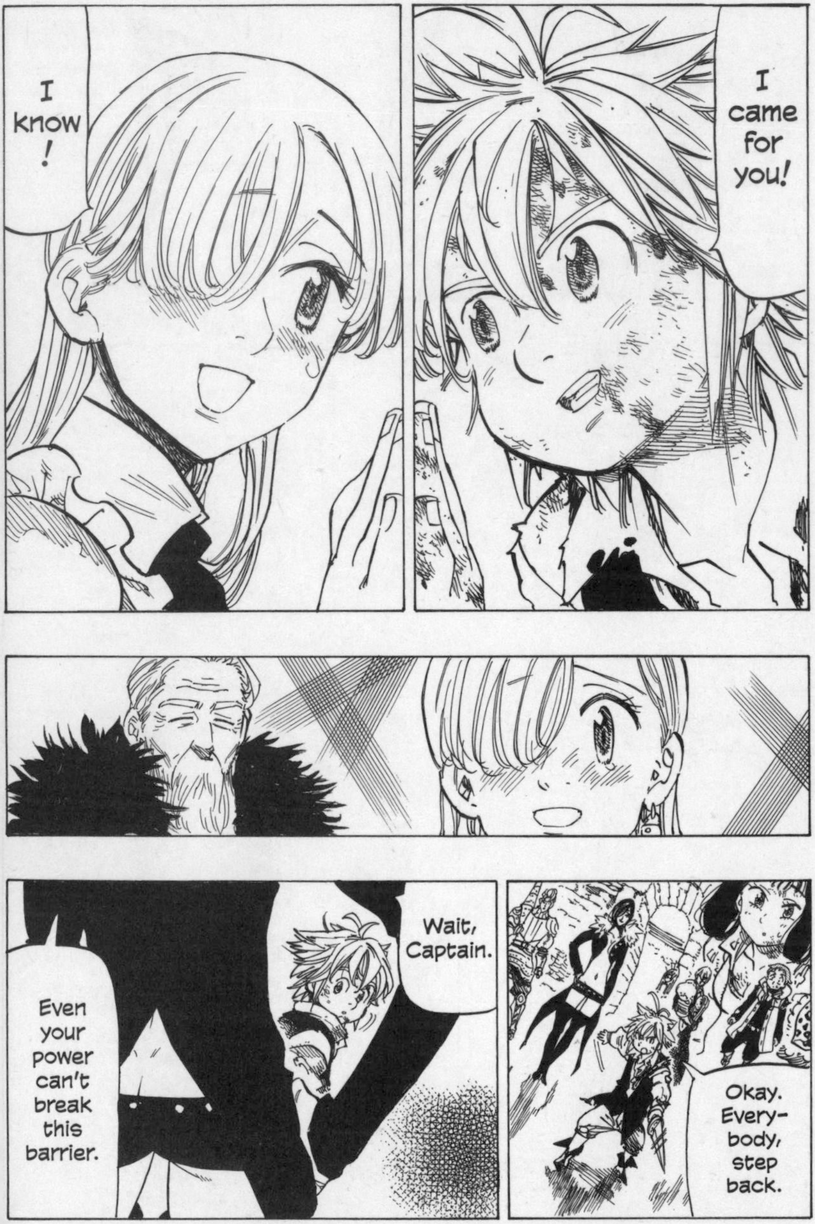
I came for you!
I know!
Okay. Every-body, step back.
Wait, Captain.
Even your power can't break this barrier.

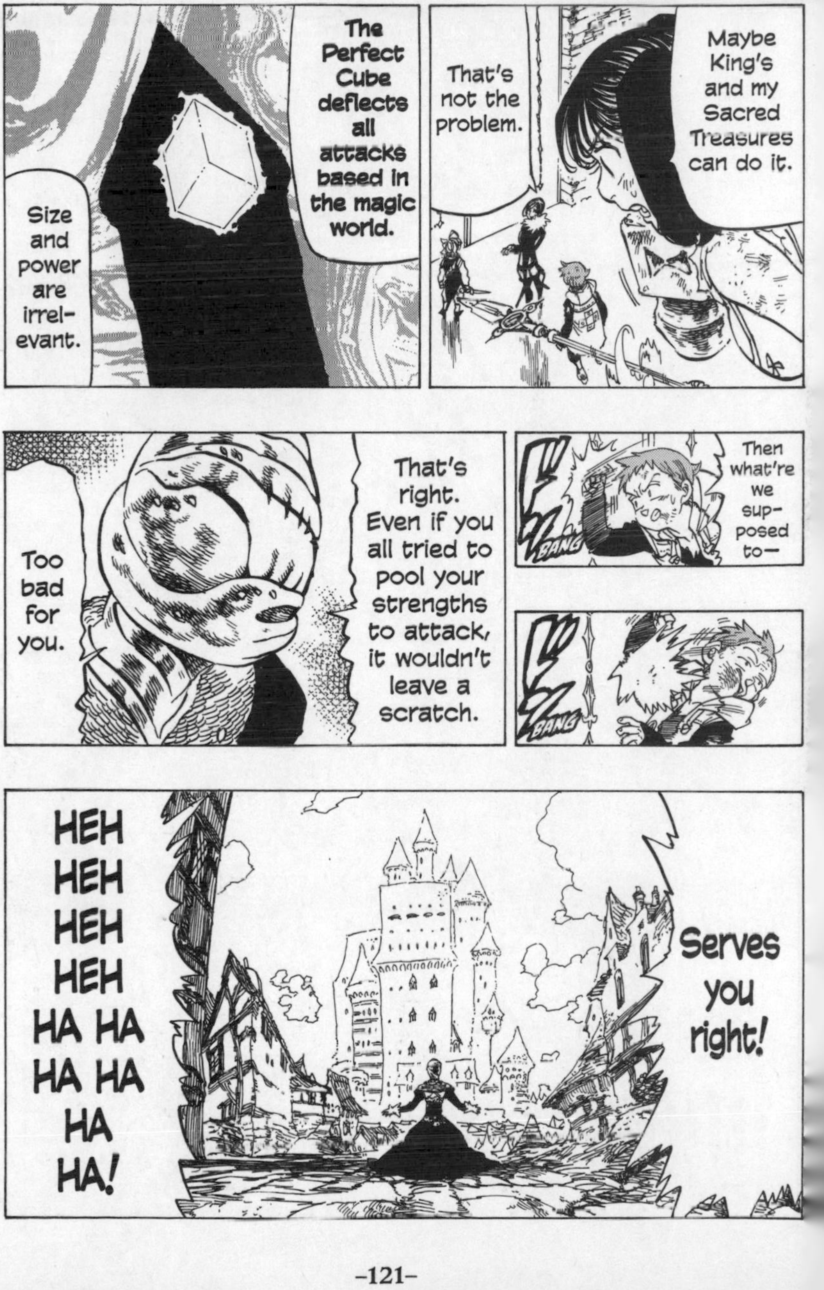
Maybe King's and my Sacred Treasures can do it.
That's not the problem.
The Perfect Cube deflects all attacks based in the magic world.
Size and power are irrel-evant.
Then what're we sup-posed to—
BANG
BANG
That's right. Even if you all tried to pool your strengths to attack, it wouldn't leave a scratch.
Too bad for you.
Serves you right!
HEH HEH HEH HEH HA HA HA HA HA HA!

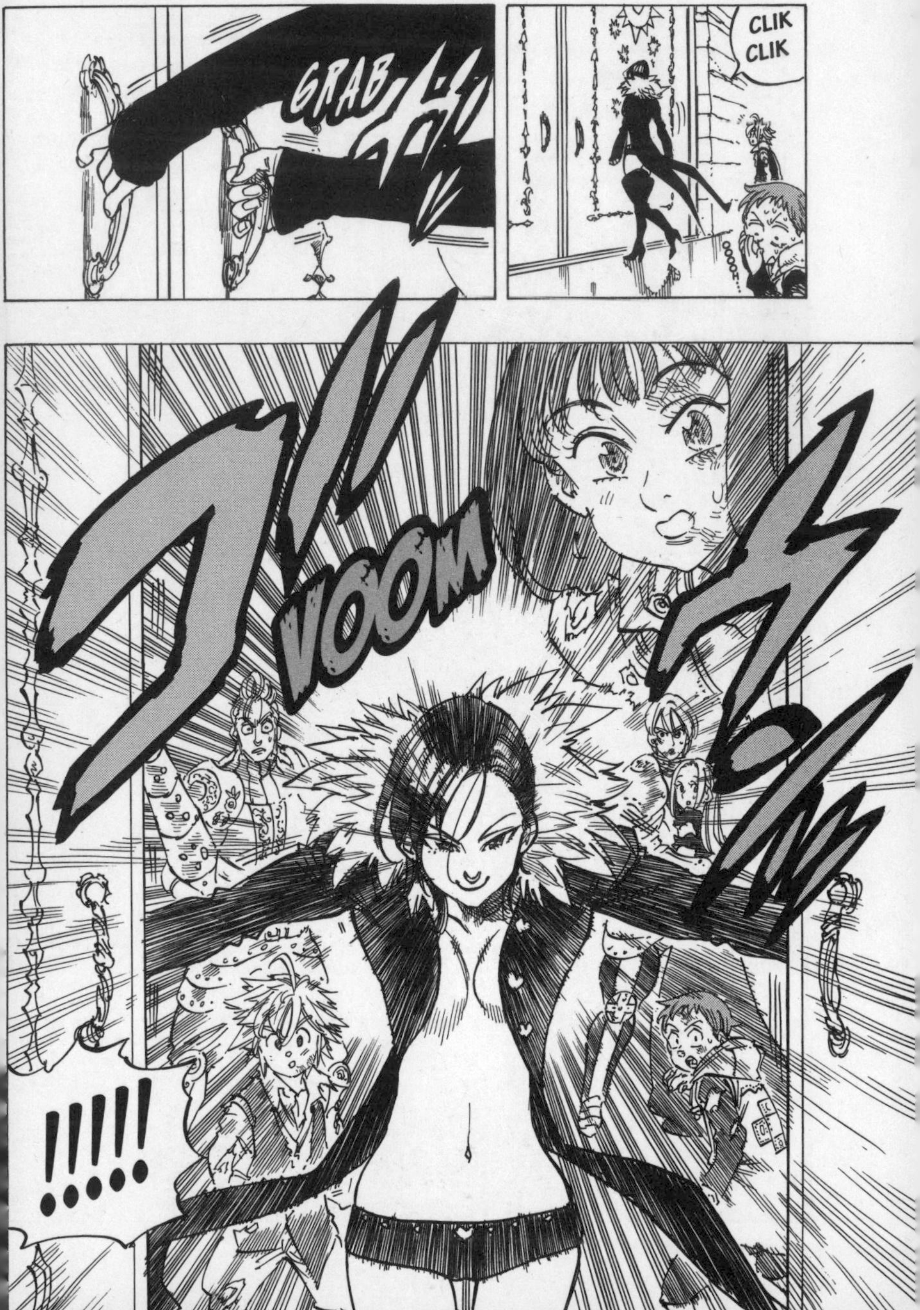
CLIK CLIK
OOOOH...
GRAB
VOOM
!!!!!

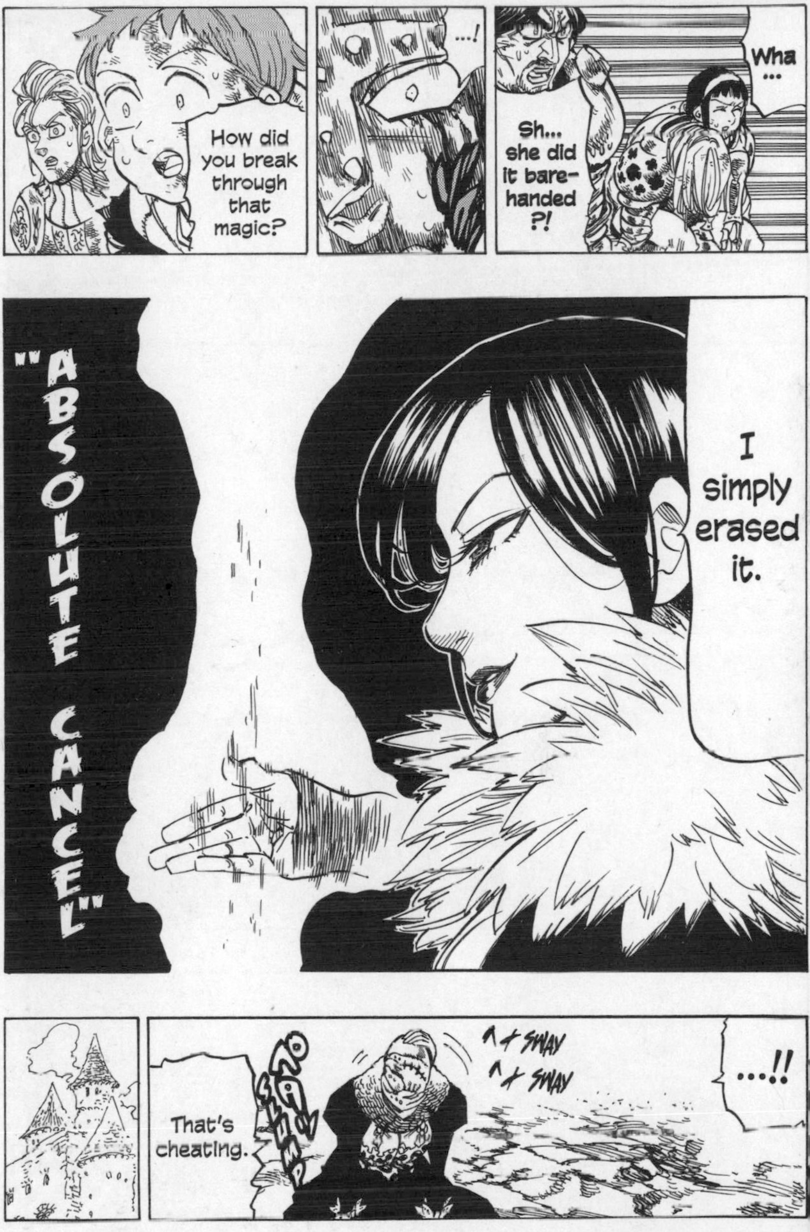
Wha ...
Sh... she did it bare-handed ?!
...!
How did you break through that magic?
I simply erased it.
"ABSOLUTE CANCEL"
...!!
SWAY
SWAY
That's cheating.

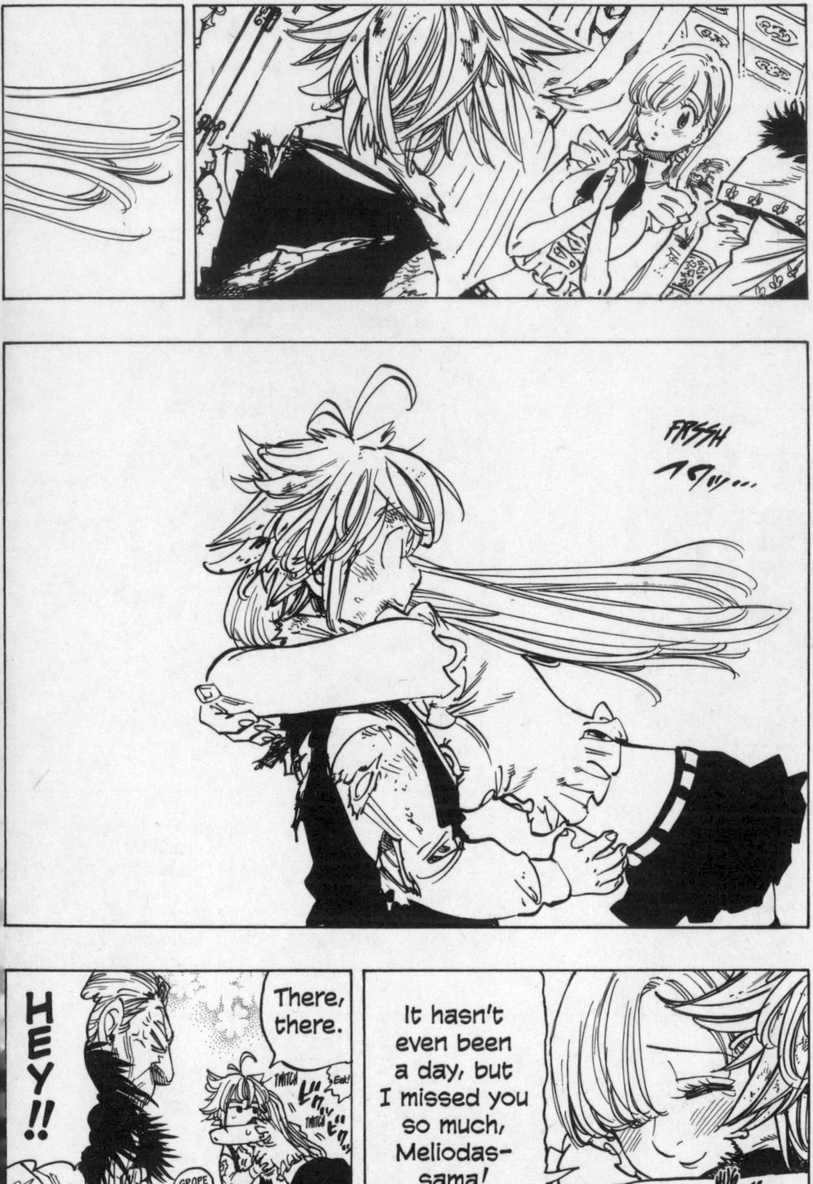
FRSSH
It hasn't even been a day, but I missed you so much, Meliodas-sama!
HUG
There, there.
Eek!
TWITCH
TWITCH
HEY!!
GROPE GROPE

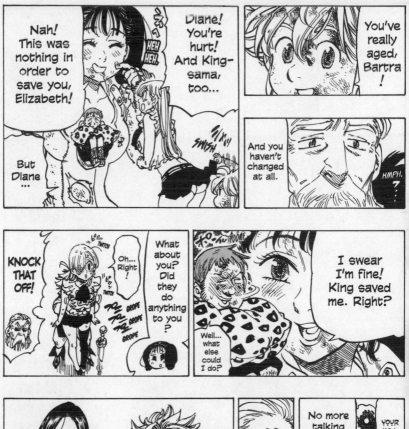

You've really aged, Bartra!
And you haven't changed at all.
HMPH.
?...
Diane! You're hurt! And King-sama, too...
HEH HEH
Nah! This was nothing in order to save you, Elizabeth!
SWISH
But Diane...
POOF
I swear I'm fine! King saved me. Right?
Well... what else could I do?
What about you? Did they do anything to you?
TWITCH
Oh... Right!
TWITCH
GROPE
GROPE
GROPE
KNOCK THAT OFF!
YOUR MAJESTY!
No more talking out of you! Attend to Slader's wounds at once!
Yes, sir!

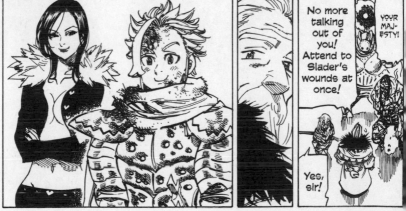

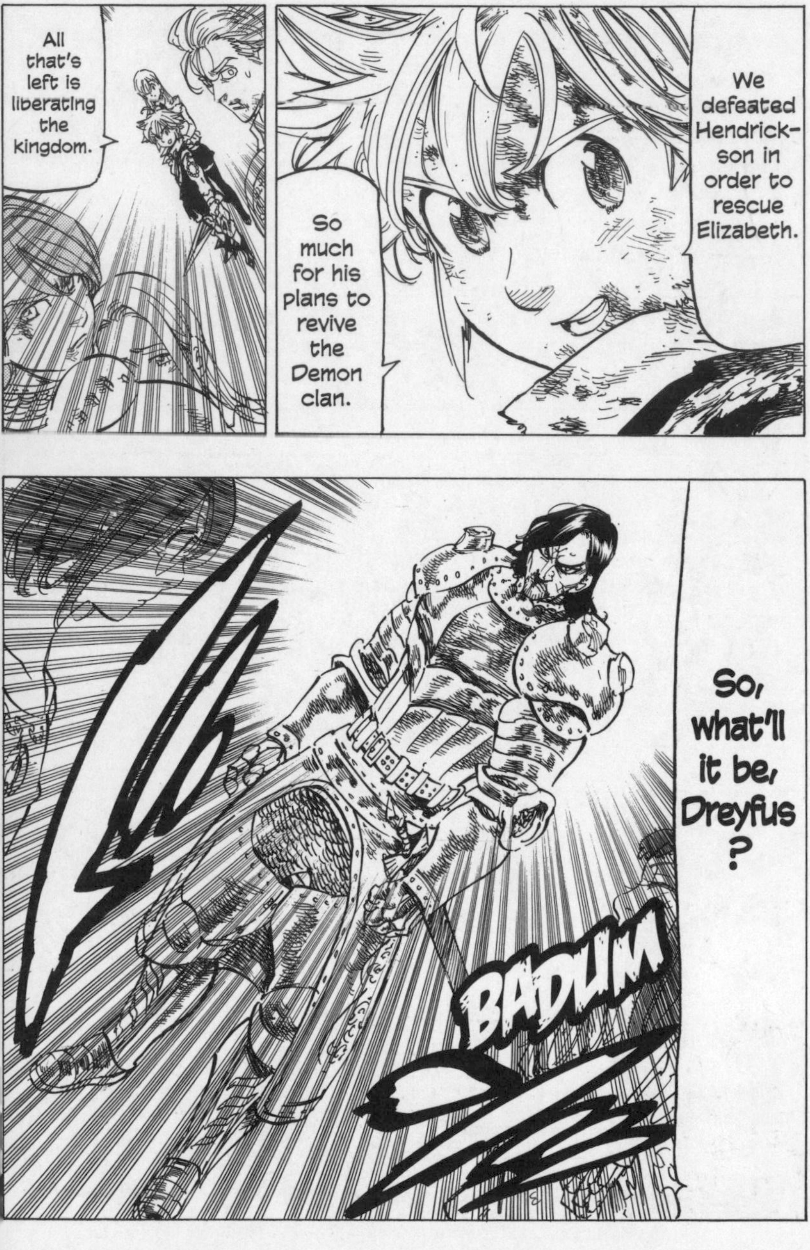
We defeated Hendrick-son in order to rescue Elizabeth.
So much for his plans to revive the Demon clan.
All that's left is liberating the kingdom.
So, what'll it be, Dreyfus?
BADUM

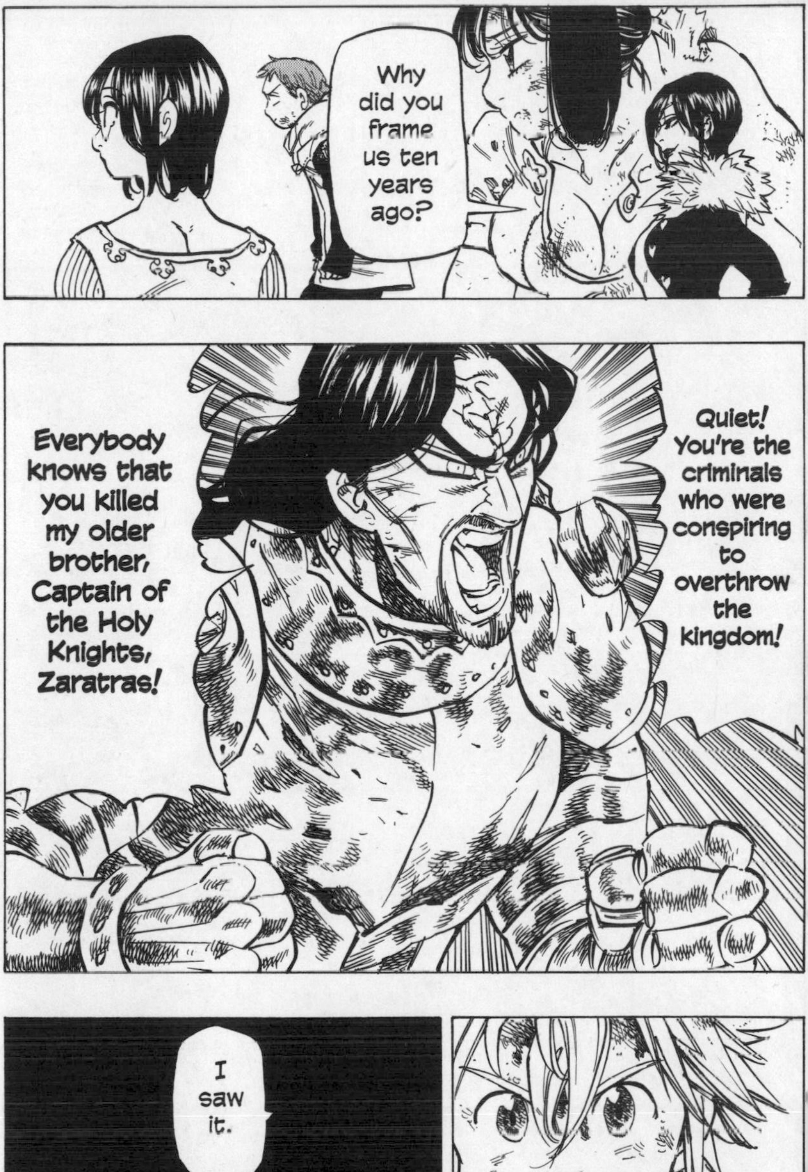
Why did you frame us ten years ago?
Quiet! You're the criminals who were conspiring to overthrow the kingdom!
Everybody knows that you killed my older brother, Captain of the Holy Knights, Zaratras!
I saw it.

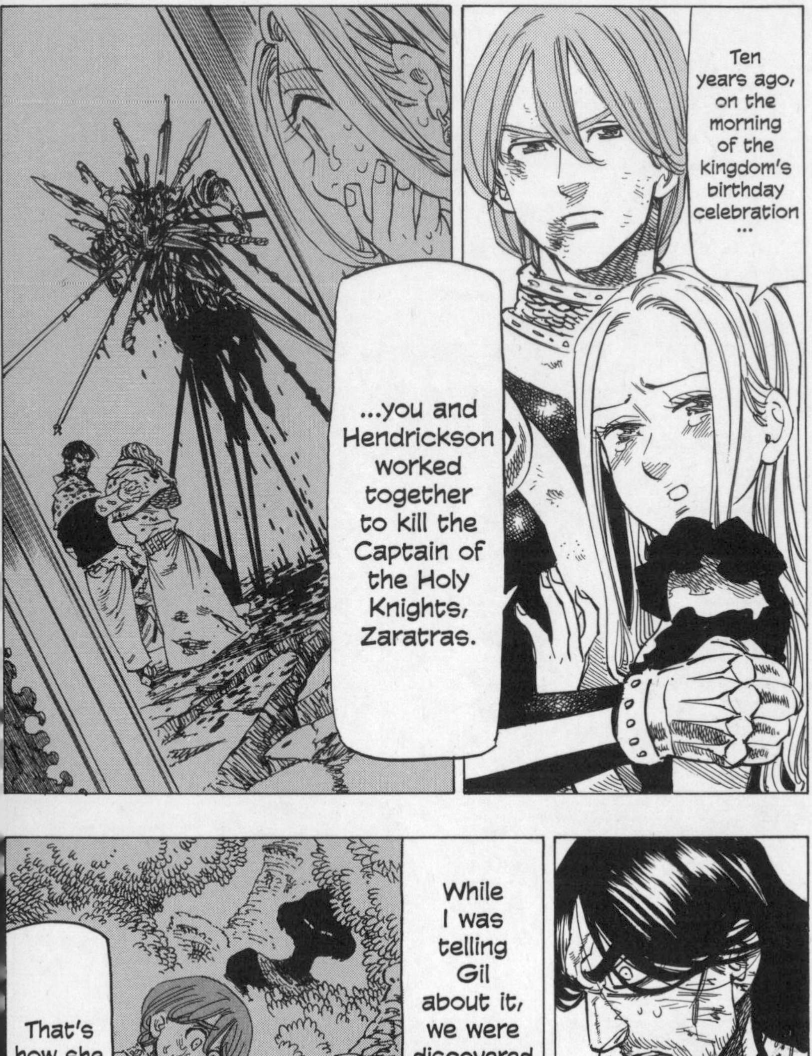

Ten years ago, on the morning of the kingdom's birthday celebration ...
...you and Hendrickson worked together to kill the Captain of the Holy Knights, Zaratras.
...!!
While I was telling Gil about it, we were discovered by Vivian.
That's how she held us captive.

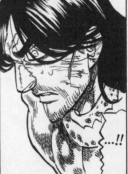

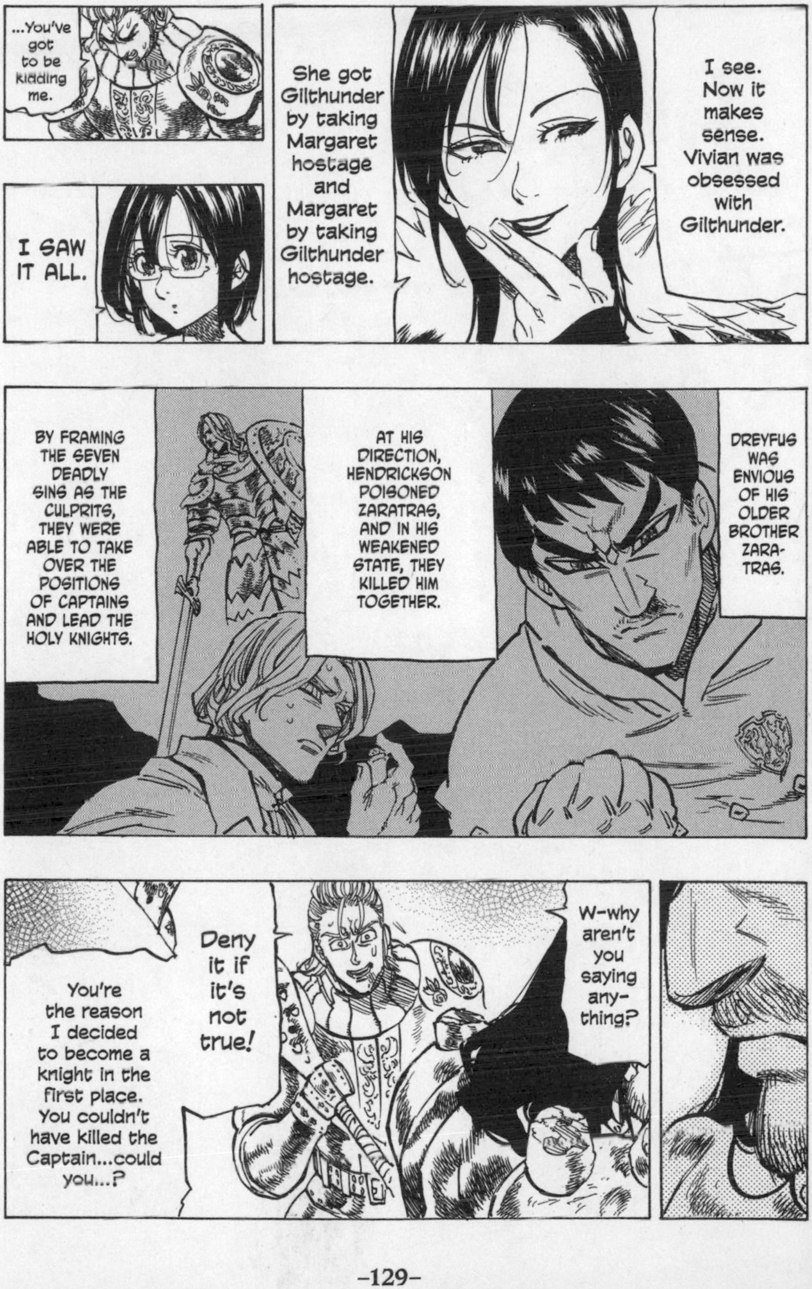
I see. Now it makes sense. Vivian was obsessed with Gilthunder.
She got Gilthunder by taking Margaret hostage and Margaret by taking Gilthunder hostage.
...You've got to be kidding me.
I SAW IT ALL.
DREYFUS WAS ENVIOUS OF HIS OLDER BROTHER ZARA-TRAS.
AT HIS DIRECTION, HENDRICKSON POISONED ZARATRAS, AND IN HIS WEAKENED STATE, THEY KILLED HIM TOGETHER.
BY FRAMING THE SEVEN DEADLY SINS AS THE CULPRITS, THEY WERE ABLE TO TAKE OVER THE POSITIONS OF CAPTAINS AND LEAD THE HOLY KNIGHTS.
W-why aren't you saying any-thing?
Deny it if it's not true!
You're the reason I decided to become a knight in the first place. You couldn't have killed the Captain...could you...?

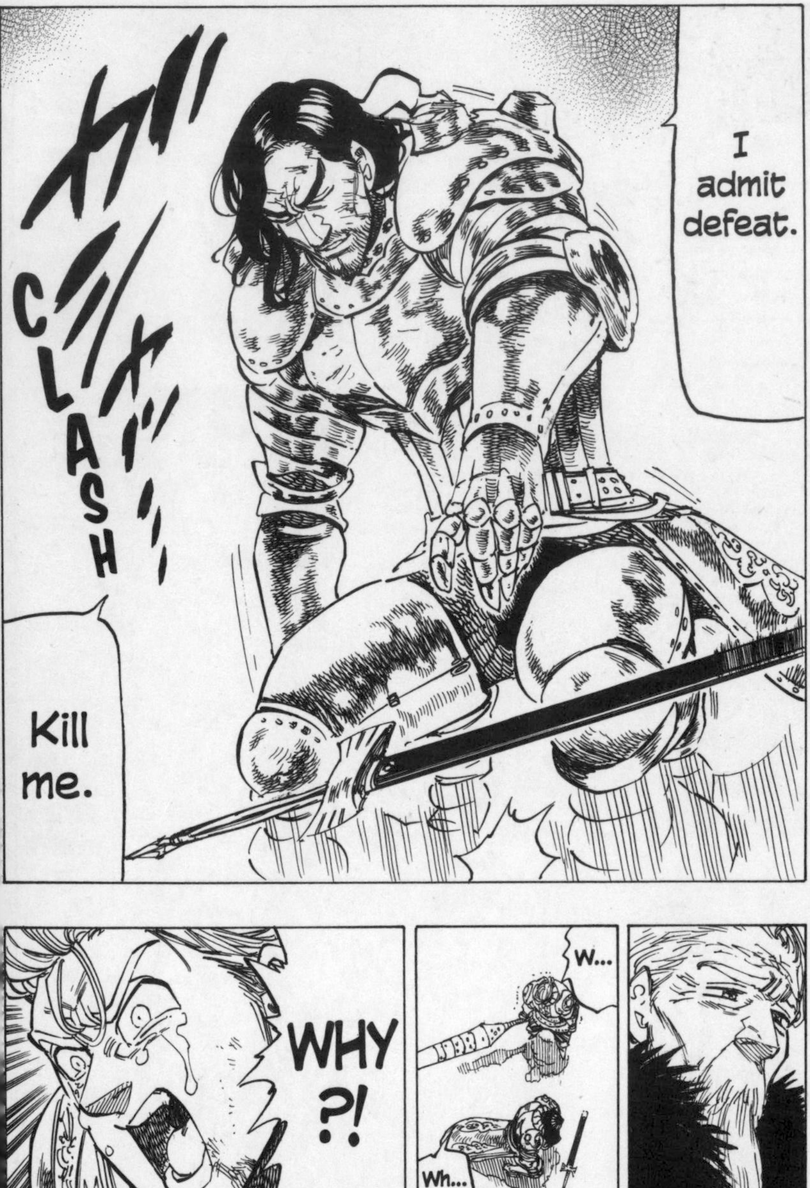
I admit defeat.
CLASH
Kill me.
W...
Wh...
WHY?!

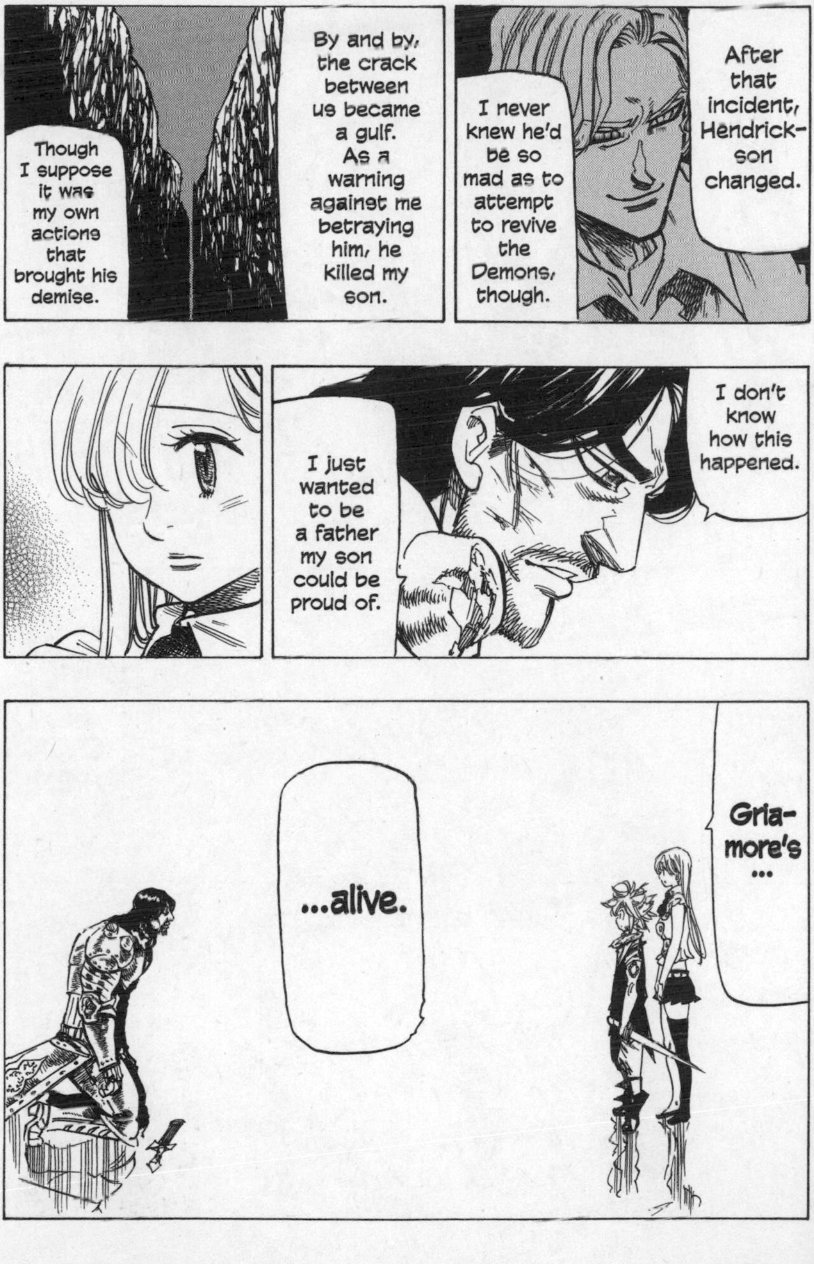
After that incident, Hendrick-son changed.
I never knew he'd be so mad as to attempt to revive the Demons, though.
By and by, the crack between us became a gulf. As a warning against me betraying him, he killed my son.
Though I suppose it was my own actions that brought his demise.
I don't know how this happened.
I just wanted to be a father my son could be proud of.
Gria-more's ...
...alive.

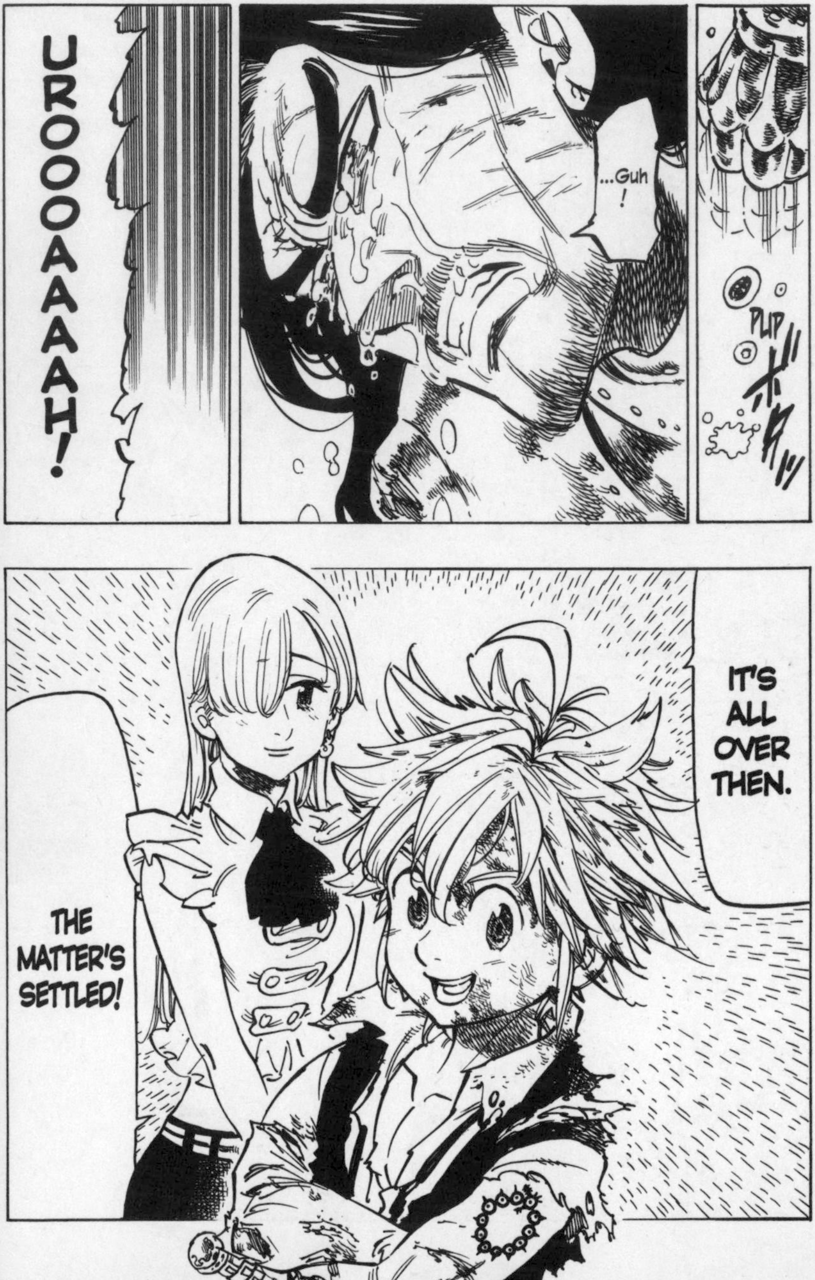
PLIP
...Guh!
UROOOOAAAAAH!
IT'S ALL OVER THEN.
THE MATTER'S SETTLED!

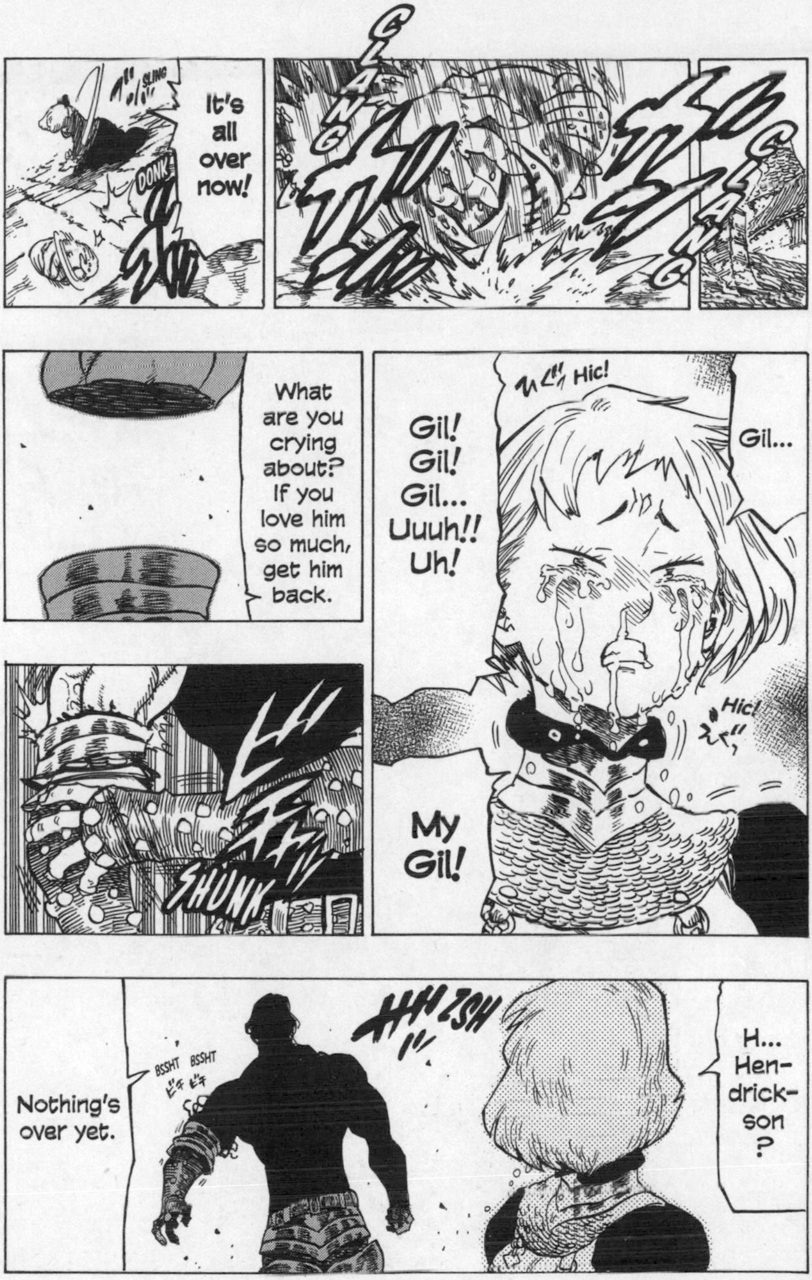
CLANG
CLANG
CLANG
SLING
It's all over now!
DONK
Gil...
Hic!
Gil! Gil! Gil... Uuuh!! Uh!
Hic!
My Gil!
What are you crying about? If you love him so much, get him back.
SHUNK
H... Hendrickson?
BSSHT BSSHT
Nothing's over yet.

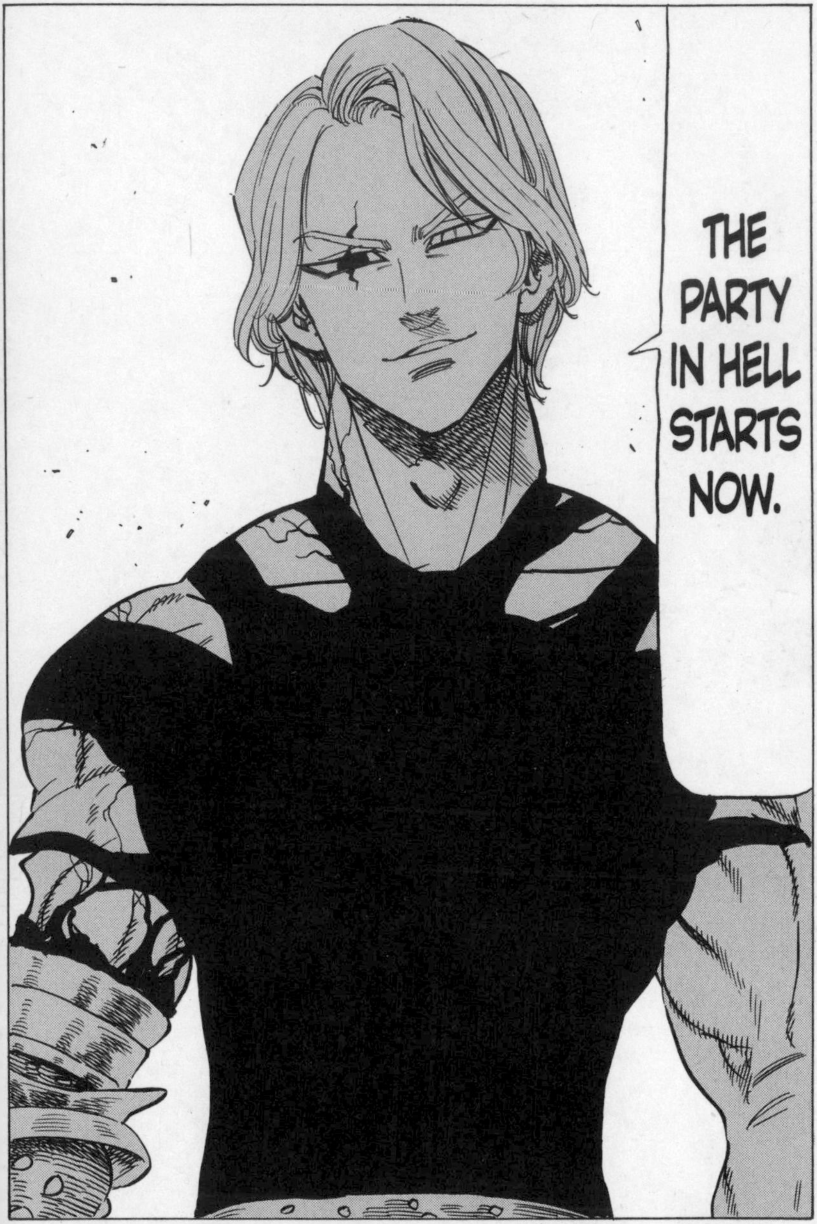
THE PARTY IN HELL STARTS NOW.

Chapter 85 - The Party Begins

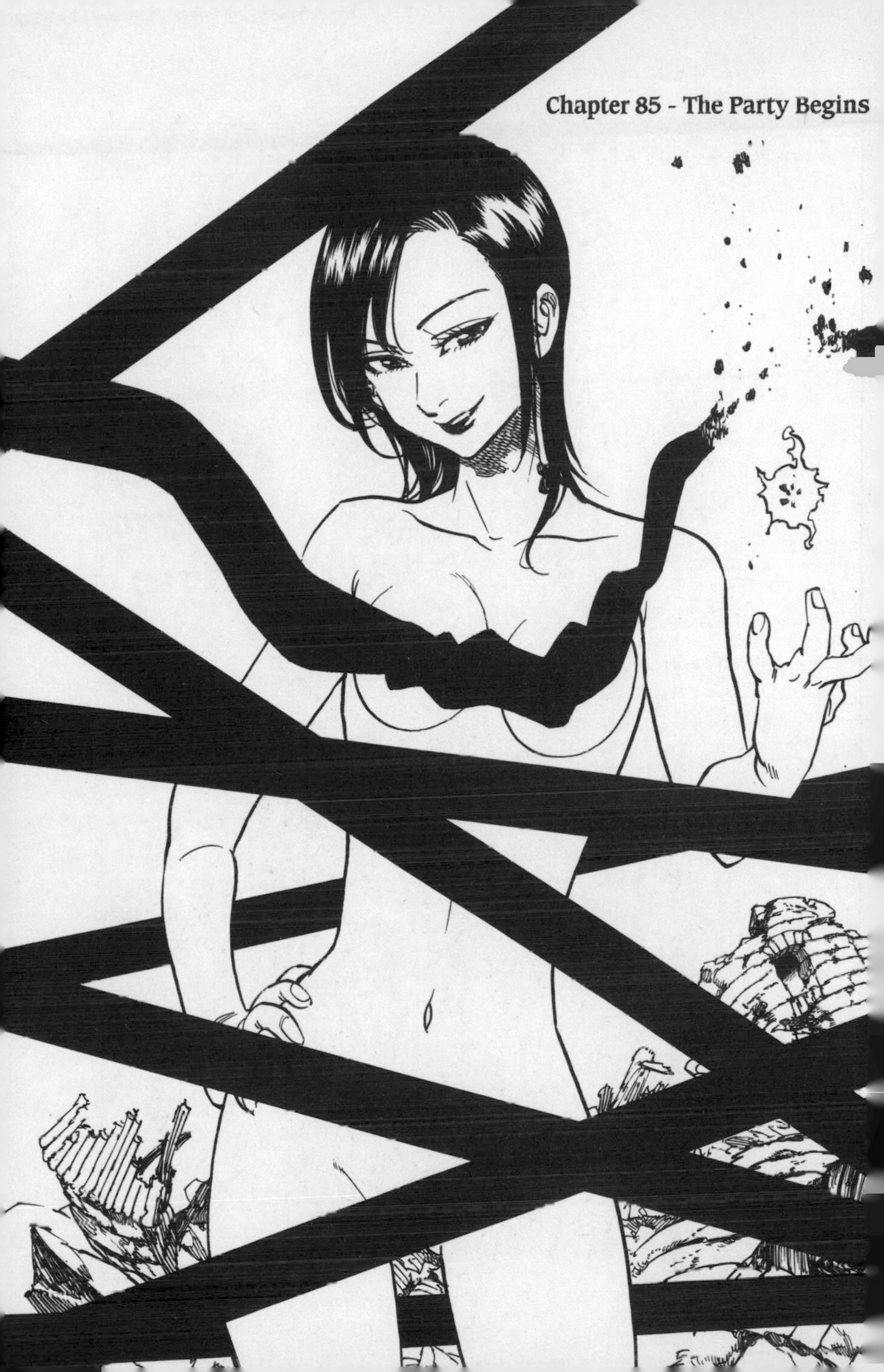

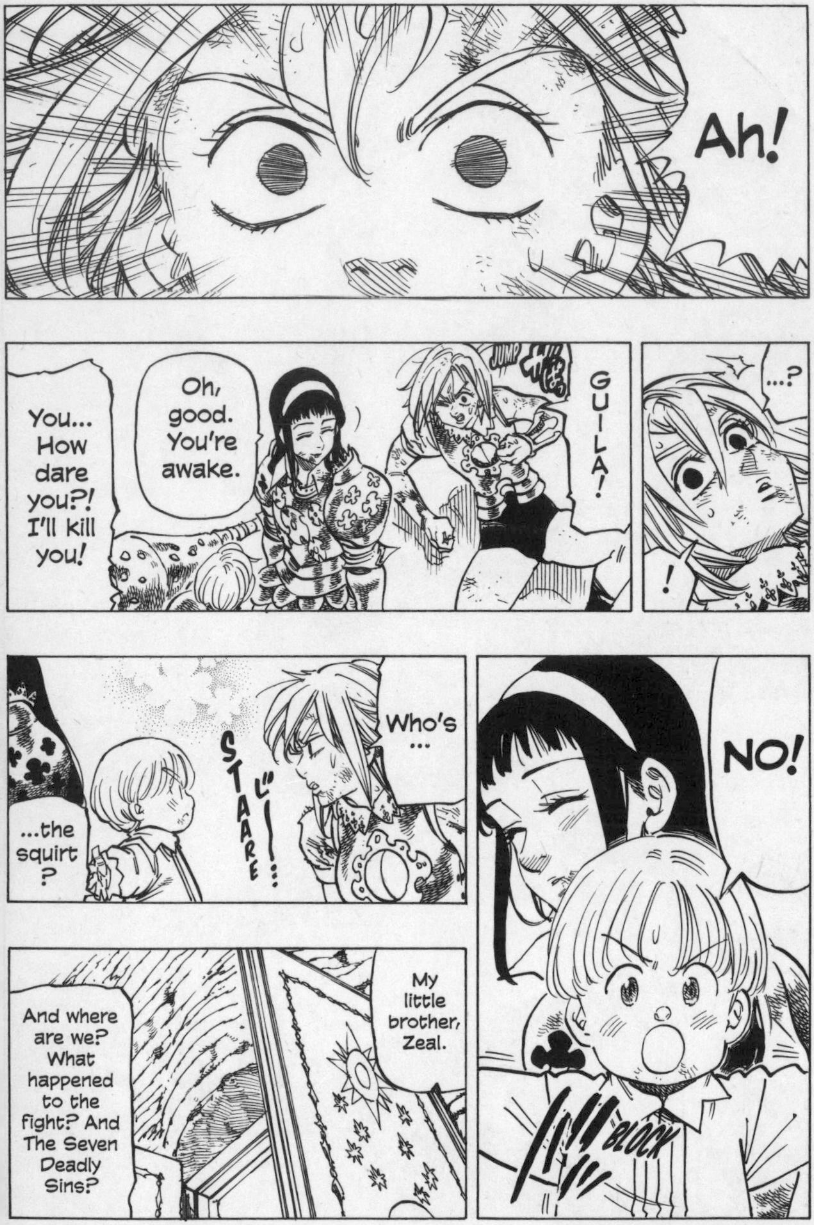
Ah!
...?
!
GUILA!
JUMP
Oh, good. You're awake.
You... How dare you?! I'll kill you!
NO!
BLOCK
Who's...
STAARE
...the squirt?
My little brother, Zeal.
And where are we? What happened to the fight? And The Seven Deadly Sins?

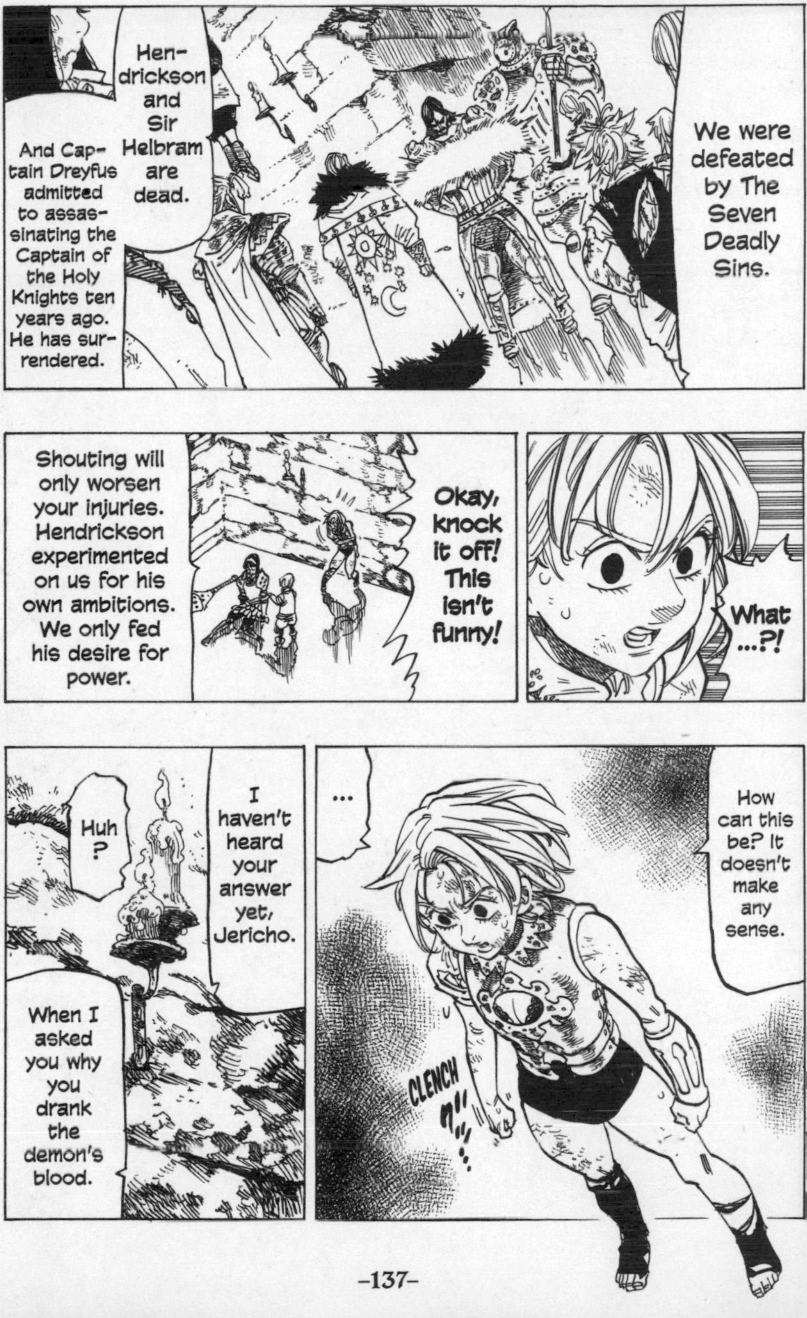

We were defeated by The Seven Deadly Sins.
Hendrickson and Sir Helbram are dead.
And Captain Dreyfus admitted to assassinating the Captain of the Holy Knights ten years ago. He has surrendered.
What ...?!
Okay, knock it off! This isn't funny!
Shouting will only worsen your injuries. Hendrickson experimented on us for his own ambitions. We only fed his desire for power.
How can this be? It doesn't make any sense.
...
CLENCH
I haven't heard your answer yet, Jericho.
Huh?
When I asked you why you drank the demon's blood.

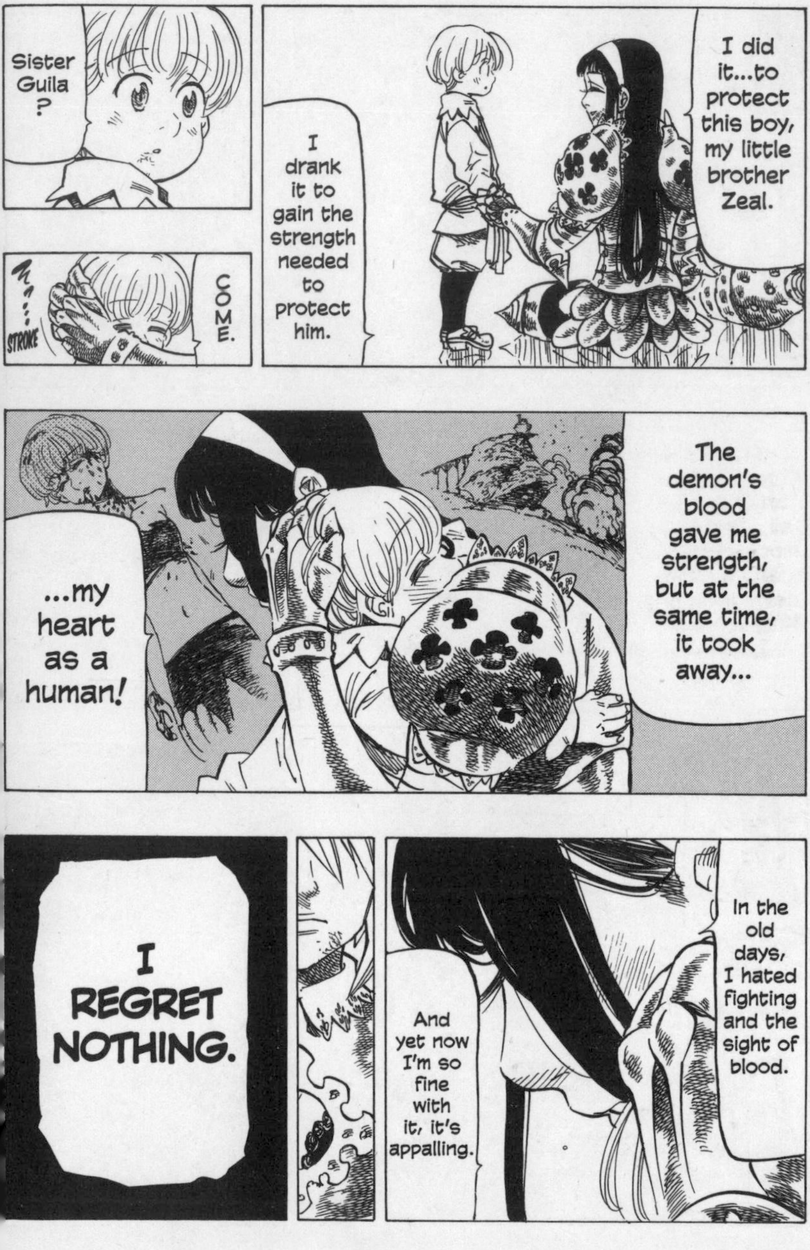
I did it...to protect this boy, my little brother Zeal.
I drank it to gain the strength needed to protect him.
Sister Guila?
STROKE
COME.
The demon's blood gave me strength, but at the same time, it took away...
...my heart as a human!
In the old days, I hated fighting and the sight of blood.
And yet now I'm so fine with it, it's appalling.
I REGRET NOTHING.

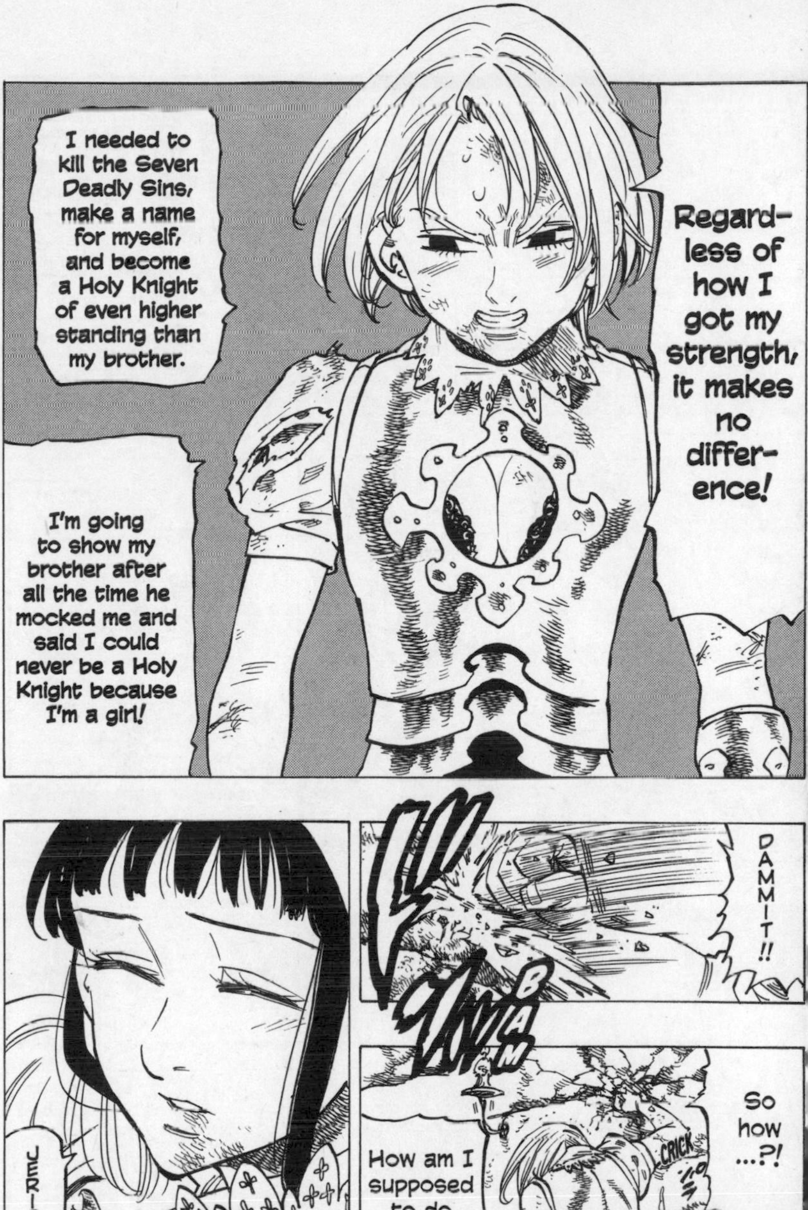

Regardless of how I got my strength, it makes no difference!
I needed to kill the Seven Deadly Sins, make a name for myself, and become a Holy Knight of even higher standing than my brother.
I'm going to show my brother after all the time he mocked me and said I could never be a Holy Knight because I'm a girl!
DAMMIT!!
BAM
So how ...?!
CRICK
How am I supposed to do that now?!
PLICK
JERICHO...

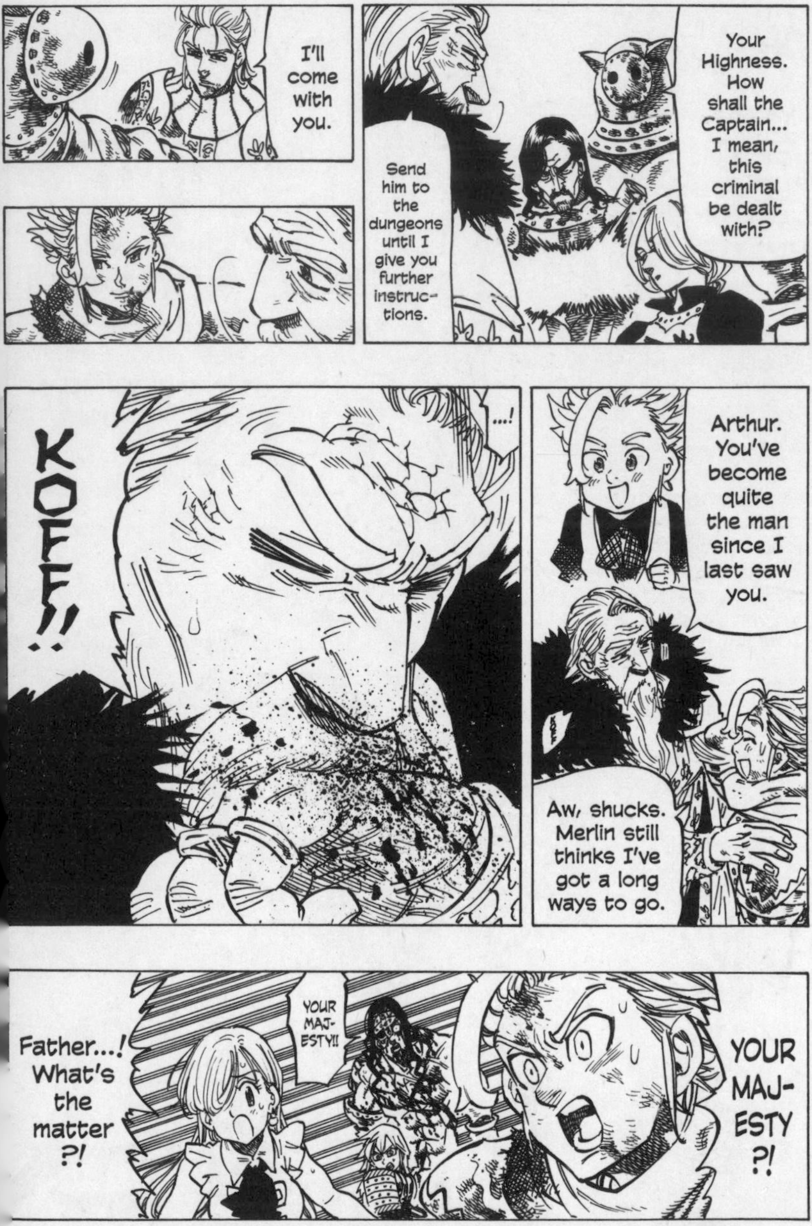
Your Highness. How shall the Captain... I mean, this criminal be dealt with?
Send him to the dungeons until I give you further instructions.
I'll come with you.
Arthur. You've become quite the man since I last saw you.
Aw, shucks. Merlin still thinks I've got a long ways to go.
...!
KOFF!!
YOUR MAJESTY ?!
YOUR MAJESTY!!
Father...! What's the matter ?!

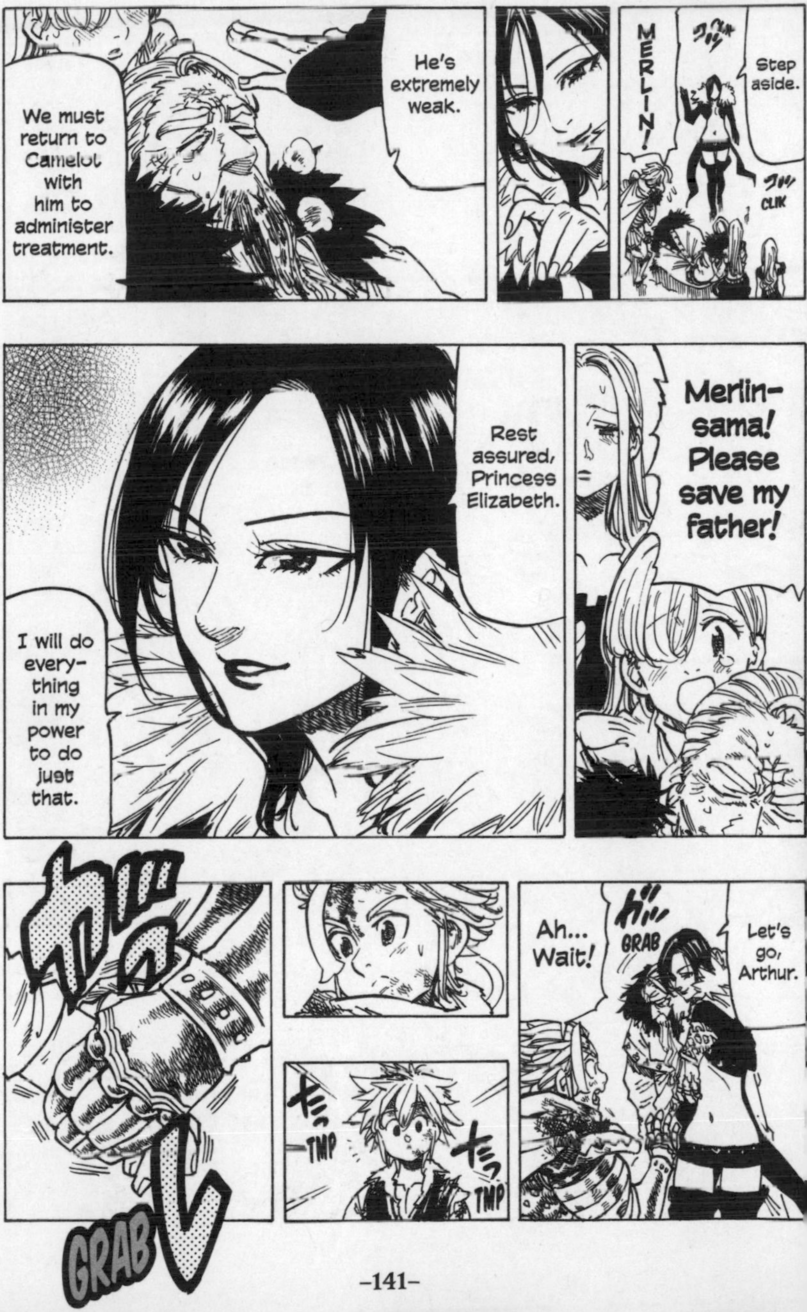

MERLIN!
Step aside.
CLIK
He's extremely weak.
We must return to Camelot with him to administer treatment.
Merlin-sama! Please save my father!
Rest assured, Princess Elizabeth.
I will do every-thing in my power to do just that.
Let's go, Arthur.
GRAB
Ah... Wait!
TMP
TMP
GRAB

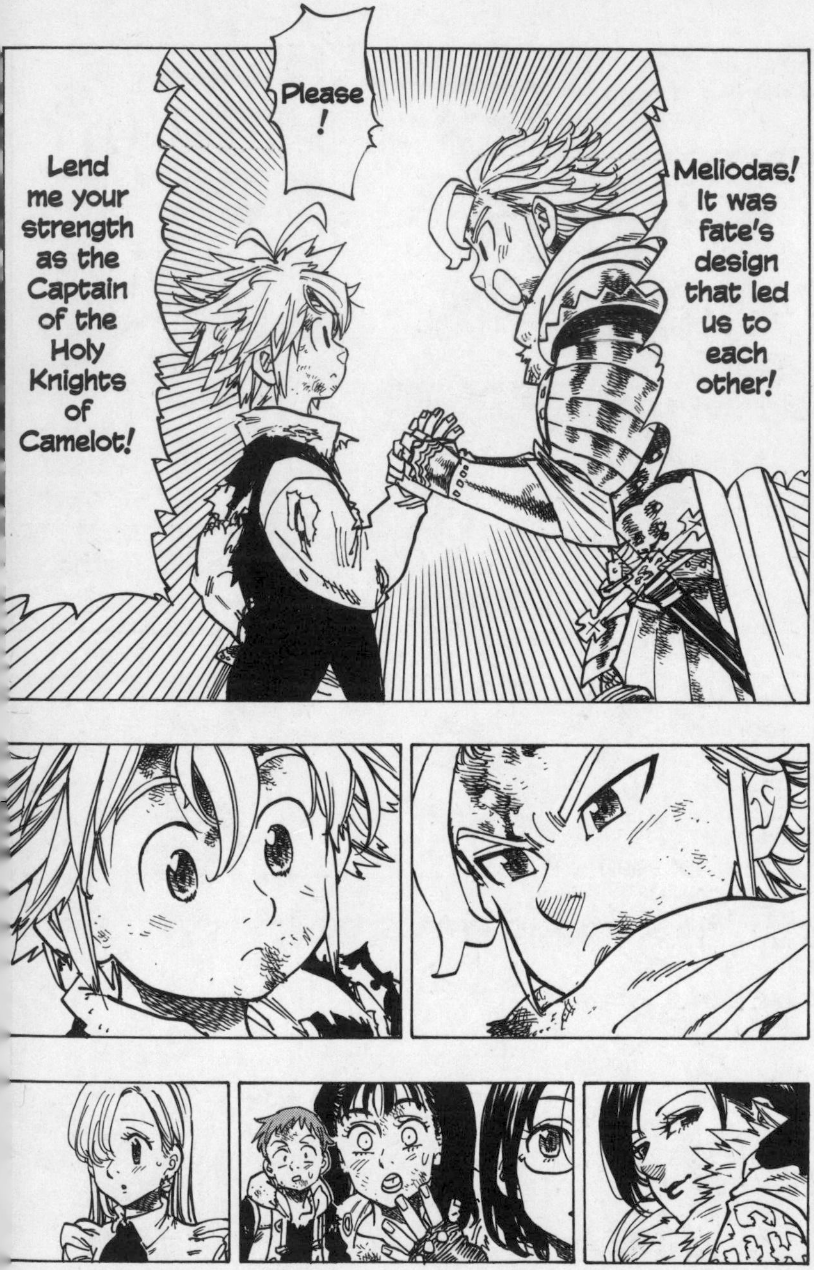
Please!
Meliodas! It was fate's design that led us to each other!
Lend me your strength as the Captain of the Holy Knights of Camelot!

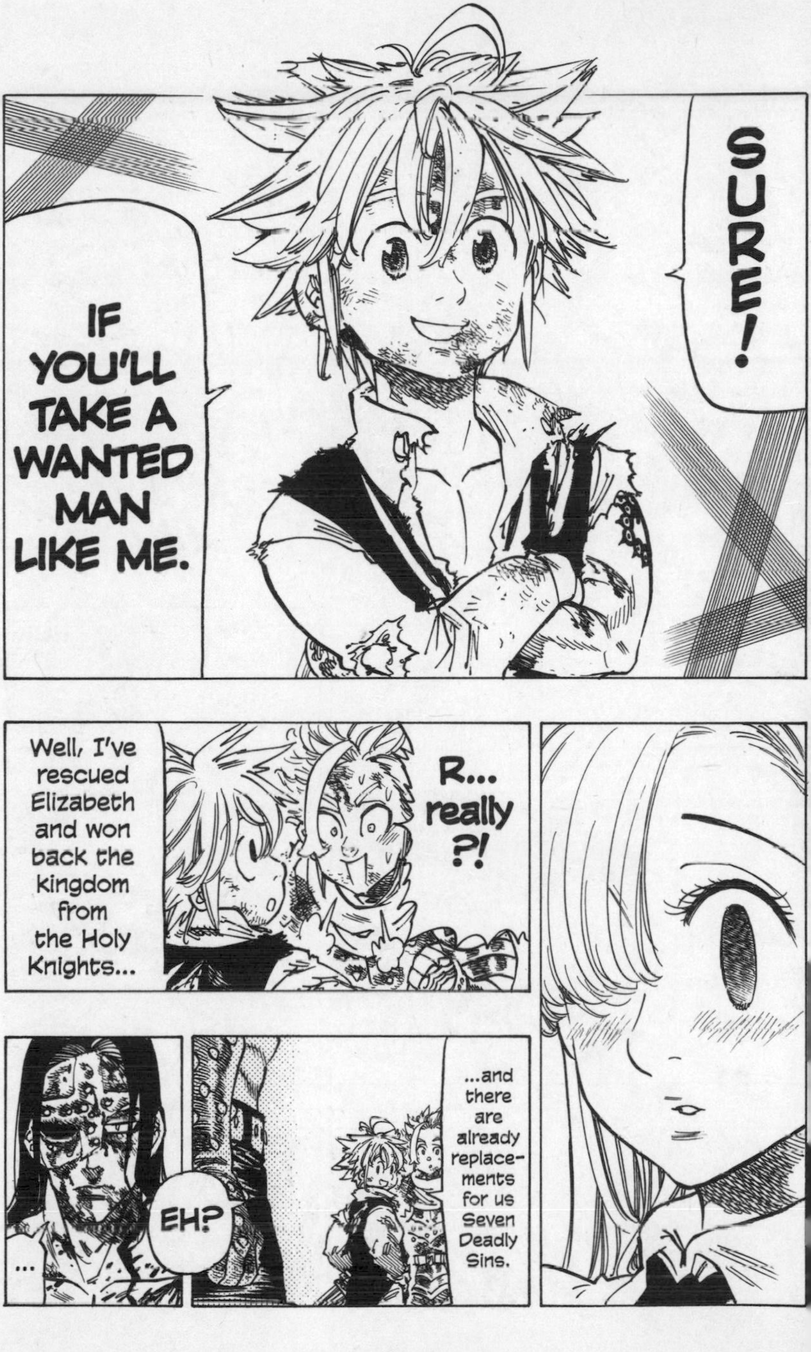
SURE!
IF YOU'LL TAKE A WANTED MAN LIKE ME.
R... really?!
Well, I've rescued Elizabeth and won back the kingdom from the Holy Knights...
...and there are already replacements for us Seven Deadly Sins.
EH?
...

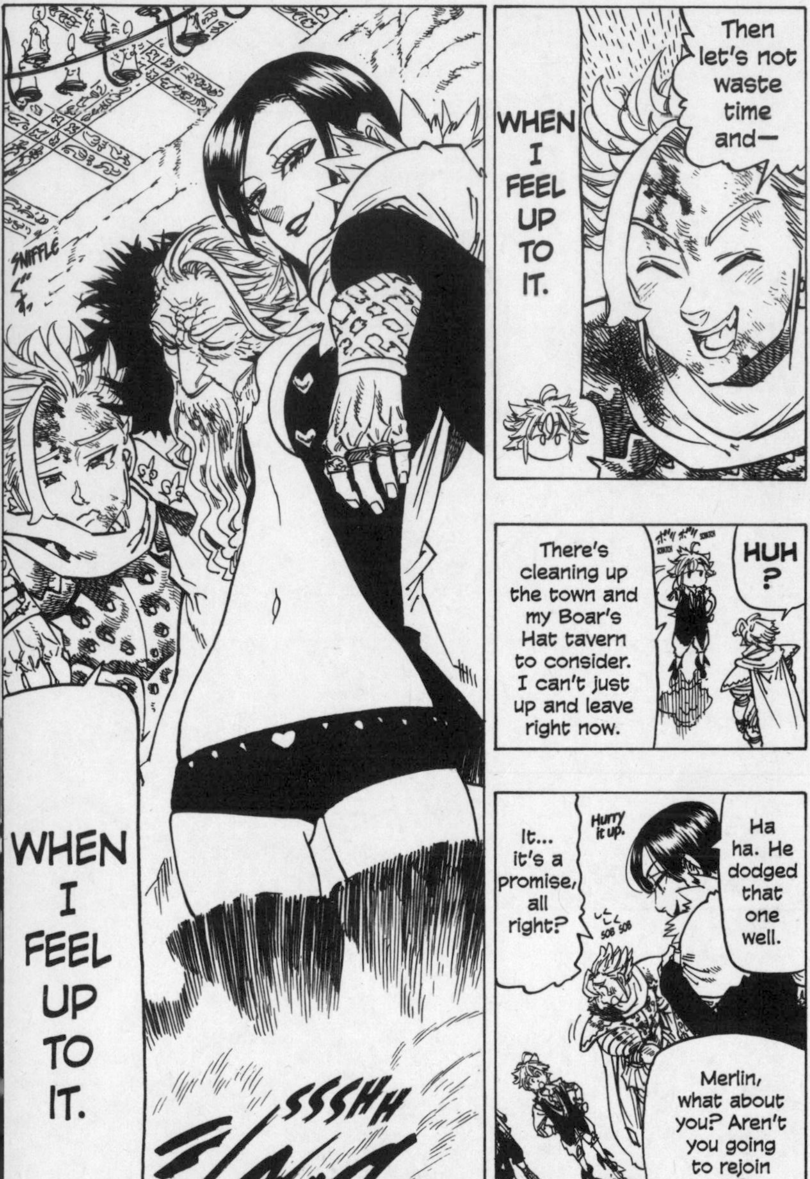
Then let's not waste time and—
WHEN I FEEL UP TO IT.
HUH?
SCRATCH SCRATCH
There's cleaning up the town and my Boar's Hat tavern to consider. I can't just up and leave right now.
Ha ha. He dodged that one well.
Hurry it up.
It... it's a promise, all right?
SOB SOB
Merlin, what about you? Aren't you going to rejoin us?
SNIFFLE
WHEN I FEEL UP TO IT.
SSSHH

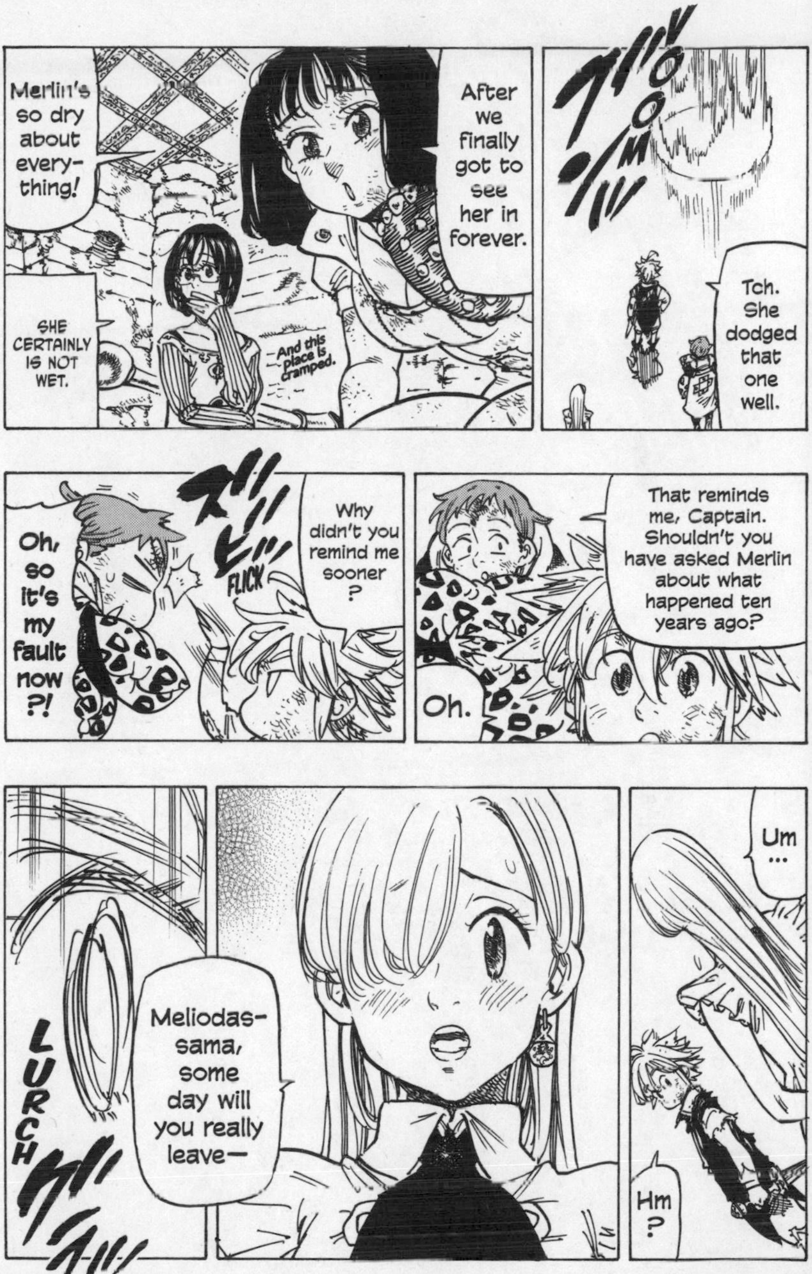
Tch. She dodged that one well.
After we finally got to see her in forever.
Merlin's so dry about every-thing!
And this place is cramped.
SHE CERTAINLY IS NOT WET.
That reminds me, Captain. Shouldn't you have asked Merlin about what happened ten years ago?
Oh.
Why didn't you remind me sooner?
FLICK
Oh, so it's my fault now?!
Um...
Hm?
Meliodas-sama, some day will you really leave—
LURCH

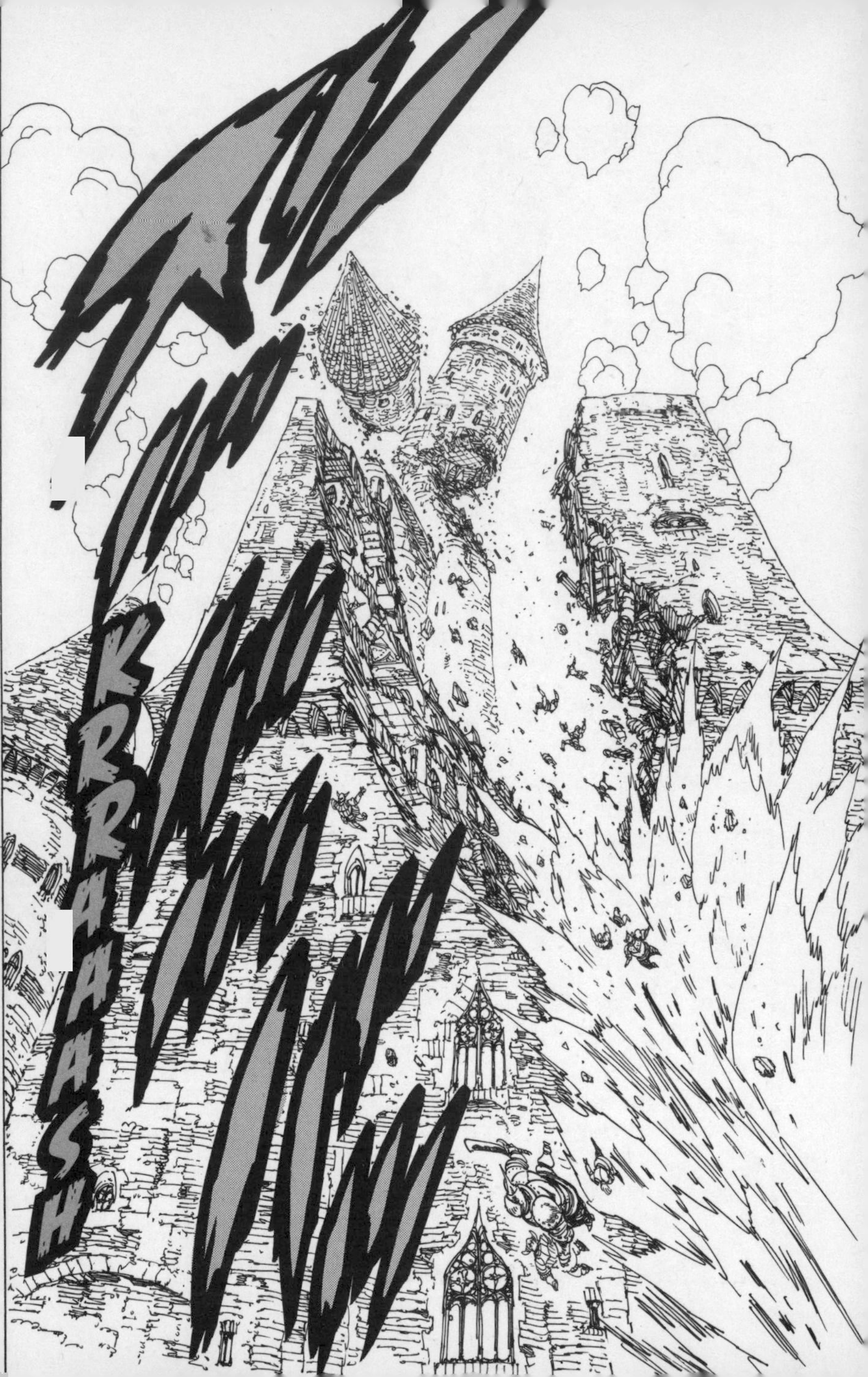
KRRAAASH

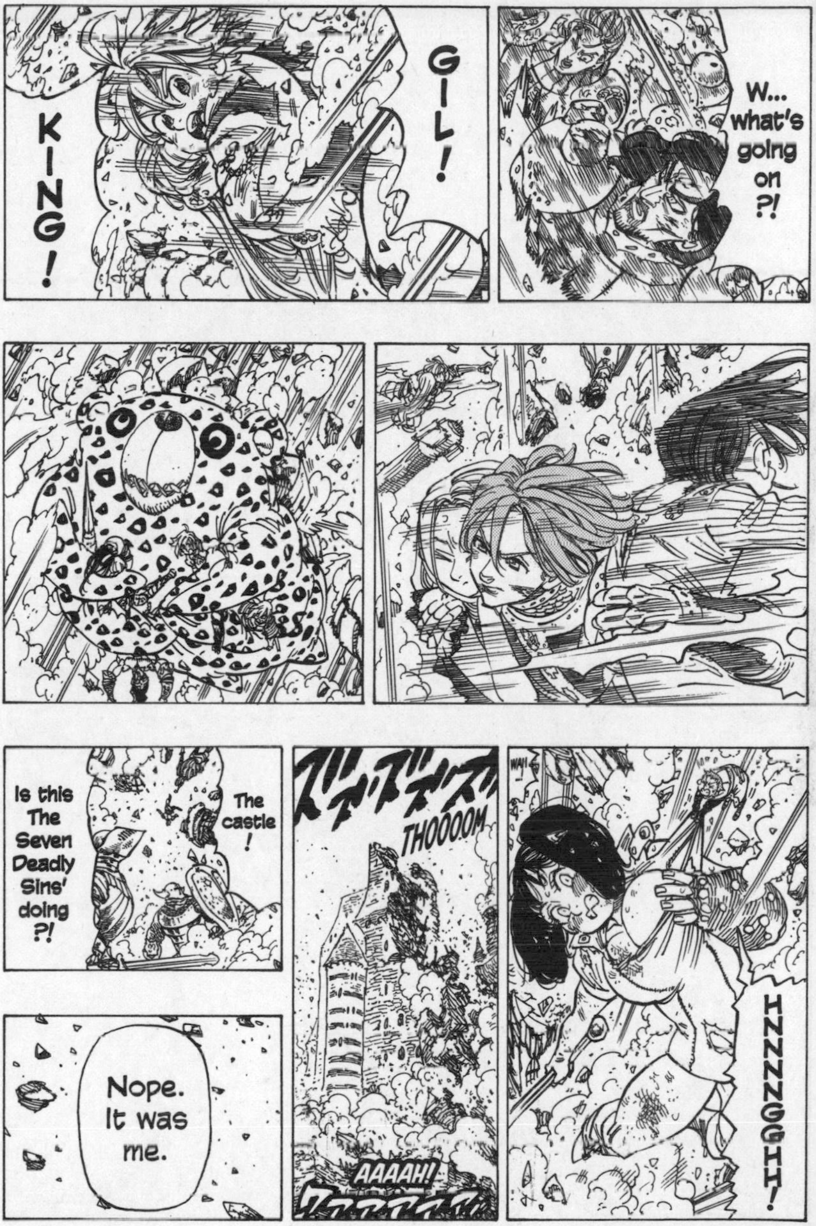
W... what's going on ?!
GIL!
KING!
WAH!
HNNNGGH!
THOOOOM
AAAAH!
The castle!
Is this The Seven Deadly Sins' doing ?!
Nope. It was me.

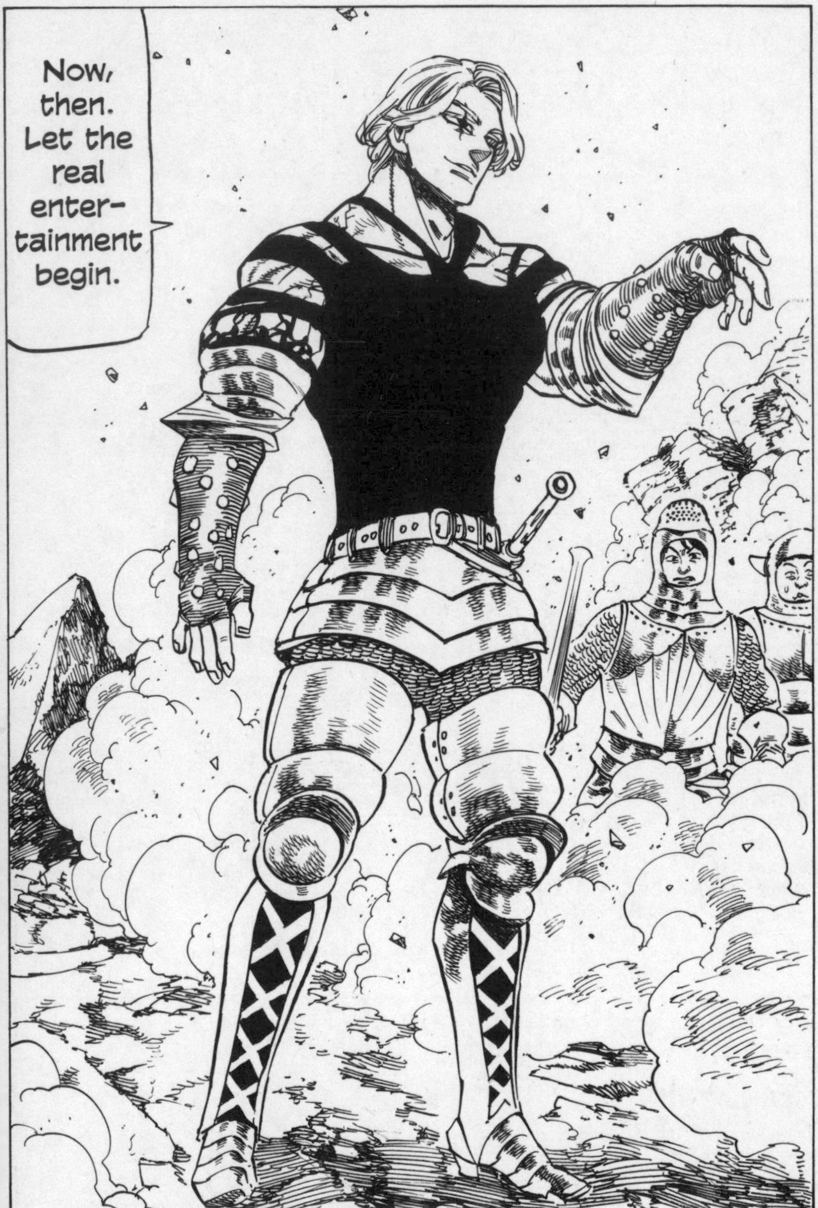
Now, then. Let the real enter-tainment begin.

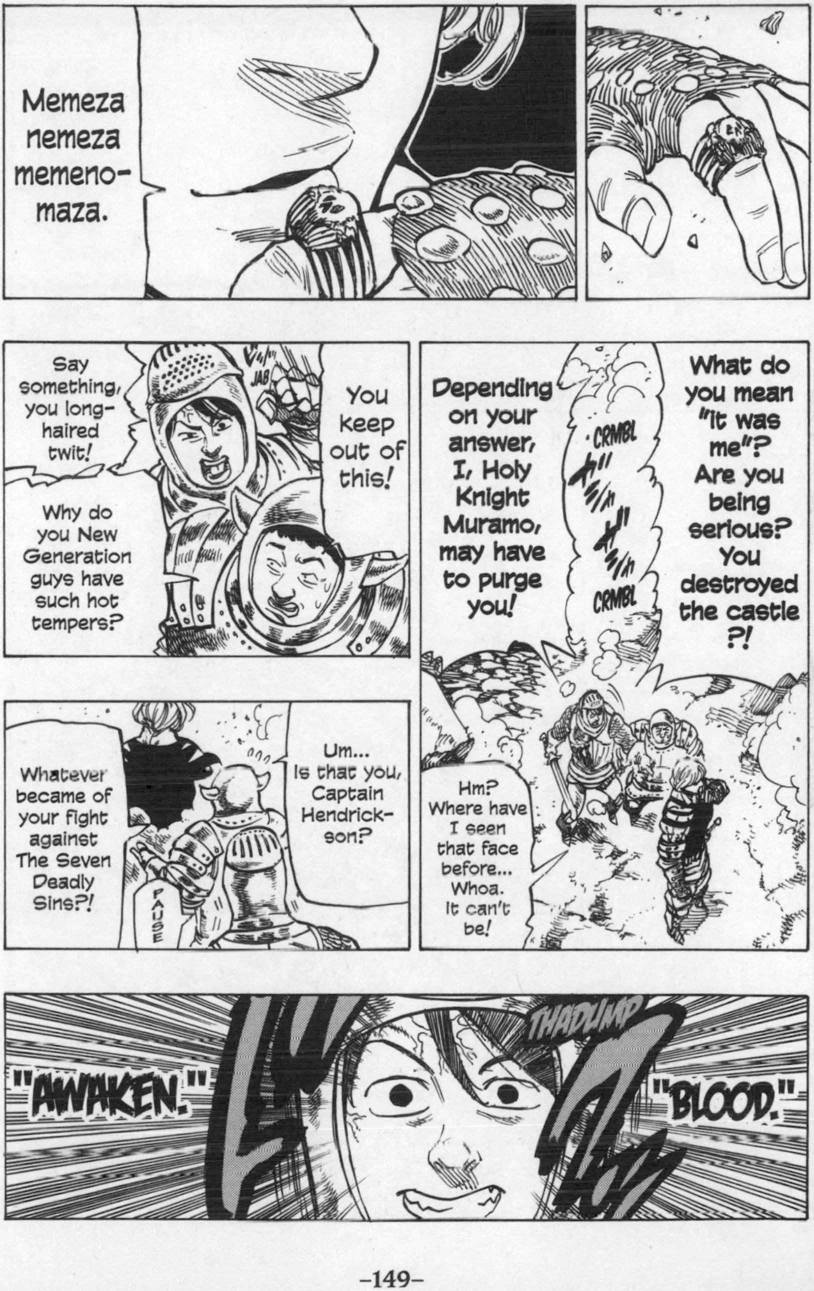

Memeza nemeza memeno-maza.
What do you mean "it was me"? Are you being serious? You destroyed the castle?!
Depending on your answer, I, Holy Knight Muramo, may have to purge you!
CRMBL
CRMBL
Hm? Where have I seen that face before... Whoa. It can't be!
You keep out of this!
JAB
Say something, you long-haired twit!
Why do you New Generation guys have such hot tempers?
Um... Is that you, Captain Hendrickson?
Whatever became of your fight against The Seven Deadly Sins?!
PAUSE
"BLOOD."
THADUMP
"AWAKEN."

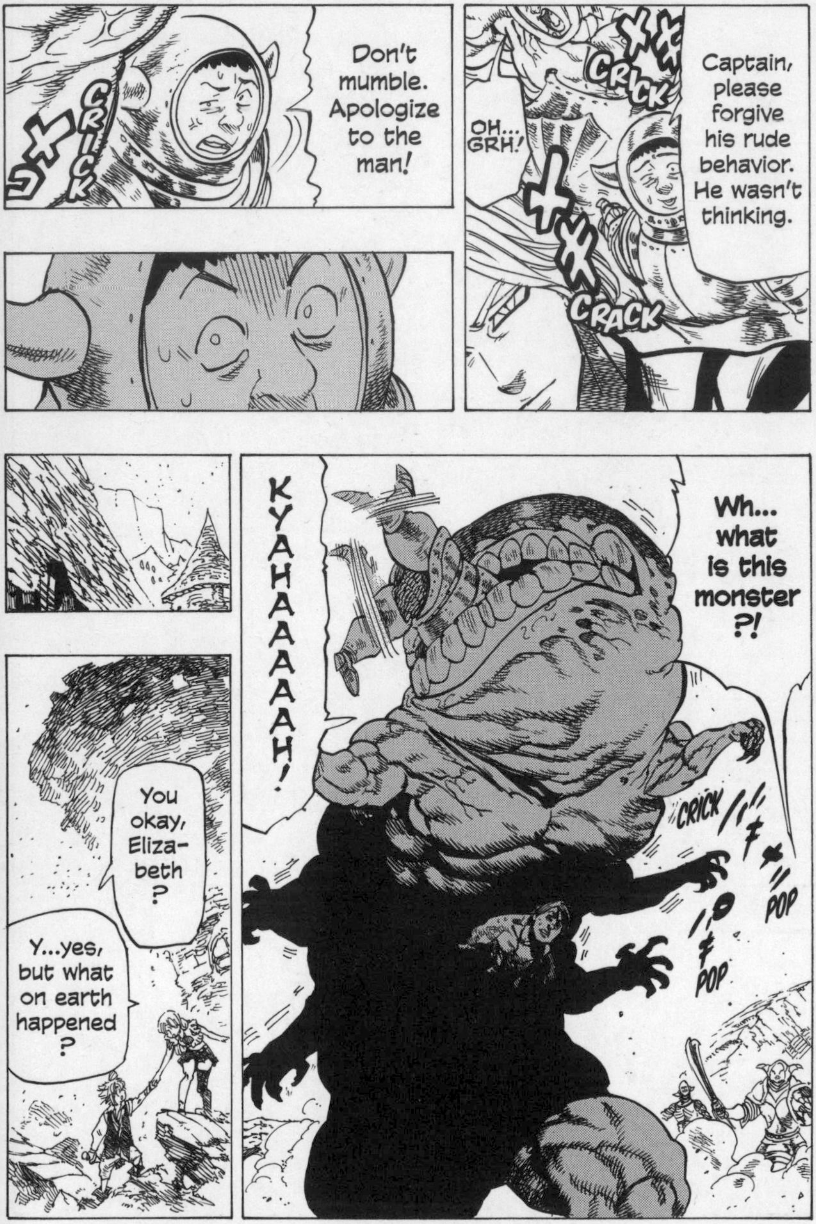
Captain, please forgive his rude behavior. He wasn't thinking.
CRICK
OH... GRH!
CRACK
Don't mumble. Apologize to the man!
CRICK
Wh... what is this monster ?!
KYAHAAAAAAH!
CRICK
POP
POP
You okay, Elizabeth ?
Y...yes, but what on earth happened ?

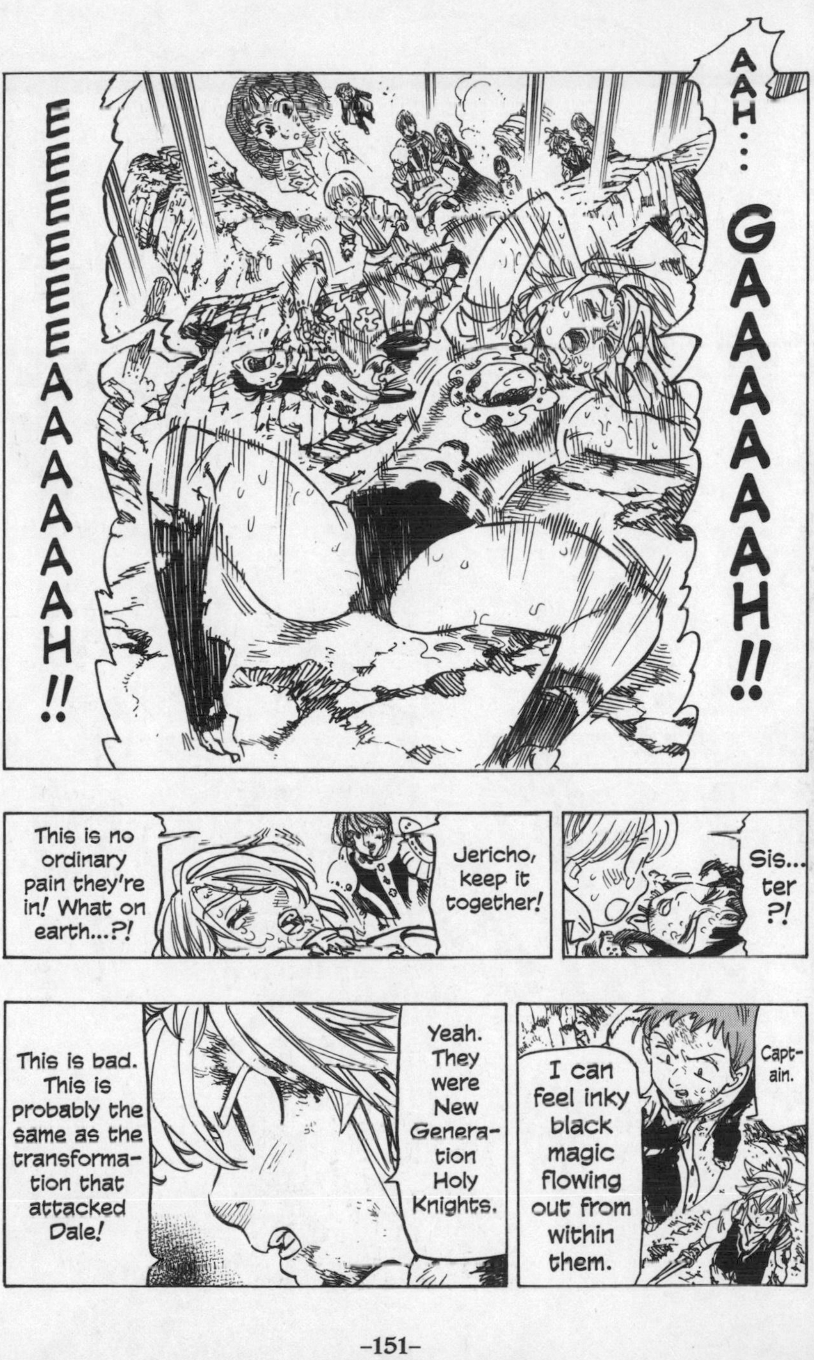
AAH... GAAAAAAH!!
EEEEEEEEAAAAAAH!!
Sis... ter ?!
Jericho, keep it together!
This is no ordinary pain they're in! What on earth...?!
Capt- ain.
I can feel inky black magic flowing out from within them.
Yeah. They were New Genera- tion Holy Knights.
This is bad. This is probably the same as the transforma- tion that attacked Dale!

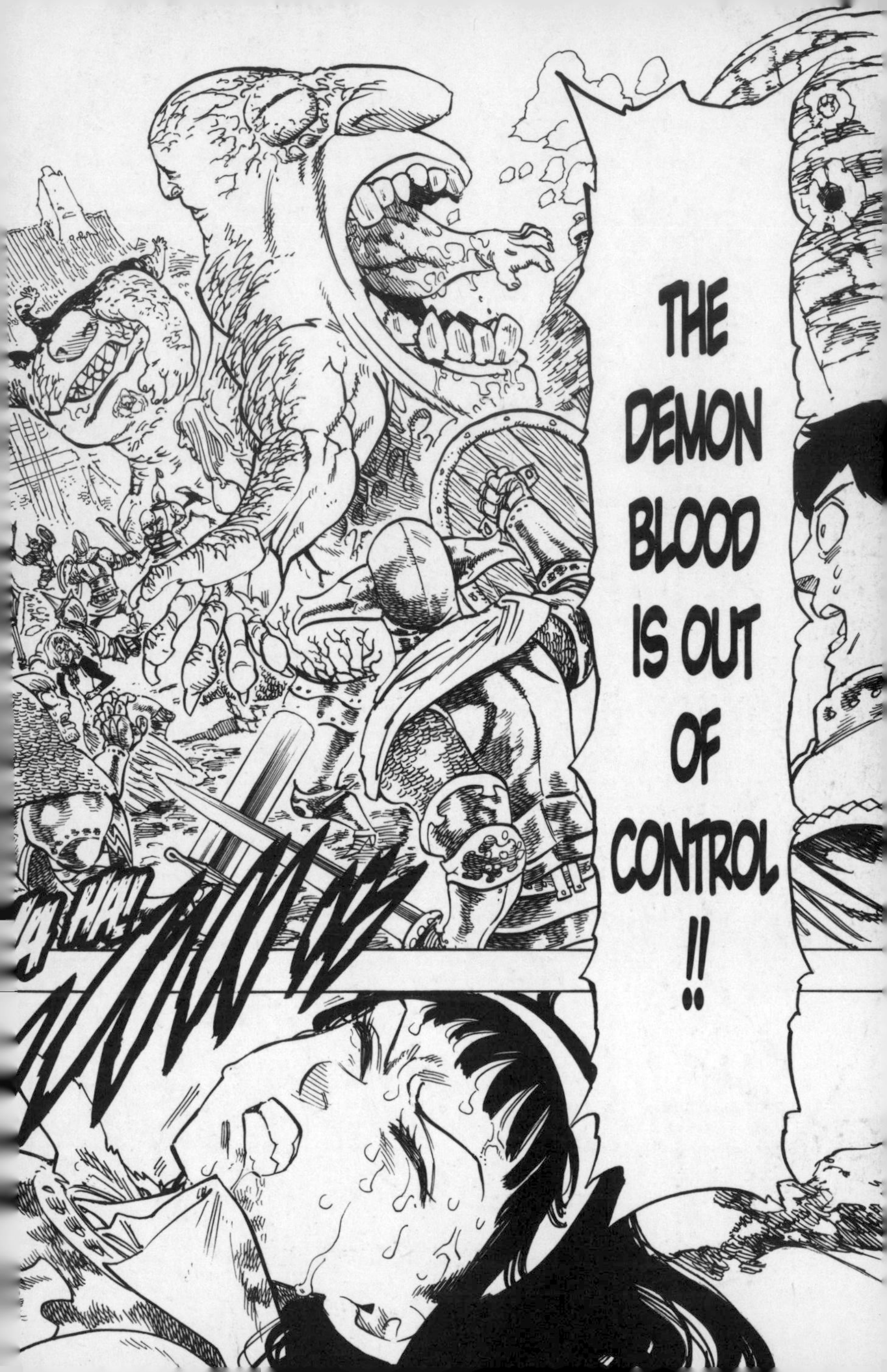
THE DEMON BLOOD IS OUT OF CONTROL !!

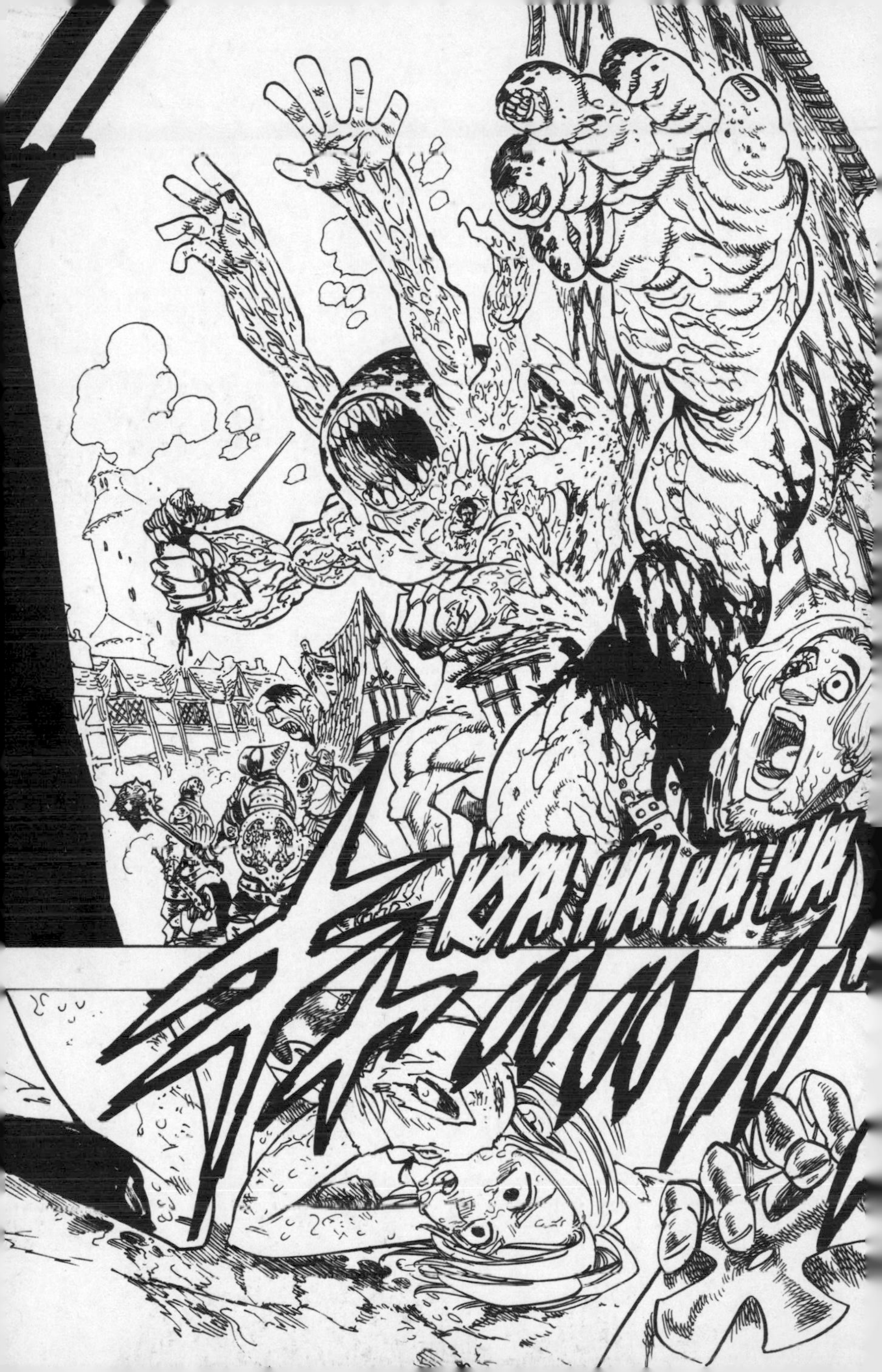
KYA HA HA HA

A Few Words on the "Initial Designs for The Seven Deadly Sins"

◆ About the "Holy Knight Ban"

He was going to be very different from the Ban that ended up in the story, with a personality that was hard to rile up. He didn't talk much, always wore a poker face, and because he was a Holy Knight, it felt like he was more like the Gilthunder we know, if anything. He seemed much more refined and classy than the Ban we know (heh).

◆ About the "Prince of the Fairy Folk Jehan"

This was King's prototype. Of course, his real name is Harlequin and Jehan was like "King", his pseudonym. His sin was going to be "Pride", which made him an annoying peak of a prince. But what makes him most different of all was what he transformed into, not an old fat guy, but a pudgy little baby.

◆ About "The Female Warrior of the Giant Race Diane"

Diane was going to have disheveled hair (like Armand), rather than her two pigtails. Her stature was also going to be a little smaller than she ended up being. She still had a crush on Meliodas, but was more hot-cold about it.

◆ About the "Warlock Jeema"

This was actually...Gowther's prototype. He was going to be one of the Deadly Sins with the role of secretly guarding Meliodas. Before I knew it, I'd turned him into a giant clad in armor, and since I figured that'd be sort of boring, I opted for him to be a lean glasses-wearing kid instead!

◆ About "The Sorceress Myrddin"

I'm sure you can already tell, but this is Merlin's prototype. Apparently, her name in Welsh is Myrddin. Do you see elements of Gowther in her here? I hadn't been drawing any mature ladies recently, though I really do like them best.

◆ About "Admired by the Sun Escanor"

This is the prototype for the Deadly Sin who has yet to make his appearance. He's...he's ripped. And with a figure like that, plus being the sin of "Lust" you just know he's a horn dog (heh). I'm sure he'll show up in the story soon enough, but keep in mind he won't actually look like that! So don't worry.

Illustrations of the initials design are found on page 114! ➡

Chapter 86 - The Threat Now Closing In

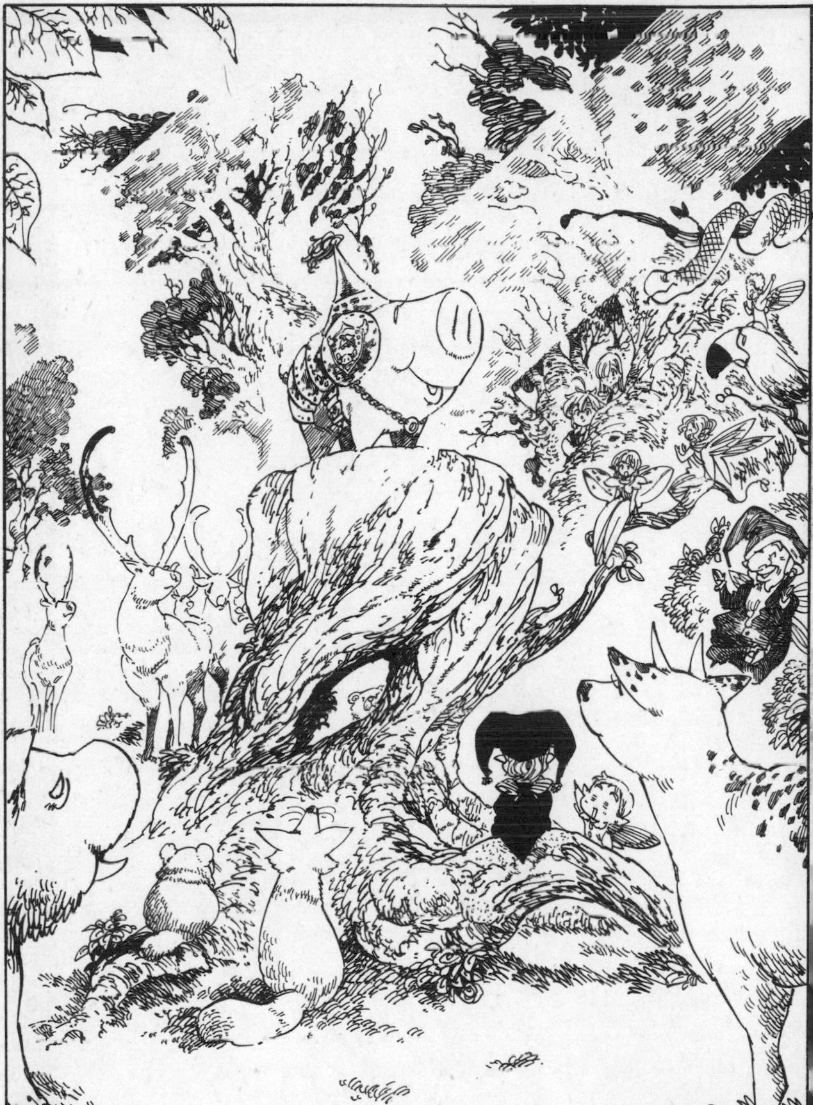

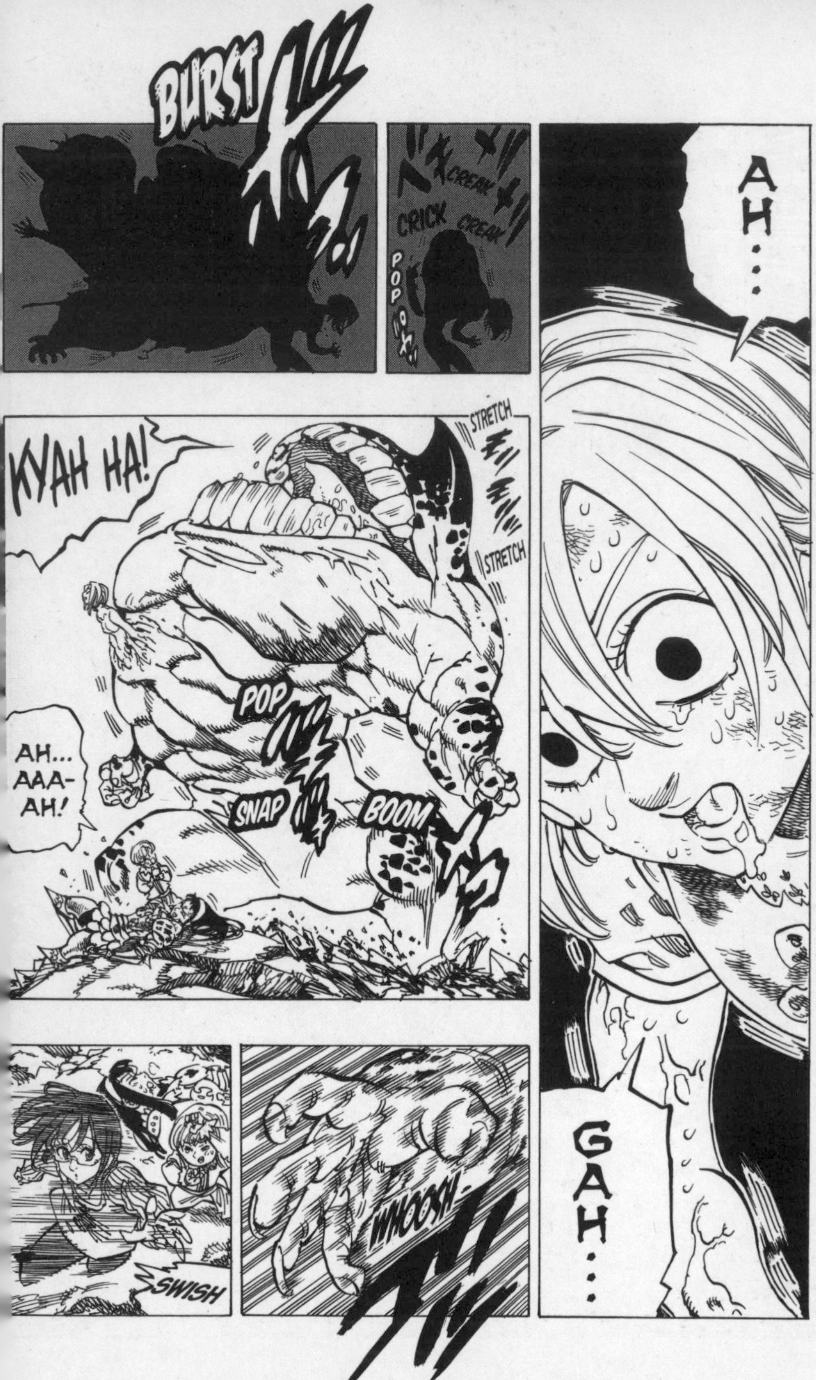
AH...
GAH...
CREAK
CRICK
CREAK
POP
BURST
KYAH HA!
STRETCH
STRETCH
POP
SNAP
BOOM
AH... AAA-AH!
WHOOSH
SWISH

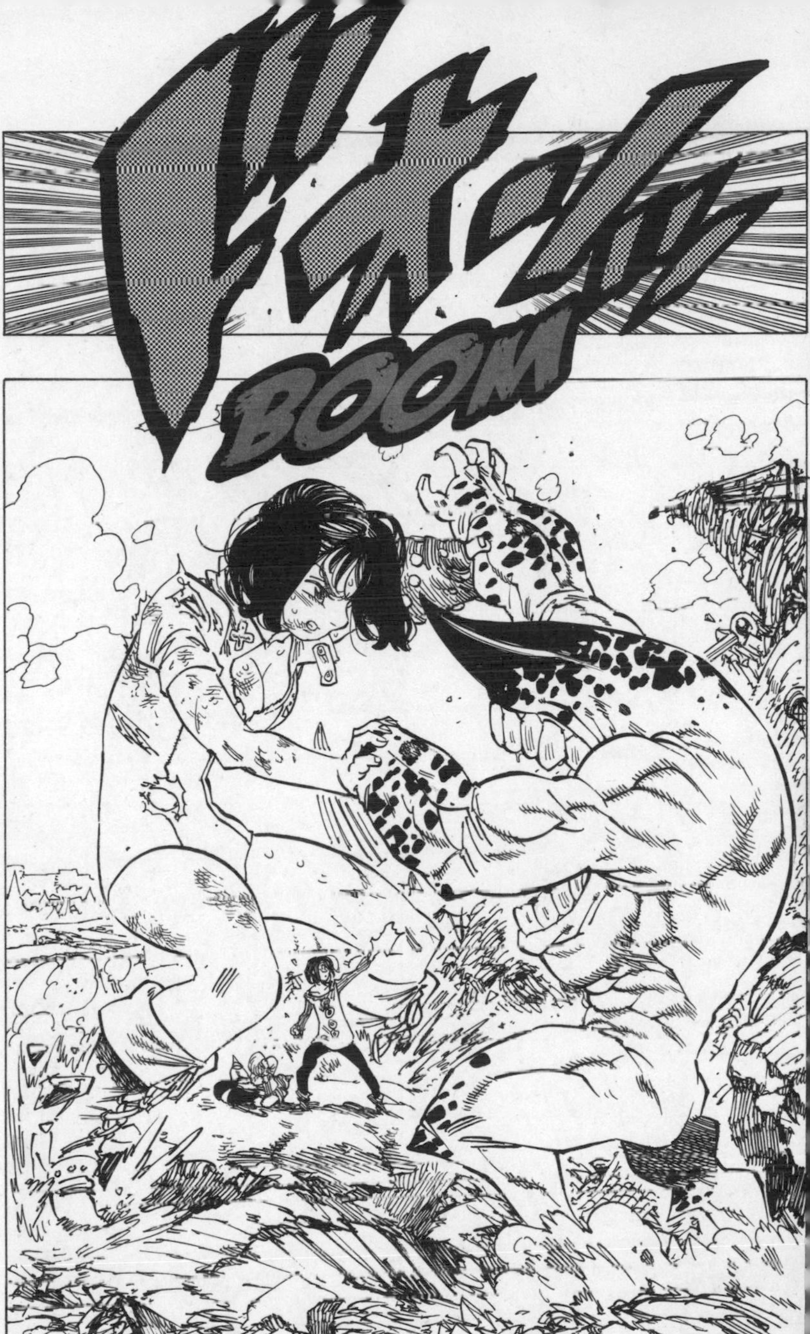
BOOM

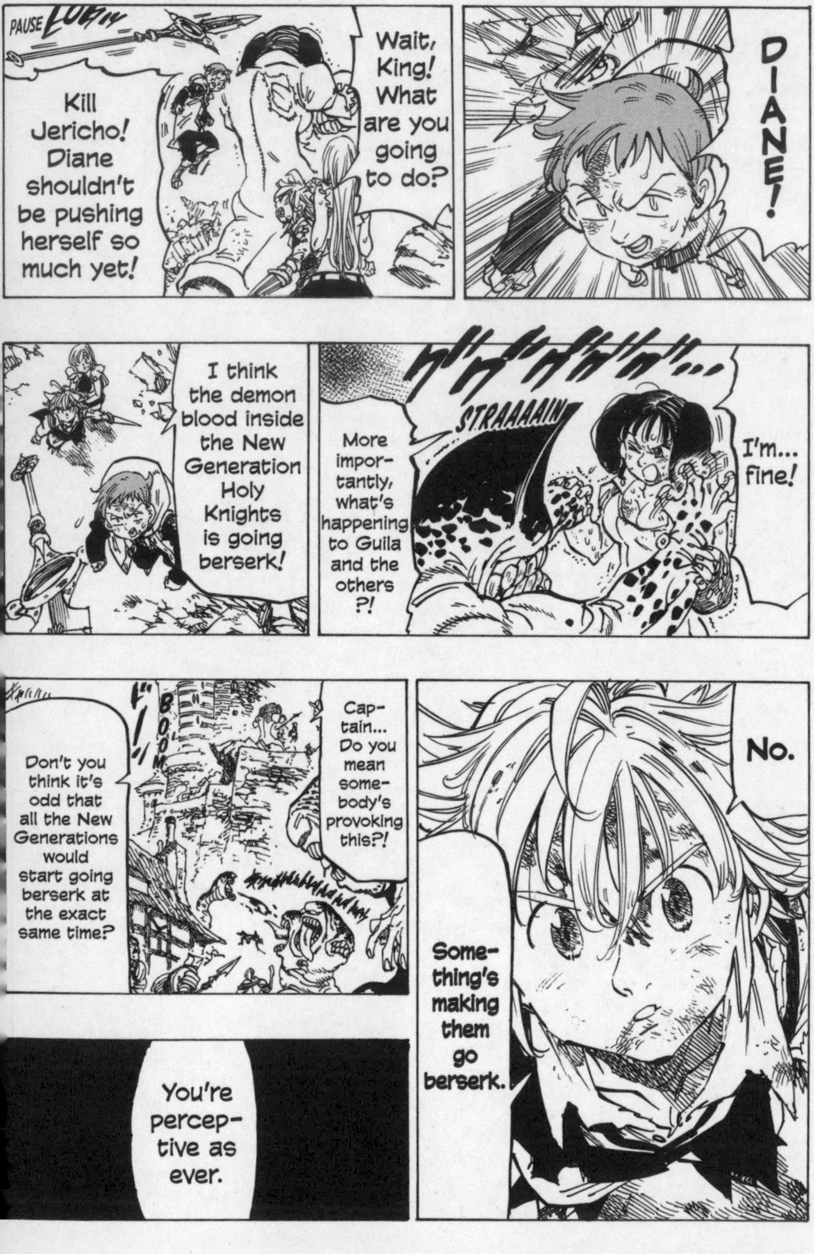

DIANE!
Wait, King! What are you going to do?
PAUSE
Kill Jericho! Diane shouldn't be pushing herself so much yet!
I'm... fine!
STRAAAAIN
More importantly, what's happening to Guila and the others?!
I think the demon blood inside the New Generation Holy Knights is going berserk!
No.
Something's making them go berserk.
Captain... Do you mean somebody's provoking this?!
BOOM
Don't you think it's odd that all the New Generations would start going berserk at the exact same time?
You're perceptive as ever.

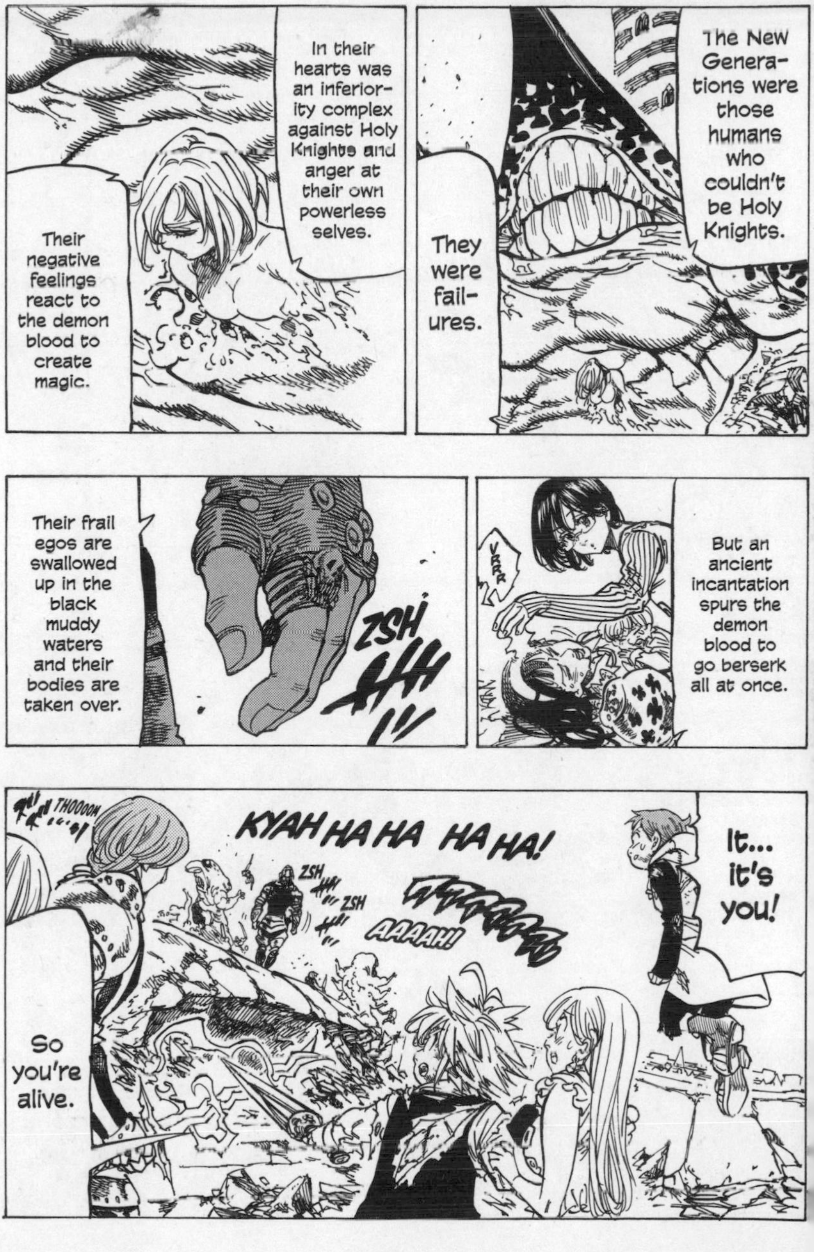
The New Generations were those humans who couldn't be Holy Knights.
They were failures.
In their hearts was an inferiority complex against Holy Knights and anger at their own powerless selves.
Their negative feelings react to the demon blood to create magic.
VRRR
But an ancient incantation spurs the demon blood to go berserk all at once.
ZSHHH!!
Their frail egos are swallowed up in the black muddy waters and their bodies are taken over.
It... it's you!
KYAH HA HA HA HA!
AAAAH!
ZSH
ZSH
So you're alive.

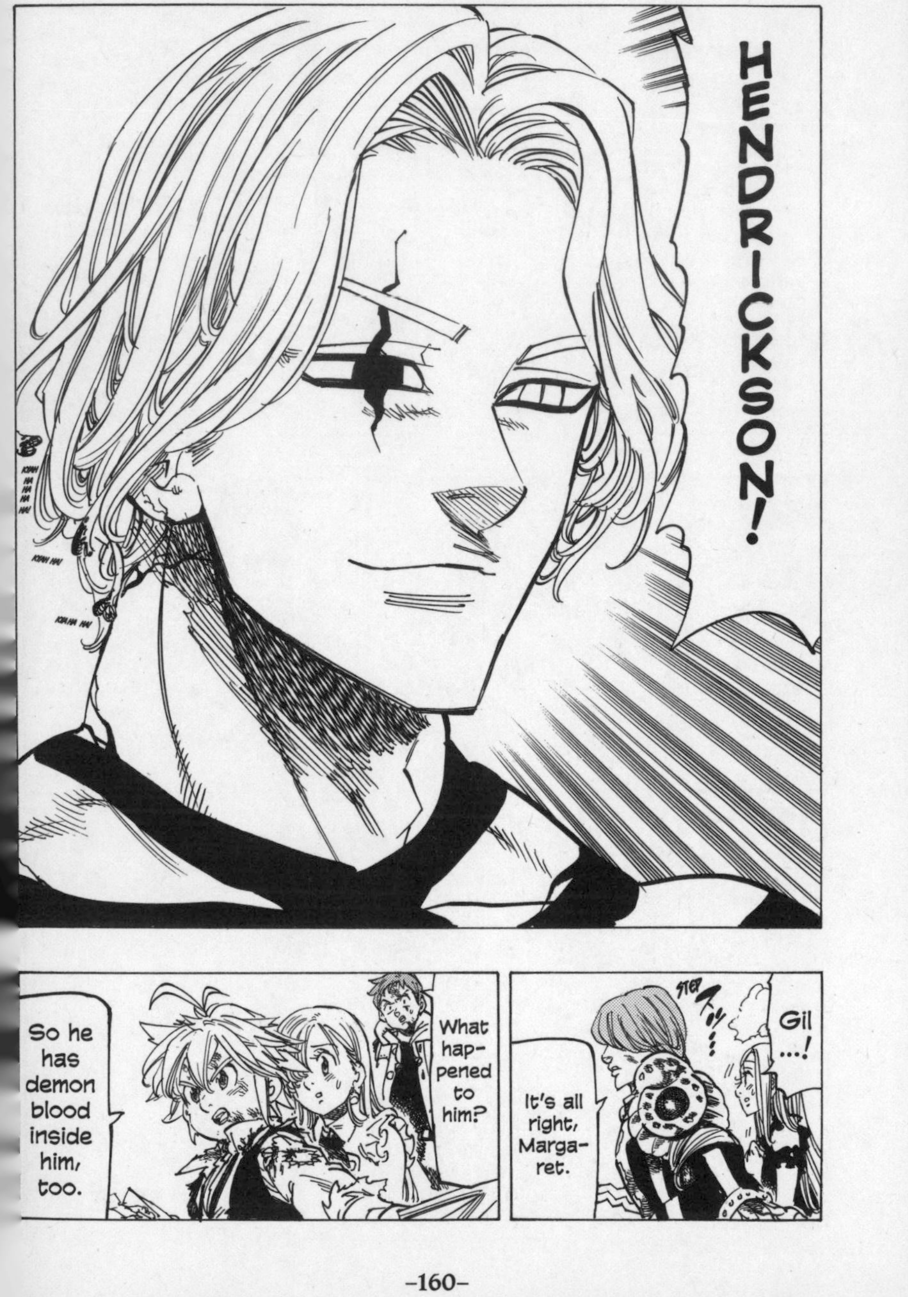
HENDRICKSON!
STEP
Gil ...!
It's all right, Margaret.
What hap-pened to him?
So he has demon blood inside him, too.

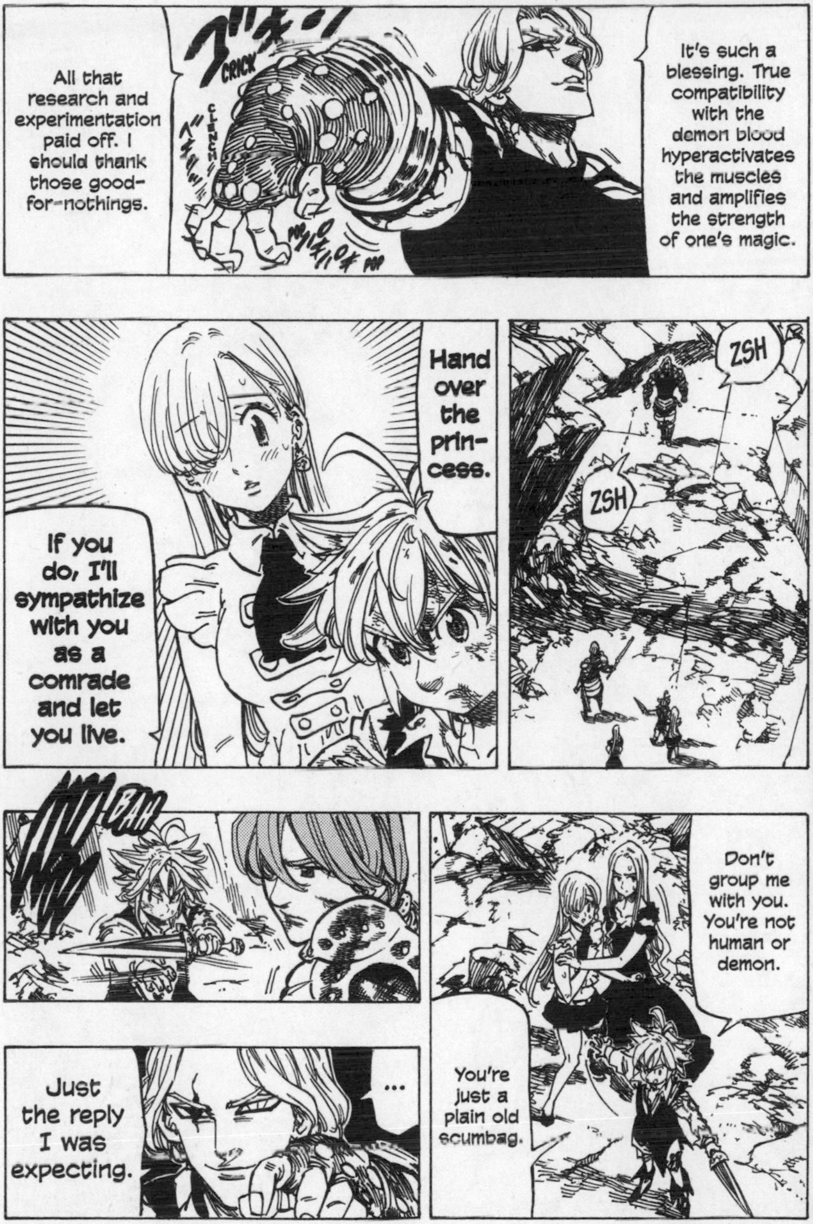
It's such a blessing. True compatibility with the demon blood hyperactivates the muscles and amplifies the strength of one's magic.
CRICK
CLENCH
POP
POP
All that research and experimentation paid off. I should thank those good-for-nothings.
ZSH
ZSH
Hand over the prin-cess.
If you do, I'll sympathize with you as a comrade and let you live.
Don't group me with you. You're not human or demon.
You're just a plain old scumbag.
BAH
...
Just the reply I was expecting.

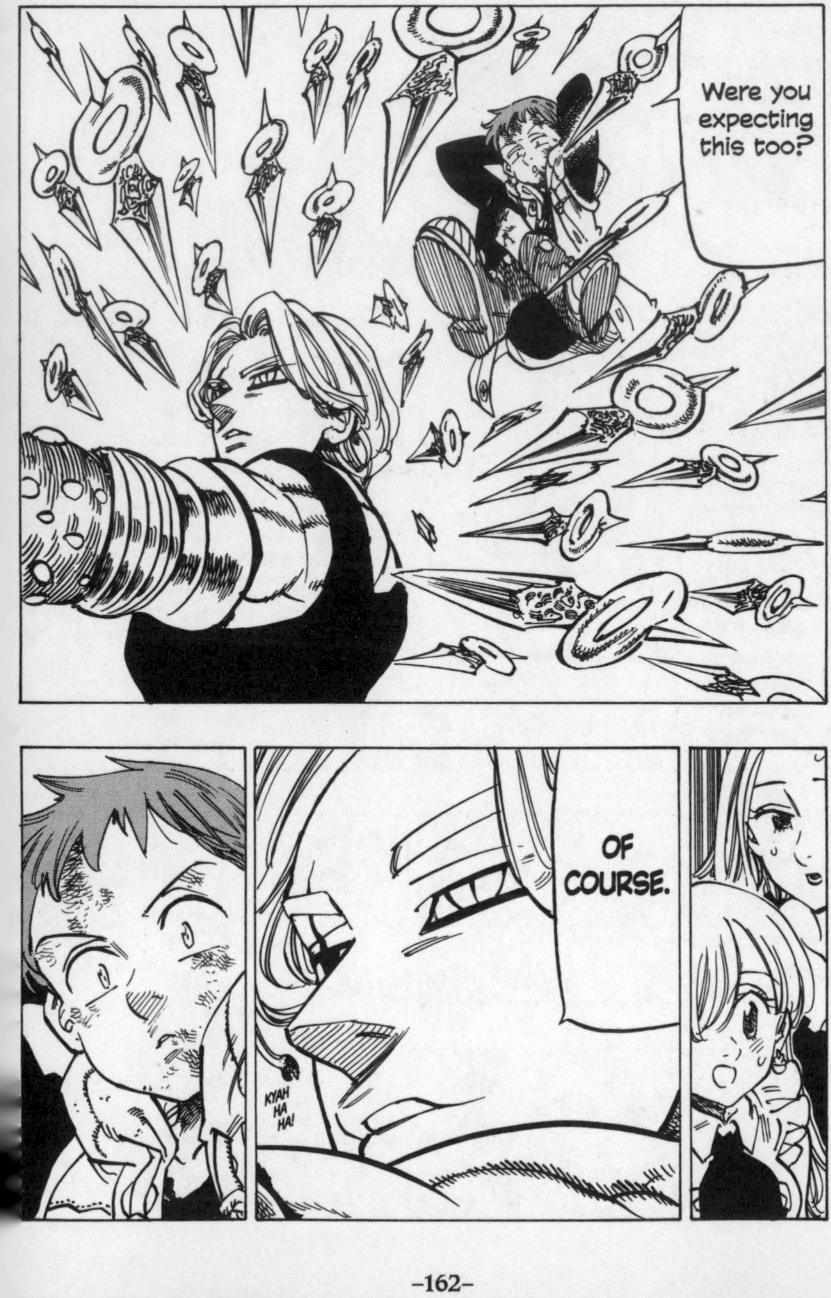
Were you expecting this too?
OF COURSE.
KYAH HA HA!

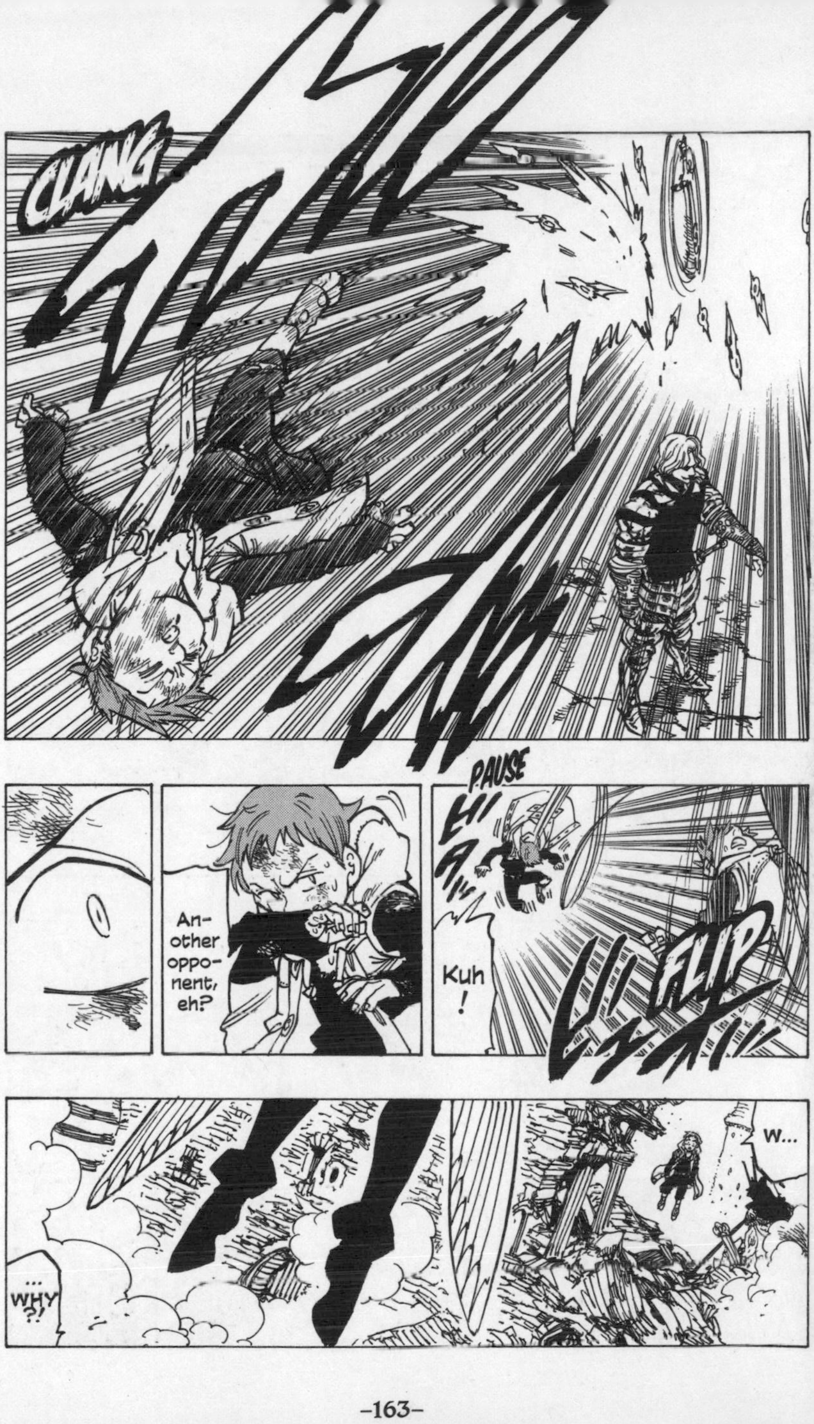
CLANG
PAUSE
Kuh!
FLIP
Another opponent, eh?
W...
...WHY?!

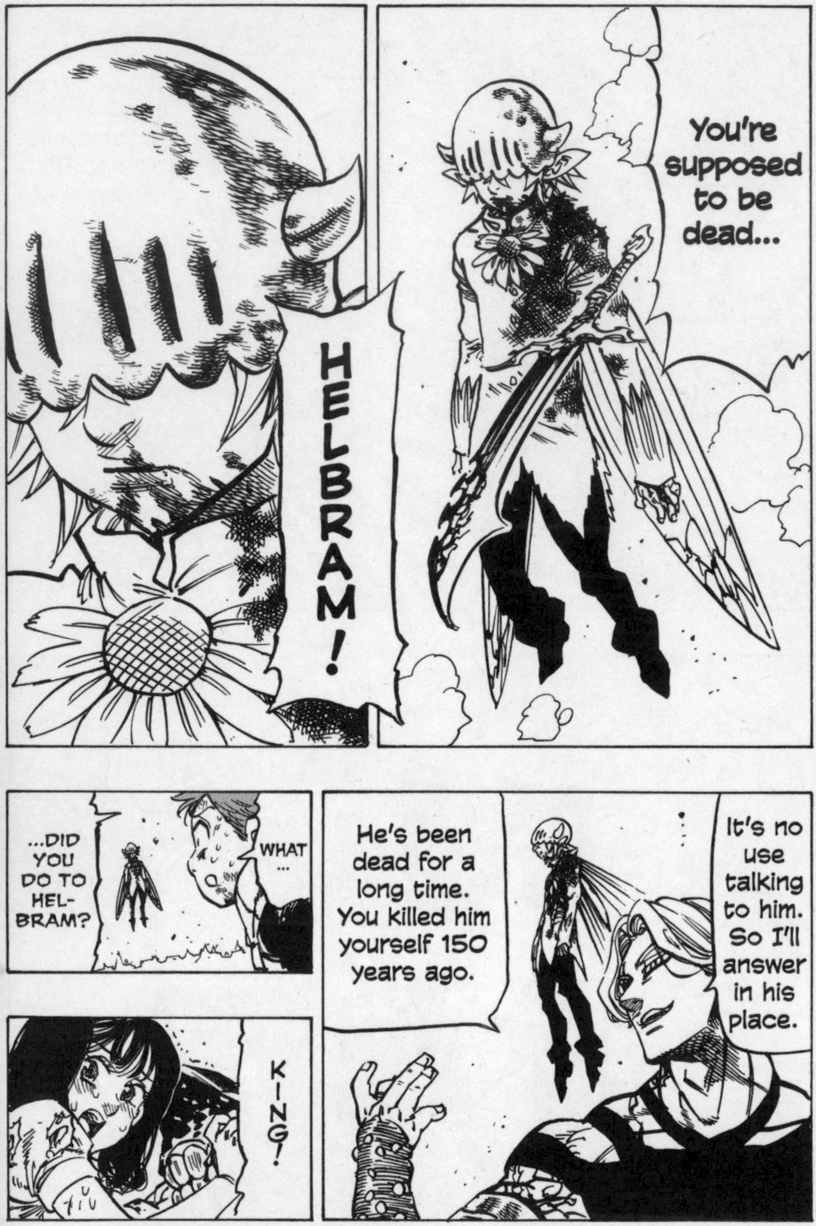
You're supposed to be dead...
HELBRAM!
It's no use talking to him. So I'll answer in his place.
He's been dead for a long time. You killed him yourself 150 years ago.
WHAT ...
...DID YOU DO TO HEL-BRAM?
KING!

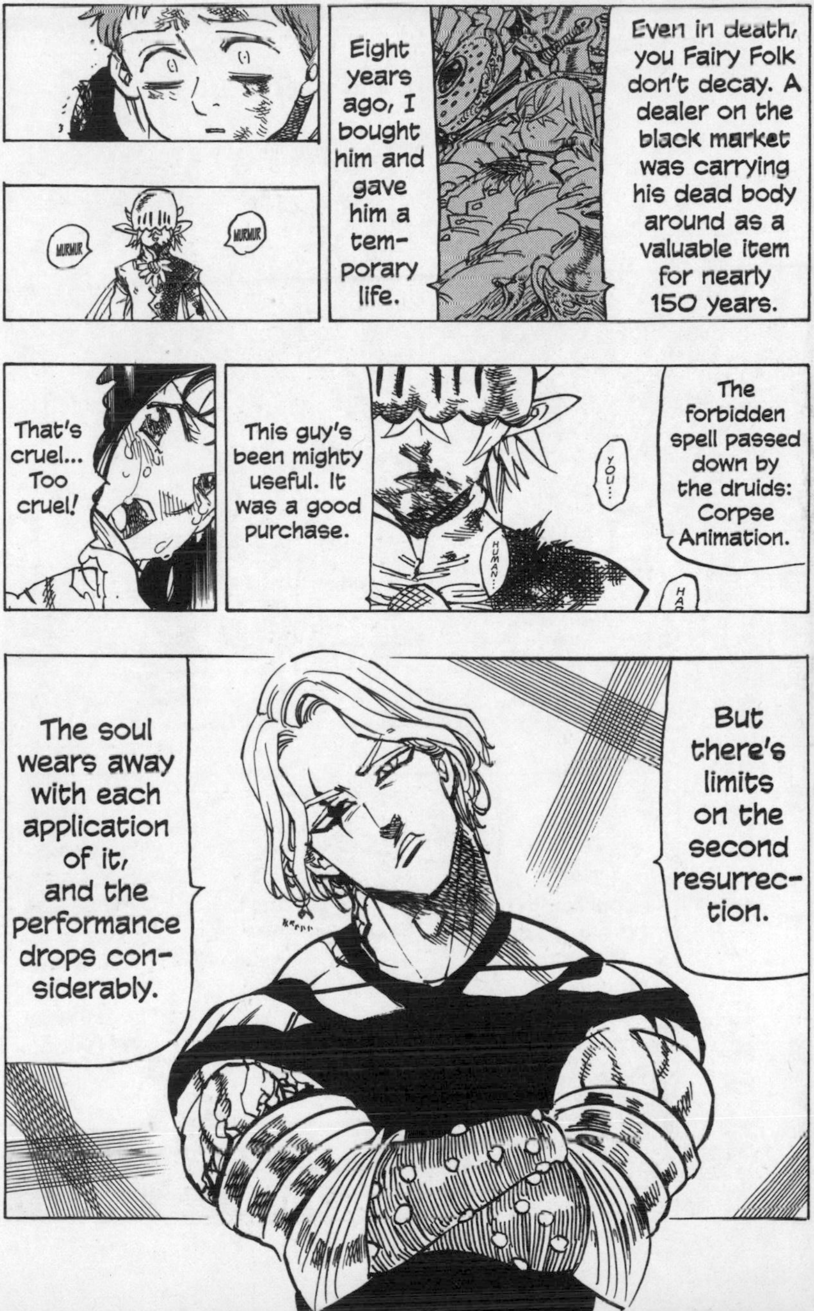
Even in death, you Fairy Folk don't decay. A dealer on the black market was carrying his dead body around as a valuable item for nearly 150 years.
Eight years ago, I bought him and gave him a temporary life.
MURMUR
MURMUR
The forbidden spell passed down by the druids: Corpse Animation.
YOU...
HUMAN...
This guy's been mighty useful. It was a good purchase.
That's cruel... Too cruel!
But there's limits on the second resurrection.
The soul wears away with each application of it, and the performance drops considerably.

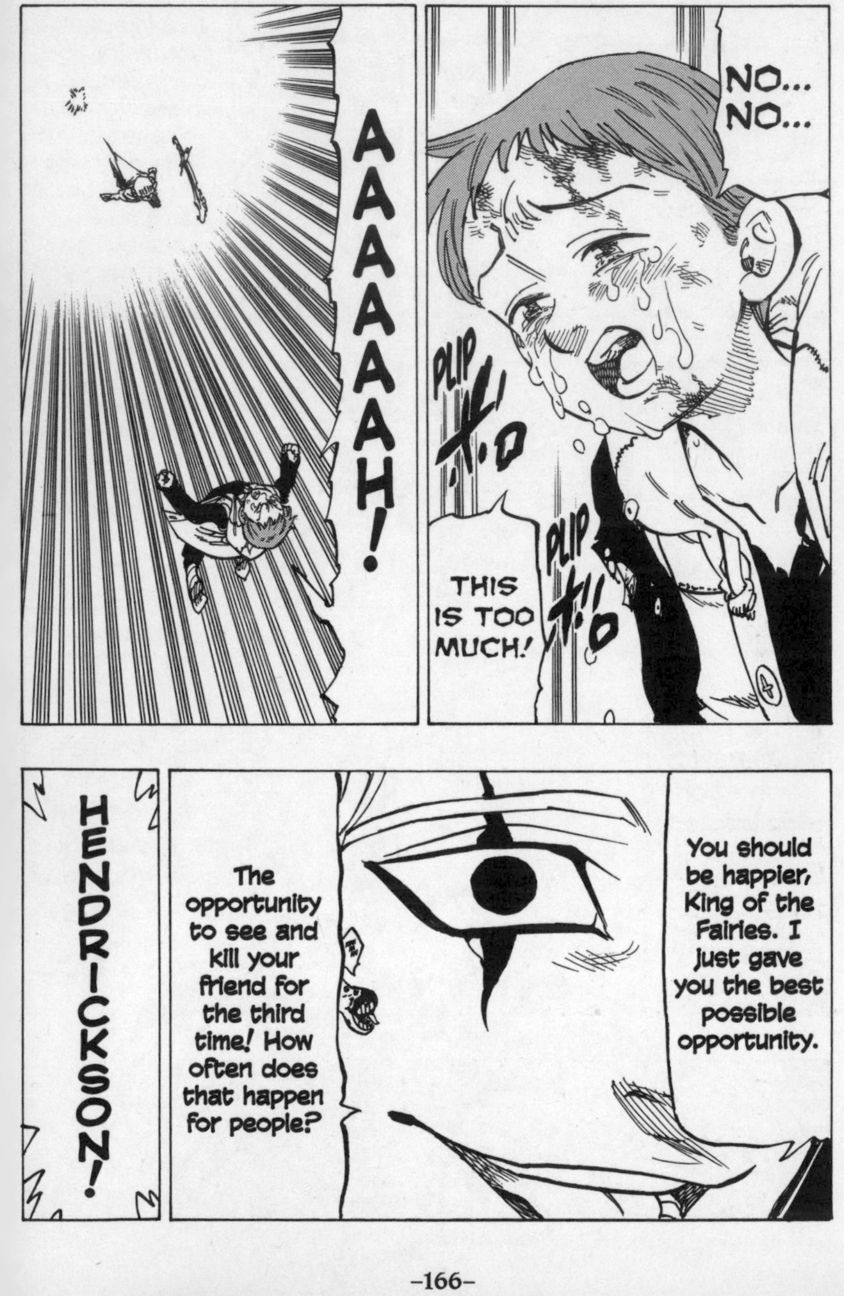
NO... NO...
PLIP
THIS IS TOO MUCH!
PLIP
AAAAAAH!
You should be happier, King of the Fairies. I just gave you the best possible opportunity.
The opportunity to see and kill your friend for the third time! How often does that happen for people?
HENDRICKSON!

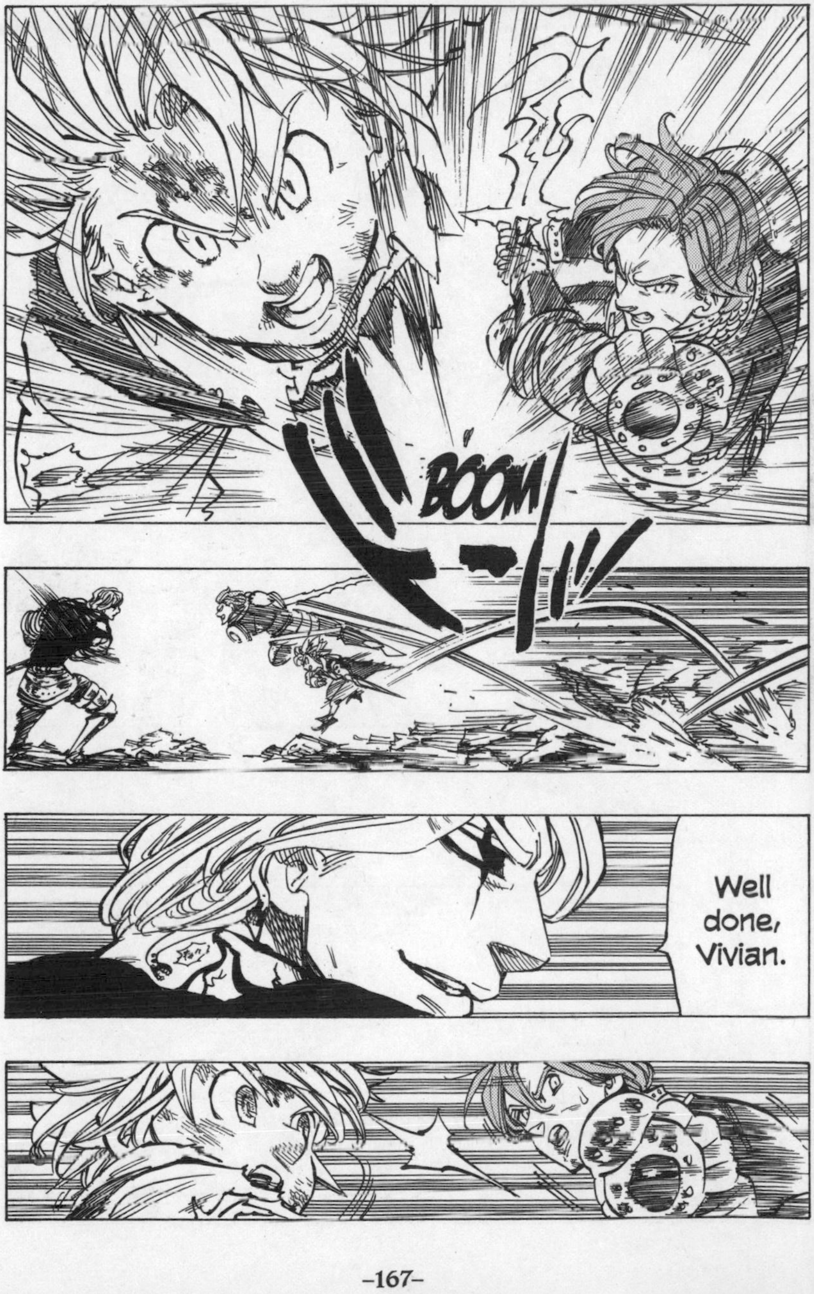
BOOM
Well done, Vivian.

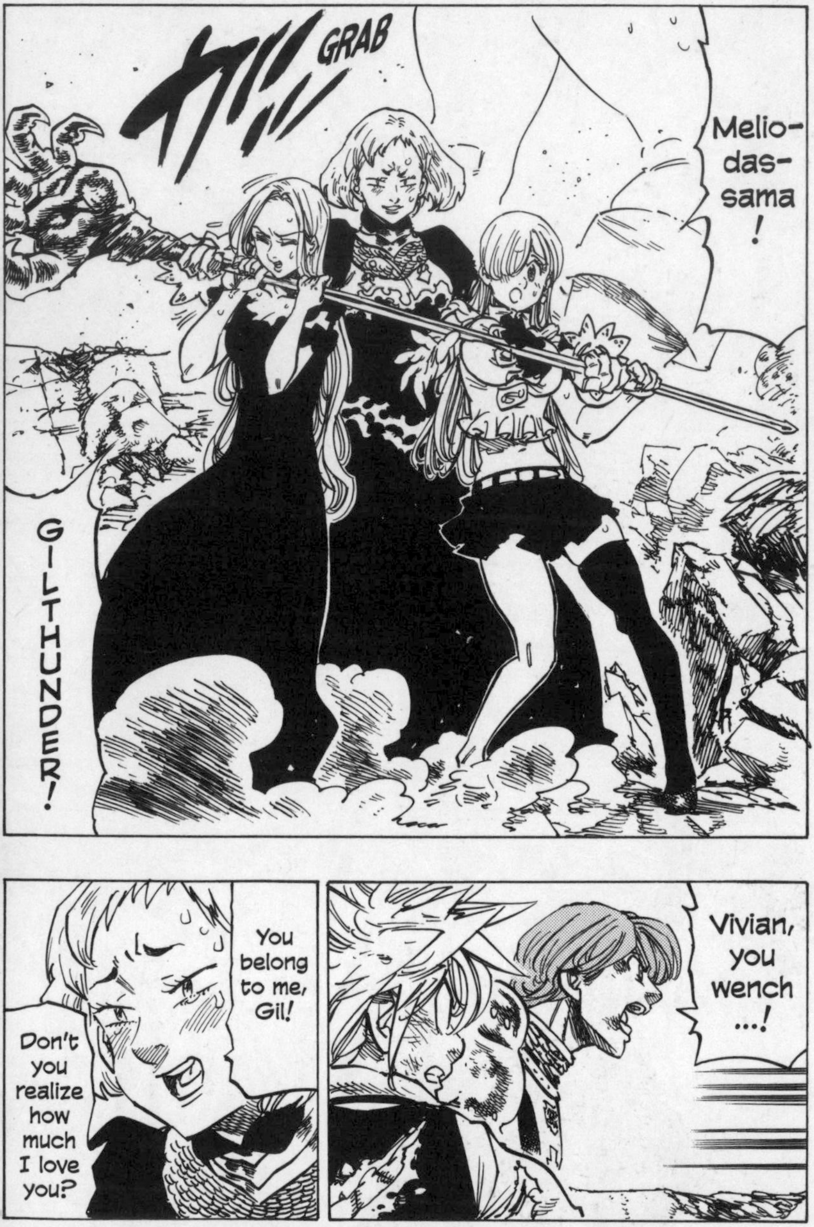
GRAB
Melio-das-sama!
GILTHUNDER!
Vivian, you wench ...!
You belong to me, Gil!
Don't you realize how much I love you?

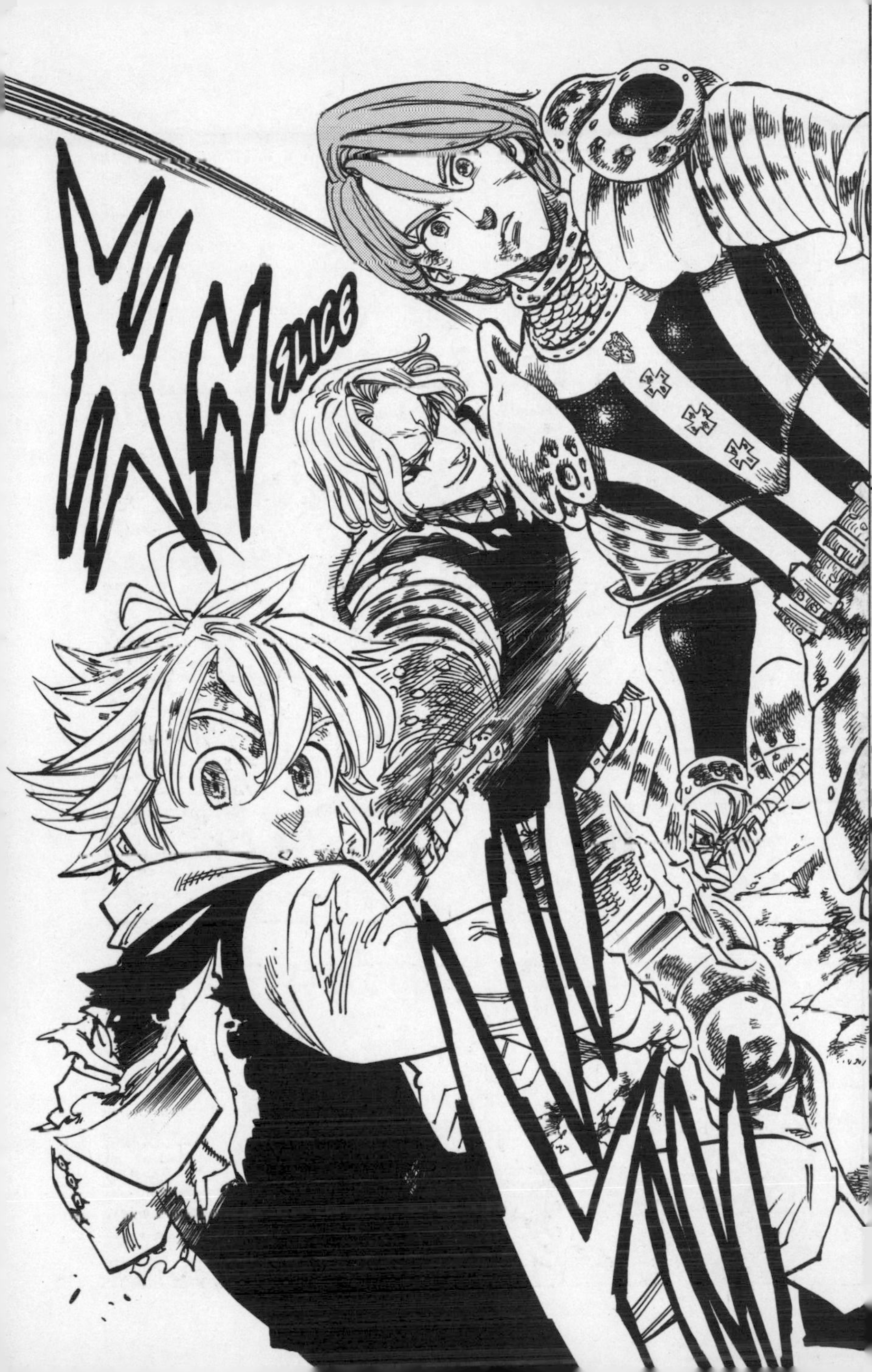
SLICE

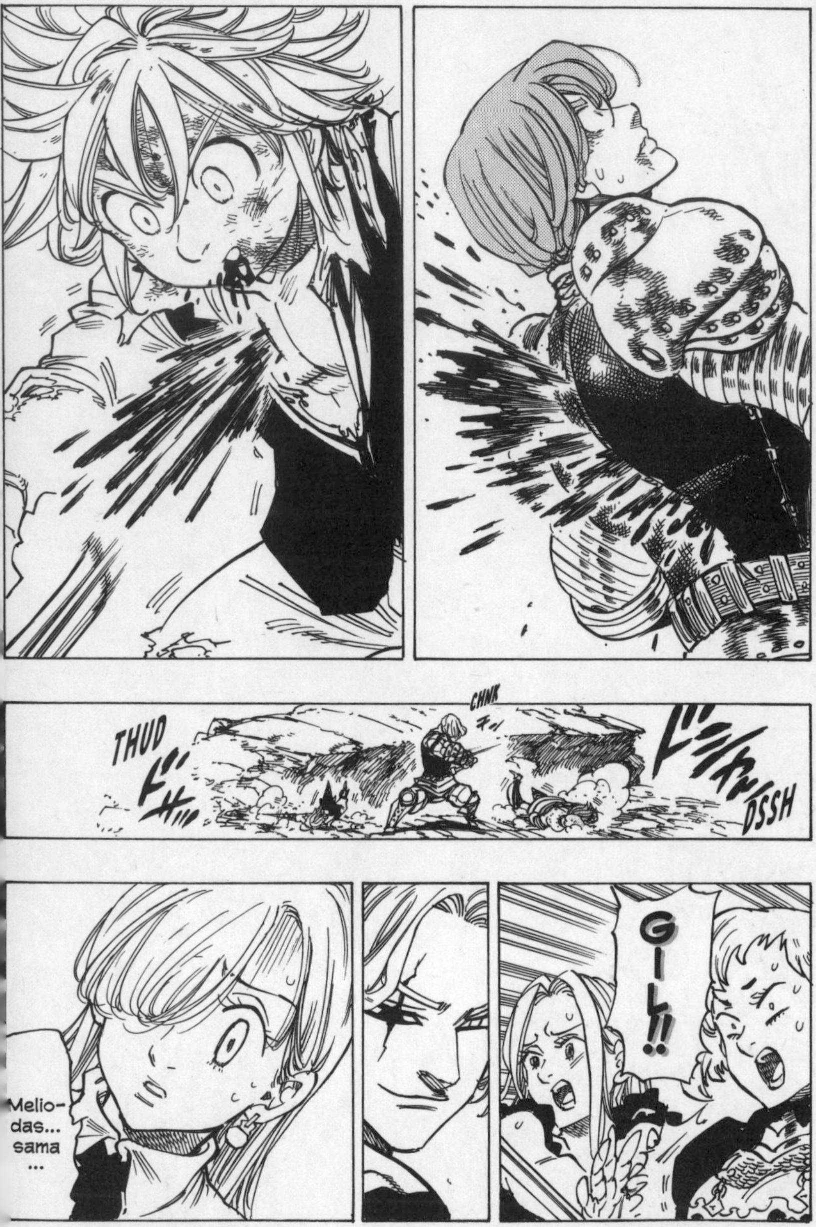
DSSH
CHNK
THUD
GIL!!
Melio-das... sama ...

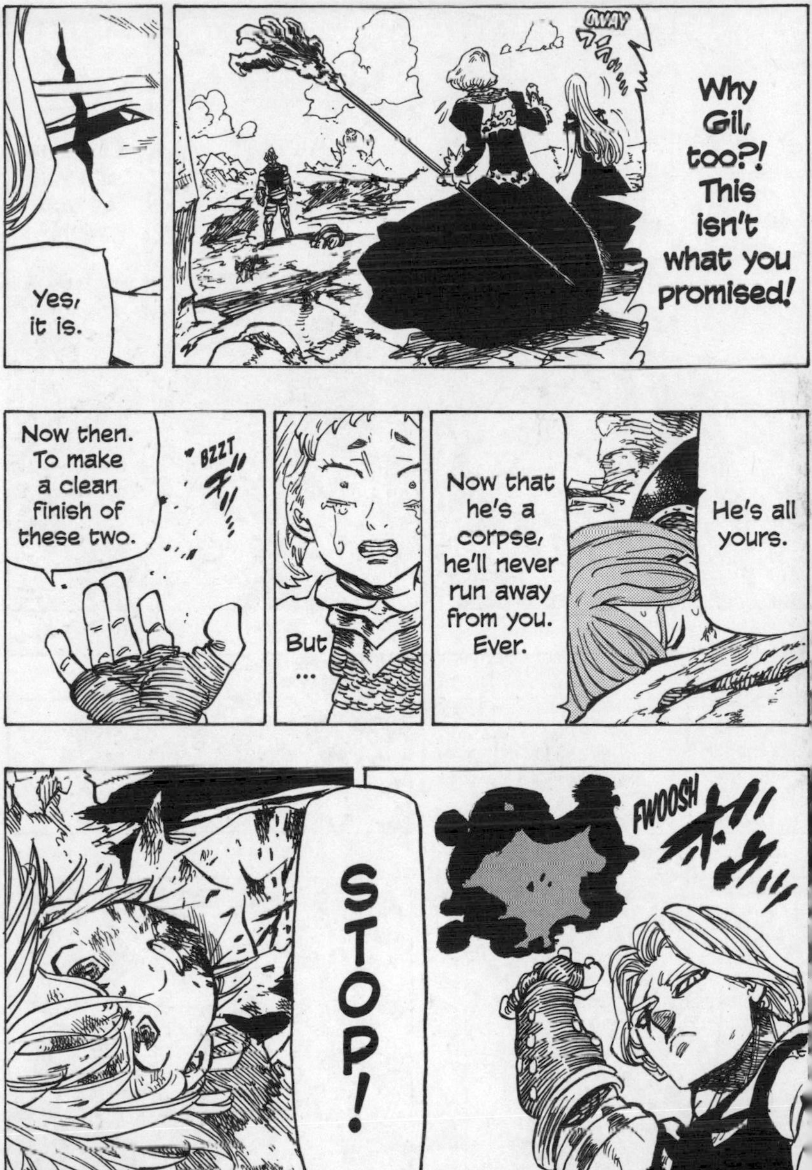
Why Gil, too?! This isn't what you promised!
Yes, it is.
He's all yours.
Now that he's a corpse, he'll never run away from you. Ever.
But ...
BZZT
Now then. To make a clean finish of these two.
FWOOSH
STOP!

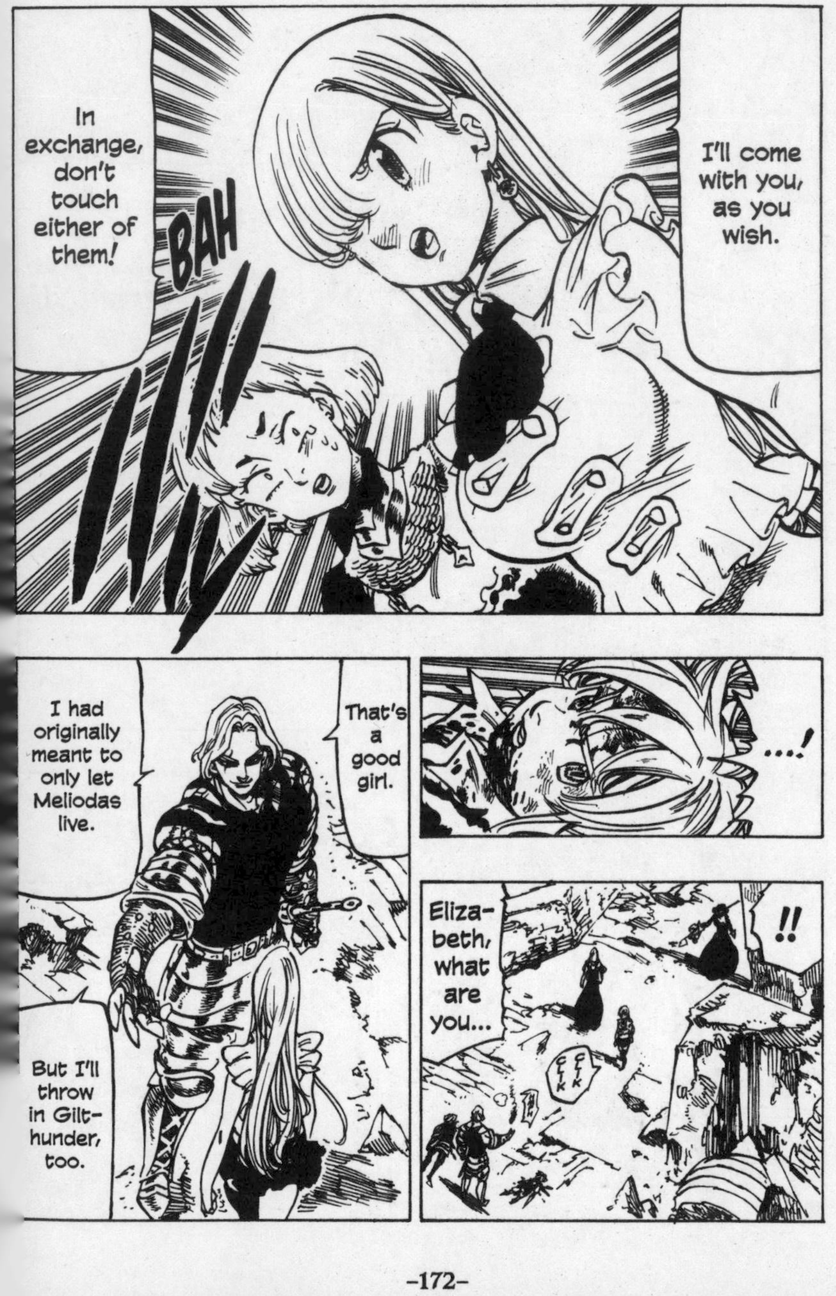
I'll come with you, as you wish.
In exchange, don't touch either of them!
BAH
...!
Eliza-beth, what are you...
!!
CLIK CLIK
That's a good girl.
I had originally meant to only let Meliodas live.
But I'll throw in Gilt-hunder, too.

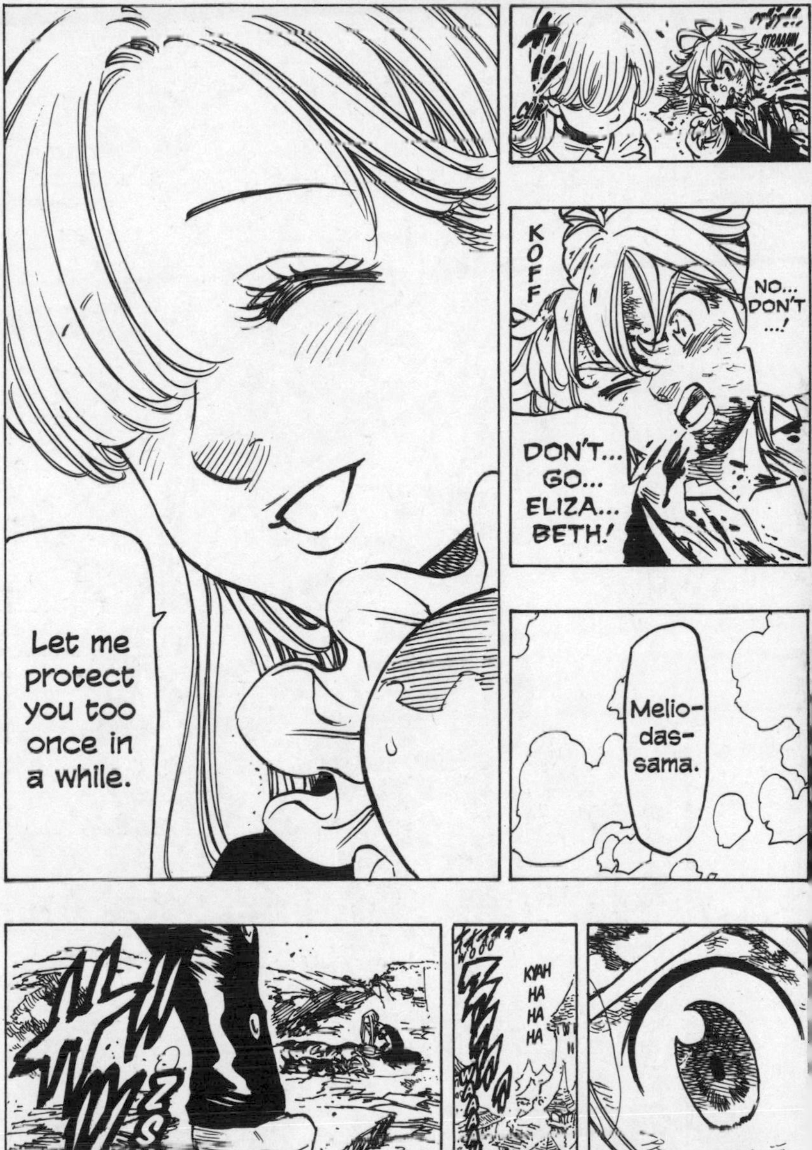
STRAAAIN
CLINK
KOFF
NO... DON'T ...!
DON'T... GO... ELIZA... BETH!
Melio-das-sama.
Let me protect you too once in a while.
KYAH HA HA HA
WOOOO
WAAAAAH
ZSH

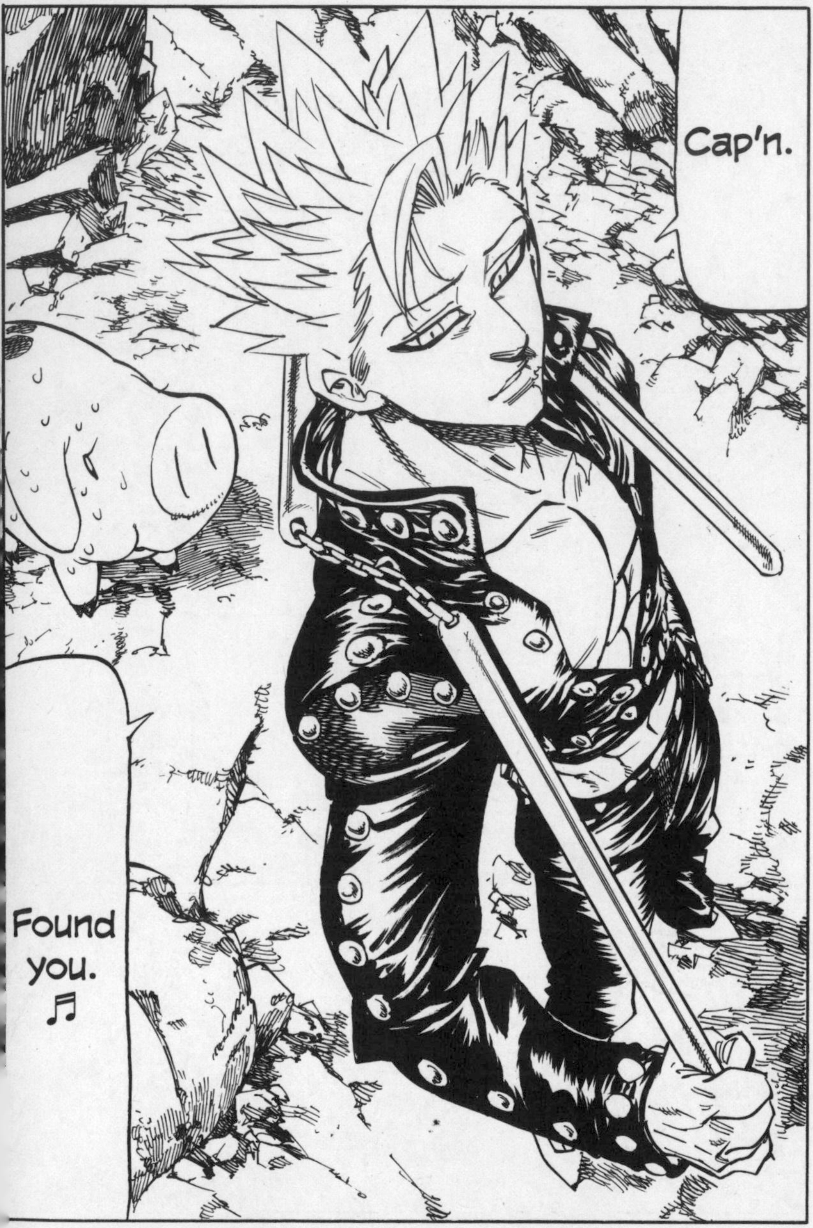
Cap'n.
Found you. ♬

To be continued in volume 12...

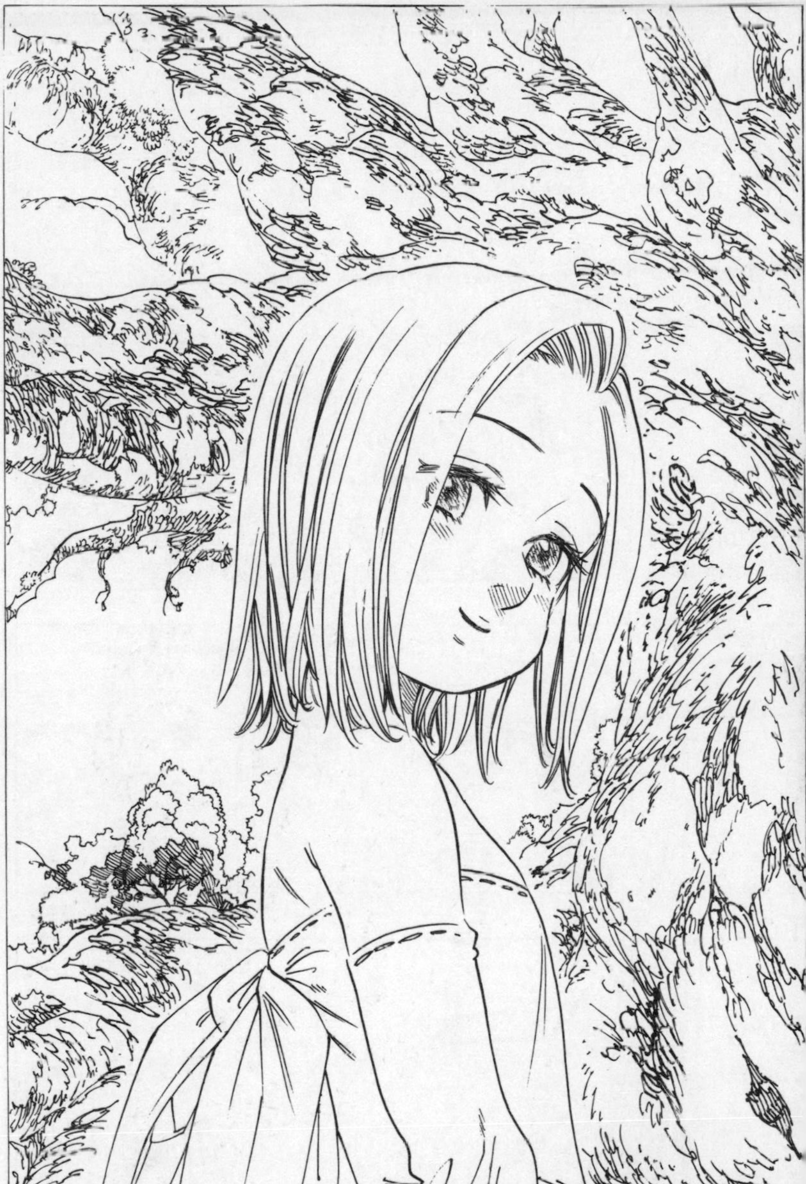

Side Story - Eternal Moment

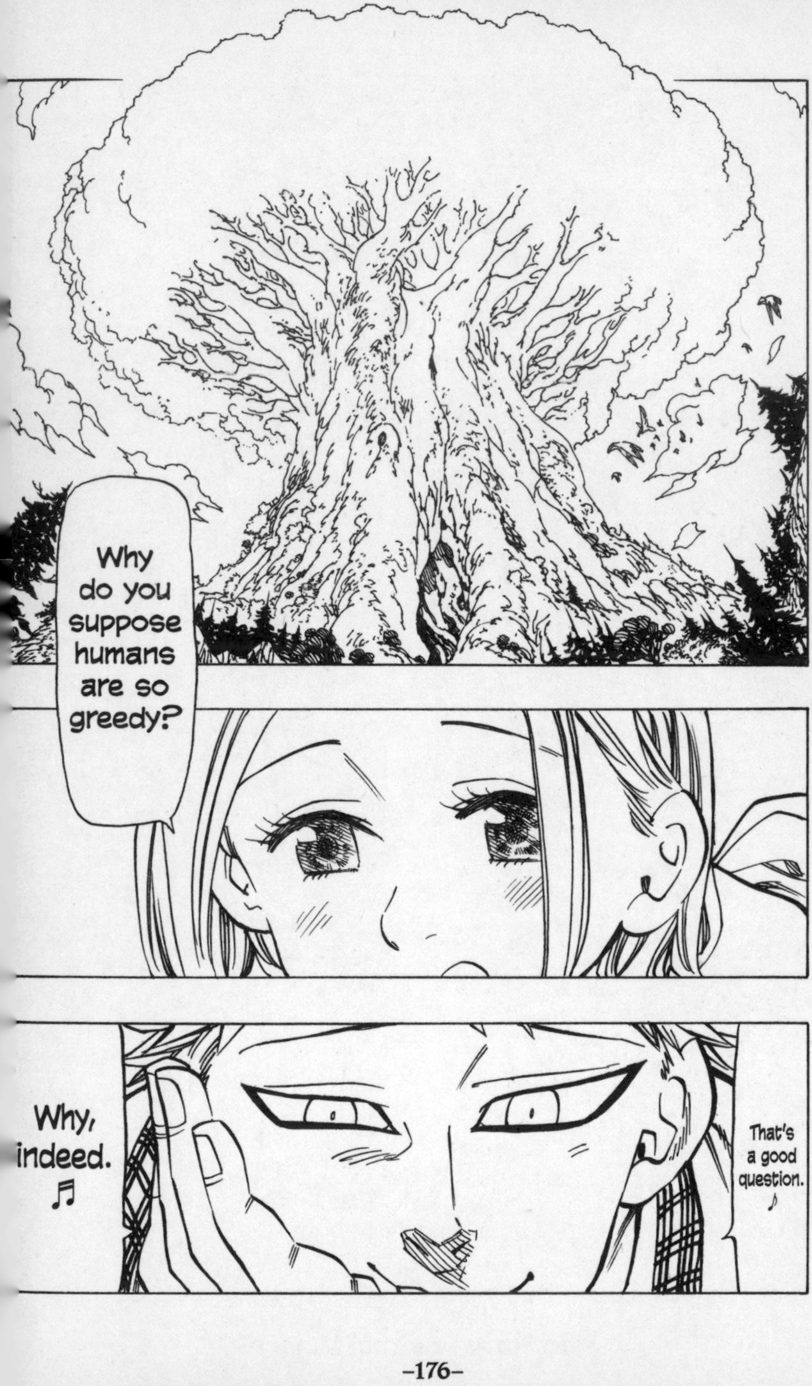
Why do you suppose humans are so greedy?
That's a good question. ♪
Why, indeed. ♬

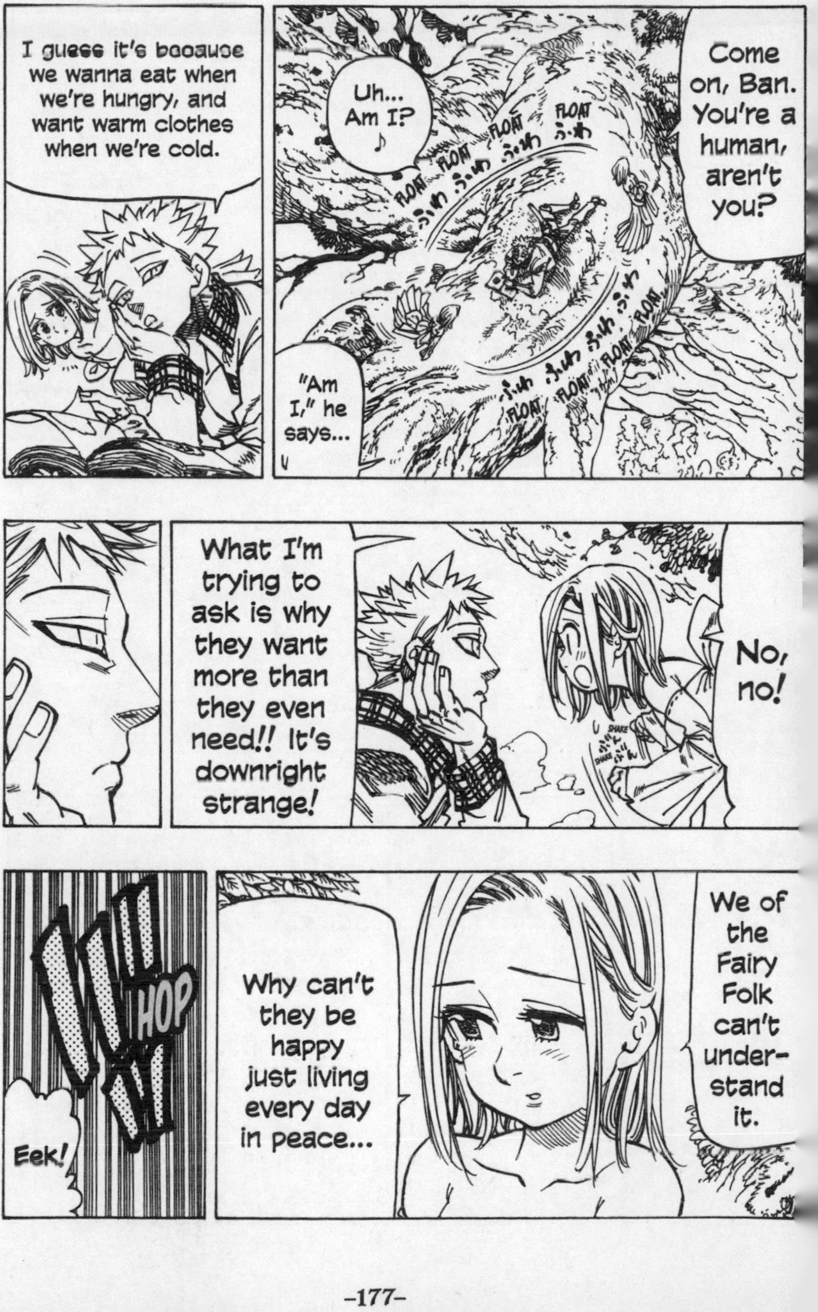
Come on, Ban. You're a human, aren't you?
Uh... Am I? ♪
FLOAT ふわ FLOAT ふわ FLOAT ふわ FLOAT ふわ
ふわ ふわ ふわ ふわ FLOAT FLOAT FLOAT FLOAT
"Am I," he says...
I guess it's because we wanna eat when we're hungry, and want warm clothes when we're cold.
No, no!
SHAKE SHAKE
What I'm trying to ask is why they want more than they even need!! It's downright strange!
We of the Fairy Folk can't under-stand it.
Why can't they be happy just living every day in peace...
HOP
Eek!

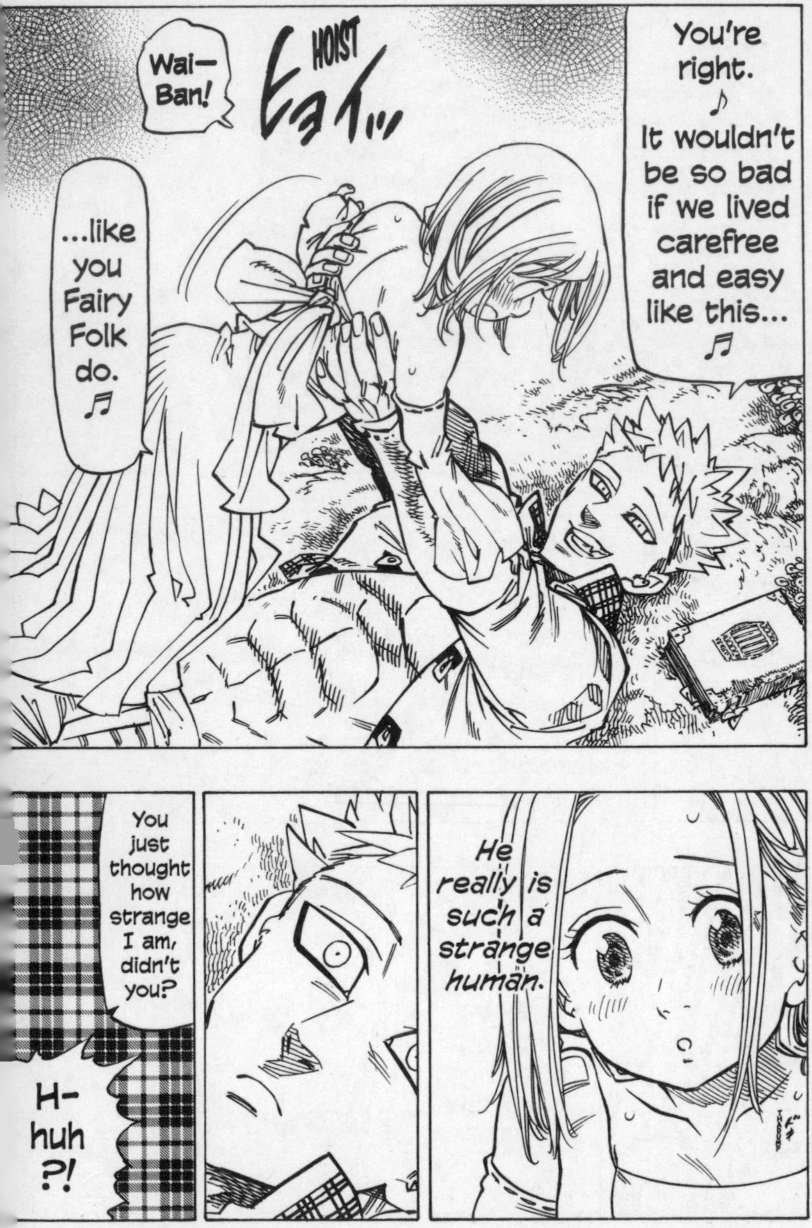
You're right. ♪ It wouldn't be so bad if we lived carefree and easy like this... ♬
Wai— Ban!
HOIST
...like you Fairy Folk do. ♬
He really is such a strange human.
You just thought how strange I am, didn't you?
H-huh?!

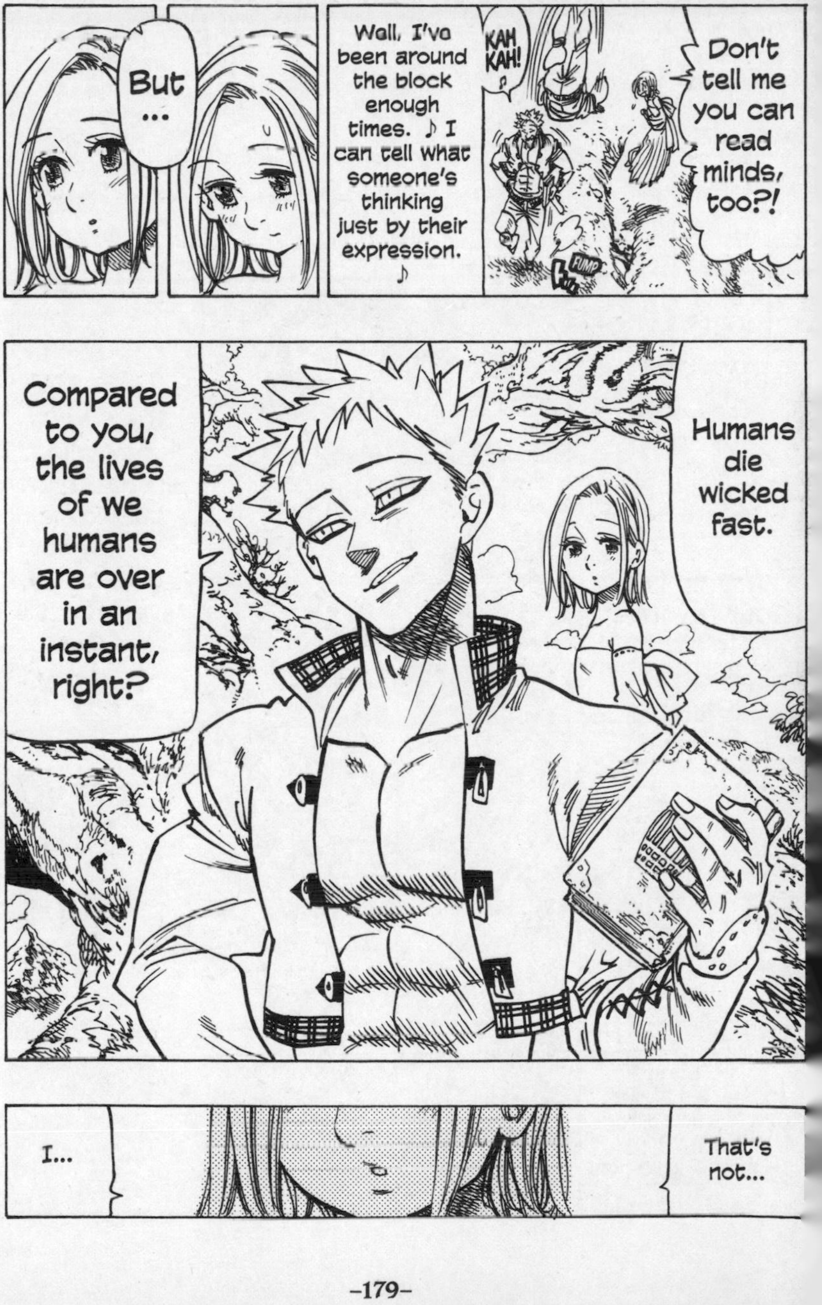
Don't tell me you can read minds, too?!
KAH KAH! ♪
FUMP
Well, I've been around the block enough times. ♪ I can tell what someone's thinking just by their expression. ♪
But ...
Humans die wicked fast.
Compared to you, the lives of we humans are over in an instant, right?
That's not...
I...

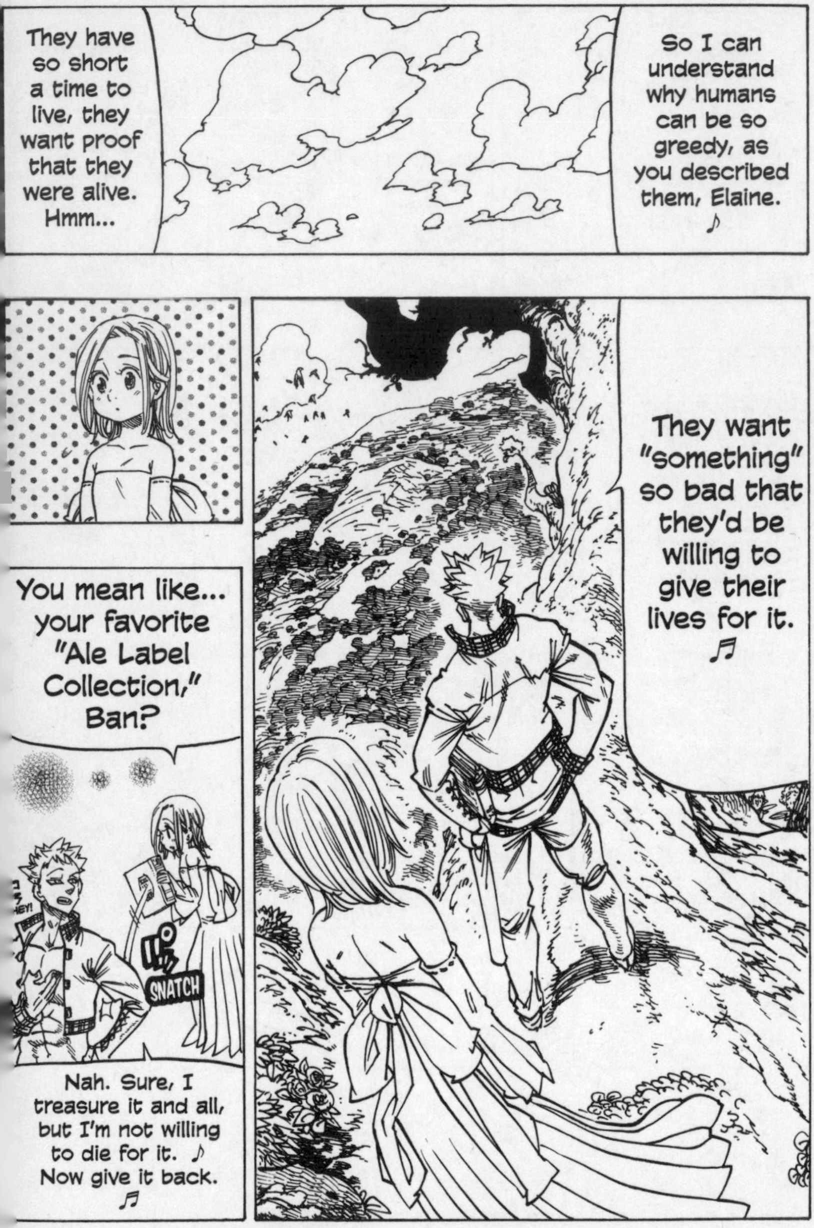
So I can understand why humans can be so greedy, as you described them, Elaine. ♪
They have so short a time to live, they want proof that they were alive. Hmm...
They want "something" so bad that they'd be willing to give their lives for it. ♫
You mean like... your favorite "Ale Label Collection," Ban?
HEY!
SNATCH
Nah. Sure, I treasure it and all, but I'm not willing to die for it. ♪ Now give it back. ♫

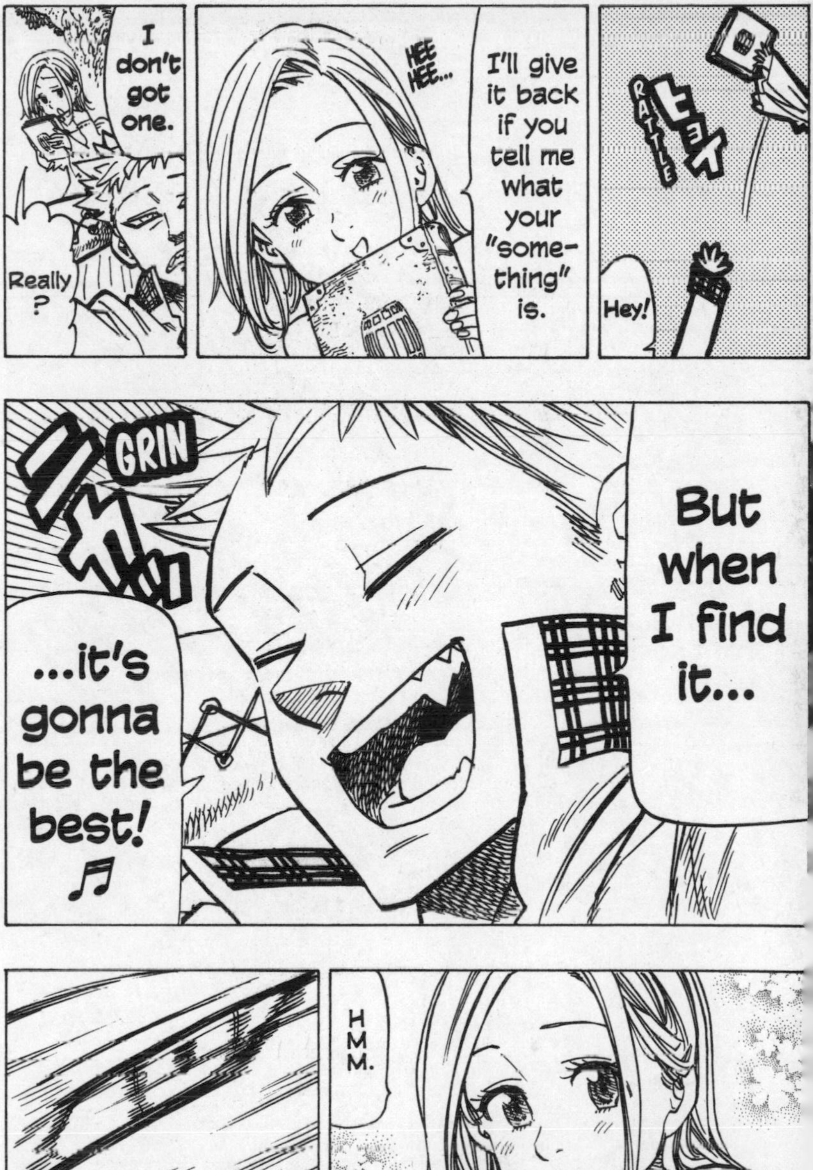
RATTLE
ヒョイ
Hey!
I'll give it back if you tell me what your "something" is.
HEE HEE...
I don't got one.
Really?
But when I find it...
GRIN
...it's gonna be the best! ♫
HMM.

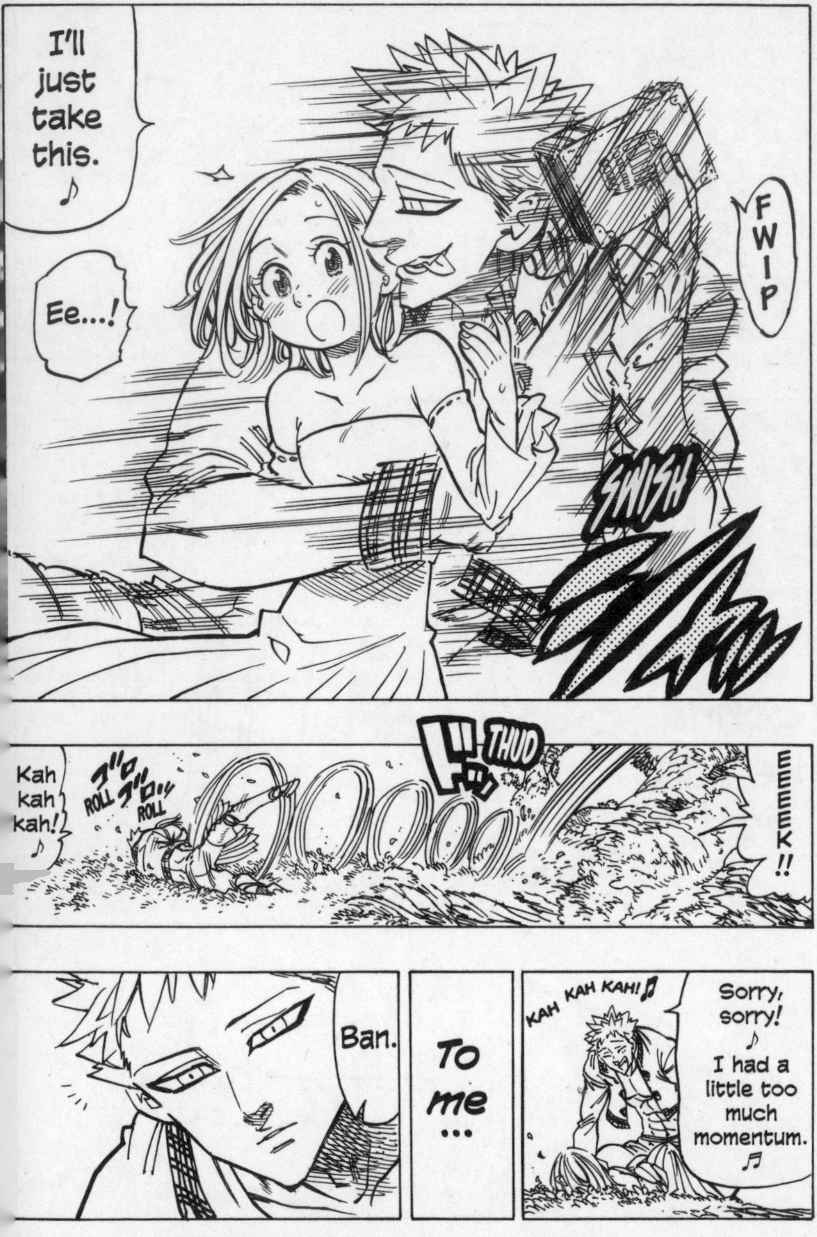
FWIP
I'll just take this. ♪
Ee...!
SWISH
EEEEK!!
THUD
ROLL ROLL
Kah kah kah! ♪
KAH KAH KAH! ♫
Sorry, sorry! ♪ I had a little too much momentum. ♬
To me...
Ban.

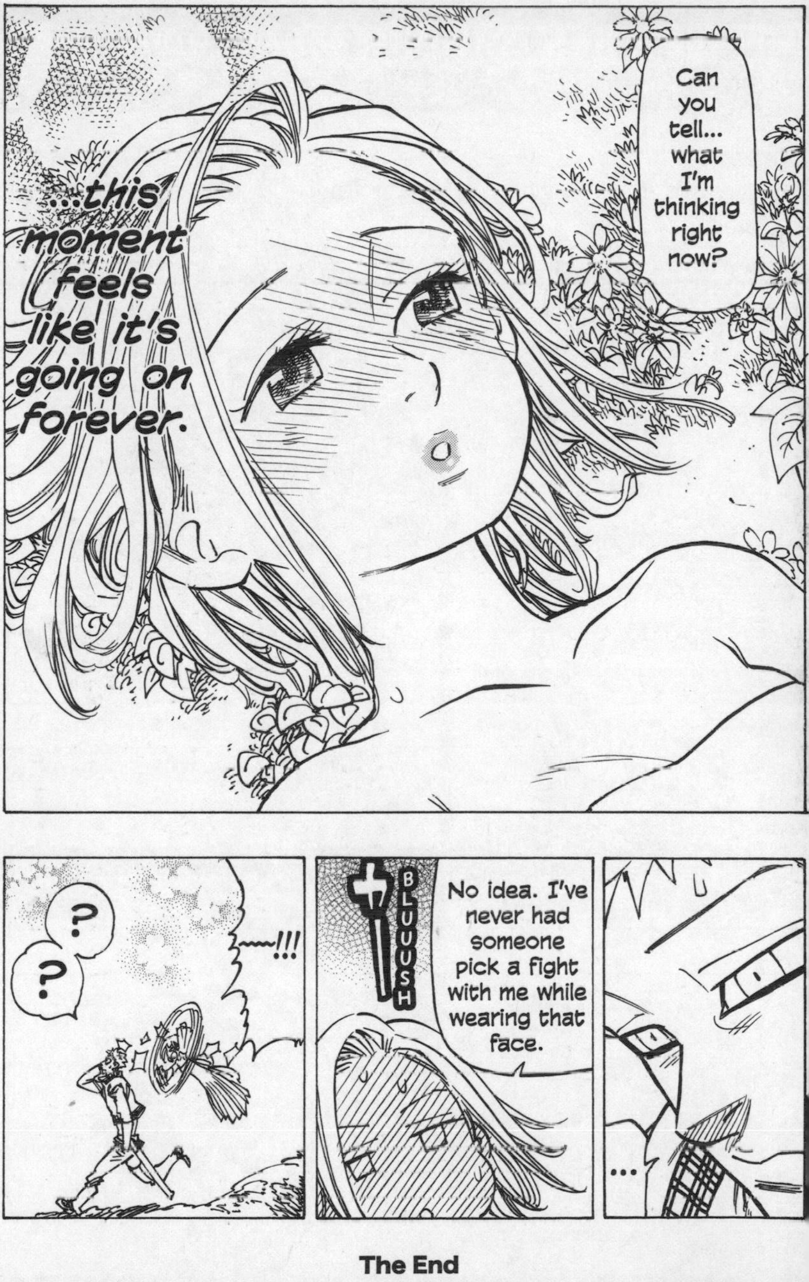
Can you tell... what I'm thinking right now?
...this moment feels like it's going on forever.
...
BLUUUSH
No idea. I've never had someone pick a fight with me while wearing that face.
~~~!!!
?
?

The End
~~~

"THE SEVEN DEADLY SINS" Q&A CORNER

"CHATTING KNIGHTHOOD"

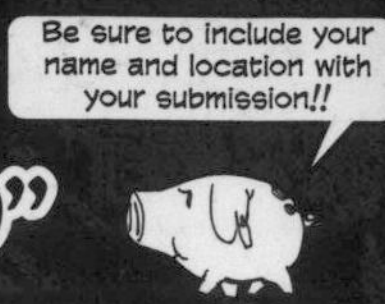
Be sure to include your name and location with your submission!!

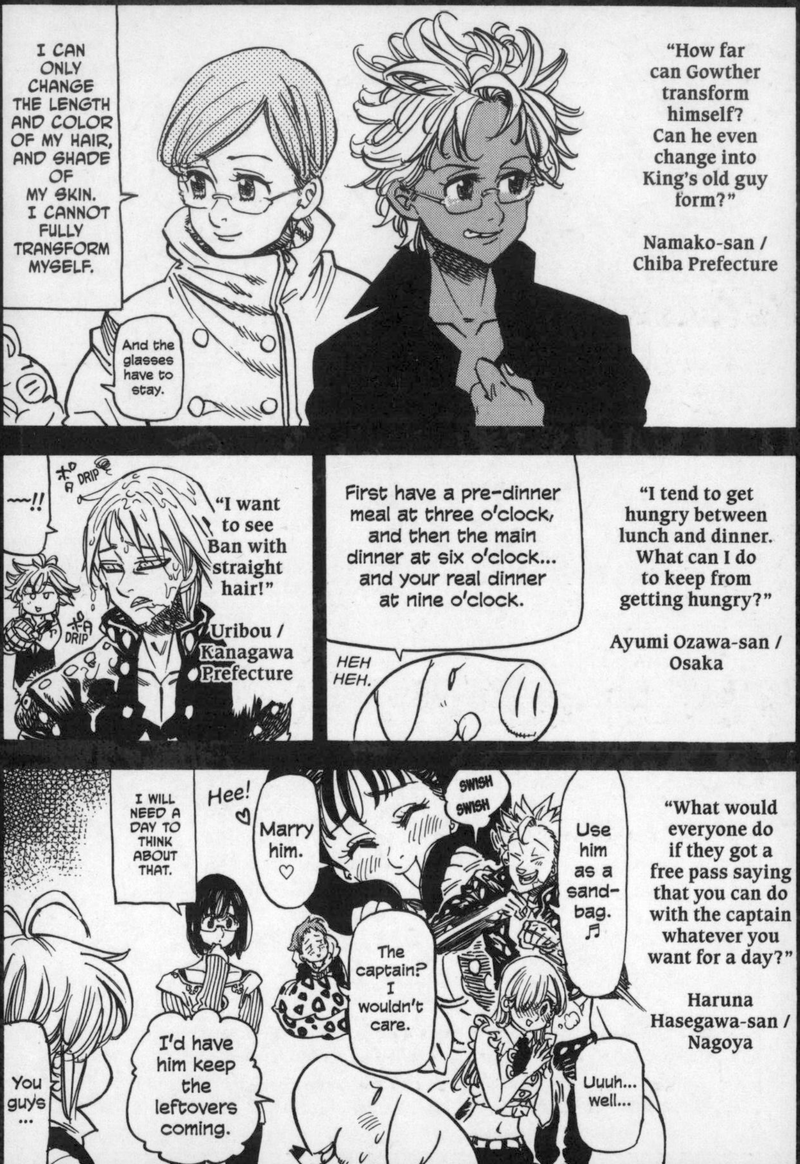
"How far can Gowther transform himself? Can he even change into King's old guy form?"
Namako-san / Chiba Prefecture
I CAN ONLY CHANGE THE LENGTH AND COLOR OF MY HAIR, AND SHADE OF MY SKIN. I CANNOT FULLY TRANSFORM MYSELF.
And the glasses have to stay.
"I tend to get hungry between lunch and dinner. What can I do to keep from getting hungry?"
Ayumi Ozawa-san / Osaka
First have a pre-dinner meal at three o'clock, and then the main dinner at six o'clock... and your real dinner at nine o'clock.
HEH HEH.
"I want to see Ban with straight hair!"
Uribou / Kanagawa Prefecture
DRIP
~~!!
DRIP
"What would everyone do if they got a free pass saying that you can do with the captain whatever you want for a day?"
Haruna Hasegawa-san / Nagoya
Use him as a sand-bag. ♬
SWISH SWISH
Marry him. ♡
Hee! ♡
I WILL NEED A DAY TO THINK ABOUT THAT.
The captain? I wouldn't care.
Uuuh... well...
I'd have him keep the leftovers coming.
You guys ...

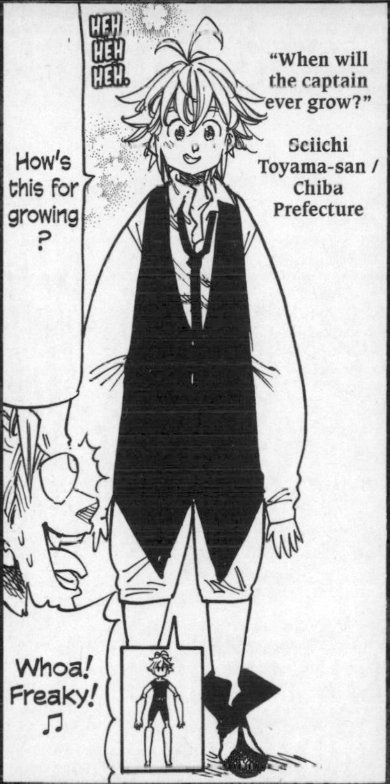
"When will the captain ever grow?"
Seiichi Toyama-san / Chiba Prefecture
HEH HEH HEH.
How's this for growing?
Whoa! Freaky! ♫

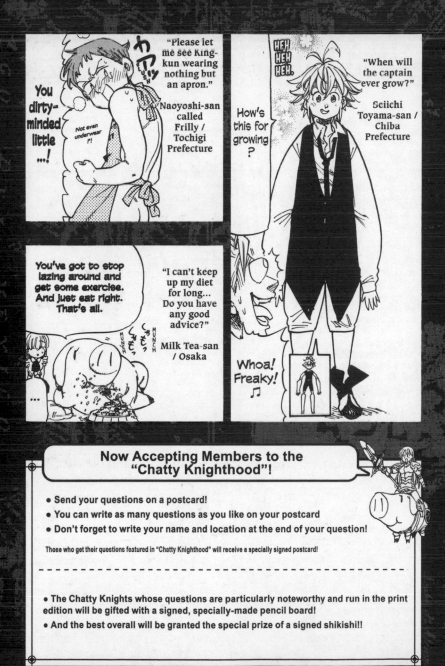

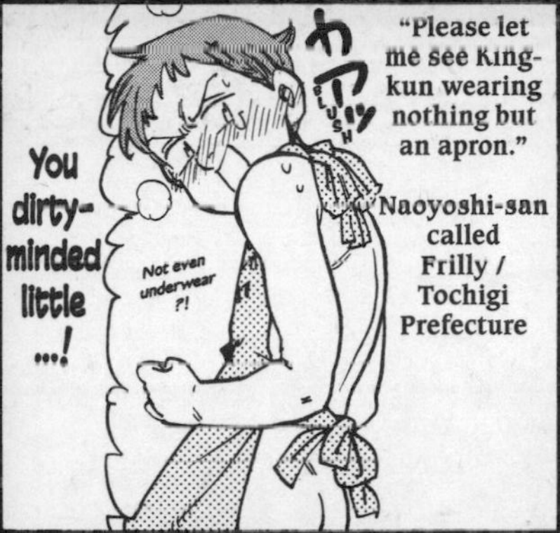
"Please let me see King-kun wearing nothing but an apron."
Naoyoshi-san called Frilly / Tochigi Prefecture
BLUSH
You dirty-minded little ...!
Not even underwear?!

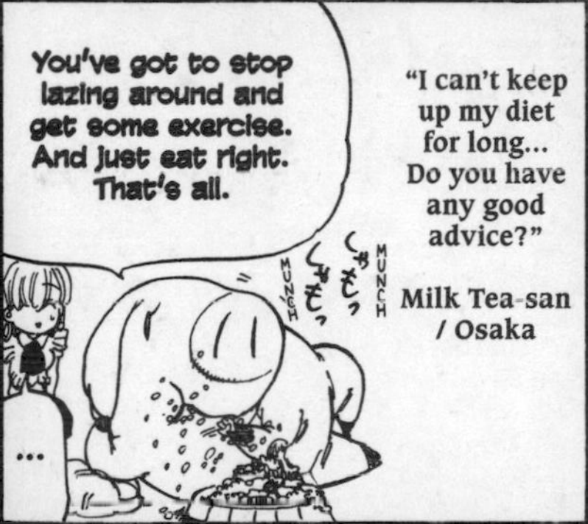
"I can't keep up my diet for long... Do you have any good advice?"
Milk Tea-san / Osaka
You've got to stop lazing around and get some exercise. And just eat right. That's all.
MUNCH
MUNCH
...

Now Accepting Members to the "Chatty Knighthood"!

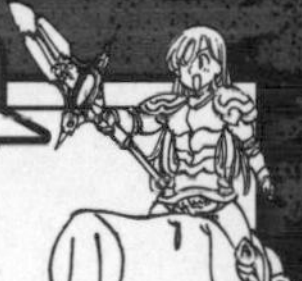

- Send your questions on a postcard!
- You can write as many questions as you like on your postcard
- Don't forget to write your name and location at the end of your question!

Those who get their questions featured in "Chatty Knighthood" will receive a specially signed postcard!

- The Chatty Knights whose questions are particularly noteworthy and run in the print edition will be gifted with a signed, specially-made pencil board!
- And the best overall will be granted the special prize of a signed shikishi!!

"THE SEVEN DEADLY SINS" ILLUSTRATION CORNER

"THE DRAWING KNIGHTHOOD" SPACE

Be sure to include your name and address on your postcard!

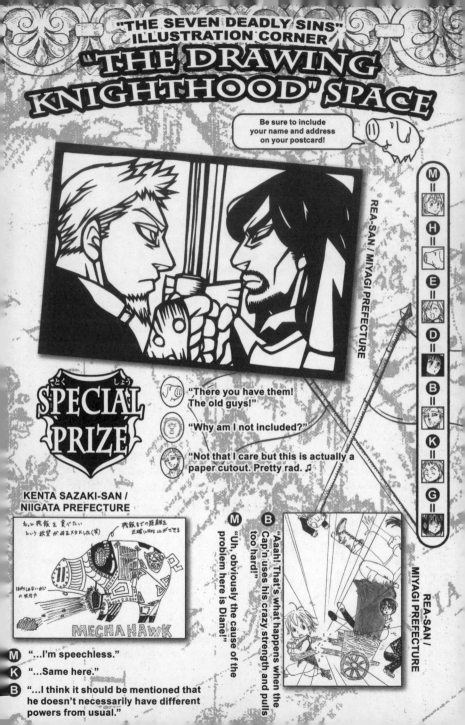

M = [Meliodas] H = [Hawk] E = [Elizabeth] D = [Diane] B = [Ban] K = [King] G = [Gowther]

REA-SAN / MIYAGI PREFECTURE

SPECIAL PRIZE

"There you have them! The old guys!"

"Why am I not included?"

"Not that I care but this is actually a paper cutout. Pretty rad. ♫"

KENTA SAZAKI-SAN / NIIGATA PREFECTURE

もっと残飯を食べたい
という欲望が体をメカにした(笑)
残飯までの距離を
正確に測ることができる
はかりしれないほどの吸引力
MECHAHAWK

M "…I'm speechless."

K "…Same here."

B "…I think it should be mentioned that he doesn't necessarily have different powers from usual."

REA-SAN / MIYAGI PREFECTURE

B "Aaah! That's what happens when the Cap'n uses his crazy strength and pulls too hard!"

M "Uh, obviously the cause of the problem here is Diane!"

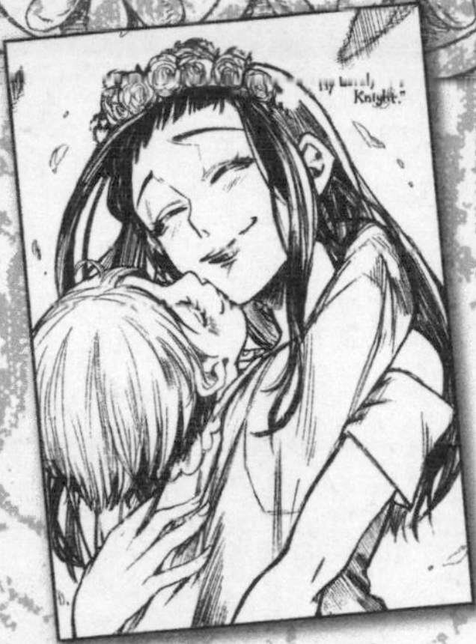

NORO-SAN / TOKYO

"Guila makes a good big sister! I wish I'd had a sister like her growing up."

"You'll always have me!"

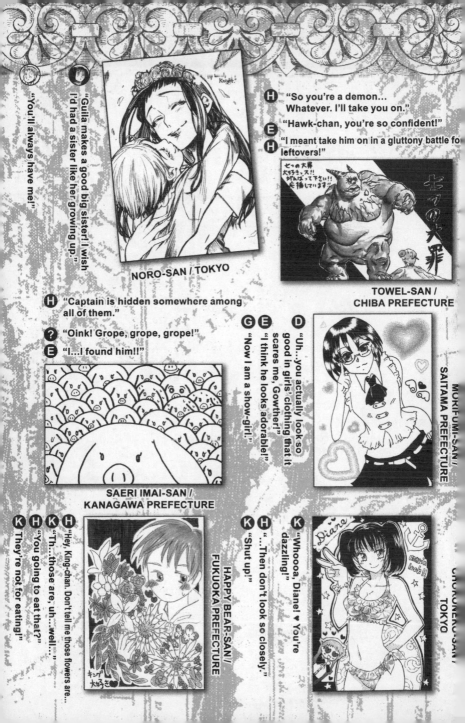

H "So you're a demon... Whatever. I'll take you on."

E "Hawk-chan, you're so confident!"

H "I meant take him on in a gluttony battle for leftovers!"

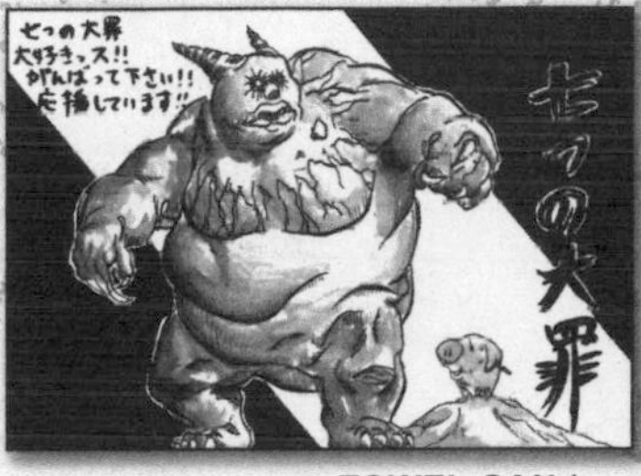
七つの大罪

TOWEL-SAN /
CHIBA PREFECTURE

H "Captain is hidden somewhere among all of them."

? "Oink! Grope, grope, grope!"

E "I...I found him!!"

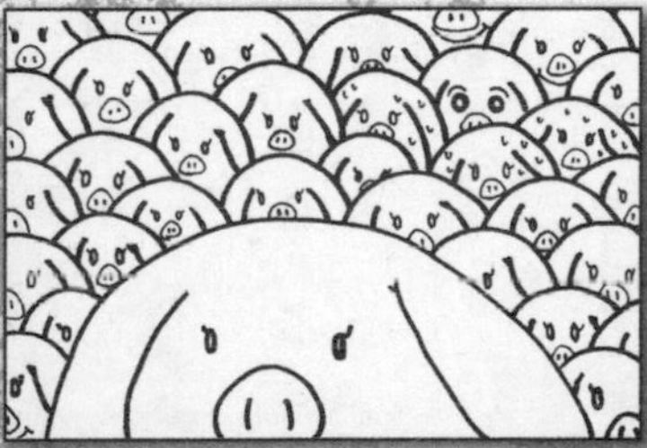

SAERI IMAI-SAN /
KANAGAWA PREFECTURE

D "Uh...you actually look so good in girls' clothing that it scares me, Gowther!"

E "I think he looks adorable!"

G "Now I am a show-girl."

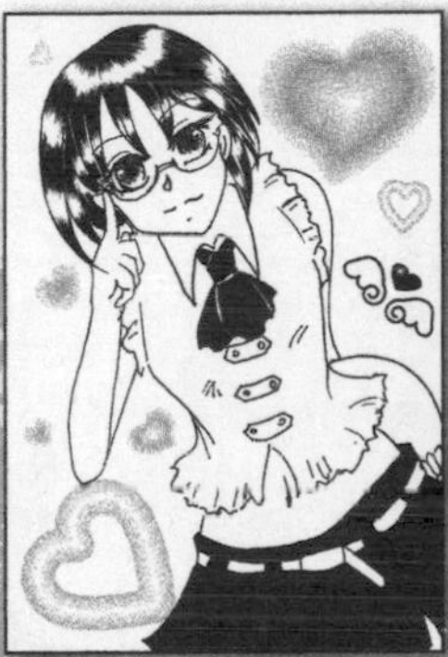

MORIFUMI-SAN /
SAITAMA PREFECTURE

H "Hey, King-chan. Don't tell me those flowers are...

K "Th...those are, uh...well..."

H "You going to eat that?"

K They're not for eating!"

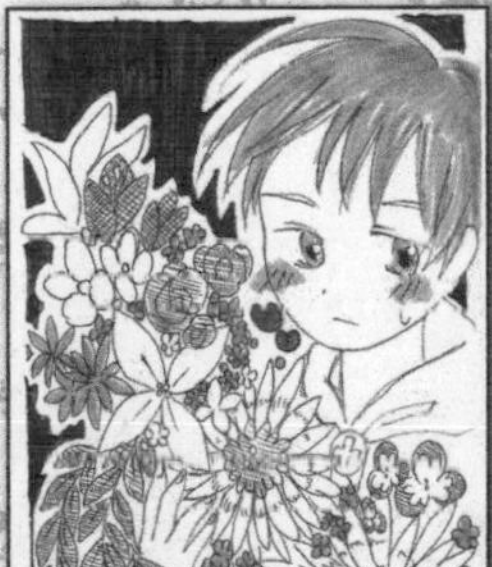
キング
大好き♥

HAPPY BEAR-SAN /
FUKUOKA PREFECTURE

K "Whoooa, Diane! ♥ You're dazzling!"

H "...Then don't look so closely."

K "Shut up!"

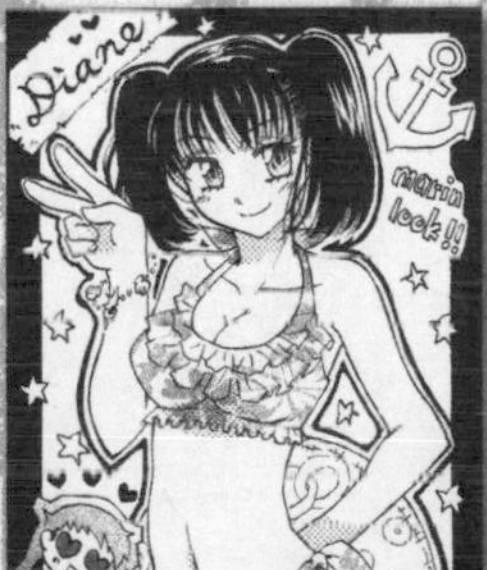
Diane
marin look!!

CHOKONEKO-SAN /
TOKYO

MAIKO MAEDA-SAN / CHIBA PREFECTURE

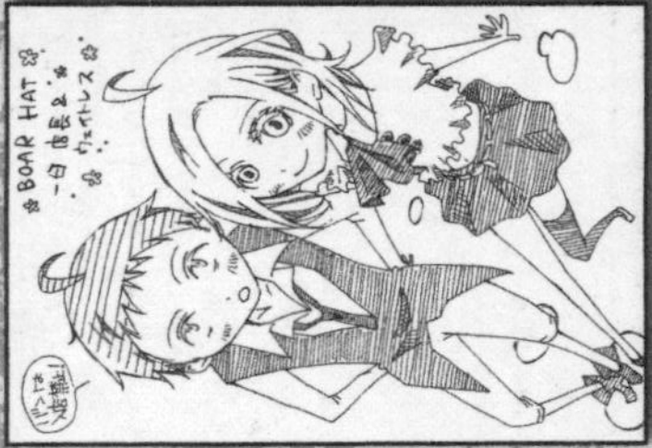
BOAR HAT
一日店長&ウェイトレス
バンは入店禁止!

K "Ban's not allowed to come into the bar."

E "Ban's fine! you're the one who's fired, brother!"

K "Huh? But I run the shop!"

CHIRORU☆-SAN / TOKYO

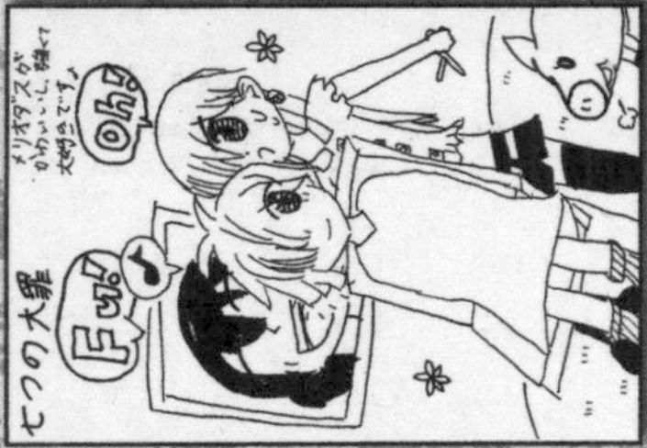
七つの大罪
Fu!
Oh!
メリオダスがかわいいし、強くて大好きです♪

E "Waaaah! I snipped off Meliodas-sama's cowlick!"

M "That calls for a speedy punishment."

E "Eeeeek! No...aah! Uuuh!!"

MANAKA TONO-SAN / FUKUOKA PREFECTURE

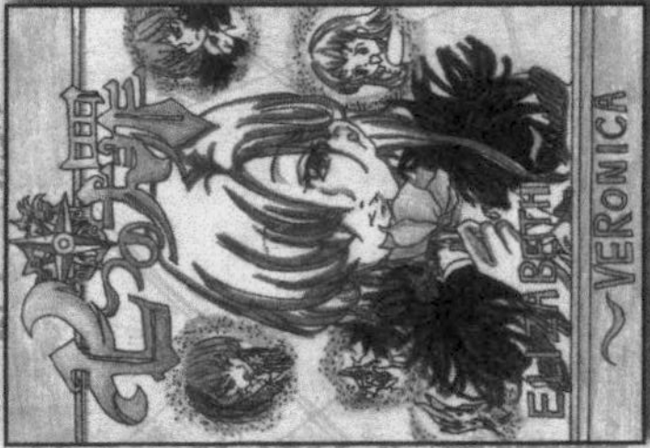
七つの大罪
ELIZABETH
~VERONICA

H "When this war's over, I want to go shopping downtown with Elizabeth.♫"

E "Yeah! Me too!"

HIRO-SAN / NARA PREFECTURE

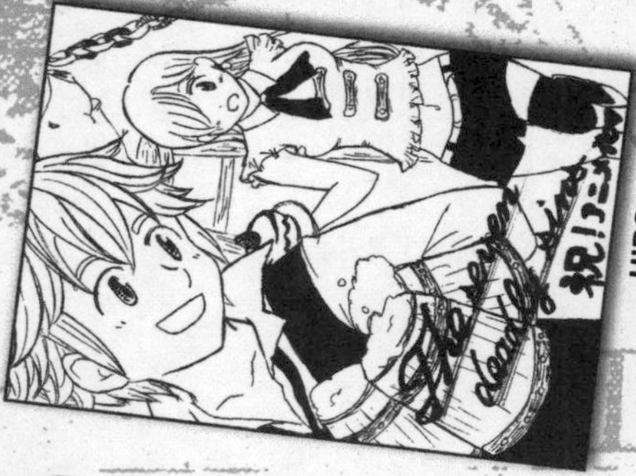
The seven deadly sins
祝!アニメ化

"The bar's definitely needs us if it's going to run."

"Yep! Let's work hard today too! Heh heh!"

MOMOKA NAKAYAMA-SAN / TOKYO

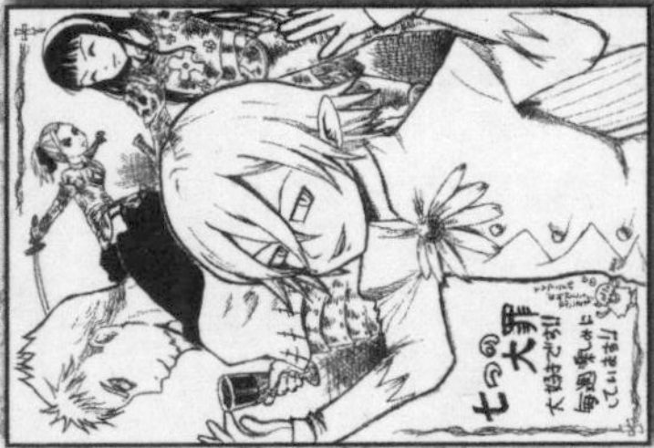
七つの大罪
大好きです!!
毎週楽しみにしています!!

K "Helbram! I swear I'll defeat Hendrickson and avenge you!"

D "...King."

FROM AKARI TAKASHINA-SAN / FUKUOKA PREFECTURE

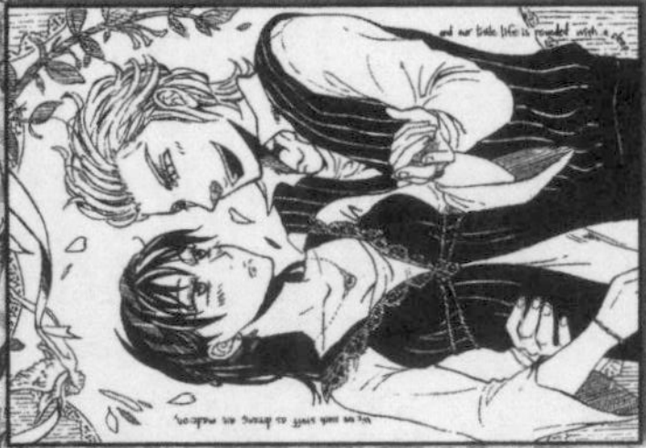

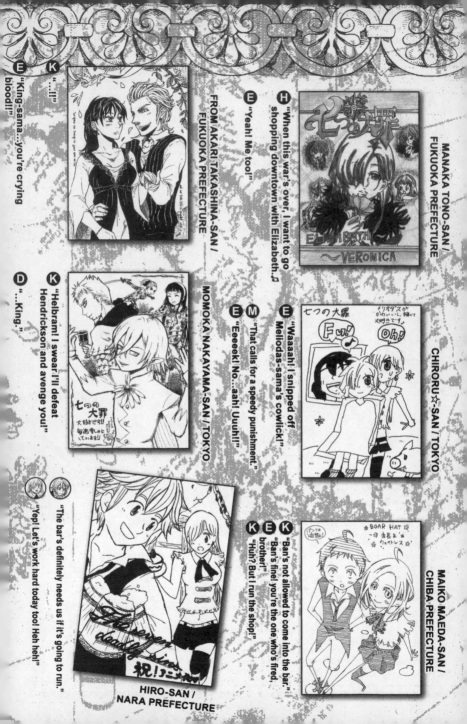

K "...!!"

E "King-sama...you're crying blood!!"

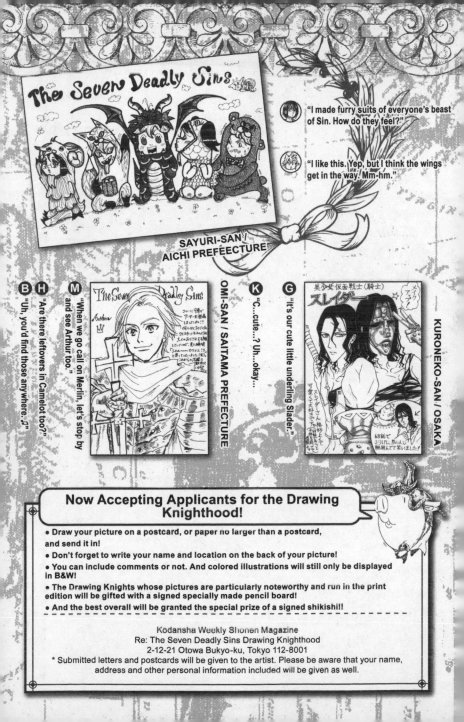

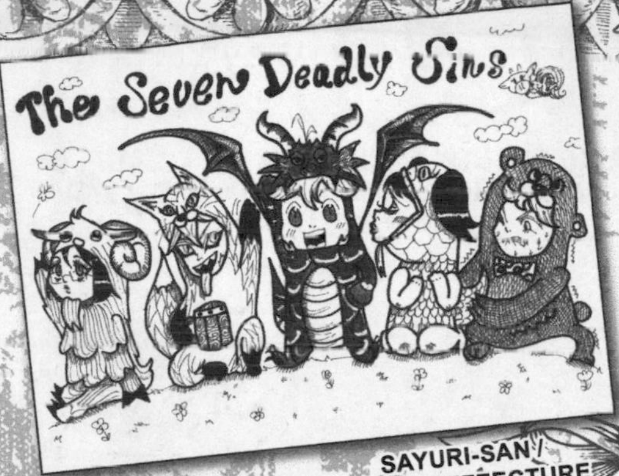
The Seven Deadly Sins

SAYURI-SAN / AICHI PREFEECTURE

"I made furry suits of everyone's beast of Sin. How do they feel?"

"I like this. Yep, but I think the wings get in the way. Mm-hm."

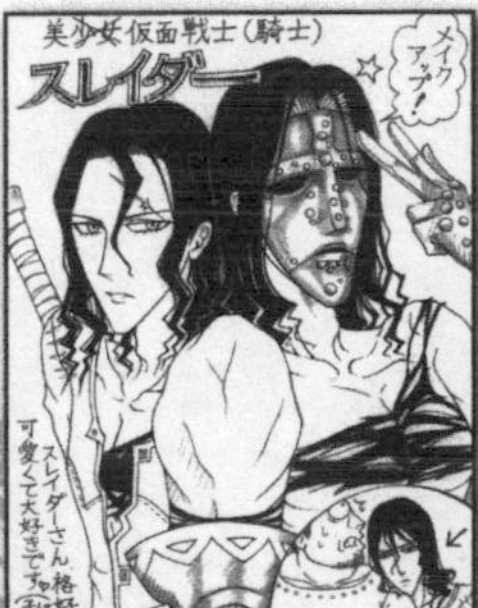
美少女仮面戦士(騎士)
スレイダー
メイクアップ!

KURONEKO-SAN / OSAKA

G "It's our cute little underling Slader."

K "C...cute...? Uh...okay..."

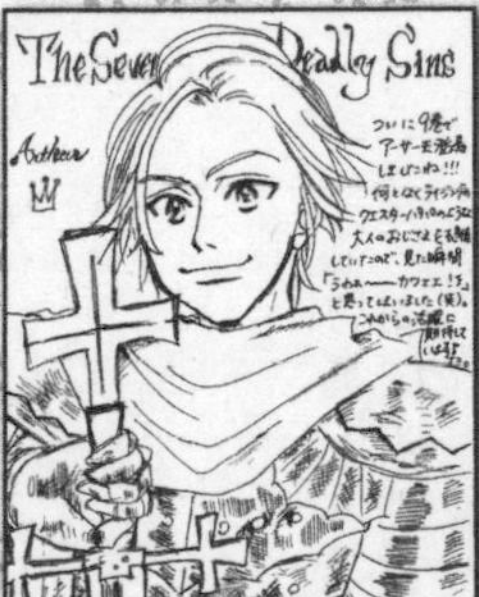
The Seven Deadly Sins
Arthur

OMI-SAN / SAITAMA PREFECTURE

M "When we go call on Merlin, let's stop by and see Arthur too."

H "Are there leftovers in Camelot too?"

B "Uh, you'd find those anywhere.♫"

Now Accepting Applicants for the Drawing Knighthood!

- Draw your picture on a postcard, or paper no larger than a postcard, and send it in!
- Don't forget to write your name and location on the back of your picture!
- You can include comments or not. And colored illustrations will still only be displayed in B&W!
- The Drawing Knights whose pictures are particularly noteworthy and run in the print edition will be gifted with a signed specially made pencil board!
- And the best overall will be granted the special prize of a signed shikishi!!

Kodansha Weekly Shonen Magazine
Re: The Seven Deadly Sins Drawing Knighthood
2-12-21 Otowa Bukyo-ku, Tokyo 112-8001

* Submitted letters and postcards will be given to the artist. Please be aware that your name, address and other personal information included will be given as well.

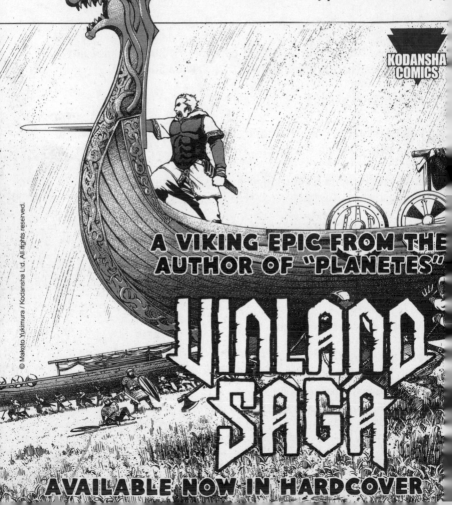

The Seven Deadly Sins volume 11 is a work of fiction. Names, characters, places, and incidents are the products of the author's imagination or are used fictitiously. Any resemblance to actual events, locales, or persons, living or dead, is entirely coincidental.

A Kodansha Comics Trade Paperback Original.

Published in the United States by Kodansha Comics, an imprint of Kodansha USA Publishing, LLC, New York.

Publication rights for this English edition arranged through Kodansha Ltd., Tokyo.

First published in Japan in 2014 by Kodansha Ltd., Tokyo.

ISBN 978-1-63236-117-2

Printed in the United States of America.

www.kodanshacomics.com

9 8 7 6 5 4 3 2 1

Translator: Christine Dashiell
Lettering: James Dashiell